D0101226

handbook of
INTERCULTURAL COMMUNICATION

handbook of
INTERCULTURAL
COMMUNICATION

EDITORS

MOLEFI KETE ASANTE

EILEEN NEWMARK

CECIL A. BLAKE

SAGE Publications / Beverly Hills / London

For information address:

SAGE Publications, Inc.
275 South Beverly Drive
Beverly Hills, California 90212

SAGE Publications India Pvt. Ltd.
C-236 Defence Colony
New Delhi 110 024, India

SAGE Publications Ltd
28 Banner Street
London EC1Y 8QE, England

Printed in the United States of America

Library of Congress Cataloging in Publication Data

Main entry under title:
Handbook of intercultural communication.
Includes bibliographical references.
1. Intercultural communication — Addresses, essays, lectures.
I. Asante, Molefi K., 1942-   II. Newmark, Eileen.   III. Blake, Cecil A.

HM258.H354   301.14   78-2468
ISBN 0-8039-0954-3
ISBN 0-8039-1074-6 (pbk.)

SECOND PRINTING, 1982

CONTENTS

Preface   9

PART I. Theoretical Considerations

1   The Field of Intercultural Communication   11
     Molefi K. Asante, Eileen Newmark, and Cecil A. Blake

2   Theoretical Directions for Intercultural Communication   23
     William S. Howell

3   On the Relevance of Cognitive Anthropology   43
     and Ethnomethodology
     Jerry L. Burk and Janet G. Lukens

4   Integrating Etic and Emic Approaches   57
     in the Study of Intercultural Communication
     Stanley E. Jones

PART II. Conceptual Frameworks   75

5   The Consciousness Theory of Intercultural Communication   77
     Tulsi B. Saral

6   Rhetoric and Intercultural Communication   85
     Cecil A. Blake

7   Demystification of the Intercultural Communication Encounter   95
     Molefi K. Asante and Alene Barnes

8   Nonverbal Behavior: An Intercultural Perspective   105
     Sheila J. Ramsey

PART III. Issues In Intercultural Communication   145

9   The Role of Values in Intercultural Communication   147
     K. S. Sitaram and Lawrence W. Haapanen

10   International Communication and Its Media: A   161
     Crossnational Study
     K. Kyoon Hur

11   An Analysis of Diplomatic Communication   179
     Eileen Newmark

12   Five Dimensions in Racial-Based Communication Stereotypes   189
     Steven M. Alderton

13   Terramedian Value Systems and Their Significance   203
     George O. Roberts

PART IV. General Problems with Data   229

14   Intercultural Communication Data Acquisition   231
     V. Lynn Tyler, Peggy Hall, and James S. Taylor

15   Still Photography: An Approach to Intercultural   253
     Communication
     Robert Shuter

16   Ethnocentric Bias in Development Research   263
     Njoku E. Awa

17   A Multidimensional Scaling Methodology for   283
     Crosscultural Research in Communications
     Oliver C.S. Tzeng and Dan Landis

PART V. Research in Specific Cultures   319

18   Communication Characteristics of Asian Americans in   321
     Urban Settings: The Case of Honolulu Japanese
     Dennis M. Ogawa

19   A Crosscultural study of Mate Recruiting Through Mass Media   339
     Erika Vora and Jay A. Vora

20   Cultural Self-Comprehension in Ethnically Plural Societies: 357
     The Case of Sub-Saharan Africa
     Akinade O. Sanda

21   Native American Communication Patterns: The Case of   373
     the Lakota Speakers
     Bea Medicine

22   Black-White Communication: An Assessment of Research   383
     Dorthy L. Pennington

PART VI. Practical Applications: Training Methods   403

23   Counseling Clients from Other Cultures: Two Training Designs   405
     Paul Pedersen

24   Case Methods in International Management Training   421
     Joseph J. DiStefano

25   Multinational Training for Multinational Corporations   447
     Melvin Schnapper

About the Authors   475

PREFACE

Intercultural communication is a field of research with applicability to a wide range of human interactions. It is significant as an intellectual and practical pursuit because it helps us to understand the nature of human beings creating meaning for other human beings.

This book has six parts: (1) Theoretical Considerations, (2) Conceptual Frameworks, (3) Issues in Intercultural Communication, (4) General Problems with Data, (5) Research in Specific Cultures, and (6) Practical Applications: Training Methods. Communication between human beings implies interaction across cultural and social barriers. What our authors have endeavored to do is to address the critical issues facing researchers and theorists of intercultural communication.

We present the work in this book as a foundation upon which to build. It is interdisciplinary and innovative. Because our intention has been to create a volume which practices what it preaches, we have included manuscripts from different cultural as well as disciplinary views. It is not enough to discuss the theory of intercultural communication; we must begin to act on the basis of our theory. A book on intercultural communication that presents views from a single perspective indicts itself. Consequently, we have tried scrupulously to avoid that posture. Hopefully other scholars will find instructive value in the structure and substance of this work.

PART I.
THEORETICAL CONSIDERATIONS

The literature on intercultural communication has been growing steadily since the early 1960s. Prosser, Saral, and Hoopes and Renwick have endeavored through invited papers and comprehensive surveys to chart its geometric as well at its arithmetic growth. There are certainly more courses, journal articles, convention papers, and professional recognition than ten years ago. In a Kuhnian sense, intercultural communicationists have burst upon the communication scene to revolutionize the traditional concepts. It is no longer acceptable for an author to write an ethnocentric communication book. Scholarship must be inclusive; this is the dictum of the era.

Yet it is impossible to say exactly where we are heading in intercultural communication. Textbooks such as *Transracial Communication* (Smith (now Asante), 1973), *Interracial Communication* (Rich, 1974), *Intercultural Communication* (Harms, 1974), *Introduction to Intercultural Communication* (Condon and Yousef, 1975), and *The Foundations of Intercultural Communication* (Sitaram and Cogdell, 1976) all represented the attempt to utilize theories of psychology, rhetoric, and anthropology to explain the phenomenon of interacting with humans from different ethnic or cultural groups. The articles in Part I of the present volume seek to establish intellectual contours in the field. We will know more expressly where we are headed when we have grasped the significance of the theoretical issues in intercultural communication.

In Chapter 1, Asante, Newmark and Blake discuss the intellectual roots of the field of intercultural communication. They see the major developmental trends as "cultural dialogue" and "cultural criticism." Analyzing the principal contributors to the field as either cultural dialogists or critics, they provide a framework from which to seek a unifying paradigm.

Howell, in Chapter 2, takes a different perspective. It is his contention that we are in need of much more observation before we can begin to build theories in intercultural communication. He endeavors to go beyond the expropriation of existing interpersonal theories to establish the ground rules for theory building in intercultural communication. This essay should facilitate the development of meaningful theories.

In Chapter 3, Burke and Lukens undertake an analysis of the relevance of cognitive anthropology and ethnomethodology to intercultural communication. They succeed in establishing the dimensions of theory and research that are applicable to an extension of the field. Thus communication traditionalists may find new growth in the area of ethnomethodology.

Chapter 4, by Jones, is a review and application of the concepts of emic and etic developed by Pike. What Jones does, however, is to point to possible uses of the concept in research and theory building. All these chapters raise theoretical issues for more fruitful analysis and directions.

1.

THE FIELD OF INTERCULTURAL COMMUNICATION

MOLEFI K. ASANTE, EILEEN NEWMARK AND CECIL A. BLAKE

State University of New York at Buffalo

This volume is an attempt to provide scholars with a theoretical and methodological orientation toward intercultural communication. Our aim is to help lay down ground rules that will direct intercultural communication into a unified field of inquiry. Psychologists, anthropologists, and communicationists have studied the various components of the intercultural communication process without reference to interrelationships. Hopefully this volume will provide the necessary framework from which to posit connections and relationships in intercultural communication.

We begin where all science must begin, with a problem: we seek to explicate the dissimilarities and similarities which impede or enhance communication across cultures. The task is to elucidate the problems and issues of intercultural communication. This volume should reduce the time necessary for each of us to discover all the answers by having scholars from a variety of disciplines present their ideas on the major problems of intercultural communication. This is done with a strong faith in the method of the social scientist, despite realizing that the broadcast and reversibility of findings are two sides of the same coin.

Theory is an attempt to explain observations in a coherent fashion. Although there have been some efforts to address the general question of communication in the theoretical terms over the last 40 years, it is only in recent times that attention has been paid to the intricacies of the communication process. The influence of culture on the communicative interaction is one of these intricacies. In a Kuhnian sense, we are about due for a revolution that would call into question some of our old assumptions about the nature of human beings. The field of intercultural communication has emerged as a response to the continuing drama of Western orientations in social science. Intercultural communication attempts to shed the trappings of ethnocentrism and explain the communicative act in its own terms. What is needed at this juncture is more description of the intercultural communication process, i.e., our scientists need to observe before they theorize. We must also work with those coherent explanations we have in order to stand higher in the asking process.

The response presented here is necessitated by the state of the field. Intercultural communication theory and research are in double states of shock. Franz Boas' (1940) collection of articles, *Race, Language and Culture* is one reason for the state of our inquiry; the other is Edward Hall's series of books on the subject of culture. Hall's latest book, *Beyond Culture* (1976), is concerned with the transference of human extensions. Boas' work is primarily classificatory, providing good anthropological description of Indian languages but no real penetration of the problems of intercultural communication. On the other hand, Edward Hall has given us a general guide to human culture, pointing to the inadequacies of Western culture as problematic. The result is that no clear lines of theoretical arguments can be discovered for intercultural communication. It is a field of inquiry without a clear tradition rooted in the social or behavioral sciences. What one finds are the tangential forays of anthropologists, communicationists, and psychologists who, while on their various journeys into their own cultural field, happen to pass by.

Two schools of thought exist regarding the value of intercultural communication: the *cultural dialogue* group and the *cultural criticism* group. Among the basic tenets underlying the cultural dialogue school are internationalism and humanism. Rooted in the conception of science as a practical tool for human use, proponents of this school argue for theories that would promote world understanding. For them, intercultural communication is one more attempt to organize human society along mutually satisfying lines. Derived from this view are such concerns as international peace organizations, transcultural perception seminars, numerous university courses, and some religious movements. The scholarly component of these concerns is usually found in communication and anthropology. Utilizing antecedents found in semi religious and quasiacademic groups, scholars have established the holistic nature of human beings. Cultural dialogue, then, is a trend toward world communication.

On the other hand, cultural criticism seeks to find the points of conflict in each culture in order to isolate them as researchable issues in transcultural interaction. For the cultural critics, there is little need to seek similarities and universals until a classificatory system that adequately describes cultures is developed. Harry Triandis' cultural assimilators and George Gerbner's crossnational study of values are endeavors to sensitize us to differences. This codification of cultural differences takes considerable time, but it is necessary research—much like naming the organic and inorganic materials of the universe. It is work which must be done before other scholars can do their work: the creation of concepts must precede their manipulation.

The concentration of scholarly interest in these two broad areas notwithstanding, there is considerable overlapping by any given scholar. Pike's *emic* and *etic* features of cultural research occur throughout Ward Goodenough's characterizations of Brazilian Indian cultures (1975). The tendency for most scholars is to seek explanation wherever it can be found, which sometimes means concentrating on problems internal or external to a communication interaction. Research that is honest and accountable has always been the objective of the best social scientists. Certainly intercultural communication theorists, armed with the cultural dialogue and cultural criticism approaches, can provide us with better blueprints for analyzing communication across cultures.

The lessons of anthropology are instructive for the general field of communication. As an area for research, cognitive anthropology has experienced problems similar to intercultural communication. Beginning with an outdated perspective on culture, many anthropologists failed to see the value of culture in other than artifactual terms. Communicationists have frequently appropriated the view of culture as artifact and thus have not been able to isolate the distinguishing factors of intercultural communication. In its most partisan cultural sense, anthropology has overcome its attachment to past conceptions of culture with Goodenough's (1956) emphasis on culture as a cognitive fact. In a similar vein, communicationists have tried to set forth a viable framework for looking at communication interactions interculturally. Culture becomes the sum total of our individual and collective beliefs and values.

Edward Stewart has provided a base from which to move ahead theoretically. One must remember that his *Outline of Intercultural Communication* (1972) was a creative attempt to define the territory. While more a sketch than anything else, it allowed debate and discussion to take place. Stewart did what Hall and Boas could not do because of their training. He explored culture as a key variable in intercultural communication and endeavored to demonstrate how it could be overcome. The components of the process, reminiscent of Leonard Doob's work (1960) on African communication, allowed communicationists to launch a more intensive inquiry.

The group of scholars whose work is drawn together in this volume is evidence in itself of the maturation of a field whose time has come. It is still not possible to set firm boundaries for the field of intercultural communication, which borrows from many disciplines, but it can be assumed to cover the relationship of culture to human interaction.

HISTORICAL ANTECEDENTS

One way to approach intercultural communication is to examine some of the historical antecedents of the two schools of thought that hold sway in the field. Both the cultural dialogue school and the cultural criticism school have been fed by numerous tributaries.

Cultural Dialogue

The interest of scholars in interpersonal behavior across cultures is not recent. Research in the general area of intercultural relations can be traced to the work of political scientists and anthropologists in the 1930s and 1940s. It was not until some time after this that sociologists and linguists became interested in culture. Communicationists came still later. It appears that few communicationists had the combined skills or interest necessary to make penetrating analyses of interactions between people of different cultures.

This should not be surprising. Communicationists have only recently been converted to the process model of human communication. Operating on a static conception, they studied Clarence Darrow's brilliant defense of Loeb and Leopold or William Jennings Bryan's "Cross of Gold" speech, but were unable to observe communication in the making and understand it. Ethel Albert fought an uphill battle with her colleagues in communication at Northwestern when she started investigating the values of Rwanda and Burundi as demonstrated in their communication. Albert became, as far as her colleagues were concerned, an anthropologist. In no journal published by communicationists, whether of the speech variety or the media type, was there any article on the relationship of culture to communication prior to 1965—except for the work done by Ethel Albert. There seemed to be an iron wall preventing communicationists from studing the impact culture had on communication. Thomas Kochman's work (1972) stretched the boundaries of the field of communication to include, for the first time, the enormous possibilities of research into human culture and the differences it makes in how humans communicate with one another. Although Kochman's work has been limited to intercultural interactions in an intranational sense, it provides us with guideposts. Much of his work was done on the streets of Chicago. Concerned about how human beings present themselves to others through communication, Kochman is basically a symbolist. Cultural dialogue research seeks to illuminate the realm of self presentation: Erving Goffman has expressed interest in this in a narrow sense; Kochman sees the necessity of enlarging our perspective in order to understand the culturally different. The publication of David Berlo's *The Process of Communication* (1960) was a major event in the field of communication. Although Berlo's work can now be seen in a much more objective light, its arrival sparked an interest in applying components of the communication process to all human interactions. Doob, in his *Communication in Africa*, used Berlo-like constituents in his analysis of African communication systems. Doob removed the process orientation, however, so that work became merely a static report. Communication is dynamic and can be studied much more profitably as a process than as a static phenomenon. Despite its shortcomings and misunderstandings, *The Process of Communication* can be singled out as the one great impetus to cultural dialogue research. Berlo had little notion of the intercultural communication dimension to his writing, but when he discussed barriers to communication he touched on cultural restraints. Thus Berlo cut loose the victims of communication provincialism. The total volume of research done as a result was extremely small. Frank E. X. Dance studied Soviet communication behavior, but beyond that nothing earthshaking moved across the journal pages in regard to intercultural communication. Most communicationists continued to study monocultural communicative behaviors.

In the late 1960s UCLA's Department of Communication Studies produced three doctoral students who began almost simultaneously to study the nature of communication across cultures. Arthur L. Smith AKA Molefi K. Asante, Dennis Ogawa and Andrea Rich produced articles and books that reflected a growing concern with communication across racial and cultural lines. These efforts were expressions of a new value orientation emerging in the field of communication. During the 1960s not one university had courses in intercultural communication. Today, almost every major university in the country teaches a course in some aspect of intercultural communication. Smith (1973) wrote about the process of normalizing communication between blacks and whites. Rich (1974) broadened her study of interracial communication to

include more American ethnic and racial groups than had been
included in Smith. The model by Rich and Ogawa (1972)
which appeared in Larry Samovar and Richard Porter's
Intercultural Communication: A Reader (1972) is an analytical approach to an intranational cultural situation. Ogawa
has further expanded on this in his work on Japanese-Americans.

In addition to these efforts, there were attempts to clarify
intercultural communication, some in political terms (Maletzke, 1970), others on a communication theory base (Harms,
1974; Condon and Yousef, 1975; and Sitaram and Cogdell,
1976). The effort of these authors was clarification of the
discipline. But clarification cannot be accomplished without
basic research into the nature of the phenomenon. How do
human beings of different cultures manage to get along verbally? What are the complexities of thinking processes which
influence what they say to each other? Are some groups more
culturally dissimilar than others but less difficult to communicate with? These and a myriad of similar questions remain for
the communicationist.

Cultural dialogists such as Condon and Yousef (1975) have
seen a relationship between rhetoric, culture, and epistemic
structures. In some respects their work is similar in content to
that of Ethel Albert, whose concept of values and rhetoric
seems to have influenced Condon and Yousef. Cultural dialogists are correct in assuming a relationship between argument, rhetoric, and culture, but their concentration on structures seldom allows the dissolution of old and the rise of new
structures. Patterns of thinking are like values, not necessarily
permanent but socially and environmentally influenced. If it
were not so, we would be minimally affected by our historical
experiences. Our patterns of thinking are influenced by educational pressures, which have a way of washing our minds with
their own intellectual detergents.

None of these observations are meant to criticize the cultural dialogue perspective, which is a proper approach to the
field of intercultural communication. If the field succeeds in
becoming practical, it will be because the cultural dialogists
have given it their best efforts. Furthermore, the type of work
which needs to be done is just now emerging, and until we have

a significant corpus of data it is premature to make a judgment. Of course the authors of cultural dialogue research and theory have usually worked independently of other influences, precisely because there was no preexisting area of specialization. What work was done had the unmistakable imprint of Aristotelianism or Neo-Aristotelianism. The best thinkers of the time had grown up with the symbolic and rhetorical theory traditions; they were cultural dialoguists almost by default. When one reads the work of Smith (1973), Rich (1974), Prosser (1974), Samovar and Porter (1973), and Condon and Yousef (1975), the overwhelming impact of rhetorical thinking on a broad group of writers is quite clear. Only Harms (1973) seems to have escaped the lure of Neo-Aristotelianism.

Thus what early communicationists wrote tended to have a rhetorical base. Argument, belief, values, structures, and poetics were considered basic branches of dialogue. Their work emerged not from concentrated study of the phenomenon of humans interacting across cultures, but rather from the application of rhetorical or symbolic categories to intercultural behavior. Concepts seem to have preceded percepts. The relevance of this work is in the application of one discipline to another or, rather, in the use of a familiar set of tools for problems for which tools had not yet been invented.

Cultural Criticism

Cultural criticism is not an attempt to broaden cultural dialogue. Often the two schools of thought have operated quite apart from each other; there has seldom been a major transfusion of thought between them. In fact, the shortcomings of the field generally may be attributed to the inability of scholars to appreciate the different perspectives contributing to intercultural communication. While it is true that the field is interdisciplinary, this fact has seldom been taken advantage of except by passers-by traveling their own disciplinary routes. Instead of seeking to broaden the work of cultural dialogists, the cultural critics have left off process to argue for understanding the barriers which separate men. In Edward Hall's *Beyond Culture*, we see the current limit of this thinking. Hall is sure we have to go beyond culture, but he is not sure of what will lead us there. Other cultural critics are not so certain that we can or indeed need go beyond culture. In his earlier work (1966), Hall had asserted the impossibility of divesting ourselves of culture. Pike (1966) believes in the advisability of etic and emic considerations in the study of culture. Determining what is and is not important in the interaction between cultures is a significant step for the cultural critic. In fact, Edward Stewart has propounded a doctrine fairly acceptable to professional trainers in intercultural communication. Stewart starts with the view that the proper understanding of cultural values will lead to resolution of intercultural communication conflict. Identification and isolation of barriers are key processes in Stewart's design. Conflict resolution becomes the principal concern of this approach. It might seem that linguistics, the first of the sciences to treat culture, would be instructive at this point. That is not the case, however. As early as 1964, Harry Hoijer bemoaned the fact that both linguistics and anthropology had failed to deal with the problems of cultural integration.

Hall may have been the first anthropologist to have recognized the possibilities of anthropology for intercultural interactions; earlier, however, Clyde Kluckhohn (1956) had undertaken a study of value emphases in different cultures. Kluckhohn did not concern himself with intercultural communication. The foundation for the cultural critical approach was being lain, but it was not until Kochman that sustained interest in intercultural communication was generated among anthropologists. What Kochman dared do was not merely to study cultural groups but to relate their communications to each other. He posed the question, "what are culturally expressive behaviors in one culture as they relate to another culture?" Kochman is principally a cultural dialogist whose research is an impetus for cultural critics. His influence is limited at this point in linguistic circles, but he has gained prominence in anthropology and sociology with his approach to method in intercultural communication. Taking the work of Hall, Kluckhohn and Kochman together, one has the basis for exploring causes and consequences in intercultural communication.

The cultural critic operates on three distinct levels: (1) classificatory, (2) analytic, and (3) applicative. At the classificatory level, the researcher attempts to identify the "barriers" to communication across cultures; at the analytic level he or she explores the barriers in terms of priority, intensity, or difficulty. When the cultural critic has made the classification and analysis, application to specific settings become possible; this level is called applicative.

Cultural critics are seeking ways to perfect the communication process across cultures by isolating the barriers. LaRay Barna (1972) writes:

> A better approach is to study the history, political structure, art, literature, and language of the country. . . . But more important, one should develop an investigative nonjudgmental attitude and a high tolerance for ambiguity—which means lowered defenses. Margaret Mead suggests sensitizing persons to the kinds of things that need to be taken into account instead of developing behavior and attitude stereotypes, mainly because of the individual differences in each encounter and the rapid changes that occur in a culture pattern. Edward Stewart concurs with this view.

Barna is correct in "reading into" Stewart's work a notion similar to her own. However, Stewart's work (1972), of all that done by cultural critics, seems to succeed most in combining classification, analysis, and application. In Barna's major statement on intercultural communication, she identifies *languages, nonverbal areas, preconceptions and stereotypes, tendency to evaluate,* and *high anxiety* as the principal stumbling blocks to intercultural communication. The contribution of Barna's evaluative work notwithstanding, it remains classificatory. On the other hand, Edward Stewart's *American Cultural Patterns: A Cross Cultural Perspective* is an attempt both to classify and to provide a perspective on crosscultural problems encountered by Americans working overseas. Thus, he is a cultural critic who understands the need for defining the components of intercultural communication without becoming a captive to componentialism.

Clearly this volume brings together authors from the two dominant schools of intercultural research as well as those (e.g. Tulsi Saral), who sing to a different muse. The breadth of this book should be its strength and value. A more specific, perhaps even more esoteric volume could have been organized, but it was the editors intention to produce a volume which would lay groundwork for reflective thinking on the critical questions of intercultural communication. The organization and structure of the book is ours; we have tried to maintain integrity as scholars and as editors who have shepherded these manuscripts through to completion. We hope, of course, that our volume will help advance the field of intercultural communication.

REFERENCES

ALBERT, E. (1964) "Rhetoric, logic and poetics in Burundi: Culture patterning of speech behavior." *American Anthropologist,* 66: 35-54.

BARNA, L. (1973) "Stumbling blocks to intercultural communication," pp. in L. Samovar and R. Porter (eds.), *Intercultural Communication: A Reader.* Belmont, Cal.: Wadsworth.

BERLO, D. (1960) *The Process of Communication.* New York: Holt, Rinehart & Winston.

BOAS, F. (1940) *Race, Language and Culture.* New York: Macmillan.

CONDON J. and FATHI Y. (1975) *Introduction of Intercultural Communication.* New York: Bobbs-Merrill.

DOOB, L. (1961) *Communication in Africa: A Search for Boundaries.* New Haven, Conn.: Yale Univ. Press.

GOODENOUGH, W. (1956) "Componential analysis and the study of meaning." *Language,* 32: 195-216.

HALL, E. (1976) *Beyond Culture.* New York: Doubleday.

HARMS, L. S. (1973) *Intercultural Communication* New York: Harper & Row.

HOIJER, H. (1964) "Linguistic and cultural change," in Pp. 142 Hymes (ed.) *Language in Culture and Society.* New York: Harper & Row.

KLUCKHOHN, C. (1956) "Toward a comparison of value-emphasis in different cultures, Pp. 135" in L. D. White (ed.), *The State of the Social Sciences.* Chicago: Univ. of Chicago Press.

KOCHMAN, T. (ed.) (1972) *Rappin' and Stylin' Out Communication in Urban Black America.* Urbana: Univ. of Illinois Press.

MALETZKE, G. (1970) "Intercultural communication" Pp. 477 in H. D. Fischer and J. Merrill (eds.), *International Communication: Media, Channels and Functions.* New York: Hastings House.

PIKE, K. L. (1966) *Language in Relation to a Unified Theory of the Structure of Human Behavior.* The Hague: Mouton.

PROSSER, M. (1973) *Intercommunication Among Nations and Peoples.* New York: Harper & Row.

RICH, A. (1974) *Interracial Communication.* New York: Harper & Row.

SAMOVAR, L. and PORTER, R. (1973) *Intercultural Communication: A Reader.*
  Belmont, Cal.: Wadsworth.
SITARAM, K. S. and COGDELL, R. (1976) *Foundations of Intercultural Commu-
  nication.* Columbus, Ohio: Charles E. Merrill.
SMITH, A. L. (Molefi K. Asante) (1973) *Transracial Communication.* Englewood
  Cliffs, N.J.: Prentice-Hall.
STEWART, E. (1973) *Outline of Intercultural Communication.* Washington, D.C.:
  BCIU.

2

THEORETICAL DIRECTIONS FOR INTERCULTURAL COMMUNICATION

WILLIAM S. HOWELL

University of Minnesota

RATIONALE

Theory building for intercultural communication will not be advanced by assuming that its process resembles a physical science, or even by beginning with quantification. Possibly we have learned this lesson from our adventures in structuring so-called "communication theory." The result of building communication theory by copying methods of other disciplines is an assortment of pretentious structures without foundations. Only recently has the absence of underpinning attracted scholarly comment. Leonard Hawes (1977: 63) summarizes the present state of commmunication theorizing with the following metaphor:

> Communication, as a discipline training social and behavioral scientists, is barely three generations old. We are rather like the young child watching his/her first international gymnastics competition on television; we immediately try to copy intricate tumbling routines and become frustrated when we can mimic only clumsily. Until there is an appreciation of the long years of training on fundamentals, the child does not see the distance from his/her ability to that of the more mature athlete. At times, the child actually believes he/she is doing quality gymnastics.

Professor Hawes (1977: 68) then provides an opinion and advice that are particularly pertinent to development of theory in intercultural communication:

We tend to be so enamored with the elegance of covering law theories we overlook the fact we may have insufficient material and inadequate questions for such theories. Let's begin at the beginning.

Events are meaningful in context, bound by time and space. Any communication event is an episode, a "film clip" with an arbitrarily selected initiation and termination. Such episodes are unique: what happens during one never happens again. We need clusters of hundreds or thousands of similar episodes to discover possible tendencies or trends. Then, cautiously, speculative theorizing can be permitted to emerge timidly from mountains of observations, description, and interpretation, most of which will be admittedly—and appropriately—subjective.

For Western scholars to accept such a procedure, the term "subjective" must be reconceptualized. Boundaries must be postulated to make clear and useful the old fuzzy blob that behavioral scientists refer to as "subjectivity." We can begin making the subjective more tangible by recognizing two levels of data processing, that within awareness and that which is out of awareness.

All perception, since it exists, in the mind, is subjective to some degree. When a perception is verified by checking it against substantial phenomena in the environment, it accumulates an objective dimension, defined as intentness on objects external to the mind. The "intentness" that makes data processing relatively more objective may be within or out of awareness. This may be done consciously or it may take place while the conscious mind is doing something else.

Both in and out-of-awareness data processing involve conative and emotional forces as well as elements of cognition. Conative forces are those that produce striving behavior, a consequence of will or volition. Emotional forces add affect to the process. Emotional tone varies from slight coloration to total domination of data processing.

Cognitive processes operate with concomitant conative and emotional influences. To the extent that conative and emotional elements are minimal, data processing tends to be objective, that is, related to verifiable external events. In-

creasing prominence of conative and emotional forces produces a relatively more subjective process. Such modification
tends to be done within the person, independent of external
reality.

Conscious and out-of-awareness data processing are equally
rational. Both range from predominantly objective to predominantly subjective, depending upon the extent of referencing to
the external world. Both are the products of cognitive, conative,
and emotive elements interacting. Thus, a person always
"reasons" with his emotions, his will and his intellect, not with
an isolated, separate logical faculty. Whether he is doing his
critical thinking within or out-of-awareness, his attempts to be
rational are shaped as much by his purposeful striving and
feelings as by his IQ. Necessarily, then, this process is holistic
rather than analytic. Because there are a multiplicity of
relationships involving internal and external events, selecting
a few for scrutiny (as we do in analysis) can only produce
deceptive distortions of the whole.

Theoretical formulations applied to intercultural communication to date have been analytical. Holistic data processing
has not been recognized as a possibility. This results from our
appropriating the quantitative, experimental methods of other
disciplines and, as Hawes points out so effectively, attempting
to omit the foundation stage of theory building, extensive
observation and description. Our commitment to analytical
procedures has been, to phrase it conservatively, premature.

In learning about intercultural communication we have been
and are most productive when we process experiences holistically. When we develop insights from either aware or out-of-
awareness responses that integrate emotions, volitions, and
cognitions, we produce informative descriptions and interpretations of events.

Perhaps far on down the line analytic treatment of minutiae
will contribute to a firmer grasp of the human condition as it
flounders in the complexities of intercultural interaction. But
for now, subjecting many informed and sensitive minds to
varied experiences and rewarding them for subjectively observing, describing, and freely interpreting will yield foundation materials on which future structures of substance may be

erected. Let us not anticipate the structures. We can better adjust to the requirements of building when the time comes and we discover what needs to be known.

To encapsulate this rationale, the most valuable material we have to theorize about is the speculation of thoughtful persons who have become interested, persistent observers, describers and interpreters of intercultural communication. If the question to be answered is, "where are we?" that is where we are.

DEVELOPING THEORY TO ORGANIZE AND SYSTEMATIZE THE STUDY OF INTERCULTURAL COMMUNICATION

If we are to move in the direction of objective-subjective theory building, recognizing the oneness of cognitive-conative-emotive data processing and the requirement of compatibility with varied cultures, agreement upon a few assumptions is desirable. These are modifications in current interpretations of communication that may facilitate and coordinate adaptation to the multicultural scene. This group of reconcep-tualizations is only a tentative beginning. If the directions advocated here prove to be productive, these assumptions will be improved and others added as work goes on.

Interaction Theory

Although many have pledged allegiance to "process" and "circu-larity," our methods of observing, describing, and interpreting communication have been linear. We assume a sender-receiver relationship. This focuses attention upon first one and then another individual rather than upon the flow of happenings between them. Such an approach is like stopping a bird in flight to see how it does it.

Communication is a social act. In the most basic sense, this implies that what occurs in participants is not as significant as what they produce together. The spotlight must be shifted from individuals to their joint ventures. Interaction theory is needed to cope with the Third World, which is a result not of what participants do, but of the chemistry of combination. The effort to interact generates something quite unique that exists independently of those making the effort. Just as H_2O differs from hydrogen and oxygen, what occurs between two persons interacting differs from what each thinks, says, and feels. Learning the properties of hydrogen and oxygen tells us little about the nature of water.

Following through on the study of interaction rather than of sending-receiving imposes a moment by moment, here and now methodology of data collection. Communication must be conceptualized as *episodic*. Every communicative act is localized in time and place. It is arbitrarily assigned a beginning and an end, and what is observed takes place on a time scale between those points. Time and space boundaries guarantee that interpretation of events in an episode will be limited to this unique happening. This makes possible accumulation of data from discrete cases for later comparison and possible consolidation.

Another consequence of relentless pursuit of the interaction approach is the realization that *the dyad is the basic unit of interpersonal communication*. No matter how many people are participating in an event, what occurs between any pair of them is unique—and important. What happens when a speaker talks to an audience cannot be understood by averaging out their responses when the speech is over. We can only approach such an understanding by collecting data that show moment by moment interaction of the speaker and *each member* of his audience from the time defined as the beginning to the time chosen as the end of the episode. Only by this method can we describe the range of dynamic variations in the way a speaker and an audience relate to each other on a particular occasion. This example suggests by analogy that the only sensible way to study interaction in intercultural communication is to observe pairs of people, continuously or at sampled intervals, within specified boundaries of time and space.

The assumptions which follow are intended to further the study of interaction rather than as a continuation of investigations within a sending-receiving frame.

Multicultural Models

An inevitable result of our being analytical in the study of communication is the increasing complexity of paradigms and models. Extended analysis identifies more variables, and since the parts are presumed to add up to the whole, none can be left out of a diagrammatic representation. Thus modern models of the communication process are not quickly and easily memorized and used.

A holistic approach to model design authorizes the designer to cluster groups of unspecified variables in ways that dramatize the point he wishes to make. This makes it possible to create simple models that say a great deal, because the mode is metaphor rather than realistic or literal symbolization. Instead of supplying all the details, the metaphoric model guides the reader into a sequence of his own thoughts, opinions, and experiences. Nonwestern cultures are, incidentally, much more comfortable with the metaphoric model than with detailed, analytical representations. Their scholars expect to have directions suggested to them rather than to be instructed literally and exhaustively.

If we accept the dyad as the basic unit of interpersonal communication, an interactive dyadic model can be constructed. It will dramatize the point that what happens between the two participants is unpredictable and changes from moment to moment. It shows also that while each person contributes to the interaction, neither controls it. We will develop the model by use of a hypothetical example.

The two circles in our simple model represent a Japanese businessman, A and an American associate, B. As our communicative episode begins, A, newly arrived from Japan, is entering B's office in Los Angeles. A is shown in by the receptionist who says "this is Mr. Nakamura" and leaves. B comes from behind his desk and advances toward A.

A sends the first message by bowing and presenting his card. B receives the message (and the card) and responds by saying, "ah, welcome to the U.S." and by grasping A's hand and shaking it vigorously.

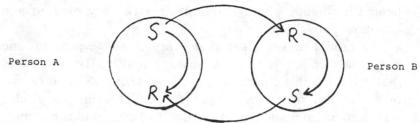

Figure 2.1: Interactive Dyadic Model, Stage 1.

The first stage of the model shows that when A opens the interaction he not only stimulates a return message from B but also prepares himself to receive that response (see S to R arrow within A's circle). The B circle shows that A's initial contribution is received (R) and precipitates the sending of B's response (S). We now proceed to stage two of the interaction.

When A receives B's verbal and nonverbal message (the greeting and handshaking), this causes him to send a nonverbal message, a smile and a nervous giggle. A is prepared to receive a warm response to his cordially intended greeting, so he perceives the smile and giggle as positive acceptance, and continues the interaction by sending another message, "well, well, Kazuo Nakamura. Kaz, it's nice to have you here," and he puts his arm around A's shoulders.

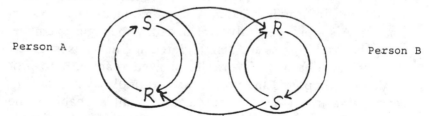

Figure 2.2: Interactive Dyadic Model, Stage 2.

The continuing interaction is represented in the second stage of the model. A receives the informal greeting and handshake with alarm, and expresses his embarrassment with the smile and giggle. B receives this as a pleased happy reaction, because that is the spirit in which he sent his greeting. This perception leads B to happily further offend A by use of a contraction of his first name and by putting an arm around his shoulders. When this is received by A, it leads to an uncontrollable laugh, hidden behind his hand, which B interprets as a very pleased and happy response, and so on.

The model makes clear that every message sent by one participant changes the next message sent by the other, and that, within a participant, any message sent prestructures his own reception of the following message. The whirling circles represent an ongoing dynamic process of continuous intrapersonal and interpersonal change. The unpredictability of interaction is dramatized, and the importance of moment by moment adaptation to unexpected events becomes obvious.

The addition of the element of stress makes the model capable of representing another important complex of variables. If A and B meet each other's expectations and the conversation proceeds smoothly, then the subject matter that is to be processed can be dealt with cognitively. But if conative and emotive forces are activated by dissonance such as results from a clash of contrasting expectations, then the smooth processing of content may not occur. In the scene we used to explain the development of the model, such dissonance became the dominant variable.

Person A, Mr. Nakamura, without thinking about it, expected to be received with the formality and reserve characteristic of his culture. When B violated A's sense of the appropriate by being informal, by using A's first name, and by physical contact, A's input was truly overloaded. A became so embarrassed he lost his poise and disintegrated into nervous laughter. B perceived this as a favorable, pleased reaction and proceeded to compound the problem. Eventually such a misunderstanding might be confronted, but in all probability the cause of the communication breakdown would not be discovered. A and B in all probability would each characterize the other as quite unreasonable foreigners, impossible of being understood. If so, they would illustrate a typical instance of the way persons from different cultures mystify one another!

What happens as the A-B disaster moves toward its climactic collapse is that a powerful extraneous element takes over the thinking mechanism of each participant. Each begins wondering, consciously, about the peculiar behavior of the other. Trying to account for apparent absurdity crowds out the business to be transacted. Such an irrelevant train of thought preventing the normal use of resources to solve problems and do other work we term an "internal monologue."

As represented above, the second stage of the model is a holistic metaphor describing dyadic interaction in which internal monologue is minimal. Participants are free to respond openly to each received message, to combine their resources impulsively, to work together in a predominantly cognitive interaction. We now must add to the model an element representing the interference caused by the failure of A and B to meet each other's expectations. In the third and final stage of our model we include internal monologue.

Person A

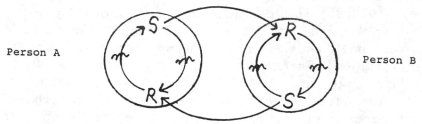

Person B

m = Internal Monologue

Figure 2.3: Interactive Dyadic Model, Stage 3.

The lower case "m" shows the distortion of internal data processing caused by disruptive extraneous concerns. When a substantial intervening monologue such as that caused by A's and B's misinterpretations of each other's behavior "takes over" the thinking of the participants, there is probably only one effective antidote. The cause of the dissonance must be identified, confronted, and resolved. Only then, when internal monologue is controlled can the interaction proceed to combine resources of participants in accomplishing their common objective.

The dyadic interaction model is included as an example of a representation that is simple, easily remembered, and truly multicultural. Other aspects of communication can be similarly dramatized. We believe that the development of simple, obvious models, each driving home a key point or two about the process of intercultural communication, are more useful to

student and practitioner than models that purport to be
analytical and complete.

Empathy Redefined

Empathy in theorizing about intercultural communication is
much talked about but little used. Why this asserted characteristic of effective interaction has not been studied more productively is a thought provoking question. A possible answer is
that empathy has been so variously and vaguely defined as to
render it an unusable element in analytical research. Typical of
definitions of empathy which defy translation into behavior is
"projecting one's consciousness into another being" (Assagioli 1973: 88). Theatrical definitions cluster around the central
idea of feeling "in." To what, with what, and how remain
unclear. Recently, a more modern metaphor has been used to
explain or define empathy—the ability or lack of ability to
"pick up the vibes."

Attempts to utilize empathy across cultures have exposed
one source of confusion. The somewhat mystical notion that
the person doing the empathizing either "picks up" or "projects into" the other person his momentary cognitive-conative-
emotive state does not allow for the different symbolizing
systems of contrasting cultures. Regrettably, empathy cannot
set aside cultural barriers. When one person feels "in" with a
person of another culture, he does so by reading in an
interpretation that would fit if the other were a member of his
own culture. The other has a different system of showing
feelings, rendering projection or picking up difficult if not
impossible.

The neglected element is this: empathy has a strong cognitive component. The knowledge stored in a person limits and
structures his empathic responses. His perceptions are a result
of his habits of making certain associations and the content of
his experiences. This explains two little noted phenomena: (1)
the fact that a sensitive person is unable to empathize with
certain particular feeling states but can empathize strongly
with others, and (2) that two persons can have powerful and
quite different empathic responses to the same stimulus.

Empathy, then, does not consist of feeling what the other person feels, but of feeling what you perceive the other person to be feeling. Two people observe a person weeping. One feels joy, thinking the person is crying with happiness; the other feels sadness, thinking the observed person has been overcome with an unendurable burden. Perceptions of the same stimulus differ, empathic responses contrast.

Redefining empathy in a way that recognizes its cognitive dimension, empathy is the ability to replicate what one perceives. Let us examine the implications of this revised definition.

We choose to think of empathy as an ability rather than a tendency because of its role in communication. Just as a person has a language to the extent he has the ability to use it, so he has empathy to the degree he is able to respond empathically.

The definition states that the empathic response is "replication of what one perceives." Perception is reading meaning into what one senses. One senses not only cognitive elements but emotions and feelings. So, the empathic person perceiving that another feels sharp pain, replicates not only the physical attitude but also feels the pain. *The pain may or may not be felt by the person observed.* As long as the observer perceives it to be there, for him it exists, and his empathy is generated from his perception.

This treatment of empathy differs from previous treatments in that it adds a powerful cognitive dimension. Information, knowledge, and understanding are critical variables that determine empathic response. Control of attention and general sensitivity are as necessary as before, but they no longer, in and of themselves, provide the key to understanding the empathetic process.

In an intercultural interaction, empathy is culture bound. Until knowledge and experience have accumulated so that a person from one culture can *live* the same feeling-behavior relationships as does a representative of the other culture, empathy is more likely to be misleading than helpful.

The popular notion that empathy is the one mode of communication which transcends cultural differences is indeed a treacherous pitfall for the student of interaction across cultures. But precisely because empathy is culture bound, training it to operate crossculturally should be a major objective.

PERSON TO PERSON INTERCULTURAL COMMUNICATION AS A CREATIVE ACT

One of the consequences of predominantly analytical methodologies in communication research is our tendency to treat interpersonal communication as though it were a mechnical phenomenon. We make the assumption that if we labor long and hard enough we will identify all the variables, measure them, and become able to predict their interaction. In effect, we assume communication to be an activity of the left hemisphere of the brain and pay little attention to the contributions of the right hemisphere.

Evidence is accumulating that the right hemisphere has a great deal to do with effective interpersonal communication. While the left hemisphere handles quantitative data and enables us to compare definite options feature by feature in conscious problem solving, it is not suited to grasping complex patterns and quick formulation of general impressions. The left hemisphere needs to be managed by conscious control while the right, left alone, picks up and processes a Gestalt of events and spews out interpretations, rearrangements, and conclusions without revealing the processes that produced them.

The interactive approach to the study of interpersonal communication has forced us to conclude that much more happens in an interaction than can be accounted for by assuming that the participants are operating analytically. For one thing, there is often no time for conscious monitoring. If a person in a fast moving negotiation takes the time to think about what he is saying and calculate its effect, he is certain to lose. The rapidity of many exchanges indicates that many appropriate responses of individuals may be described as automated, i.e., not consciously directed.

Postulating internal monologue and its predominantly negative effects on purposeful communication further discredits analytical theories. A person who proceeds to be analytical during a conference does so by creating an internal monologue which (1) gives him two tasks, to maintain his internal monologue and carry on the conversation per se, and (2) makes him a bad listener. He is no longer able to devote his full energy to picking up clues he needs to create appropriate responses.

When we observe and describe highly effective interpersonal communicators we find that, like Maslow's self-actualized people, they have few self-centered thoughts during an episode of communication. Their attention is directed outside themselves. There is no concern about what or how they perform; they trust themselves to do the appropriate thing when the time comes. Because their total effort is devoted to collecting data, from the environment, their internal monologue is negligible or nonexistent. They absorb the complex flow of events in which they are involved and process it out-of-awareness. Responses come when needed and are given without being monitored. The process is aptly described by the adjective "automated." Adjustment to events is accomplished holistically rather than analytically. Patterns rather than parts of the process are ingested, an activity that is insulated from interference caused by the conscious mind.

Why do we claim that this sort of communicative interaction is a creative act? Because the activity described above, in which internal monologue is controlled and fresh responses combine cumulatively, resembles inventive or artistic creativity.

The result of creativity is the generation of significantly new concepts. This happens after the limits of analytical thinking have been reached. When linear thinking is no longer possible, when the data run out, people resort to holistic processing of clusters of impressions. The rules of systematic treatment of evidence are suspended. The thinker is free from the usual obligation to repeat the past. He becomes able to receive messages from his out-of-awareness critical thinking center. In effect, he stops conscious work on the problem (quiets the left hemisphere) and permits the right hemisphere to proceed holistically, accepting and using its output. The "flashes of insight" artists and inventors have in common often consist of simply knowing something is so without being able to explain its origin. Such a solution to a problem is not the result of trying to combine known variables. In fact, attempting to follow usual procedures tends to ensure against creativity. The creativity that occurs in communication is in the here and now, invariably surprising the participants who produce it, and the process by which complex patterns of events generate spontaneous response is little understood.

Westerners seem obsessed with related elements they persistently intrude into an interaction. Consequently, they respond as much to extraneous items as to what happens from moment to moment. The ability to choose to exist in the present and respond to it in context, spontaneously, varies from culture to culture. Creativity cannot happen in communication unless interacting persons control their internal monologue, that is, rid themselves of their scripted expectations and become free to respond as the circumstances of the moment dictate. Americans find this more difficult than do most of the peoples in the world.

We are belaboring the point that holistic processing of experience is difficult for Westerners to accept because this limitation has crippled our efforts to understand intercultural communication. An American interacting with a Japanese is ridigly inflexible, relatively speaking. He can deal only with what he anticipates, in ways he has rehearsed, by rearranging and replaying the past. The Japanese can drift into the here and now much more easily, maintaining his ability to adjust to changing circumstances sensitively. In an effort to cope with the difficulties that arise when these two patterns of behavior come together, Americans have tried to induce Japanese to behave like Americans, while the Japanese have postulated two theories of the life styles that produce these dissonant behaviors. These are termed erabi and awase.

The *erabi* view is that, ideally, man can freely manipulate his environment for his own purposes. This view implies a behavioral sequence whereby a person sets his objective, develops a plan designed to reach that objective, and then acts to change the environment in accordance with that plan.

Awase, on the other hand, rejects the idea that man can manipulate the environment and assumes instead that he adjusts himself to it....the environment consists of a constantly changing continuum of fine gradations. *Awase* is the logic of seeking to apprehend and adapt to these fine gradations of change [Kinhide, 1976: 41].

The mere enunciation of erabi and awase assumptions demonstrates what Watzlawick, Weakland, and Fisch (1974: 92) term "the gentle art of reframing." If the Japanese attempt to provide an illuminating context for our communication problem is not satisfactory, our cue is not to ignore the problem but to reconceptualize it in a way that is more insightful. Until we develop theory more compelling than the *erabi-awase* hypothesis, we may well use it to promote deeper understanding and ultimately, more and better theory.

By and large, other peoples in the world are more creative in their interpersonal communication than are we in the West. This significant difference seems associated with their greater reliance upon holistic processing of data. If we wish to relate to them more effectively (and our pursuit of the study of intercultural communication suggests that we do), then we might well attend to improving our utilization of holistic methods and procedures.

A first step is to assess our competence in responding holistically to the present. Edward T. Hall (1976: 34) comments:

> The danger is that real-life problems are dismissed while philosophical and theoretical systems are treated as real. I see this everyday in my students. It has been my experience that after students have spent sixteen or more years in our education system they have been so brainwashed that it is impossible to get them to go out and simply observe and report back what they heard, what they felt, or what went on before their eyes. Most of them are helpless in the face of real life, because they have to know beforehand what they are going to discover and have a theory or a hypothesis to test. Why? Because that is the way they have been taught.

If Hall is accurate in his observation that Western education produces scholars who can use only analytical approaches and procedures, then theory building requires major revision if it is to cope with global communication phenomena. Historically and presently, the study of intercultural communication assumes that we live in an erabi world, a classic instance of the "self reference criterion" (Lee, 1966: 106-114) in action. Until we include the elements of creativity that most of the world's people know to be the essence of interpersonal communication in our conceptualization of that process, our theory will continue to be an insufficient one. Balancing erabi and awase perspectives is a clear challenge to those who would guide our study towards a more productive future. Reframing intercultural communication by conceptualizing it as a creative act rather than as a mechanical process is only a beginning.

THE RELATIONSHIP OF ANALYTIC AND HOLISTIC DATA PROCESSING

Either-or, true-false Aristotelian thinking poses a problem to those who would integrate holistic processes with Western behavioral science. As Charles Hampden-Turner (Samples, 1976: 161) wisely stated, "the act of dichotomization was the original sin." To think of analytic and holistic processes as incompatible or mutually exclusive misses the main point. By relying on holistic data processing, Eastern thought has accomplished a great deal; by relying upon analytical procedures, Western thought has made significant advances. The time has come to place these systems in a supplementary relationship. By combining Eastern and Western approaches, we should be able to create theory that interprets life facts more competently than either does alone. The natural proving ground for the combination may be the symbolic intermingling of East and West we encounter in intercultural communication.

Westerners writing about holism strain to find words for largely out-of-awareness, nonlinear creativity and problem solving. Bob Samples refers to this human resource as the "metaphoric mind," a fitting label because the concept of metaphor is openended and nonlinear. He shows the necessity for both holistic and analytic operations in two deceptively simple sentences: "Attempting excursion into the metaphoric mind is not an attempt to discredit the rational mind. Without rationality, how could the excursion be made?" (Samples, 1976: 56). Somewhat abstractly, we have suggested the possibility that holistic and analytic methods may enhance and extend each other when blended into a joint venture. Perhaps we can be more specific as to how this unification can be implemented.

The analytic and holistic capabilities of a person manifest themselves in two distinctly different kinds of competence in communication or other types of human performance. *Conscious competence* is always analytic. It is a process of identifying variables involved, developing meaning for them, and, ultimately, putting the parts together to increase understanding of the total event. This requires a supply of theories and procedures to enable one to adjust to a range of circumstances. Conscious competence uses continuous monitoring, within-awareness calculation of the effect of what has and is being done, and specific planning of coming events.

Unconscious competence, a holistic phenomenon, is ideally unmonitored. A person relying upon unconscious competence is free to use his total resources to collect information from his environment and respond to it. He knows that when he feels the impulse to say something it will be more appropriate and effective than what he might say after thinking it over. He adjusts rather than anticipates. He simply depends upon his out-of-awareness critical thinking, trusting his ability to make unpremeditated, spontaneous responses.

Two applications of the division of communicative competence into conscious and unconscious categories suggest themselves. Interactions can be studied to find the circumstances under which each one is most effective. Second, persons can learn to choose to use conscious or unconscious competence and to shift from one mode to the other at will. The ability to sense which competence is appropriate and use it comfortably may become important to intercultural communication.

Another application may turn out to be multicultural. Preparation for an interaction should probably be predominantly analytic. Extensive internal monologue, with much conscious judgmental experimentation, is necessary to "program the internal computer" for the coming event. All sorts of possibly useful materials, facts, units of reasoning, illustrations, rhetorical devices, and so on are weighed and filed. Such analytic preparation cannot be too extensive or thorough, but an important restriction must be observed if the option to become holistic is to be preserved, namely, none of this material should be sequenced. If any is placed in a sequential arrangement, a script is developed and the freedom to respond spontaneously is lost. The result of the preparation period is a well-filled data bank, the contents of which can be drawn upon when and if appropriate during the communicative event.

The person who has prepared shifts to the unconscious competence mode when the interaction begins. His total attention is on the other person, his responses come without anticipation or later assessment. He uses material from his data bank when it meets the need of the moment, and finds himself using totally different content when it does the job better than anything he put in the bank. If things go wrong, he may need to shift to analysis and consciously evolve a change in his procedures. When this is done, he returns to the holistic mode of unconscious competence, which contains his maximum potential for adjusting, adapting, and collaborating with the flow of events.

When a person shifts from analytical preparation or trouble-shooting to holistic interaction, he does so by mind control. In Zen this is called "emptying the mind." In the present context, emptying the mind is simply turning off the internal mono-logue, eliminating extraneous thoughts, so that total attention can be directed outside the self. Then the out-of-awareness assets (data bank, critical thinking) can deal with changing circumstances via the apparently automated data processing of unconscious competence.

Intercultural communication intensifies our need for emphasis upon holistic data processing (unconscious competence, out-of-awareness critical thinking) because it involves interaction with representatives of many cultures wherein that is the norm. Fortunately, a beginning has been made, and the relation of out-of-awareness holism and conscious analysis within American culture are receiving increasing attention. (Mintzberg, 1976: 49-58; Ornstein, 1975). Communication theory for the future must account for creativity in interaction by placing analytic and holistic data processing in collaborative juxtaposition.

SUMMARY

We have noted the fragmentary nature of theorizing in the study of intercultural communication; the theory we do have is sparse, monocultural, analytic and not very helpful in promoting understanding of real life interactions across cultural boundaries. The directions suggested involve reconceptualizing intercultural interpersonal communication as a creative act. This will necessitate working through tthe relationship of analytical and holistic activities.

REFERENCES

ASSAGIOLI, R. (1973) *The Act of Will.* New York: Viking.

HALL, E.T. (1976) *Beyond Culture.* Garden City, N.Y. Anchor Press/Doubleday.

HAWES, L. (1977) "Alternative theoretical bases toward a presuppositional critique," *Communication Quarterly* 25: 63-68.

KINHIDE, M. (1976) "The cultural premises of Japanese diplomacy." P. 41 in Kano Tsutomu, (ed.), *The Silent Power: Japan's Identity and World Role.* Tokyo: Simul Press.

LEE, J.A. (1966) "Cultural analysis in overseas operation." *Harvard Business Review,* 44 (March/April): 106-114.

MINTZBERG, H. (1976), "Planning on the left side and managing on the right," *Harvard Business Review,* 54 (July/August): 49-58.

ORNSTEIN, R. (1975) *The Psychology of Consciousness.* New York: Penguin.

SAMPLES, B. (1976) *The Metaphoric Mind.* Reading, Mass.: Addison-Wesley.

WATZLAWICK, P., WEAKLAND, J. and FISCH, R. (1974) *Change: Principles of Problem Formulation and Problem Resolution.* New York: W.W. Norton.

3

ON THE RELEVANCE OF COGNITIVE ANTHROPOLOGY AND ETHNOMETHODOLOGY

JERRY L. BURK
Boise State University
AND
JANET G. LUKENS
University of Wisconsin

Two major problems have beset social science researchers in attempting to make comparisons across cultural boundaries: their apparent inability to construct scales capable of making valid and equivalent comparisons across cultures, and the lack of systematic controls for effectively eradicating their biases and selectivity. Mehan (1973) equated the problems of crosscultural research with those of educational researchers who have tried to discover a concept of "intelligence" across persons and failed. Both crosscultural and educational researchers have sought interviewing techniques and nonverbal tasks in the hope of designing measures that are valid and reliable. Both have failed for lack of valid equivalences of meaning or reliable measures of the concepts under study, whether crosscultural comparisons or measures of persons within the same culture.

Researcher subjectivity and the potential of selective perception created dissatisfaction with earlier research methods in crosscultural research. This prompted some anthropologists and sociologists to depart from the traditional methods of their respective disciplines in order to achieve a more objective understanding of cultures and thus the goal of cultural comparison. Cognitive anthropology and ethnomethodology were developed for the purpose of obtaining insight into the cognitive "reality" of members of various cultures. Cognitive anthropologists contended that their ethnoscientific approach would transform anthropology from a social science into a formal science, lending increased objectivity to the information secured from native informants about their culture. Ethnomethodologists, on the other, assumed that by going to cultures themselves and becoming immersed in the problems of everyday life, they could discover what constitutes cognitive reality for the members of a given culture.

Both methods were developed in response to the inadequacy of previous approaches to provide either insight into the subjective reality of individuals or greater control for the selectivity of researchers, who are steeped in their own cultural traditions. Cognitive anthropologists, or ethnoscientists, were dissatisfied with the approach of traditional anthropology, which emphasized fieldwork and data collection but neglected to provide a systematic description of the world as viewed through the eyes of natives. Very often anthropologists tried to fit the data to their own theoretical models with little or no regard for native classification systems. Ethnomethodologists were at similar odds with traditional sociology because it, too, was seen as failing to present the insider's point of view. In essence, ethnomethodologists maintained that traditional sociology was divorced from the "lived social realities" of the everyday lives it sought to describe.

Although there are distinctions between the approaches of these two methods of studying cultural groups, the similarities in their ultimate goals outweigh the differences. With this in mind, we will explore the utility of ethnoscience and ethnomethodology as methods for research in intercultural communication. There may be considerable value in being able to probe a particular culture and learn the perspective of cultural members through the revolutionary methods of cognitive anthropology and ethnomethodology.

Both cognitive anthropology and ethnomethodology have been critically examined in the literature of various disciplines, but those analyses have not been specifically concerned with their usefulness to intercultural communication research. Such an undertaking must be entered into wiith an open mind, as Chomsky (1972: 102) suggested:

For those who wish to apply the achievements of one discipline to the problems of another, it is important to make very clear the exact nature not only of what has been achieved, but equally important, the limitations of what has been achieved.

It is our intention to clarify both the achievements and limitations of these methods both through an explication of their major tenets' application to intercultural communication research, and through projections concerning their future usefulness to intercultural communication research.

AN EXPLICATION OF COGNITIVE ANTHROPOLOGY

Cognitive anthropology is a recent specialty in the field of anthropology. Goodenough (1956) is credited with the founding treatise, in which he discussed componential analysis as a means of discovering the structures and hierarchies of informants' minds. Componential analysis became one of the prominent research methods used by cognitive anthropologists; it was designed to revolutionize the concepts, research methods, and theoretical formulations of traditional ethnography.

The revolutionary nature of this new field increased the potential misunderstanding of the new ethnography. Three major claims are made by researchers in the area: (1) cognitive anthropologists claim to provide a new focus for ethnography; (2) cognitive anthropology research methods are designed to develop a formal analytical model of culture; and (3) cognitive anthropologists claim to transform culture through the ethnography using their research methods.

New Focus

Ethnographic investigations by cognitive anthropologists are significant departures from traditional ethnography because their focus is not overt, material phenomena but covert, cognitive concerns. "Culture" is not equated with cultural materials or other byproducts of human behavior. Instead, it is discussed as a cognitive construct capable of being understood only through the methods of cognitive anthropology. Those methods are generally designed to answer two fundamental questions: (1) what material phenomena are significant for the people of a given culture? and (2) how do the people of a given culture organize these material phenomena?

Cognitive anthropologists study the material phenomena of a culture insofar as it is revealed in the speech of an informant; they use those linguistic items in mapping the cognitive system. Linguistic items, together with their relative use in varying contexts, lead them to what they claim is the cognitive structure of the culture. Researchers in this area contend that the methods of cognitive anthropology allow the researcher to conceptually experience and describe events as the informant experiences them. Frake (1968: 514) has stated that:

> The intended objective of these efforts is eventually to provide the ethnographer with public, nonintuitive procedures for ordering his presentation of observed and elicited events according to the principles of classification of the people he is studying. To order ethnographic observation solely according to an investigator's preconceived categories obscures the real content of culture: how people organize their experience conceptually so that it can be transmitted as knowledge from person to person from generation to generation.

Elicited speech is the avenue through which cognitive anthropologists claim to "get inside the human brain" and discover cognitive systems which constitute the "culture" of a new group.

Formal Analytical Model

The ultimate goal of cognitive anthropology is to develop formal analytical methods which may be applied to elicited speech in order to discover the informant's category system. The perceptual categories of the culture under study are then used to describe the conceptualization of the natives. In this process, verbal behavior and the native's semantic domain appear to be equivocated because the elicited speech is used to discover cognitive domains.

Methodologically and conceptually, ethnoscientists seek to render anthropology a "formal" rather than a "social" science. Accordingly, they feel that ethnography will become a formal science when a general theory of culture emerges. To achieve this goal, new research methods have been devised to separate cognitive anthropology from linguistic and ethnological studies using traditional ethnographic methods. According to Tyler (1969: 12),

> new fieldwork techniques and methods have had to be devised. Most important among these are techniques of controlled *eliciting* and methods of *formal analysis*. Controlled eliciting utilizes sentence frames derived from the language of the people being studied. The aim of such eliciting is to enable the ethnographer to behave linguistically in ways appropriate to the culture he is studying.

Neither the traditional ethnographic methods nor the refinement of methods from this paradigm would satisfy cognitive anthropologists in their search for a formal science of culture.

Culture Transformed

The concept of culture was supposed to be transformed by the revolutionary methods and theoretical constructs of cognitive anthropologists. In this respect, ethnographic data became the organizational, structural, and perceptual processes of informants because traditional ethnographies did not provide sufficient data for a substantive, formal, analytic foundation for crosscultural comparison. Tyler (1969: 15) concluded that,

> if culture is the unit of comparison, then we must compare whole systems which are bounded in space and time or demonstrate that the parts of systems we are comparing are justifiably isolable. Since most ethnographies are not sufficiently complete for either of these possibilities, the whole comparative approach based on substantive variables must be abandoned if our claim is indeed cultural comparison.

For the purposes of this paper, the advantages claimed by cognitive anthropologists over traditional ethnographic methods may be summarized as follows (Frake, 1968: 154):

1. Cognitive anthropology gives a central place to cognitive processes of natives.
2. Reliable data will be generated for better understanding of the relationship between language, cognition, and culture.

3. Meaningful crosscultural comparisons will be possible.
4. Description of cultural behavior will make it possible for researchers to perform appropriate and acceptable behaviors within a given culture.

AN EXPLICATION OF ETHNOMETHODOLOGY

The term "ethnomethodology" was coined by Garfinkel in the 1960s to refer to the study of how people make decisions in everyday life. He identified this method as an organized study of common sense knowledge of how members of cultures structure their ordinary affairs by discovering invariant properties of everyday behavior, practical activities, or regularities.

Ethnomethodology emerged out of the dissatisfaction with traditional sociological research methods. Traditional sociology, it was claimed,was confined to the static model of social institutions, having no concern for the "social structuring activities" (i.e., practices, methods, procedures) that are the focus of ethnomethodologists. Whereas traditional sociologists focused their attention on social structures, increasing numbers of researchers saw a need for studying the relationships among the variables investigated by sociologists at the empirical level. They perceived a need for discovering how social reality is created out of dynamic relationships among human social agents.

Whereas traditional sociology is exclusively concerned with macrostructures, ethnomethodologists study the structuring activities that operate in the "real world" of individuals in social and institutional settings. These structuring activities include conversational openings, turn taking, classroom behavior, decisionmaking, power play, and so forth. Ethnomethodologists believe that knowing how these social structuring activities operate in everyday life increases the researcher's understanding of macrosocial structures. Mehan and Wood (1976) contrasted traditional sociology and ethnomethodology and concluded that ethnomethodologists had demonstrated a greater interest and explanatory power in the analysis of interpersonal behavior activities, including "oppression," "dogmatism," "racism," and "absolutism."

The increased explanatory power of ethnomethodology comes from its claim to have discovered how members of cultures construe reality. Researchers are not bound by formal analytical methods as cognitive anthropologists appear to be. Rather, ethnomethodologists rely more heavily on phenomenology to discover the subjective reality of individuals through systematic analyses of aspects of everyday life that are, otherwise, taken for granted by the individuals under study. Research methods are employed to discover how the world is interpreted by individuals in their daily lives and how "social reality" is shared among members of a particular culture. The phenomena under study are communication behaviors, verbal and nonverbal, which are replete with meaningful constructions.

Unlike cognitive anthropologists, ethnomethodologists have not confined themselves to static linguistic phenomena in the analysis of cognitive domains. Rather, they maintain that through the application of phenomenology one can discover the rules underlying *all* of man's experience, including linguistically organized experience. The ethnoscientist's approach is viewed by ethnomethodologists as limited to the discovery of rules underlying the verbal and cognitive realms of a given culture. The ethnomethodologist, on the other hand, contends that he can provide a grasp of the rules that underlie the culture's nonverbal and affective domains. In essence, the ethnomethodologist seeks to discover the rules underlying the structures and structuring of everyday life.

For the present purposes, the advantages claimed by ethnomethodologists over traditional sociological methods may be summarized as follows:

1. Ethnomethodologists discover the cognitive mapping of people's minds.
2. The "taken for granted rules" employed in everyday activities are uncovered.
3. Social and affective meanings can be analyzed through attention to verbal and nonverbal communication.
4. Researchers are no longer bound to macrostructures and the analysis of static social institutions.

APPLICATIONS OF COGNITIVE ANTHROPOLOGY AND ETHNOMETHODOLOGY

The research methods of cognitive anthropology and ethnomethodology can contribute to intercultural communication research by providing insight into native perceptual systems. This sort of awareness would facilitate the present conceptualizations of what intercultural communication failures are, as well as provide guidelines for how intercultural communication could be more effective. Such methods might, for example, help us understand how values function in communication transactions across cultures as well as within a culture. We will briefly discuss other potential contributions of these methods to a better understanding of race, language style, abstraction, nonverbal behavior, personality, and measurement.

Race

Methods of cognitive anthropology may prove relevant in intercultural communication researchers' concerns for cognitive variables that are concomitants of race. Studies using folk taxonomies within a particular race might reveal perceptual and attitudinal sets which would interfere in communication transactions with other racial groups. Ethnoscientific research methods may be used to discern how other racial groups are ranked within the social structure of a given race. Ethnomethodology might be employed to discover the emotional reactions that accompany communication transactions with various racial groups. These methods could, further, discover the foundations for stereotypes which racial group members have of outgroups and the attribution of characteristics to outgroup members based upon racial or biological characteristics.

Language Style

The outgroup status of cultural group members may be signaled by the speech pattern and language style used by the individual. Cognitive anthropology and ethnomethodology could be used to create a taxonomy of language styles and then ask native speakers to identify which styles would be most effective and appropriate in particular settings. Data from such studies could certainly be useful to persons doing other types of research within a culture by enhancing their ability to match cultural context and language style.

Abstraction

Tests may be developed for making systematic comparisons of how cultures differ on a continuum from abstract to concrete concepts of reality. Many extant experimental designs, according to Price-Williams (1974: 102-103), ask members of a culture to draw distinctions between levels of abstraction even when the culture is *not* oriented to discriminating at the levels required by that test or requested by the experimenter. Consequently the results may not be valid for the culture under study, and they certainly do not lend themselves to comparisons across cultures. Yet the research methods of cognitive anthropology and ethnomethodology may be able to generate instruments that are capable of cognitively measuring the abstraction level used by many cultures. Otherwise, the concept of "abstraction level" becomes meaningless for lack of valid instrumentation for crosscultural comparison.

Nonverbal Behavior

Little progress in the field of intercultural communication is possible unless some systematic account is taken of the role of nonverbal communication behavior. For our purposes, nonverbal communication behavior ranges from overt behavior, intentional and unintentional, to silence—each being as important as the other. These phenomena must be interpreted from the perspective of the individual in order to be meaningfully understood and described. Methods of cognitive anthropology and ethnomethodology could facilitate systematic intercultural communication of nonverbal behavior by developing a taxonomy of nonverbal behaviors that impede the development of meaningful relationships between members of different cultures. Of course ethnomethodology, with its focus on affective and cognitive dimensions of culture, would provide greater insight than cognitive anthropology.

Personality

Both methods could prove useful in the assessment of personality through an identification of particular traits founded in the cognition of culture group members. Ethnoscientists could construct folk taxonomies to be used as instruments: informants would be asked to rank the traits according to their preferences in people. Foreknowledge of these distinctions and cultural preferences could be used by practitioners who live in other cultures or by persons who plan to do so. Armed with this knowledge, intercultural communication researchers could prepare more accurate theoretical models of the interaction of cultural behavior and communication behavior.

Measurement

Intercultural communication researchers could profit from the development of "culture free" measuring instruments by ethnoscientists. Cognitive anthropological research methods could be used in the development, refinement, and validation of such tests through comparisons of the phenomena measured by the instruments in different cultures. It is to be expected that what an instrument measures in one culture will not be the same as what it measures in another. For example, tests have been made to modify intelligence instruments, but there has been an overall failure to recognize that cultures differ with respect to what constitutes intelligence. Cognitive anthropology and ethnomethodology may be useful in addressing these problems systematically.

THE FUTURE OF INTERCULTURAL COMMUNICATION RESEARCH

There is no doubt that we need to know more about cultural patterning, the role of communication in the patterning process, and the effects of that patterning and communication upon interactions with members of a given culture. That cultural patterning occurs as a result of communication patterning in the learned environment of every well enculturated individual cannot be denied. As a result, differences in perception and perspective emerge, separating one culture from another and thus creating the plurality of cultures which exist today.

Fundamental questions are generated when we recognize the interaction of communication and culture and our seeming inability to deal with these concepts systematically. Consider the following, for example: how does a language differ from a dialect? when do dialects stop and languages begin? how does a dialect or language patterning affect the cultural patterning? is cultural patterning signaled by the use of language by members of a given culture? is culture the sum total of symbolically learned and functionally observable phenomena? are the structuring of cultures and the functioning of communication sufficiently correlated to lead one from overt behavior to covert cognition? These are questions that must be addressed by researchers who wish to facilitate the conceptual and theoretical growth of intercultural communication.

Intercultural communication researchers have failed, like anthropologists and sociologists before them, to answer such questions in the comparison of cultures. Continued failures of this ilk will cause "intercultural communication" to be relegated to the study of "culture and communication" because of an exclusive dependence upon anecdotal rather than substantive crosscultural comparisons. This limitation may be checked, however, through the application of ethnoscience and ethnomethodology. Each is designed to move beyond the superficial to the "deep" or "embedded" structures within cultures, and so may be useful in the development of intercultural communication research methods.

Researchers must recognize that the methods from other disciplines that have made advances have limitations too. The limitations of ethnoscientific and ethnomethodological research methods for intercultural communication may well be caused by their differences in theoretical focus. Ethnoscience and ethnomethodology differ from one another, as we have explained, and each differs from the concerns of intercultural communication research. Neither method is a ready made solvent for the conceptual, methodological, or pragmatic problems of intercultural communication research.

The differences in focus are readily apparent when we recognize that many intercultural communication scholars seek a pragmatic approach to communication across cultures. They look at communication behavior, verbal and nonverbal, to understand how relationships between individuals are influenced by the communication transactions. Intercultural communication scholars are concerned with the *human relationship* rather than with the discovery of a *covert reality*. At this writing, the central question pertains to whether the reality of an individual is necessarily subject to explicit codification and subsequent analysis. Condon and Yousef (1975: 185) addressed this issue and concluded that, "it is by no means a universal assumption that *reality* can be apprehended and expressed in *words*." Likewise, we are not of the opinion that the reality of the individual is signaled by either verbal or nonverbal behavior.

The pragmatic approach to intercultural communication does not require that the researcher discover the reality that exists for a particular individual. A great deal can be learned about the communication behaviors that facilitate or retard the development of trust, for example, in communication transactions. Yet there may be considerable value in exploring the cognitive domain of individuals through the use of ethno-scientific and ethnomethodological research methods. And even if the "objective reality" of the individual is not discovered, one may still gain insight into the salience of certain objects and values for members of a particular culture.

REFERENCES

BASSO, K.H. (1970) "To give up on words: Silence in Western Apache culture." *Southwestern Journal of Anthropology*, 26: 213-230.
BECKER, S.L. (1969) "Directions for intercultural communication research." *Central States Speech Journal*, 20: 3-13.
BERREMAN, G.D. (1972) "Is ethnoscience really relevant?" in J. Spradley (ed.) *Culture and Cognition,* Toronto, Ontario: Chandler.
BERRY, J.W. (1969) "On crosscultural comparability." *International Journal of Psychology* 4: 119-128.
BRACE, C.L. (1967) *The Stages of Human Evolution and Cultural Origins*, Englewood Cliffs, N.J.: Prentice-Hall.

BRISLIN, R.W. and HOLWILL, F. (1976) "Indigenious views of the writings of behavioral/social scientists: Toward increased cross-cultural understanding." Paper presented at the Binational Conference on Intercultural Communication, Manila, Philippines.

BURK, J.L. (1975) "An explication and evaluation of cognitive anthropology." *Communication Annual*, 1.

BURLINGS, R. (1964) "Cognition and componential analysis: God's truth or hocus pocus?" *American Anthropologist* 66: 20-29.

CARROLL, J.B. (1956) *Language, Thought and Reality*. Cambridge, Mass.: MIT Press.

CHOMSKY, N. (1972) *Language and Mind*. New York: Harcourt Brace Janovich.

CONDON, J.C. and YOUSEF, F. (1975) *An Introduction to Intercultural Communication*. Indianapolis: Babbs-Merrill.

EASTMAN, C.M. (1975) *Aspects of Language and Culture*. San Francisco: Chandler and Sharp.

FRAKE, C.O. (1968) "The ethnographic study of cognitive systems," in R. Manners (ed.), *Theory in Anthropology: A Sourcebook*. New York: Aldine.

GARFINKEL, H. (1967) *Studies in Ethnomethodology*. Englewood Cliffs, N.J.: Prentice-Hill.

GOODENOUGH, W.H. (1956) "Componential Analysis and the Study of Meaning." *Language* 32: 195-216.

GOODNOW, J. (1969) "Problems in research on culture and thought," in D. Elkind and J. Flavell (eds.), *Studies in Cognitive Development: Essays in Honor of Jean Piaget*. London: Oxford University Press.

HEWES, G.W. (1966) "The Domain of Posture." *Anthropological Linguist* 8, 8: 106-112.

JENSEN, S. (1969) "How much can we boost IQ and scholarly achievement?" *Harvard Educational Review* 39: 1-123.

JONES, A. (1976) "Integrating emic and etic Approaches in the Study of Intercultural Communication." Paper presented at the International Communication Association, Portland, Oregon.

JOOS, M. (1967) *The Five Clocks*. New York: Harcourt, Brace & World.

HSU, F.K. (1900) "Prejudice and its Intellectual Effect in American Anthropology: an ethnographic report." *Anthropological Linguistics* 75: 1-19.

LANTZ, D. and STREFFRE, V. (1900) "Language and cognition Revisited," in S. Moscovici (ed.), *The Psycho-Sociology of Language*. Chicago: Markher.

MEHAN, H. (1973) "Assessing Children's Language Using Abilities: Methodological and Cross Cultural Implications," in M. Armer and A.D. Grimshaw (eds.), *Comparative Social Research: Methodological Problems and Strategies*. New York: John Wiley and Sons.

MEHAN, H. and WOOD, H. (9176) "De-secting ethnomethodology." *The American Sociologist* 11: 13-21.

PATERSON, D. (1900) "The Linguistic Analogy in Anthropology." Unpublished seminar paper, University of Washington, Seattle, Washington.

PENG, F.C.C. (1974) "Communicative distance." *Language Sciences* 31: 32-38.

PHILIPS, S. (1970) "Acquisition of Rules for Appropriate Speech Usage," in J.E. Alatitis (ed.), *Georgetown University 21st Annual Roundtable*. Washington, D.C.: Georgetown University.

PIKE, K.L. (1947) *Phonemics*. Ann Arbor: University of Michigan Press.

PRICE-WILLIAMS, D. (1974) "Psychological Experiment and Anthropology: The problem of categories." *Ethos* 2: 95-114.

PSATHAS, G. (1972) "Ethnoscience and Ethnomethodology," pp. 206-222 in J. Spradley (ed.), *Culture and Cognition.* San Francisco: Chandler.

SARLES, H.B. (1966) "The Dynamic Study of Interaction as Ethnoscientific Strategy." *Anthropological Linguistics,* 8, 8: 66-70.

SPRADLEY, J.P. (1970) "Ethnoscience and the Study of Urban Images," Paper presented at the Conference on Anthropological Research in Cities, University of Wisconsin-Milwaukee, Milwaukee, Wisconsin.

STEFFLRE, V. (1972) "Some Applications of Multidimensional Scaling to Social Science Problems," pp. 211-243 in K. Shepard, A.K. Romney, and A. Nerlove (eds.), *Multidimensional Scaling: Theory and Applications in the Behavioral Sciences.* New York: Academic Press.

STURTEVANT, W.C. (1972) "Studies in Ethnoscience." pp. 129-167 in J. Spradley (ed.), *Culture and Cognition.* San Francisco: Chandler.

TYLER, S. (1969) *Cognitive Anthropology.* New York: Holt, Rinehart and Winston.

WAX, M., WAX, R. and DUMONT, R.J. (1970) "Formal education in an American Indian community." *Social Problems Monograph No. 1,* Society for the Study of Social Problems, Kalamazoo, Michigan.

INTEGRATING ETIC AND EMIC APPROACHES IN THE STUDY OF INTERCULTURAL COMMUNICATION

STANLEY E. JONES

University of Colorado

TWO BASIC APPROACHES TO THE STUDY OF CULTURAL PHENOMENA

There are two traditional approaches to making discoveries about cultural differences, and communication scholars have tended to follow the lead of other disciplines by adopting one or the other. The distinction was originally inspired by Sapir (1925) but given further examination by Kenneth Pike (1960), who coined the words "etic" and "emic" from the linguistic terms "phonetic" and "phonemic." The etic approach looks at behavior from the outside for the purpose of comparing cultures. Categories of behavior are imposed on observation. Objective observation is the method of study, and interobserver reliability and replication are the criteria for validity. The emic approach, on the other hand, attempts to discover how a system looks from the inside, so ordinarily only one culture is studied at a time and comparison is not a matter of immediate interest. The categories and rules of behavior are derived from the user's point of view. Participant observation is the primary method of investigation, and intersubjective reliability is the test of validity.

The purpose of this paper is to suggest a way in which the etic and emic approaches might be combined in the process of generating information of value to an understanding of intercultural communication. In order to do this, I will first describe some of my own research on cultural differences in proxemic behavior within the United States as an example of the comparative etic approach. In the process, I will try to show how some of the problems of such research can be overcome, especially underlining the notion that the distinction between "field" and "laboratory" studies is not an absolute one. In the latter part of the paper, I will suggest how I might have done this research in a different manner, employing both the etic and emic means of gathering data.

FIELD STUDIES OF DIFFERENCES IN PROXEMIC BEHAVIOR AMONG AMERICAN ETHNIC GROUPS

The investigator conducting a comparative study of communication behaviors of cultural groups immediately faces two problems. First, a situation must be found in which the conditions for observation will be relatively equivalent for members of each cultural group. This would seem to call for studies conducted under carefully controlled laboratory conditions, but there is a second issue with which one must deal. Investigators risk producing invalid results whenever they study interaction apart from the physical and social situations that give rise to the behaviors. It certainly creates a problem in the study of ethnic minorities when the experimenter takes individuals off to a strange laboratory environment and implicitly asks them to perform while a middle class Anglo observer looks on; a similar difficulty in interpretation may also exist when an American investigator observes subjects of a different country in a laboratory environment. An exception may be Michael Watson's laboratory studies of proxemic behavior of foreign and American students, because he has obtained results that compare favorably with field observations of Arabs and members of other groups (Watson and Graves, 1966; Watson, 1968). Foreign students in the United States become rather accustomed to interacting in a variety of strange surroundings, but even here one may well be doubtful of the validity of findings.

Studies of Street Behavior

I first attempted to overcome these problems in two studies of street behavior in lower income black, Puerto Rican, Chinese, and Italian neighborhoods in New York City. In the initial study (Jones, 1971), three trained observers recorded interaction distances and body axis (the degree to which bodies are turned toward or away from one another) of two-person groups, using an adaptation of a notation system designed by Hall (1963). Recordings were made at the first moment when each interactant was stationary. Interactions were sampled so as to maintain equivalence across cultural groups in times of the day, days of the week, and types of locations in which recordings were taken.

In the second study (Jones, 1972), two observers with stopwatches recorded "mutual head orientation" (the amount of time when the faces of both interactants were turned toward one another), while two other observers made distance and axis recordings at ten second intervals. Interjudge reliabilities were acceptably high for recordings in both studies.

Contrary to expectations based on Edward Hall's theories (1966), the results showed that the four cultural groups were rather similar in their distancing and body axis behavior, although there were sex differences (females in all cultures turned toward one another more and maintained more mutual head orientation than males). Black males did have less mutual head orientation than members of other groups, as predicted. There were three apparent explanations for why the expected cultural differences were not found. First, it is possible that the measurement scales were not sufficiently precise or that situational variations were so high that error factors accounted for the lack of significant differences. Second, it might be that poverty groups are rather alike in some aspects of their proxemic behavior. Third, these cultural groups might not differ from one another very much in the context of public street behavior. In any case, more research was called for, and each of these possible explanations provided some direction for further investigations.

Studies of Elementary School Children

In a second series of two studies, my colleague John Aiello and I investigated cultural differences among grade school children. In the first study (Aiello and Jones, 1971), a methodology similar to that of the street studies was employed to observe first and second grade children interacting in dyads on school playgrounds in lower income black and Puerto Rican and middle class Anglo schools. As in the street studies of adults, recordings of distance and axis were taken at the first moment when both children were stationary. The results showed that both of the lower income groups used much closer interaction distances than the middle class Anglos, average distances being about six inches for the black and Puerto Rican children and one foot for the Anglo children. No cultural differences were found in axis orientation.

In a second study (Jones and Aiello, 1973), we employed a somewhat different situation for observation in order to better control environmental conditions, the relationship among the interactants, and the topic of conversation. We were also interested in seeing how cultural differences might change from the first to the third to the fifth grade levels of school. Pairs of children of the same sex and race from each grade level at a lower income black school and middle class Anglo school were matched according to whom they would ordinarily choose for talk or play. The pairs of children were taken one at a time to a classroom in each school which was used for out of class activities. These classrooms were similar in appearance and identical in physical dimensions. The observer invited each pair of students to jointly select their favorite television commercial "to act out," and then proceeded to "grade papers" while the children talked, looking up unobtrusively to make recordings on distance and axis behavior every 20 seconds.

Because of the times of year when the playground study and the classroom study were conducted, the first and second grade children from the first study had an average age close to the average age of the first grade children in the second study. The findings essentially replicated those on interaction distances from the first study. The black children stood closer than the

Anglo children at the lowest grade level. At the third and fifth grade levels investigated in the second study, however, the difference in interaction distances disappeared, and actually appeared to be crossing over by the fifth grade. Thus the black children seemed to be more distant at the highest grade level, although this result was not statistically significant. While no significant cultural differences in axis were discovered in the first study, the use of a more precise scale for measuring body orientation in the second study showed that the blacks maintained less direct orientations than the Anglos across the grade levels, as predicted.

Our primary objective in these studies had been to test Hall's assumption (1966) that proxemic norms are "basic to culture and subculture" because they are "learned at an early age." In both studies we found evidence that cultural differences did appear at an early age. But we also found that not all cultural differences in proxemic behavior were "set" at an early age, because distancing behavior changed as children grew older, while body directness (axis) remained rather stable. Since this study, Aiello and Aiello (1973) have been able to demonstrate that distancing behaviors of middle class Anglo children continue to change up until age 12 (around the seventh grade), and then tend to stabilize as they grow older.

In the second study, we were able to demonstrate that the results of the first study concerning behavior in the early grade school years were replicable in a different setting in which various aspects of the communication context were more controlled. In the process, we were also able to show the feasibility of creating conditions which were, at the same time, a "field" and a "laboratory" situation.

A Study of Cultural and Social Class Differences

In our most recent study (Aiello and Jones, 1977), we explored both cultural and social class differences of blacks and Anglos in proxemic behavior by employing a "classroom laboratory" methodology similar to that of the second study of children, this time with tenth grade students from predominantly working class black, working class Anglo, middle class

black, and middle class Anglo schools. We used sociometric
measures as a basis for pairing students with members of their
same sex, race, and social class; the topic for discussion was
"the value of television." The results showed that blacks were
more distant, less direct in body axis, and maintained less
mutual head orientation than Anglos. The only significant
difference attributable to social class was that working class
students, both black and Anglo, stood farther apart than middle
class students.

The findings on cultural differences were quite consistent
with expectations derived from our own research, etic compar-
isions conducted by others in field situations (Willis, 1966;
Baxter, 1970), and one emic study which touched on the
subject of black proxemic behavior (Cooke, 1972). The surprising result was that social class played such a small role. In
short, there was very little evidence of any assimilative trends
on the part of blacks as we looked from the working class to the
middle class data. This study was crucial to our entire program
of research because we were able to both establish predicted
differences in behavior among subjects who had presumably
acquired adult norms and separate cultural or racial factors
from the variable of social class.

DIRECTIONS FOR FUTURE RESEARCH: INTEGRATION OF THE ETIC AND EMIC APPROACHES

The research program described above has progressed to the
point where some signs of progress can be listed, and these
illustrate the kinds of information that can be gleaned from etic
studies. Some widely held notions about cultural differences in
proxemic behavior based on the theories and impressionistic
accounts of Edward Hall have been tested. Hall's expectation
that adult blacks, who are supposed to constitute a "high
involvement culture," would stand closer together than Anglos
was not born out. In addition, the picture of cultural proxemic
differences which emerges is more complex than that originally
painted by Hall. Cultural differences seem to be more apparent
in some contexts than others. Some cultural norms of proxemic
behavior appear to change with age, at least from the early

years of school until some point in adolescence, and are not "set" at an early age. Social class appears to play some role in the development of proxemic norms, although perhaps its influence is not as pervasive as assimilation models might lead us to expect, at least in the case of blacks.

However, there is one particularly perplexing fact that must be taken into account. While the findings described are consistent among themselves and match the findings of most other investigators, there have been studies which produced somewhat different conclusions. Hall himself (1974), in a field study of working class black and middle class Anglo adults, and Forston and Ericson (1973), in a laboratory study of middle class black and Anglo college students, both found that blacks maintained closer interaction distances than Anglos. Not all the findings of these studies contradict other research: Hall and Forston and Ericson also found that blacks faced one another less directly than Anglos, a difference not yet inverted in any studies. But the weakness of the exclusive use of the etic approach can be seen.

How can we explain these discrepancies in the findings of different investigators? Where students have failed to produce significant differences, the results might be traceable to faulty measurement and observation techniques. All we can do to overcome this problem is to refine measurement and observation techniques. But where findings of different researchers are statistically significant and contradict one another, something is being measured. Apparently, cultural differences are not absolute, but vary with the context in which observations are made. This suggests that we must know more about the cultural significance of the situations that are used as a basis for comparison, which requires an emic approach.

How might the etic and emic strategies be integrated? One approach widely recommended by linguists is for the investigator to go from etic to emic analyses. This is the procedure suggested by Pike (1966) in his initial proposal of the etic-emic distinction, and by Hymes (1964) in his recommendations on the methodology of ethnographic studies of speech acts. According to this approach, research begins with etic analysis, which provides a "preliminary grid and input to an emic (structural) account," but which necessarily goes on to the inherently more accurate emic analysis (Hymes, 1964). The reverse order makes just as much sense when one is concerned not just with language, but with communication in its broadest sense—as verbal and nonverbal code enactment in social situations. Nor does such research need go only in one direction, i.e., toward increasing emphasis on the emic approach. I can demonstrate this best by reexamining my own research, but first it is necessary to evaluate the suppositions of the etic to emic recommendation.

The assumption beneath the approach which goes from etic to emic analysis is that the study of communicative acts in general should follow the same method used by structural linguists for the study of language. The linguist begins by employing a system of categories presumed to apply to all cultures, such as the International Phon*etic* Alphabet. This is only the first step, however, since the linguist must go on to use informants to discover which sounds are phon*emic*ally distinct from one another for members of a given culture. Eventually, larger meaning units are discovered, including words and sentence structures.

The application of this approach to other-than-linguistic aspects of communication runs into two difficulties, however. First, assuming one accepts the idea that language can be profitably studied apart from other communication phenomena, it can be seen that the etic transcription system's value to language study is that it permits the description of all (or nearly all) potentially relevant elements in linguistic acts (Francis, 1958). Later, when the linguist asks informants to help in the process of discovering structure among those sounds initially recorded, it can be assumed that nothing has been left out. It is not clear that this principle can be applied when nonverbal and contextual elements are also studied. At present, there is no transcription system that can record all potentially relevant elements of body motion, facial expression, vocal intonation, personal appearance, spatial relations, environmental conditions, and other aspects of social encounters. Even if an approximation to such a system were employed, it could not be used in most field situations because multiple cameras would be required to produce an audio-visual recording that would permit accurate coding of the data. Of course, it can be argued that the investigator may only be interested in the "proxemic system" of a given culture, and that a notation system such as the one provided by Hall (1963) will generate all the data needed for this task. But some investigators (cf. Argyle and Dean, 1965) have suggested that proxemic behavior, unlike language, is highly sensitive to a wide variety of behaviors in the communication flow (e.g., facial expression). If this is so, then the "building block" approach of the structuralists tends to break down because it stipulates that we cannot go on to higher levels of abstraction until we have obtained a complete record of related behavior on a more microscopic level.

This leads to the second difficulty in applying the linguistic analogy. The strict use of the structural approach assumes that the smallest unit of study must be exhaustively investigated before one can move on to the next level. Even for the linguist, this makes it virtually impossible to move beyond the level of the sentence: structural linguists have, at least, tended to operate within the realm of the sentence (Birdwhistell, 1970). Likewise, the investigator who studies broad aspects of communication cannot insist upon starting with a complete description of the most minute aspects of body position and movement (and other communicative behaviors) and hope to study entire face-to-face encounters in any appreciable numbers. Therefore, the exclusive use of this methodology would considerably delay the discovery of cultural differences, since a wide variety of contexts would have to be examined structurally before any conclusions could be drawn.

It should be stressed that the etic-emic distinction is drawn by analogy from the concepts of phonetics and phonemics. It is not tied to the structuralist approach. In linguistics, etic research is traditionally concerned with microscopic units, while emic analysis builds on etic description and is necessarily concerned with a higher level of abstraction. When used more broadly to refer to communication research in general, etic categories can be microscopic or rather macroscopic (e.g., types of social gatherings found across cultures). The investigator might indeed begin with (broad) etic categories, but these can be revised later: no assumption need be made that the investigator is working with building blocks toward a complete emic analysis. The major point of contrast between the etic and emic approaches is that the former can be used for purposes of systematic comparison, while the latter attempts to discover how the events appear to the persons within each culture.

I propose that in future studies of cultural differences in proxemic behavior, and in studies of other types of communicative behavior as well, the etic phase of controlled data collection for purposes of comparison ought to be preceded by a stage of emic analysis of contextual factors in each culture. Although some degree of etic analysis might go before an emic approach, especially in the use of broad categories for the observation of behavior, the investigator ought not spend too long in this stage of the investigation. He or she ought to go on to the task of doing a partial emic analysis and then return to etic comparisons, thereafter going back and forth between each approach.

For example, in each of the studies of proxemic behavior in which I was involved, a more nearly exhaustive description of the nature of the activities engaged in by members of each culture at each location might have helped to explain the results more fully and might have led to different choices about the sampling of behaviors. In the studies of street behavior, these problems were overcome to some degree by simple observation. For example, I discovered after many long hours of observation that Italians simply did not "come out" very often to stand around and talk in the early afternoons, and that on Saturday mornings, black women had rather brief interactions on the street and then passed on to stores where they did their marketing. This suggested that observations made at these times might not be comparable to other occasions. I was also able to glean some information directly from informants about what was going on when. Meeting in front of the church after services on Sunday morning in the black community and working on cars on Sunday afternoons in Puerto Rican neighborhoods, for example, were quite distinctive kinds of social occasions, and observations at those sites on those occasions were avoided.

Although I did do some analysis using an emic approach as groundwork, I did not approach the step of constructing a "social map" of locations in each community. At the very least, such a map would have required extensive interviewing of informants, including getting residents of each area to walk through the neighborhood with me, pointing out what was likely to be going on in various places at various times. Eventually, a good deal of direct participation in interaction would have been desirable to verify this information. In other words, I would have had to employ an emic approach to discern how members of each community categorized contextual variants in behavior.

If I were to do my research over again, the extensive emic phase of investigation suggested above would eventually give way to etic comparative analysis. Having developed some notions about differences among cultural groups while studying neighborhoods (whether concomitantly or one at a time), I would want to put my ideas to a test. I would not want to depend solely on my impressions about differences based on my perceptions of my informants' perceptions; I would want to objectify my observations in the form of an etic category system and systematic collection of data. A method of recording and notating behavior would be selected and a strategy for getting into position to observe behavior would be devised, much as in my original studies. But the choice of hypotheses of locations for comparison across cultural groups, and perhaps of what situations to compare within each cultural neighborhood would be strongly influenced by the previous participant observation phase of research. In the process, of course, some information about the unique character of proxemic communication within each culture would be temporarily ignored, but a valid comparison with limited objectives would be possible.

How far to go with an emic analysis before proceeding to the step of etic comparisons is a matter for the judgment of the investigator. At the very least, a contextual analysis should determine the range of situations for interaction, as distinguished from one another by the members of the community. If the objective of study were the delineation of forms of street behavior, the categories might include gambling, "hanging out," stopping to pass the time of day while shopping, and so forth. Closely related to this first step of analysis would be the identification of times, locations, and participants for each situation. Finally, the analysis could go on to the details of the events within each setting and occasion, including the role relationships of participants, topics of discussion, the specific purposes of interaction and, ultimately, the specific patterns of exchange within face-to-face groups. These latter types of observations would most likely involve some direct partic- ipation on the part of the investigator. In some cases, help in performing each of these steps of emic analysis can be gained by reference to other emic accounts of similar settings by previous investigators. But researchers would also need to familiarize themselves with the specific communities they were studying and to test the validity of prior accounts.

The exact point at which to objectify the analysis with an etic comparison of behavior among different groups is difficult to determine. Presumably it would be when he or she has begun to solidify hypotheses about the nature of cultural differences in various social contexts. In my own proxemic research on street behavior, for example, this point might have come when I was quite confident that I had discovered equivalent (or nearly equivalent) interaction situations among the various ethnic communities, and when I had some clear idea of how interac- tion behavior varied across groups for each context. Non- equivalent situations within and across cultural groups could also be compared to test the contextual variability of ethnic differences.

This etic analysis would in turn feed into further study employing an emic approach. If the etic data did not verify the hypotheses, or if some unexpected incidental results were obtained, reexamination of the conclusions of the participant observation stage of research might be indicated. For ex- ample, in my second study of street behavior, despite the lack of cultural differences in average interaction distance, I dis- covered that the blacks had greater variability of distances within encounters than other groups. Had I pursued this lead, I would have done further participant observation work to explore this "in and out" behavior and what it signifies in black conversation. Perhaps this pattern provides the basis for a more important communicative distinction between blacks and others than the question of average interaction distance. (In fact, subsequent discussion with Anglo informants who had spent some time among blacks suggested that this frequent changing of distance orientation was one of the characteristics of black interaction behavior that confused them most.) I would have returned to the task of collecting etic data among cultural groups when I was more confident of the nature of the behaviors I wanted to compare and the conditions under which I expected cultural differences to exist.

I am hard pressed to identify appropriate models in past research for this kind of approach. The closest example comes from urban sociologist Gerald Suttles' study (1968) of black, Mexican-American, Puerto Rican, and Italian communities in the Addams area of Chicago. Suttles lived in this area for nearly three years while he conducted an extensive parti-cipant observation study of patterns of behavior, going back and forth among the various neighborhoods. Although he concentrated on an emic analysis of each cultural group, from time to time he also gathered comparative data in an etic manner in order to test his developing conclusions about cultural differences.

For example, in order to examine his hypothesis that com-munication patterns reflected different levels of sociocultural integration among the various groups, Suttles conducted sys-tematic counts in selected locations of the use of various clothing styles by teenage boys. He found that blacks seemed to address their self-presentations to the wider community, favoring clothes that were sufficiently "dressy" to be worn outside the Addams area, while Italians preferred very casual and unstylish garb worn only within their own community, and Mexican-Americans and Puerto Ricans were intermediary, "borrowing" items of style from both groups. (Suttles, 1968: 67-72.)

Suttles also identified some differences in other aspects of communicative behavior, although he did not verify these observations with etic comparisons. He noted that residents were vaguely aware of certain variations in nonverbal behavior found in the Addams area (including gestures, patterns of eye contact, and walking behavior), but that they tended not to identify these as cultural differences and instead assigned meanings on an individual basis. For example, the characteristic lack of eye contact on the part of blacks and the higher amount among Italians was interpreted by members of each culture as a sign of impoliteness on the part of those from the other group (Suttles, 1968: 66-67). From the point of view of intercultural communication research, it is disappointing that he did not follow through on his approach by systematically comparing these behaviors across cultures, and that he did not measure the responses of members of each group to the nonverbal behaviors of their own and the other groups. In short, while his work is admirable for its use of etic comparisons as a check on emic analysis, he did not always follow through on this approach.

APPLICABILITY OF FINDINGS TO THE ANALYSIS OF INTERCULTURAL COMMUNICATION EVENTS

The combination of etic and emic approaches has two distinct advantages over both the prevailing practice of using one approach to the exclusion of the other and the practice recommended by linguists that investigators proceed solely from etic to emic analysis. First, each approach provides a check upon and a method of generating new directions for the other. More progress will be made when an investigator or team of investigators goes back and forth between both approaches. Second, combining the approaches in this way maximizes the usefulness of data for making practical applications to intercultural communication situations.

We may conceive of research related to intercultural communication concerns as falling into three types. These can be arranged in an ascending order in terms of their contribution to our understanding of what happens in the process of intercultural message exchange. They may also be seen as rough stages toward an analysis of intercultural events if no rigid assumptions are made that one stage must be entirely completed before the next one is entered.

Studies of Individual Cultures

Studies of individual cultures focus on emic analysis. The investigator may begin observations using etic categories, but this is not essential. Ultimately, the goal is to discover how the communication system of the culture functions. In practice, of course, the entire system is not explored, but only selected elements are examined. Examples include, in the area of sociolinguistics, Gerry Philipsen's study (1975), "Speaking 'Like a Man' in Teamsterville" and in the realm of proxemics research, Albert Scheflen's study (1971), "Living Space in an Urban Ghetto." Although this approach has the obvious advantage that cultures are studied in some depth, there are two disadvantages from the standpoint of intercultural communication theory. First, we must rely heavily on the insights of the individual investigator, and we seldom have information with which to judge whether two independent investigators would reach the same conclusions about each culture. Second, judgment about how the two systems will "fit together" in actual cases of culture contact is highly speculative.

Crosscultural Comparisons

Crosscultural comparisons focus on etic analysis. Comparisons are made across cultures by using some measure (such as the semantic differential or a category system for the observation of interaction behavior) and some method of equating conditions for data collection. From this kind of information, we can begin to infer how members of each cultural group might respond to the same stimulus situation. We become more confident about the nature of cultural differences and more precise in our guesses about how behaviors of one cultural group match those of another. If the research has been based on emic investigations of each culture, we are also reassured to some degree that the situations studied are comparable, and become more confident in our projections about what meanings would be assigned by members of each culture. For example, if we know on the basis of an etic comparison that under certain circumstances Arabs will stand closer than Americans, and we also know something from emic studies about the cultural relevance of these circumstances—i.e., what distances are seen as distinctly different within each culture, and how standing "too close" or "too far away" is likely to be interpreted—then we can begin to hypothesize about sources of understanding and misunderstanding between these cultures stemming from proxemic behavior. Ideally, after this phase of research, the investigator would return to each culture for further study, especially if the data indicated that prior analyses in the individual cultures did not lead to accurate predictions about cultural differences. While this is comparatively easy to do with contiguously located ethnic communities, it is difficult with societies which are geographically distant from one another, although team research efforts might overcome this problem.

Studies of Intercultural Contact

Studies of intercultural contact involve the investigation of how members of different cultures behave in relation to one another. Such studies are rather rare because of the difficulty of getting in position to examine such events. They may be conceived of as emic in approach if we are willing to view a situation of intercultural interaction as a cultural system within itself. Sara Winter's analysis (1971) of interracial self-analysis groups is an example of this, but for the most part, studies of intercultural contact are etic in nature, relying on some sort of categories for the description of interaction or the assessment of outcomes. An example is Collett's experimental study (1971) of contact between English students and Arab foreign students. Some Englishmen were trained to act proxemically in a manner similar to Arabs—maintaining a high degree of eye contact, sitting close, and shaking hands at several points in a conversation. Other Englishmen were not trained and simply behaved like Englishmen—maintaining less eye contact, employing a comparatively distant position, and not touching at all. As one might expect, post-test questionnaires revealed that the Arabs liked the "Arab-like" Englishmen better. In studies of this type, if previous work has provided both comparative data on the specific kinds of behavior in question (from etic studies) and information on how members of each culture are likely to perceive messages within the situation (from emic studies), the investigator is in a better position to make predictions and to interpret results.

As progress is made in the field of communication toward a methodology for a science of intercultural communication, it is natural that there will be some borrowing from the approaches of anthropologists, linguists, and social psychologists. But it will also be necessary for communication scholars to develop their own ways of pursuing their unique interest in the process of message exchange among members of diffcrent cultures. I suggest that an integration of the emic and etic standpoints involving alternation of these approaches constitutes a strategy which serves this purpose.

REFERENCES

ARGYLE, M. and DEAN, J., (1965) "Eye contact, distance, and affiliation." *Sociometry,* 28: 289-304.
_____ (1971) "Field study of the proxemic behavior of young school children in three subcultural groups," *Journal of Personality and Social Psychology* 19: 351-356.
AIELLO, J. R. and JONES, S. E. (forthcoming) "Race, social class, and proxemic behavior."
BAXTER, J. C. (1970) "Interpersonal spacing in natural settings." *Sociometry,* 33: 444-456.
BIRDWHISTELL, R. L. (1970) *Kinesics and Context.* Philadelphia: Univ. of Pennsylvania Press.
COLLETT, P. (1971) "Training Englishmen in the non-verbal behavior of Arabs." *International Journal of Psychology,* 6: 209-215.
COOKE, B. G. (1972) "Nonverbal communication among Afro-Americans: An initial classification," in Kochman (ed.), *Rappin' and Stylin' Out.* Urbana: University of Illinois.
FORSTON, R. F. and ERICSON, J. L. (1973) "Black-white nonverbal communication: Personal space analysis." *Iowa State Journal of Research,* 48: 1-6.
FRANCIS, W. N. (1958) *The Structure of American English.* New York: Ronald Press.
HALL E. T. (1974) *Handbook for Proxemic Research.* Society for the Anthropology of Visual Communication.
_____ (1966) *The Hidden Dimension.* Garden City, N.Y.: Anchor.
_____ (1963) "A system of notation of proxemic behavior." *American Anthropologist,* 65: 1003-1026.

HYMES, D. (1964) "Toward ethnographies of communication." *American Anthropologist,* 66: Reprinted in Michael H. Prosser [ed.] (1973) *Intercommunication Among Nations and Peoples.* New York: Harper and Row.
JONES, S.E. (1972) "Subcultural and sex differences in proxemic behavior." New York: Queens College, Unpublished paper.
_____ (1971) "A comparative proxemics analysis of dyadic interaction in selected subcultures of New York City." *Journal of Social Psychology* 84: 35-44.
_____ and AIELLO, J. R. (1973) "Proxemic behavior of black and white first-, third-, and fifth-grade children." *Journal of Personality and Social Psychology* 25: 21-27.
PHILIPSEN, G. (1975) "Speaking 'like a man' in teamsterville: Culture patterns of role enactment in an urban neighborhood." *Quarterly Journal of Speech* 61: 13-22.
PIKE, K. L. (1966) "Etic and emic standpoints for the description of behavior," in *Language in Relation to a Unified Theory of the Structure of Human Behavior.* The Hague: Mouton. Reprinted in Alfred G. Smith (1966) *Communication and Culture.* New York: Holt, Rhinehart & Winston.
SAPIR, E. (1925) "Sound patterns in language." *Language* 1: 37-51. Reprinted in D. G. Mandelbaum [ed.] (1949), *Selected Writings of Edward Sapir.*
SCHEFLEN, A. E. (1971) "Living space in an urban ghetto." *Family Process* 10: 429-449.
SUTTLES, G. D. (1968) *The Social Order of the Slum* Chicago: Univ. of Chicago Press.
WATSON, O. M. (1972) "Conflicts and directions in proxemic research." *Journal of Communication* 22: 443-459.
_____ (1968) "Proxemic behavior: A cross-cultural study." Boulder: University of Colorado (Ph.D. dissertation). Reprinted by University Microfilms, Inc., Ann Arbor, Michigan.
_____ and GRAVES, T. D. "Quantitative research in proxemic behavior." *American Anthropologist* 68: 971-985.
WILLIS, F. N. (1966) "Initial speaking distance as a function of the speakers' relationship." *Psychonomic Science* 5: 221-222.
WINTER, S. K. (1971) "Black man's bluff." *Psychology Today* September: 39-43, 78-81.

PART II.

CONCEPTUAL FRAMEWORKS

Human beings have gone through 4,000 years of introspection, but it is only within the last 300 that we have begun to explore our horizons. We have not feared to traverse the most dangerous terrain or to cross the most violent seas. But we have also sought by understanding to improve our minds. The ability to meditate and to explore the self is responsible for a great deal of sanity in the twentieth century. Perhaps to know ourselves, in every respect, is positively correlated to intercultural communication.

The essays in this section are focused on conceptual problems. Saral's "Consciousness Theory of Intercultural Communication" seeks to broaden our traditionally Western concept of consciousness by explaining that *in-culture self-knowledge* is a prerequisite for effective communication. Unitive thinking, flowing with the world, and intuition are his choice terms. What is clear for Saral is that "a state of consciousness is a unique dynamic pattern or configuration of psychological structure designed to enable us to sense the external and internal environment."

In "Rhetoric and Intercultural Communication," Blake brings to our attention the whole area of comparative rhetoric. His purpose is to suggest how the comprehensive scope of human discourse could be profitably studied. Blake's treatment of comparative rhetorics allows us to find heuristics for more detailed analyses. Providing discussions of procedure and scope, he warns of the pitfalls of both if we approach the subject with a Western frame of mind. Asante and Barnes' "Demystification of the Intercultural Communication Encounter" provides a conceptual framework for examining the intercultural encounter experience. Beginning with the idea that self identity, relatedness, and power are significant factors of the self, they show how this works in an encounter.

Finally, Ramsey presents an extensive evaluation of research on nonverbal communication in "Nonverbal Behavior: An Intercultural Perspective." Her work reviews the most relevant materials in the field in relationship to intercultural communication. A remarkably thorough treatment, Ramsey's piece anchors the conceptual framework section with new views of nonverbal behavior.

5.

THE CONSCIOUSNESS THEORY OF INTERCULTURAL COMMUNICATION

TULSI B. SARAL

Governors State University

The study of consciousness has recently sparked considerable interest in Western psychology. Psychologists like Ornstein (1972) and Tart (1975) are beginning to recognize that beyond the ordinary state of consciousness, there lie potential but unexplored forms of consciousness entirely different from our normal mode of consciousness. It is further acknowledged that our ordinary state of consciousness is limited by our societal assumptions about the world and the reality. The effect of our well learned categories on the content of our awareness is far reaching. We construct a model of the world, expect certain correspondence of objects, ideas and events to occur, and then consciously or unconsciously attempt to fit our experience to our predetermined categories. Consciousness can thus be defined as a subjective experience within the organism in which the organism is aware of some sensory input or of the associative processing of such input.

It is interesting to note that during the last few years, the study of intercultural communication has also received great impetus. Communication scholars such as Porter (1972), Prosser (1973), Condon and Yousef (1975), Rich (1974), and Sitaram and Cogdell (1976) have attempted to explore the area of intercultural communication from various perspectives. Intercultural communication is described as the form of

AUTHOR'S NOTE: *I am grateful to Mary Kenny Badami, Dale Gilsdorf, David Matteson, Michael Real, Sharon Ruhly, and Alfred Smith for their constructive comments on the initial drafts of this paper, which was first presented at the International Communication Association Conference in Portland, Oregon, April 14-17, 1976.*

77

interaction that takes place when speaker and listener come from different cultures. It often involves racial and ethnic differences, but it also exists when there are gross cultural differences without accompanying racial and ethnic differences.

Inquiries into the nature of intercultural communication have mostly concerned themselves with current socioethnic concerns, with definitions of intercultural communication, and with general cultural variables—such as language, values, norms, and role expectations—that affect communication. Several models have been constructed to effectively demonstrate how intercultural communication operates in various situations, and projects have been proposed to train students and scholars of intercultural communication in techniques and methods of communicating effectively across cultures.

Most of this work, by necessity, is descriptive; this is natural in any newly evolving discipline and is extremely valuable in that it provides a critical data experience base. Yet, the very act of describing an event, an experience, or a phenomena tends to segment both knowledge and human identity into meaningless fragments. Any description that regards human beings as aggregates of skills, behaviors, roles, or fragmented faculties tends to segment the processes of human living and runs the danger of distorting humanness beyond recognition.

Intercultural communication has been described as communication among members of two or more different cultures. However, culture is a living dynamic process. It develops and lives as a continuum. It is kept alive by a constant flow of exchanges among its members and their environments, all of which are in a process of continuous change. In other words, individuals and their environments are inextricably meshed and involved within a transactional process which fundamentally prevents knowing either one unless they are viewed as a part of a whole system.

What I am proposing here is a way of looking at the world that is very different from the one to which we who have grown up in print-dominated linear culture are accustomed. The culture to which most of us raised and educated in Western tradition subscribe is one that emphasizes individual rational thinking and linear reasoning for achieving dissociative, contrasting categorization conducted with an air of detachment and personally uninvolved objectivity—a culture that encourages competition and views accumulation of material goods as reward for achievement.

The way of viewing the world suggested here is neither dissociative nor a linear work of syllogistic reasoning, but one of unitive thinking, of intuitively appreciating the commonality of events and objects by subjectively experiencing, with the whole body, oneself as necessarily connected with an environment and the universe. The followers of this world view approach the environment not to control or manipulate it, but simply to flow with it. In such an orientation, there is no place either for an extensive or elaborate designation of bipolar cultural value clusters or for contrasting objects and characteristics with other objects and characteristics. One simply experiences the continuous flow of events and objects and the unity of all, even of so-called opposites. The focus of study within such a framework is not on developing catalogues of habit patterns of various cultures, but on facilitating a process, *in-culture self-knowledge,* which is a necessary prerequisite to any effective communication.

This approach highlights the two major modes of functioning which Deikman (1971) terms the "action mode" and "receptive mode." The action mode is a state organized to manipulate the environment. The principal psychological manifestations of this state are focal attention, object-based logic, heightened boundary perception, and the dominance of formal characteristics over the sensory. The action mode is a state of striving.

The receptive mode, on the other hand, is a state organized around intake of the environment rather than manipulation. Its principal attributes are diffuse attending, paralogical thought processes, decreased boundary perception, and the dominance of the sensory over the formal. Color and texture have preference over shape and meaning. As Deikman points out, the receptive mode is not a regressive ignoring of the world or a retreat from it, but a different strategy for engaging the world for pursuit of a different goal.

Ornstein (1972), summarizing evidence from split brain research, arrives at a similar conclusion. He suggests that man's two cerebral hemispheres process different kinds of information and that the operating characteristics of the two are likewise different. The left hemisphere is predominantly involved with analytic, logical thinking, especially in verbal and mathematical functions. Its mode of operation is primarily linear; it seems to process information sequentially. The right hemisphere is more holistic, relational, and simultaneous in its mode of operation. It coordinates our orientation in space, and is responsible for integration of many inputs at once.

Anthropologist Lee (1950) has discovered an enlightening extension of this holistic, relational, and simultaneous mode of operation in Trobriand culture. Trobrianders do not arrange their events or experiences chronologically, nor do they organize events and objects in a sequence which is climactic in size and intensity, in emotional meaning, or according to some other principle. There is no boundary between past Trobriand existence and the present; past, present, and future are presented, linguistically and existentially, as the same.

Lee (1950: 96) poses a challenging question: "Are we then right in accepting, without question, the presence of a line in reality? Are we in a position to say with assurance that the Trobrianders are wrong and we are right?" The insight offered by Lee is neither novel nor surprising. As far back as 1911, anthropologist Boas (1911: 232, 242, 243) attempted to underline a somewhat similar difference between the so-called primitive and civilized cultures:

> When the same concept appears in the mind of primitive man, it associates itself with those concepts related to it by emotional states. This process of association is the same among primitive men as among civilized men, and the difference consists largely in the modification of the traditional material with which our new perceptions amalgamate. Thus, an important change from primitive culture to civilization seems to consist in the gradual elimination of what might be called the social associations of sense-impressions and of activities, for which intellectual associations are gradually substituted.

LeShan, an Einsteinian physicist (1974), proposes two general ways of conceptualizing and experiencing the world: (a) sensory reality—the way the world appears to most of us, most of the time; and (b) clairvoyant reality—a nonordinary way elaborated in the literature of mystical tradition. The sensory reality emphasizes individuality and separateness and regards time as a very real unidirectional flow. In clairvoyant reality, however, the unity and interrelationships of things are emphasized; time is considered illusory, and time concept and time experience are subject to continuing change.

It is thus apparent that there is no absolute reality, nor is there a universally valid way of perceiving, cognizing, or thinking. Each world view has different underlying assumptions. Our normal state of consciousness is not something natural or given, nor is it universal across cultures. It is simply a specialized tool, a complex structure for coping with our environment. As psychologist Tart (1975: 4) aptly puts it:

> We are creatures with a certain kind of body and nervous system, a large number of human potentials are available to us. But each of us is born into a particular culture that selects and develops a small number of these potentials, rejects others, and is ignorant of many. The small number of experiential potentials selected by our culture, plus random factors, constitute the structural elements from which our ordinary state of consciousness is constructed. We are at once the beneficiaries and the victims of our culture's particular selection.

A state of consciousness is a unique dynamic pattern or configuration of psychological structure designed to enable us to sense the external and internal environment and to automatically select and abstract sensory input so we perceive and cognize only what is "important" by personal and cultural (consensus reality) standards. The problem of intercultural communication, therefore, is essentially a problem of communication among varying states of consciousness. Let us examine an interaction between two states of consciousness— the normal waking state and a dream state. The logic and rules that govern the manipulation of information and the assumptions about time and space are entirely different in each of the two states. In order to really appreciate the dream, one has to suspend the logic, rules, and assumptions governing the normal waking state. Then can one relish the bliss of dream state. The same holds true for communication among members of different cultures.

Commenting upon the scope and method of crosscultural research, Frijda and Jahoda (1966: 102-127) observe that we can compare only when we have dimensional identity. That is, only when two behaviors fall on a single dimension is it legitimate to relate one to the other for comparative purposes; otherwise, we descend to the proverbial comparison of apples and oranges. The same is true for communication among various states of consciousness and, for that matter, among various cultures. States of consciousness, like cultures, vary along many dimensions. To bring about any meaningful communication among these varying states of consciousness, we need to identify the various dimensions involved and the locations of various states on each of these dimensions. Communication among various states is possible only to the extent that they share some common dimensions, albeit with varying locations. In situations where no such commonality exists, no communication will be possible until and unless one of the communicants is willing to suspend his or her mode of sensing, perceiving, and attending to reality.

What I am proposing then, is that we view the intercultural communication process as analogous to the process of communication among various states of consciousness. This means asking an entirely different set of questions than we have been asking so far. Rather than occupying ourselves with the surface structure of cultural features such as attitudes, norms, values, role perceptions, and language, we will begin to focus upon the deep structure of cultural experience characterized by the reception, organization, and utilization of information gained through contact with environment.

We homosapiens are partly creatures of our own images. Our perceptions of ourselves affect how and what we communicate:

> Man is a multiple amphibian and exists at one and the same time in a number of universes, dissimilar to the point, very nearly, of complete incompatibility. He is at once an animal and a rational intellect; a product of evolution closely related to the apes, and a spirit capable of self-transcendence, a sentient being in contact with minute data of his own system, and the physical environment, and at the same time the

creator of a home-made universe of words and other symbols, in which he lives and moves and has anything from thirty to eighty percent of his being. . . .

Living amphibiously in numerous incommensurable worlds at once, human beings (it is hardly surprising) find themselves painfully confused, uncertain where they stand or who they really are. To provide themselves with a recognizable identity, a niche in the scheme of things that they can call "home," they will give assent to the unlikeliest dogmas, conform to the most absurd and even harmful rules of thought, feeling and conduct, put on the most extravagant fancy dress and identify themselves with *masks* that bear almost no resemblance to the faces they cover. [Huxley, 1962: 270-280]

Could it not be, then, that intercultural communication is merely human beings' desperate attempt to communicate with their many known and not-yet-known selves? What I am suggesting is that intercultural communication is ultimately nothing but explanation of one's many selves. Scholars and students of intercultural communication have begun to realize that at different times, in different contexts and situations, they experience their different selves. In order to become integrated individuals, we need not suppress one self or identify with an other; rather, we need to create an environment in which we can flow back and forth among our various selves without feeling stuck at one place or addicted to a particular mode of experiencing. Each of us is a combination of various cultures in the form of our multiple selves; each of us, like a distinct culture, is governed by unique dimensions of reality. If we want communication across our multiple selves, we need not only to acknowledge the uniqueness of these distinctive dimensions, but also to free ourselves from our deep rooted addiction to sensing and coding reality in rigid and narrow patterns. Then, and then alone, can we allow ourselves to experience the rare ecstasy of encountering ourselves in our entirety.

REFERENCES

BOAS, R. (1911) *The Mind of Primitive Man.* New York: Macmillan.

CONDON, J. C. and YOUSEF, F. (1975) *An Introduction to Intercultural Communication.* New York: Bobbs-Merrill.

DEIKMAN, A. (1971) "Bimodal consciousness." *Archives of General Psychiatry* 25. Reprinted in Robert Ornstein [ed.] (1973) *The Nature of Human Consciousness.* San Francisco: W. H. Freeman.

FRIJDA, N. and JAHODA, G. (1966) "On the Scope and Methods of Cross-Cultural Research." *International Journal of Psychology,* I.

HUXLEY, A. (1962) "Education of the nonverbal level." *Daedlus* Spring. Reprinted in R. M. Jones [ed.] (1967) *Contemporary Educational Psychology.* New York: Harper & Row.

LEE, D. (1950) "Codification of reality: Lineal and nonlineal." *Psychosomatic Medicine,* 12. Also in Robert Ornstein [ed.] (1973) *The Nature of Human Consciousness.* San Francisco: W. H. Freeman.

LE SHAN, L. (1974) *The medium, the mystic and the physicist.* New York: Viking.

ORNSTEIN, R. (1972) *The Psychology of Consciousness.* San Francisco: W. H. Freeman.

PORTER, R. E. (1972) "An overview of intercultural communication" in L. A. Samovar and R. E. Porter (eds.), *Intercultural Communication: A Reader.* Belmont, Cal.: Wadsworth.

PROSSER, M. H. [ed.] (1973) *Inter-communication among nations and people.* New York: Harper & Row.

RICH, A. L. (1974) *Interracial Communication.* New York: Harper & Row.

SITARAM, K. S. and COGDELL, R. (1976) *Foundations of Intercultural Communication.* Columbus, Ohio: Charles Merrill.

TART, C. T. (1975) "States of consciousness." New York: E. P. Dutton.

6.

RHETORIC AND INTERCULTURAL COMMUNICATION

CECIL A. BLAKE

State University of New York at Buffalo

Rhetoric is a study of communication—effective communication. It is usually associated with the study of suasory discourses. (Bryant, 1953). Its roots are firmly grounded in classical scholarship and enjoyed a tremendous era of repute (and disrepute) throughout classical times. Rhetoric's age, if nothing else, renders it a revered subject matter. More important, however, is the fact that each society on earth practices the art of effective and suasory communication. We may not find as much literature on non-Western rhetoric as on Western rhetoric but, needless to say, people in other parts of the world do communicate. Thus the rhetoric remains an important area for investigation and speculation. Indeed, the universality of rhetoric ought to be more fully recognized now than ever before because of the changing drama of world relations: we have gone from a world divided between colonizers and the colonized to one of independent nations seeking to enhance their various societies. The absence of any significant body of knowledge that treats the subject matter of effective and suasory expression in the developing nations only makes rhetoric more germane for the non-Western scholar.

The primary purpose of this paper is to initiate a discussion on what may be broadly referred to as comparative rhetoric. Although there is no body of knowledge to serve as a foundation for studying the breadth and depth of rhetoric around the world, this should not prevent at least a heuristic treatment of comparative rhetoric. Some may argue that, in order to deal successfully with a subject matter of such magnitude, one would have to travel the world over in search of peculiar rhetorical histories, oral or literary. This argument is sound, and it is precisely this troubled nature of the subject that prompts discussion of the topic of comparative rhetoric.

A review of the history and development of Western rhetoric leads to several conclusions, namely: (1) in order for a society to practice effective rhetoric and acquire a rhetorical tradition, there ought to be argumentation, discussion, and debate as we understand these terms in the West; (2) all major human components in the rhetorical situation—i.e., audience and rhetor—ought to be involved in such discussion and debate, implying active participation by the audience in decision-making that affects the future of the populace; and (3) such requirements could only function in what we vaguely refer to in the West as "free societies," "democracies," or the "free world." Such requirements seem restrictive because they could simply dismiss societies that do not practice or abide by them. If rhetoric or effective suasory expression is existent in all societies, then the philosophies peculiar to those societies govern the rhetorical structure and practice of each. Applying stringent Western requirements for effective investigation into non-Western rhetoric would result in warping the non-Western society to suit the narrow whims of the scholar.

An appropriate start for a discussion on comparative rhetoric is a working definition of rhetoric. Rhetoric can be defined as effective expression in all discourse, or simply as discourse with persuasive intent. Donald C. Bryant (1953) defines it as "the rationale of informative and suasory discourse." Douglas Ehninger (1972), however, argues that

> Bryant's definition is confining. Rather than limiting rhetoric to a consideration of how oral or written language may be used to convey information or effect persuasion, the current practice is to extend it to encompass all of the ways in which, and all of the ends for which, symbols of any sort may be used to influence or affect another's mind. . . . Also regarded as appropriate subject matter for rhetoricians to study and evaluate are such non-discursive phenomena as art, architecture, music, dance, parades, mass gatherings, sit-ins, and public demonstrations of all sorts, as well as hair, dress, and bearing on the part of the individual.

Looking at rhetoric in such a broad perspective, one could investigate these various communication strategies in different societies. Even the most so-called primitive societies exhibit forms of music, dance, and art. Ehninger's approach commits rhetoric to being an integral part of all human communicative interaction. This view could save us from the pitfalls of inaccurate analyses of rhetorical traditions, patterns, and strategies in other cultures. Morrison (1972), for example, misunderstood the crucial difference between East and West in his essay, "The Absence of a Rhetorical Tradition in Japanese Culture," contending (as the title of his article suggests) that Japanese culture is arhetorical. Oliver (1971), on the other hand, recognized the strong cultural and philosophical influences in the growth and development of any rhetorical tradition, pointing out that "any attempt to discover in Asia prototypes of the Western rhetorical canons would be unavailing," and that "the East is not the West."

The remainder of this paper will discuss key issues that shed light on the nature of comparative rhetoric and suggest some guidelines for future research in this area. Among the issues to be considered in any discussion on comparative or intercultural rhetoric are the following: (1) what is it that we look for when we attempt to do a study on comparative rhetoric? (2) where do we start?

I

As the expression suggests, comparative rhetoric is the comparative study of rhetorics of different societies. This definition does not exclude contrasts, but simply stresses the comparative aspect of the approach to the subject matter. What is it that we look for when we attempt to do a study on comparative rhetoric? To answer this question, we need to identify what we generally refer to as rhetoric. We have stated earlier that rhetoric is a study of communication. We have already noted that communication can take many forms. So the first answer to our question is that we look for the communication patterns, strategies, and vehicles peculiar to the cultures or societies under investigation. But there is another side to this answer: we also need to know the general culture, tradition, folklore, philosophy, and social organization of each society being studied.

The wide range of areas covered above is important. When we study Western rhetoric, for example, we study the earliest writings of the fathers of the art, coupled with the prevailing philosophies of the times. Besides the study of Western philosophy and its influence on the conceptualization of Western rhetoric, we also study the influence of the other institutions, such as the church, the educational system, and so on. Added to all of these, we attempt to understand the prevailing epistemology. It is precisely this rigorous set of standards that we have to satisfy in order to theorize satisfactorily about Western rhetoric that makes it incumbent on the would-be comparative rhetorician to account fully for all of these facets in the cultures he wishes to study.

Besides the above items, which constitute the context within which our study of rhetoric is set, we must look for the constituent parts of the rhetoric peculiar to each society studied. It is not necessary for us to repeat the constituent parts of Western rhetoric in their entirety, but simply identifying key parts of Western rhetoric will facilitate our discussion. Aristotle tells us that the essential constituents of rhetoric are the modes of proof, i.e., ethos, logos, and pathos. He assigns priority status to the first two. As comparative rhetoricians, we ought to be able to unearth the constituent parts of the societies we intend to study and attempt to account for the parts that receive most emphasis. It could be revealing, for example, to discover that in an average African or Asian society, the priority of ethos over everything else renders a different picture of what we are accustomed to seeing, hearing, or believing. Morrison (1972) apparently could not understand why issues are not debated in the elective process in traditional Japan; his interpretation was simply to say that Japan lacks rhetoric. But we cannot afford to judge other cultures in that manner. Instead, we must identify the primary and secondary constituents and, through our examination of the culture as a whole, attempt to conceptualize the peculiar rhetorical theory exhibited by each society under investigation.

Another problem area is that of the predominant rhetorical strategies and vehicles in each society under investigation. The developing nations of Africa and Asia present excellent laboratories for such research. Africa, Asia, and the rest of the developing world are desperately searching for the most effective means of communicating innovations to their populations. But in order to communicate successfully, there must be common symbols of communication. Such symbols may simply be termed "identifiable symbols." A second major constraint is the necessity for "communicable symbols."

Identification of common or identifiable symbols is necessary because we usually find ourselves communicating messages that seem identifiable to us, but which are alien to the African farmer and other members of the developing societies. This is seen in many African countries where farm broadcasts are made that use complex technical language, accompanied at times by demonstration.

How does one go about uncovering identifiable symbols? What is entailed in reaching the masses by a vehicle they can easily recognize? In societies dominated by distinct language code systems, the knowledge of the language itself is not sufficient: the knowledge of the structure through which the people amplify their messages—use of parables, story-telling, drama, to mention just a few—is also essential.

Simplistic as the above may seem, it is remarkably practical. In order to communicate effectively in Western culture, we have to understand that argumentation and discussion are the primary communication strategies to master. We must understand, to a degree, the workings of logic; the use of warrants; the identification and application of evidence; the identification and application of credible sources to enhance our communication efforts; the identification and application of amplification devices to illustrate our points, and so on. These form part of the rhetorical structure and pattern of Western societies. If we do not understand how these structures and patterns operate, we cannot communicate effectively. The comparative rhetorician has to make an intense effort to identify the rhetorical patterns and structures prevalent in the particular groups of people he is studying. Bordenave (1971), for example, conducted a study among the peasants of Northeast Brazil and discovered a peculiar rhetorical vehicle, a vehicle that he himself accepts as being sophisticated.

Bordenave relates a story about a program he conducted in Northeast Brazil. He states that "the results of the first test dramatized the need for communicators to know about rural people's modes of perception and learning." Leaflets were sent out regarding brucelosis control. When a test was conducted to determine how farmers treated the leaflets, it was found that they did not react to them as expected. They selected portions of the information contained in the leaflets at random instead of reading it all in an orderly and systematic manner. No orderly regard for illustrations "indicated by arrows" was observed. Subtitles were ignored, and drawings were interpreted literally.

The situation changed, however, when a different communication form was used. Bordenave utilized a common Northeast Brazilian communicative form called the "folhetos" to channel his messages. The messages were received better because Bordenave utilized the rhetorical pattern that was common to all. Explaining the alternative approach, Bordenave (1971) states:

> the high degree of comprehension of literary flowerish and romantic materials by the peasants has surprised many people. I refer particularly to the "folhetos" popular in Brazilian Northeast. . . . Folhetos do not follow our rational criteria for simplified writing: simple words, concrete meaning, short sentences, straightforward sentence structure. . . but they "communicate!" The peasants not only understand the stories but memorize them and repeat them to their illiterate friends and relatives . . . . This falls under the general nature of "folkcommunication."

To utilize a rhetorical structure and pattern that peasants recognize and understand is one aspect of a complex problem. The other is dealing with "communicable symbols." The persuasive structure can be identified, we can discover a common tool, but are all the symbols manipulable? This question asks about the degree of convertibility of the message structure into the rhetorical structure identified. Are there available symbols or words that will suit our intended messages? Does the symbol structure discovered have the capacity

to accommodate scientific instruction, or does the form discovered lend itself to such a vehicular operation? These are
some of the questions the comparative rhetorician ought to
examine. Long term studies of the rhetorical structures,
patterns, and vehicles of different cultures will greatly enhance
our understanding of other cultures and their methods of
effective expression and communication. The implications for
intercultural communication are many. One major implication
stands out, however—we could communicate better if we
understood "those other people."

II

Where do we start? Of all the issues of importance in
comparative studies, the most crucial is selecting areas of the
world that will give us the opportunity to conduct our studies,
serve as a representative model for the geographical area, and
have the facilities to make such an investigation possible. This
central problem of choice is even more profound for the
comparative rhetorician because language structure and rhetorical patterns, vehicles, and strategies could all differ significantly from area to area within the same geographic region.
This problem is particularly acute in Africa. In Sierra Leone
alone, the rhetorical patterns of the Western area are significantly different from those of the rest of the country because of
the heavy influence of British rhetorical strategies and patterns
in Freetown and the surrounding villages. Because of the above
situation, one could not easily generalize about Sierra Leonean
rhetorical patterns, much less on African rhetorical strategies.
Thus, the question of where we start stands as a central issue
for the comparative rhetorician. Broadly associated with this
key question are problems of procedure for gathering of data
and problems of scope.

Problems of Procedure

The procedure referred to here is that of selecting an area in
the world in which to start our work. As mentioned earlier, we
have an abundance of literature on Western rhetorical history

and thought. Armed with these materials, it should not be difficult to examine the rhetorical traditions of England, France, Italy, or any of the major Western countries. But when we come to Asia, we have to start from the grassroots. Robert T. Oliver (1971) started at the grassroots of Asian culture and tradition, and wrote on rhetoric in ancient India and China. His long association with Asian culture practices and philosophy prepared him to venture into his investigation. Yet, he was cautious to identify only ancient India and China, and not the whole of the Asian continent. This procedure is sound, because it portrays the limitations of generalizing about geographic regions where there are significant cultural and philosophical disparities. If we attempt to study African rhetorics, it would hardly be worthwhile to simply go to the libraries, do research at a distance, and generalize. Rather, it would be necessary to isolate a country and study the philosophy and general cultural patterns of its regions (particularly so because of the various ethnic groups that could exist in a given African state). This procedure may seem tedious, but to gain a better understanding of the conceptualization of rhetoric across cultures, extensive field research is the logical method of accumulating primary data. We could then attempt to classify rhetorical strategies, vehicles, and patterns. If, for example, we initiated field studies in Sierra Leone, we would have to assign research personnel to at least four regions in the country, selecting the four largest language groups. If we discovered a popular rhetorical vehicle such as story-telling or parables among these groups regardless of language and cultural heritage, then we would have the beginnings of a classification of Sierra Leone's rhetorical system.

Problem of Scope

The problem of scope involves demarcating our areas for study. Anthropologists used to isolate race as their primary emphasis in their studies of various cultures. We cannot afford to isolate one factor in a culture to account for its communication or rhetorical system. With rhetoric, the problem becomes acute because we cannot simply isolate speechmaking patterns, structure, and organization as our primary emphases. Rhetoric is not just speechmaking: Bryant (1953) believes it is "the function of adjusting ideas to people and people to ideas." If we agree with that function, such adjustments cannot be achieved simply by speechmaking alone. There are other means of communication, such as writing, drama, dance and music, all of which assist in adjusting people to ideas and ideas to people—and, as Oliver notes (1971), people to people. Thus, the comparative rhetorician must deal not only with speechmaking but also with all the other various forms of communication utilized in the cultures of his choice.

To emphasize only the communication component of a culture would be defeating our purpose of understanding fully the processes, functions, and structures of its rhetoric. Communication occurs in a cultural context comprised of many factors—sociopsychological, historical, epistemological, and philosophical—all influenced by the traditions of the culture. To study these factors from a distance, as suggested by Elingsworth (1963), is fruitless for the comparative rhetorician if he indeed intends to fully account for the processes, functions, structures, and patterns of rhetoric prevalent in a given culture. This task may well seem insurmountable, but if we are to do an effective job of studying rhetoric crossculturally, our work at the beginning is necessarily heavy and demanding. We cannot afford to miss major or even minor influences that shape the rhetorical traditions of any given culture.

CONCLUSION

This exploratory paper has discussed the concept of comparative rhetoric, a topic of undeniable importance in the world today. The problem is to pinpoint a series of approaches that are consistent in their objectives and that lead us to some concrete understanding of the subject matter we call comparative rhetoric. This paper represents a first stage—i.e., thinking and speculating about the subject. Much remains to be done that cannot be undertaken here due to time and space constraints.

The implications for a continued interest in speculating, conceptualizing, and theorizing on comparative rhetoric are many. As stated earlier, the world context demands a better understanding of communication patterns outside of the Western tradition. Such an understanding could conceivably change the diplomatic scene. Diplomatic problems that arise partly because of cultural communication misunderstandings could be reduced; foreign exchange programs involving students and professionals from various cultures could also benefit. Continued efforts on the part of scholars and others will provide information and resources that contribute to effective intercultural communication. We have a long way to go before we can actually experience such benefits, but we need to start somewhere.

REFERENCES

BORDENAVE, J.D. (1971) "New approaches to communication training for developing countries." Inter American Institute of Agricultural Sciences of the OAS.
BRYANT, D. (1953) "Rhetoric: Its function and its scope." *QJS.*
EHNINGER, D. [ed.] (1972) *Contemporary Rhetoric.* Glenview, Ill.: Scott, Foresman.
ELLINGSWORTH, H.W. (1963) "Anthropology and rhetoric: Toward a culture-related methodology of speech criticism." *Southern Speech Journal,* Summer.
MORRISON, J.L. (1972) "The absence of a rhetorical tradition in Japanese culture." *Western Speech,* 2.
OLIVER, R.T. (1971) *Communication and Culture in Ancient India and China.* Syracuse, New York: Syracuse Univ. Press.

7

DEMYSTIFICATION OF THE INTERCULTURAL COMMUNICATION ENCOUNTER

MOLEFI K. ASANTE AND ALENE BARNES

State University of New York at Buffalo

Extensive international travel makes intercultural adjustment a topic of special significance to social scientists. Among the problems identified in adjusting from one culture to another has been use of a second language. MacNamara (1966), Christian (1970), and Nostrand (1966) have suggested that failures to adequately communicate or adjust may occur even if people have the same language but different cultural frames of reference. Tucker and Gadaloff (1970) have contended that even with the same language proficiency, individuals may have difficulty communicating. Although it can be argued that absolute proficiency in language is not necessary for efficient communication, it is apparently true that individuals must have the ability to "demystify" the linguistic and symbolic experience if they are to be efficient communicators in a given society. Students who sojourn in foreign countries may experience difficulties relating to second languages, frames of reference, and cultures. Students from foreign countries bring with them their own mystic and cultural realities.

Public encounters are extensions of our mythic and cultural realities. What we say and how we behave during intercultural encounters are the cumulative results of our relationships, heritage, and status perceptions. Cultural shock, the disconcerting consciousness experienced by those entering a strange environment for the first time, results from the initial contact of cultures in conflict. Personal cultural expressions, as outgrowths of our socialization processes, can create intercultural dissonance.

This essay provides an approach to demystifying the interracial communication encounter in an effort to effect cultural
harmony based upon an understanding of the mythic realities
of different cultures. Axiological clashes between individuals
of the same composite cultural backgrounds must be distinguished from the axiological differences or similarities of those
from different composite cultural backgrounds. The composite
cultural background is comprised of the cognitive patterns,
familial considerations, and artificial manifestations of a group
of people. Individuals within such a composite culture may
have similarities with people of another composite culture and
dissimilarities with those in their own. But these individual
differences are exceptions to the composite culture and do no
violence to the individual's identity with the composite culture
as a whole. For example, it is possible to find an American
whose values on nature are similar to the Ashanti's reverence
for trees and rivers. Although such value concentration may
differ from the American composite culture, acceptance of that
value does not make an American an African. One could speak
of the individual as an American with an African sense of
reverence for nature. These exceptions are found in every
culture, but it is the totality of the cultural manifestations—as
determined by cognitive patterns, familial factors, and artificial
considerations—that determines the composite culture. Environment, education, and religion are some artificial considerations.

Demystification unravels the shock of the initial intercultural
communication encounter. An intercultural communication
situation may be hostile, neutral, or friendly in terms of one's
own cultural values. Harry Triandis' concept of contrast
cultures is instructive for an analysis of our feeling of difference. The greater the cultural contrast, the more likely the
hostility between cultures. Whether the shock is momentary or
lengthy, demystification creates the potential for an effective
encounter.

Alex Haley, author of *Roots*, has said that when he visited
Juffure, his ancestral home in Gambia, he was struck by how
uniformly black the people were at the village. It was unlike his
Afro-American experience. Demystification, deshocking

always occurs after the communicator realizes the difference is unstaged and natural. Haley's experience suggests that he overcame momentary disconcerting consciousness to achieve an effective communicative situation.

The triggering devices for the shock effect may be physical, structural, sensual, or psychic. Physical triggering devices may include how people of different races or cultures dress, how different they appear to us physically, and what actions of theirs are significantly different from ours to be recognizable as cultural rather than personal idiosyncrasies. For example, American students in foreign environments, such as Africa and the Asian subcontinent, may find themselves objects of curiosity for village people. Americans may find Africans and Indians physically different. This fact in and of itself does not mean that the shock effect will occur. Our historical content determines to what extent we are affected by the intercultural experience in a physical sense.

Sensual triggering devices include smell, touch, and taste. When an American student steps off the plane in Senegal and inhales the pungent smell of peanut oil, she or he is liable to associate it with nothing in his or her background. This is a difference, perhaps, brought on by economic rather than cultural conditions. Even so, the American stranger may have a sensual awakening. Tactile behavior can be different in various cultures. The lack of tactile involvement seems more characteristic of some societies and not so characteristic of others. Societies which have more touching and embracing may appear to be too tactile for the American. Food taste can also trigger the shock effect. Culinary habits and delights differ widely. Although one may anticipate difference, there can never be enough anticipation for the strikingly different food. To some extent, sensual and physical triggering devices overlap: sight is, after all, one of the senses.

The fact that the shock effect is triggered by physical, structural, sensual, and psychic devices within a host environment means that all strangers abroad for the first time are initiated the same way. The psychic triggering devices are included in the anticipation, apprehension, and even nervousness which may occur. No orientation program can anticipate all of the intricacies of a culture. An American in a foreign culture is both herself and her circumstances. This means that while you bring yourself and all the memories that constitute you to the setting of a foreign culture, you are also, in that culture, in the peculiar circumstances of that setting.

There are two principal ways to deal with the shock experience. One can make assumptions or ask questions. The first course of action is quicker though not safer. Our assumptions about a foreign society may be correct or incorrect. Although making assumptions allows us to continue our engagement with a society, sooner or later we must have our assumptions validated. Validation is essentially a problem of demystifying the shock experience in order to arrive at the central facts of an intercultural encounter.

Such validation dispenses with the bifurcation between dynamics of cultural shock on one hand and adjustment on the other. Adjustment is preeminently a component of shock. A person, however, may adjust negatively or positively. By understanding the dimension of crosscultural effectiveness from a person centered concept, it is possible to begin demystification.

Crosscultural effectiveness is more than knowledge of a job and of successful dissemination of facts. It is fundamentally a demystification of role in a given society. Thus, knowing one's information and getting such information across to members of a given society cannot be evaluated as a positive state of crosscultural effectiveness. Information has been successfully disseminated in some places although it has violated the cultural values of the recipient culture. It is almost as if some people have been knocked over the head and made to accept an idea or belief in their state of incapacitation. Dissemination efficiency is source determined; attitude toward the information is audience determined.

Segmental or componential theories have served useful purposes in intercultural literature. For example, Barna (1972) has been quoted widely among writers and lecturers in the field of intercultural communication as identifying barriers or stumbling blocks to intercultural communication on an interpersonal level; Davis (1967) has discussed function points of

American technicians abroad; and as early as 1958, Oberg was concerned with the problems of adjustment in new foreign cultures. However, most of these studies have dealt with purely ethnocentric configurations regarding culture. Similar theoretical essays for isolating problem areas, stumbling blocks or friction points can be employed by other cultures vis-à-vis American society. As it now stands, the window looks out to cultures other than American in an effort to determine cross-cultural effectiveness. It is not surprising therefore that the Centre Monchanin group has opposed the theoretical concept *intercultural communications* on the grounds that, as traditionally presented, it is a Western notion. What is needed is a method to cross the boundary of ethnocentricism in theory and so develop a system for demystifying shock.

Admonitions to be careful how you greet others, to be sincere in your approach to others' customs, to be open to their manner of doing things, to use the appropriate nonverbal gestures, and to refrain from making judgments about the others' customs, have some validity in terms of interpersonal protocol. However, such admonitions do not go far enough to utilize one's own axiological basis and structure. The segmental approach, unfortunately, is based upon the narrow structure of Western social and economic assumptions. As in theory, in evaluation of programs it is necessary to understand that most of the programs evaluated or discussed in the literature (Arensberg and Niehoff, 1964; Brislin and Pederson, 1976; Tucker, 1973) have dealt with Americans entering foreign cultures. The research on others entering American society is just beginning to start (Pruitt, 1977). In the studies that have been done, one can see the assumptions of the American orientation clearly. The idea behind Barna's stumbling blocks or Arensberg and Niehoff's "thou shalt nots" is that in order to be a successful person working in a foreign environment you cannot be yourself. You must sell yourself. The sojourner becomes a commodity or makes him or herself a commodity to be packaged, shined, wrapped in the best paper for presentation. It is an economic arrangement which says, "I do this in order to get you to buy." This leads to some "success" stories about how certain persons trained in this or that program used all of the tools to overcome the barriers and stumbling blocks of a foreign society. But it also leads to charges of insincerity, salesmanship, and paternalism. Our Western orientation to overcoming barriers must be understood as much more intense than, say, in Africa. The positing of barriers in the first place is an activity which finds its source in our attempt to break through, break down, tunnel, bridge, and climb on top. These notions are consonant to the values we have created to accompany them.

In the West, we assume that nature must be overcome; it must give way to the power and knowledge of human beings. Mountains must be tunneled through, trees must be cut down, and rivers must be bridged if we are to achieve our objective. This is a driving force, a part of the Western character. Some societies however, do not see nature as a barrier. Mountains, trees, and rivers are a part of the environment in a similar fashion to ourselves. The notion of stumbling blocks, friction points, and barriers is a notion from a particular orientation.

Therefore a discussion of training programs in intercultural effectiveness tends to lead to barriers. It is an inevitable idea in human relationships to nature. How to get through to the other person, how to get over and how to overcome obstacles occupy a considerable amount of our time. Personal relationships are commercialized to the extent that a man or a woman seeks to perform so that the other will find him or her acceptable. Human beings thus become commodities to be bought, sold, or exchanged. An extension of this concept is seen in our segmental orientation toward crosscultural training. The questions we ask, probably because we can formulate more empirically restable hypotheses, have little to do with a person using personal perceptions to aid the demystification process. Knowledge can never be being. It is not possible to substitute what you know for who you are.

Demystification of crosscultural experiences must begin with who you are. Apart from rootedness in an ontological base, the encounter becomes commercial and superficial. It is possible to identify methods for assessing behaviors that may be meaningful in a foreign culture. But identification of behaviors such as *respect* for the host, *empathy*, and *role* can only be presented as worthwhile; any attempt on the part of a training program to teach respect, empathy, and so on begins at the wrong place. The contention that knowledge of self is the basic philosophical necessity for demystifying an experience means that the person is defined by being, relationships, and power. The process of demystifying begins with an understanding of *being*, *relatedness*, and *power*.

Demystification Chart

	Survey	Inquiry	Action
Self Identity	Feel more myself when	Why do they feel that way?	This is the way I choose to be
Relatedness	Feel related when	Why do others relate differently?	I choose to relate this way
Power	Feel powerful when	Why do others feel powerful in other ways?	I choose to act this way

Figure 7.1: Demystification Chart

In demystifying the shock effect, we must concentrate on the reality that exists rather than attempt to substitute reality. Being is basic. A person begins with this ultimate reality as a basis for a reaching out to others. "Who am I?" becomes the fundamental question in the demystification process. A person develops his or her knowledge of self by contrasting and comparing. In addition, self identity, relatedness, and power are keys in demystifying the shock effect (Figure 7.1).

In a foreign environment, the American negotiates demystification by going through the process of surveying, inquiring, and acting in regard to self identity, relatedness, and power. If we take the demystification process in terms of self identity, we see that once a person thinks about herself in connection with the shock effect, in that initial moment, she knows by surveying herself that she feels more herself when certain other conditions not foreign to her obtain.

This can be carried through the inquiry phase by asking, "why do people in this culture feel the way they do about themselves?" Answers to this question, of course, may take a long period of time. Nothing is guaranteed by asking ourselves questions about other cultures. Self identity in a foreign situation is finally the ability to survey the situation, inquire into the host nation's culture, and act according to how you choose to be. Similarly, relatedness must be looked at in terms of survey, inquiry, and action.

What makes an American feel related? Are the behaviors of the hosts antithetical to the American's needs? Communicationists are interested in what makes some people feel comfortable in foreign interaction situations and others not. Furthermore, we need to know what peculiar characteristics held either by the sojourner or the host make for comfort in one place but discomfort in another. The model of adjustment being described is, therefore, concerned with relatedness.

The third element in an orientation toward demystifying the shock effect is power. We all have a certain orientation to power. Some may not be as strong or urgent as others, but we look for those things that make us feel or look good. When an American goes to a foreign country, he is an entity with certain attributive powers. They may be negative or positive attributes, but they exist. But insofar as demystification begins with the person entering a new nation, it is necessary to go through the survey, inquiry, and action phases of the model. These are not mechanical motions; the American does them automatically, as foreigners in the United States must also do. Our response to these phases may take longer, may distort our perceptions, or may produce depression, but we do respond. An American might survey the situation and say to herself, "I feel powerful when I can be in command, show dynamic leadership, or exhibit a take-charge attitude." However, in some Eastern cultures, she may discover that her attitudes are contrary to the cultural norms of the people hosting her. In that case, one must inquire as to what situations, conditions, and circumstances make others feel powerful. By asking questions, the foreigner learns not only what attributes are powerful but what questions are proper. Finally, action occurs when the student says, "this is the way I choose to act on the basis of my information."

Now that the fundamental explanation of the shock effect is accomplished, how does it operate in a specific case? Take yourself or someone you know and imagine the scenario. When a person, say an American student, enters a foreign environment and experiences the shock effect, several options are opened to him psychologically. He could reject the culture and withdraw, ignore the culture, or move toward the culture by demystifying. If he rejects and withdraws, say from the Bolivian culture, he is no longer obligated to the situation.

In such instances, the student either returns home to "sweet ole America" or turns to an American community in Bolivia for solace, companionship, and validation. If he ignores the host culture, he will continue to receive the shock effect, but it will be like water on the back of a hippopotamus—it will not matter to him. In that instance, the Bolivian people might consider it strange that he fails to learn after so many shocks. This is similar to the phenomenon of the 1960s, when the word "black" was gaining prominence among African-Americans as a racial designation. Numerous whites who had always said "colored" or "Negro" could not bring themselves to say "black." They ignored it, although blacks frequently used it deliberately in conversation with them. If the student is properly advised and so proceeds to learn more about the culture through decodifying the shock effect, he develops a track record which allows him to adjust from one shock to the next—a frame of mind is set. A similar process takes place when a person from a rural area visits a place like New York City: anticipation can help to allay some of the shock. This happens to the American student in Bolivia (or anywhere else) who builds up a catalog of attitudes, reactions, and assumptions. Success grows geometrically in such cases. You do not have to have a hundred experiences before you start to "feel" the culture. Sensitivity is developed when you begin to anticipate ways to decodify the shock effect. It makes sense for the stranger to learn the ground upon which the host culture is based.

Adjustment should begin with a focus on decodifying experiences that produce the shock effect. If you run simulations, exercises, or critical incidents to teach a person how to adjust to a different culture, utilize the demystification process. Reduce the mystery by providing the student with an opportunity to experience domestic situations, created or actual, which simulate the effect of shock (though not necessarily the culture itself). It is not so much the culture that must be the focus of training as it is the demystification of the shock effect.

REFERENCES

BARNA, L. (1972) "Stumbling blocks in interpersonal intercultural communication" p. 47 in David Hoopes (ed.), *Readings in Intercultural Communications,* Vol. 1. Pittsburgh: University of Pittsburgh.

BRISLIN, R. and PEDERSEN, P. (1976) *Cross Cultural Orientation Programs.* New York: Gardner.

CHRISTIAN, C.C. (1970) "The analysis of linguistic and cultural differences: A proposed model," pp. 149-162 in J. Alatis (ed.), *Georgetown Monograph Series on Language and Linguistics* 22.

DAVIS, D. (1969) "Cultural frictions of American technicians abroad." *Texas Business Review* 43: 210.

MacNAMARA, J. (1966) *Bilingualism and Primary Education.* Edinburgh: Edinburgh Univ. Press.

NOSTRAND, H.L. (1966) "Describing and teaching the sociocultural context of a foreign language and literature." p. 4 in A. Valdman (ed.), *Trends in Language Teaching.* New York: McGraw-Hill.

OBERG, K. (1958) *Culture Shock and the Problem of Adjustment to New Cultural Environments.* Washington, D.C.: U.S. Department of State.

PRUITT, F. (1977) "Adaptation of African students to American education." *Report to the Bureau of Educational and Cultural Affairs.* Washington, D.C.: U.S. Department of State.

TUCKER, G.G. and GEDALOFF, H. (1970) "Bilinguals as linguistic mediators." *Psychomonic Science,* 20: 118-127.

TUCKER, M. (1973) *Improving Cross Cultural Training and Measurement of Cross Cultural Learning.* Denver: Center for Research and Education.

8

NONVERBAL BEHAVIOR:
AN INTERCULTURAL PERSPECTIVE

SHEILA J. RAMSEY

International Christian University

"It doesn't sound like French when you see it."
(Hayes, 1964)

INTRODUCTION

It is presently accepted by most of those oriented toward both research and application in the area of intercultural communication that an understanding of any communication event is incomplete without consideration of meanings conveyed through nonverbal behavior. In presenting a selected review of research, the subdivisions of posture, gesture, touching, and spatial behavior are points of focus. This is done for logistical reasons and should not be taken as advocating a compartmentalized focus.

For those who approach research and applied interests from a communication framework, the choice of nonverbal events is largely dependent upon the purposes and contexts of exploration. When investigating intercultural interaction, it is vital that the definition does not limit the events to be studied or used in educational programs. Barnlund's definition (1975) embues all behaviors with potential code capacity: he holds that communication involves exploration of all the factors and forces by which meaning is created. Here "communication" does not imply understanding, successful completion of goal, or conscious intent.

AUTHOR'S NOTE: *The author is on the communication faculty at International Christian University, Tokyo, Japan. She is indebted to Dean Barnlund, John Condon, Toby Frank, Nan Sussman, and Paul Ventura for their suggestions and support.*

A more restrictive definition involves the necessity of intention on the part of the sender in order for an act to be labeled communicative. If it is necessary that A consciously intends to create meaning in another, then one examines only those acts based upon one point of view at one point in time. Out-of-awareness actions of A which may be creating meaning in B are not integrated into an explanation of the encounter. This is hardly a complete perspective even when interactants share cultural membership; that is, when they share a common coding system that relates specific signs to meanings. Within an intercultural encounter, however, the degree of code sharing can vary along a continuum from nearly identical to very dissimilar. It is to be expected that A will be creating meaning in B of which A, evaluating the interaction through his or her own cultural coding system, cannot consciously be aware. Thus it becomes impossible to predict, a priori, what behaviors should "count" as a communicative. This framework grows from the thesis that one "cannot not communicate" (Watzlawick, Beavin and Jackson 1967:49).

One may either view all behavior as communicative or philosophically separate communicative behavior from informative behavior (Wiener et al., 1972).[1] In either case, the limitations of any definition which places restrictions upon what "counts," and in doing so narrows the spectrum of events to be studied, must be made clear before research proceeds.

While all behaviors should be understood as potential messages, analysis aimed at cultural explanations of behavior requires the search for order and patterning in behavioral sequences:

> were it not that interactions were patterned, behavior would be unpredictable and unreliable, and it would be impossible to sustain, mediate and form human relationships, complete co-ordinated tasks and transmit a common culture. [Scheflen 1968: 47]

Analysis, then, must be centered around deciphering the conscious and out-of-awareness codes[2] which guide encoding and decoding of nonverbal behavior in any particular culture. Patterns grow from common experience and are the basis of shared expectations and intentions, that is, predictability.

Analysis on the individual or idiosyncratic level does not serve the pragmatic needs of the consumers for whatever knowledge can be accumulated about nonverbal behaviors between cultures.

One very useful approach to pattern identification has been the concept of display rules. The concept, developed by Klineberg (1940), was first related to facial expression and was a challenge to Darwin's theory that facial expressions were universal. Ekman and Friesen (1969) continued to explore the contingencies that govern behavioral display. Such rules are socially learned and specify what management techniques are applicable for any context. There are four major management techniques: one can intensify, deintensify, neutralize, or mask a behavior. Management is accomplished in relationship both to static and dynamic contextual characteristics and to the particular meaning to be communicated. As illustration, Friesen (1972) discovered that, when alone, both American and Japanese subjects showed similar affect when watching stressful films, but in the presence of cultural peers, the Americans showed more negative affect than did the Japanese. Boucher (1974) suggests that, if display rules are as ingrained as we think they are, experimental intervention can be performed with minimal loss of normal data

There are particular characteristics of meaning conveyed via nonverbal behavior. While the identification of these characteristics arises from a research base, they also represent important philosophical perspectives which guide both the questions asked about nonverbal behavior and how nonverbal issues are handled in educational and training situations.

Nonverbal behavior communicates a different form of information than does verbal. While the spoken word is exclusively digital, nonverbal behavior is primarily analogic in form (Watzlawick et al., 1967: 60-67; Wilden, 1972). The distinction between the two relates to the characteristics of information flow and use in computers. Digital form involves a precise, abstract, "yes-no/on-off/all-none" relationship between a sign and its referent. Through management of signs, or syntax, it is possible to represent negative statements and "nothing." Quantities represented in the analogic form are much less precise than those in the digital; they are of the "more-less," "both-and" quality—"analogic differences and differences of magnitude, frequency, distribution, pattern, organization and the like" (Wilden, 1972: 62). Examples of simple analog computers include the slide rule, the thermometer, and maps.

Both the analogic and digital forms of information are applied in understanding information flow within human relationships. Obviously, words are in a digital relationship to their meanings: because there is nothing "thing-like," no direct relationship, between the animal pig and "p-i-g." There are at least three very distinct meanings of p-i-g; the correct application is a matter of semantics and contextual convention. It is also possible to be silent—a "zero representation"—and for one digital sign or word to negate another. Nonverbal behavior is much more analogic than speech. Many of our gestures, postures, facial expressions, and paralinguistic cues actually look or sound like what they mean. An example of such a relationship, widely accepted in Western cultures, is that people tend to get physically closer to others whom they like. Another is that facial expressions and postures of sadness and depression often have downward direction. "In shame. . . there is an implosion of the self. The body gestures and attitudes include head bowed, eyes closed, body curved in on itself, making the person as small as possible" (Lewis, 1971: 37). Whether the gesture for "come here" involves a palm up or down, movement with the fingers, hand or entire arm, the motion is usually from an outward to an inward position, as if to draw the other toward the self.

> In displaying himself, man always tries to make himself larger and, by coloration, ornaments, and noisy behavior, more impressive. Submission is the antithesis. One tries to be inconspicuous, to make oneself smaller, by bending the head or even falling prostrate to the ground. [Eibl-Eibesfeldt, 1964: 305]

However universal some analogues may be, it is also the case that, "with a different logic quite different analogical expressions can express the same meaning" (Condon and Yousef, 1975: 133). An example involves using the fingers to count to five. Most Americans begin with a closed fist and extend one finger per number. Members of other cultures begin with an open fist and withdraw one finger per number so that "five" is represented by a closed fist. These appear to be variations of an analogic representation. This makes it necessary to learn the different analogic bases of behaviors in various cultures. Condon and Yousef (1975: 134-140) suggest that many analogues may be based in value orientations. It thus becomes possible to tie nonverbal meanings to individualism versus group identity and to status-respect versus equality of rank. For example, behavioral qualities of bowing are a visible representation of the status relationship between two parties.

Even though a cultural analog must be learned, initially analogic learning is faster and easier than digital learning. While a traveler may not be able to speak a particular language, if the analogue of behavior can be understood, he or she can "get along" using primarily nonverbal behavior. There are, of course, instances in which nonverbal behavior seems to have as arbitrary and abstract a relationship to meaning as does digital communication. Examples include particular emblems, costuming, and cosmetic codes—those behaviors which serve regulatory or monitoring functions.

The translation of analogic into digital information has serious implications for interpersonal communication. How is one to accurately formulate a precise translation of a "more or less," "both-and" behavioral statement? To move from the digital to the analogic involves a loss of precise message content, while the reverse change involves loss of meaning on the relationship level. First, it is difficult for one to verbalize behavioral manifestations of a feeling, attitude, or other subjective experience. Second, when disagreement or miscommunication occurs about some analogic, nonverbal behavior, it is difficult to obtain agreement because both parties translate into the digital, verbal mode via their personal and cultural views about the relationship (Watzlawick et al., 1967: 99-102). The translation is also affected by what one is allowed to verbalize about personal relationships. Theoretically, meanings are often conveyed nonverbally when there are restrictions on their verbal expression. Cultural restrictions include norms governing levels of self-disclosure, gender differences, and the appropriateness of direct negative and positive feedback. We know very little about how such restrictions channel particular meanings into the nonverbal mode. Nonverbal ramifications of the definitions of private and public self are beginning to be explored (Barnlun, 1975). In particular, taboos against direct verbal negation are explored in such articles as "How to tell when someone is saying no" (Rubin, 1976) and "Sixteen ways to avoid saying 'no' in Japan: a survey of the function and frequency of Japanese patterns of declining requests" (Ueda, 1974).

As previously mentioned, the analogic mode lacks an expression for "not:"

> To illustrate, there are tears of sorrow and tears of joy, the clenched fist may signal aggression or constraint, a smile may convey sympathy or contempt, reticence can be interpreted as tactfulness or indifference . . . . Analogic communication has no qualifiers to indicate which of two discrepant meanings is implied, nor any indicators that would permit a distinction between past, present and future. [Watzlawick et al., 1967: 65]

Meaning assigned to nonverbal behavior must then be a function of behavioral analogues, selective perception, specific views of the relationship, rules governing the meanings allowed expression in the verbal and nonverbal modes, and the available digital system.

Human communication occurs on two levels. The content level involves information about ideas, facts, events, feelings; it is the substance of the verbal form. In addition, information about the relationship between participants is also being exchanged. This is termed the "relationship" or "command" function; it is primarily through nonverbal behavior that we communicate on this level. In addition to presenting a lecture on communication, by the way she moves, stands, gestures, uses eye contact and vocal inflection, a teacher also tells her class about herself, how she feels toward the subject matter and the very act of lecturing, and how she feels about them.

In any attempt to completely understand meaning, each level must be interpreted within the context of the other. But at one point in time we may pay more attention to one level than the other. We tend to believe that the verbal always carries the "main" meaning, while the nonverbal serves as modifier. Such is not always the case. While a kiss nonverbally communicates affection, if it is accompanied by the words "I am supposed to kiss you," the verbal becomes the modifier of the nonverbal. Thus, most researchers agree that the two modes relate in interactional, integrative ways rather than being consistently autonomous or subordinate (Melbin, 1974).

Another belief revolves around contradictory or discrepant information. People have quite precise opinions about what others will "do" when verbally lying; about which nonverbal behaviors are easy and difficult to fake, and about which subjects lies are most often told. Such determinations seem to arise through experience, and are thus culturally influenced and often topic-related. While we tend to think that "the truth" is ultimately revealed via nonverbal behavior, the case for such an overall claim is not conclusive (Shapiro, 1968; Wass, 1973).

It must be understood that verbal and nonverbal behaviors are inextricably intertwined; speaking of one without the other is, as Birdwhistell says, like trying to study "noncardiac physiology." Whether in opposition or complementary to each other, both modes work to create the meaning of an interpersonal event. According to culturally prescribed codes, we use eye movement and contact to manage conversations and to regulate interactions; we follow rigid rules governing intra and inter personal touch, our bodies synchronously join in the rhythm of others in a group, and gestures modulate our speech. We must internalize all of this in order to become and remain fully functioning and socially appropriate members of any culture. However, when asked to explain the rules which govern such behavior, it is often found to be impossible.[3] Thus it is through violation of those norms which produce clear behavioral contrast that the first steps toward awareness begin. The majority of nonverbal exercises used in communication training programs today are based upon this very principle.

There is an important interpersonal consequence of the out-of-awareness nature of nonverbal behavior. Meanings originating from nonverbal behaviors are often the primary, if not sole, basis for impression formation and attribution about another (McMahan, 1976). The attributions made often determine whether there will be any verbal interaction. There are innumerable accounts of miscommunication triggered by nonverbal behavior. If the problem can be traced to such behaviors, participants can approach at least an intellectual, if not an emotional, reconciliation. Often, however, since the nonverbal mode is not explicable as an option in analysis of what went wrong, the cause is attributed to some internal aspect of the other. The problem is connected to personality, intelligence, or attitudes rather than to a mismatch of learned nonverbal codes. Educational programs which stress behavioral description as a first step in analysis of miscommunication can do much consciousness-raising about the role of nonverbal behavior in the total communication system and can contribute to an understanding of the nature of interpersonal attributions based on nonverbal behavior.

Mary Ritchie Key's book, *Paralanguage and Kinesics* (1975), places nonverbal acts within an all-encompassing theory of context. A complete analysis of context includes the choice of channel of communication; temporal aspects; location, position, and space or distance relationships; descriptions of speaker/hearer (age, sex, culture, role); description of audience; physical conditions (noise/silence, light/darkness, artifacts); Zeitgeist; individual idiosyncracies of participants; and style of communication (Key, 1975: 122-134). These determinants of nonverbal behavior interact and overlap:

> One aspect cannot be analyzed in isolation, nor as a static condition, because features change along with the interaction. The context of situation, then, is the controlling influence in the choice in language, from pronunciation features to syntax to larger structures, and to nonverbal behavior. An analysis without these considerations could only be done in an extremely narrow sense, and this might be almost useless with regard to meaning. [Key, 1975: 134]

Key also stresses the necessity of obtaining baseline or "idio-movements" of any individual before assessing meaning. In her final discussion on the scientific method, she points to the need for solid descriptive study with an eye toward identifying universals.

In a much more theoretically oriented book, *Man Beyond Words* (1976), Poyatos proposes a model of total bodily communication. Every message-producing aspect of the body is categorized and an exhaustive accounting of conditioning background, or context, modifies each category. Emphasizing paralinguistics, kinesics, proxemics, and chronemics, Poyatos stresses the necessity for an integrative approach to the study of nonverbal behavior that includes exploring the relationship of behavior to context and of one nonverbal subcomponent to another.

While almost every text on nonverbal behavior considers the cultural dimension to varying extents, Argyle's text, *Bodily Communication* (1975), includes a particularly instructive chapter, which claims that nonverbal behavior patterns differ across social class boundaries within one culture as well as across international cultural boundaries. Argyle uses the Japanese and Arab peoples as case studies for detailed descriptions of cultural differences in all nonverbal subcomponents. Discussing the influence of ideas and languages on nonverbal behavior, Argyle suggests that the verbal repertoire of a culture may influence both encoding and decoding of behavior. Acts focused around the concepts of "machismo" and "chutzpah" are examples. He spends a good portion of the chapter dealing with the issue of cultural universals. He describes diverse greeting forms used in 17 cultures, but also points out their common behavioral components: close proximity, direct orientation, the eyebrow flash, smiling, mutual gaze, bodily contact, presenting palm of hand (either for visual or tactile contact), and the variant of the head toss (1975: 80). Every culture selectively manages this repertoire of components in what seems to be a universal greeting sequence of four phases: 1) the direct salutation; 2) approach and preparation, 3) close phase; and 4) attachment phase (Goffman, 1971; Kendon and Farber, 1973).

Raising culturally specific analysis to a theoretical level, Argyle (1975: 95) points out certain features of nonverbal behavior characteristic of all cultures: (1) the same body parts are used for expressive purposes; (2) similar information, attitudes, emotions, and self-disclosing messages are communicated on the nonverbal channel; (3) nonverbal behavior supports speech production and is used in art and ritual; (4) the nonverbal channel is used for similar reasons; ie., when speech is impossible or would be too direct, while bodily communication is more immediate and stronger; (5) nonverbal behaviors are used to manage identical ranges of situations and relationships; and (6) meaning, on the nonverbal channel, is usually analogic.

In turn, most intercultural texts have chapters on nonverbal behavior. There is an excellent chapter in the Condon and Yousef text (1975) which is theoretically sound and full of culture-specific examples illustrating theory. In discussing the analogic nature of nonverbal information, the reader is cautioned against becoming caught up in trying to discover the origin of behaviors. Questions of "why" are less practical then questions of "how" and may be only slightly disguised forms of ethnocentrism. Within the chapter, the form of many nonverbal behaviors are related to value orientations; particular taboos are explained and there is a section on crosscultural meanings sent by unchangeable physical traits such as skin color and height. The authors suggest that we do not yet understand well enough how perceived differences in appearance affect interpersonal relationships across cultures.

While there are numerous discussions which examine the totality of nonverbal behaviors within one cultural context, those emphasized here are especially useful as overviews because they clearly illustrate how nonverbal behaviors relate to each other and to context. An excellent article of this type is "Aspects of Nonverbal Communication in Japan" (Morsbach, 1973). The author begins by relating the historical development of behavioral styles. In detailed discussion, aspects of posture, gesture, facial expression, paralanguage, proxemics and artifacts are directly related to such social factors as ranking and hierarchy, mother-child relations, and intragroup solidarity. Morsbach continually draws parallels between specific behaviors and the Japanese language, especially proverbs. He emphasizes that nonverbal behavior in Japan differs both quantitatively and qualitatively from that of the West. In other words, not only are there culture-specific differences, but there are differences in the importance and function of the nonverbal mode.

In Search of What's Japanese about Japan (Condon and Kurata, 1974) explains aspects of dress, facial expression, silence, color, architectural and personal space, posture and gesture in terms of value orientations. The vertical nature of Japanese culture, the emphasis on group orientation, and the philosophy that "seeing is also a way of not seeing," are three such orientations that appear to be analogic principles upon which many nonverbal actions are based.

Contextual analysis is the theme of Gorden's *Living in Latin America: A Case Study in Cross-Cultural Communication* (1974). Gorden's purpose is to

> demonstrate the importance of the situationally determined assumptions in the process of cross-cultural communication, discover some of the specific non-linguistic barriers between North Americans and Colombians and sensitize the reader to some of the symptoms and results of communication blockages typical among people in daily cross-cultural contact. [1974: xii]

Insightful comments on space, appearance, gesture and time are woven throughout an ethnographic-like account of living patterns in a Colombian household. Particular nonverbal behaviors are analyzed within spatial and action contexts—the bathroom, the bedroom, and the dining area. Nonverbal behaviors are also shown to be integral parts of maintaining the "guest" role relationship with specific family members.

In *Communication in Africa* (1961), Doob pays special attention to the appearance of the body and how changes are accomplished via piercing, removal of parts, deformation, and other permanent modifications of the skin. He claims that in some parts of West Africa it is often possible to identify ethnic groups by facial markings. There are, however, many factors which mediate against such labeling: scarification due to slavery, lack of marking due to missionary influences, style changes in marking aross generations, and marks made for personal gratification. Within one ethnic group, however, facial markings are clear signs of age grades, status, and mobility, and are used to indicate changes in these variables.

There are two major articles which analyze the nonverbal behavior of black Americans: "Nonverbal Communication Among Afro-Americans: An Initial Classification" (Cooke, 1972), and "Black Kinesics: Some Nonverbal Communication Patterns in the Black Culture" (Johnson, 1971). Both studies are descriptive. According to Johnson, since the existence of black English has been widely demonstrated, it sensibly follows that nonverbal communication patterns of black Americans should differ substantively from that of the dominant culture. He hypothesizes two reasons for the existence of differences: nonverbal patterns could have their origin in African behaviors, and they could have taken on distinctive qualities during the periods of isolation of black Americans from other Americans. Research is needed to verify the role of one or both of these theories of origin.

Cooke's descriptions (1972: 33-43) are based on observations of teenagers from Chicago's West Side during 1968-1969. He presents a detailed analysis of one particular behavior, "skin: giving-and-getting." He identifies four major kinemes: greeting skin, parting skin, complimentary skin, and agreement skin. All may be performed in four modes: on the sly, empathic, superlative, and regular.

Both Cooke and Johnson describe stances and walks of young males; Cooke's description of walks is more detailed, identifying five types (chicken, sluefoot, basic soul, cool, and pimp), while Johnson deals only with the pimp walk. Eye movement patterns, such as "rolling the eyes" to communicate hostile disapproval of another in a superior role or avoidance of eye contact to communicate respect, are analyzed only in Johnson's article. His article, too, is the one which points up appropriate behavior when black males are gathered in a nonserious small group discussion. The boundary of the group fluctuates as members move in and out of the center; a group member may

> turn his back to the center of the group and walk away, almost dance
> away, with great animation to nonverbally communicate his confirma-

tion of what has been said and his recognition of the creative way in
which it was said. [Johnson, 1971: 265]

Johnson's brief comments emphasize an area much in need of
investigation. In educational, business and training endeavors,
much intercultural contact occurs in the small group context. It
is vital to identify cultural influences on nonverbal behavior
styles deemed appropriate and inappropriate within this context. It is also important to understand the effects of culturally
inappropriate behaviors on task completion and socioemo-
tional tone of a group.

While both articles do discuss eye movement and stance of
black females, there is much less attention paid to their
behavior than to that of males. There is also a lack of
discussion of differences in behavior that may be due to age.
Cooke (1972: 42) stresses that all kinetic elements are tools
used by individuals to suit their own needs and purposes, and
that the only way to interpret the meaning of an act is to
"analyze the entire communication event." His article also
contains a warning (1972: 54) that is essential to have in mind
when describing nonverbal behavior:

> It is certainly erroneous to ascribe a certain kind of walking style,
> clothes, and vocabulary with just one role or type of personality. This
> results in a gross stereotyping of the blacks (similar to the Sambo myth)
> which ignores the true diversity and richness of communication patterns
> which exist in the Afro-American culture. Herein possibly lies one of the
> pitfalls of "ethnic studies."

REVIEW

The majority of material available on intercultural aspects
of nonverbal behavior focuses on only one or two subcomponents. While integration of subcomponents is the ideal, at
this point in the state of the art, this single focus approach
seems to be the most appropriate way to organize existing
material and the smoothest framework through which to
comprehend the large amount of data.

Posture

The choice of postural options appropriate for particular functions and contexts is culturally influenced. One of the most well known assessments of postural options in use around the world comes from the work of Hewes (1955, 1957). There appear to be close to 1,000 static postures which are comfortable enough to be held over time. Hewes enumerates variables upon which choices of postures may be based: gender differentiating conditions (pregnancy, lactation, child carrying), fear of genital exposure, clothing and footgear, artificial supports, house construction, activity, terrain, physiologic functions, and burial norms. Hewes does not explore the social context of these postures, but if such data are to have practical application, it is necessary to understand the social component of appropriate and inapproprite usage. In particular, it is universal that a person of higher status has more postural flexibility than does one of lower status (Kendon 1973: 47).

The bow is a posture about which much has been written (Morsbach, 1973; Okawa, 1974; Befu, 1975). In a vertical society like Japan, misbehavior signifies a certain social relationship between participants; if performed according to ritual, it also indicates that both participants will abide by the interpersonal rules of that relationship. Appropriate bowing is a complicated process. There are two basic positions from which to bow—sitting on tatami and standing—and each bow can be divided into three levels—deep, intermediate, and light.

Total bowing behavior is dependent upon the status relationship of participants; the inferior must begin the bow, and his or her bow is deeper, while the superior determines when the bow is complete. When participants are of equal status, they must both bow the same way and begin and end the bow at the same time. Synchronization is extremely important:

> the matter of synchrony, in fact perfect synchrony, is absolutely essential to bowing. Whenever an American tries to bow to me, I often feel extremely awkward and uncomfortable because I simply cannot synchronize bowing with him or her. . .bowing occurs in a flash of a second, before you have time to think. And both parties must know precisely when to start bowing, how deep, how long to stay in the bowed position, and when to bring their heads up. [Befu, 1975]

How do Japanese manage this behavior; how and when do they develop this "sense" that approaches perfect synchrony? What are the ritual behaviors in other cultures that are similar to the bow in terms of synchrony and of the need for a heightened awareness of the other?

Face-to-face interaction analysis provides a framework through which much intercultural analysis could be accomplished. Synchronous movements between same cultural members have been the subject of much study. "To move with another is to show that one is with him in one's attention and expectations" (Kendon, 1970: 125). To what extent is synchrony possible between members of different cultures? If it is accomplished, whose rhythm dominates, or is a third created? If a Japanese can become comfortable bowing with an American, what exactly have they both learned?

A very intriguing study by Dabbs (1969), which examined the interpersonal effects of gesture similarity, has ramifications for intercultural posture sharing and synchrony. Dabbs discovered that mimicking (of posture, gestural mannerisms and touch patterns) increased identification with the actor and resulted in the perception that the actor was persuasive and well informed. During deliberate antimimicking, liking was especially low. Generally, similarity seemed to improve communication, while dissimilarity was very disruptive. This latter finding has obvious intercultural relevance. Dabbs also hypothesized that this effect was especially related to expectation; posture discrepancy may be especially upsetting when two people believe that they are similar. This supports the need for general "consciousness raising" about nonverbal differences so that people do not expect movement sameness.

There are, of course, postures that accompany particular interpersonal events—listening, arguing, explaining, begging, and so forth. What kind of frameworks are available to describe culturally variant behaviors that accompany such speech acts? Are Scheflen's (1965) divisions of body movements into the point, the position, and the presentation universally applicable? Participants in a focused interaction must signal how committed they are to the total engagement, who they are "with," to whom they are speaking, and that they are listening.

In other words, in having a conversation, the participants must
cooperate together to maintain a system of relationship, an organization
within which talk, whatever it may be concerned with, can be carried out.
We shall say that conversationalists enter into and maintain a "working
consensus" which specifies the "ground rules" for their conduct in a
conversation. [Kendon, 1973: 30]

We know very little about how culture influences the way
posture is used to regulate social interaction. For example, the
degree to which two people face each other is related to their
sex, the topic, any activity they are involved in while talking,
the place, their level of acquaintance, the distance between
them, and the cultural rules about how all these variables fit
together. While two white Americans may be able to walk and
talk with an occasional turn of the head, Hall (1966: 161)
found this not to be the case when walking and talking with an
Arabic friend. As they would walk, it was necessary for the
Arab to stop Hall and directly face him when speaking. Hall
discovered that viewing his friend peripherally was rude and
not sufficiently involving.

According to Mehrabian (1972), there are two dimensions
of posture which are associated with communication of attitudes: the factor of immediacy and that of relaxation. Forward
lean is suggestive of greater immediacy, as in the presence of
someone liked. Asymmetry of arms and legs plus sideways and
backwards lean is indicative of relaxation that may be present,
for Americans, with another of lower status. While these
dimensions may have crosscultural validity, it has not been
clearly shown that the postural variables indicative of a
particular dimension are universal.

Bond and Shiraishi (1974) manipulated body lean and
status to determine the effect on male and female Japanese
interviewees. While U.S. subjects have reacted with increased
vigilance and tension when interacting with another of higher
status, there are no known behaviors that are universally linked
to tension and vigilance. Bond and Shiraishi's dependent
variables were eye contact, pauses during speech, total speaking
time, "ah" and "nonah" ratios, self-manipulation, gesture,
torso shift, smiling, and a person perception scale. The
confederates were male; they dressed as either high or equal

status and assumed a forward or backward lean during the entire four minute interview. Results indicated that Japanese women seemed to respond with more anxiety than did men to a person of higher status.

Gesture

Gesture is one of the areas in which most intercultural work has concentrated over the longest period of time (Tylor, 1878; Mallery, 1880 and 1881; Scott, 1893; Phillot, 1907; Klineberg, 1935; Boas et al., 1936; Hayes, 1941; Bailey, 1942). Until fairly recently, reports were mainly anecdotal and concerned with description of emblems.

Darwin (1872: 235, 246-272) was interested in showing that many gestures were universal. He saw the shoulder shrug, for example, serving three purposes: to show that one cannot do something or cannot prevent something from happening, to accompany a statement like "it wasn't my fault," and to express patience or the absence of any intention to resist. He did not, however, claim universality for the head movement accompanying "yes" and "no."

Both Klineberg (1935, 1938) and Labarre (1947) amassed data to illustrate that emblems are culture-specific and learned. In his review of Chinese literature, Klineberg (1938) found a number of behaviors that Americans would use and understand. Many others would be unfamiliar: sticking out the tongue to indicate suprise; widening eyes for anger; and scratching ears and cheeks to show happiness. Klineberg was also interested in how cultural rules managed the expression of nonverbal behavior. His questions set the foundation for the development of the crucial concepts of display rules (Ekman and Friesen, 1969a; Boucher, 1974). The anthropologist LaBarre (1947) has provided an exhaustive amount of culture-specific data describing how people around the world signal "yes" and "no," walk, laugh, kiss, greet, and act in a variety of situations. His descriptions are generally concerned with emblems and bodily actions.

As research on emblems has continued, most agree that these signs vary with culture, are socially learned and conventionalized, and thus can be organized and classified for study. Ekman (1976) has defined emblems very precisely as follows: (1) emblems have a direct brief verbal translation; (2) most members of a particular class or culture share meaning for this movement; (3) messages are deliberately sent: (4) the receiver is aware of the message and that he or she was the desired receiver; and (5) the sender usually takes responsibility for the behavior. Ekman and Friesen are presently involved in a major effort to construct an emblem dictionary. (Ekman, 1976; Johnson et al., 1975).[4] A dictionary will make possible research into ontogeny, how emblems vary with speech, how usage varies with age, gender, and role, and the degree to which some emblems may approach universality.

It is necessary to place performance of emblems within context to understand shades of meaning, modifications of usual form, and the pragmatics of usage—i.e., from whom, to whom, and when use is appropriate. There are many "lists" available which describe a particular motion and how it is to be verbally translated. These descriptions include a concern for contexts and pragmatics to differing degrees (Hughes, 1941; Devereux, 1949, 1951; Walker, 1953; Meggit, 1954; Feldman, 1959; Saitz and Cervenka, 1962; Schnapper, 1969, 1975; Condon, 1973; Nine-Court, 1974; Mathai, 1975). In studies of these types, it is often unclear whether meanings were uncovered through anecdotal or controlled observation, or to what population within a culture the meaning relates. Studies without such concerns do not provide much information beyond the "isn't it quaint" and "do they really do it that way?" level.

The methodology used to discover and validate culture-specific emblems must be very precise. Johnson et al., (1975) delineate three major steps. First, informants perform emblems of their culture. Since even these more obvious aspects of nonverbal behavior can be out-of-awareness, Ekman and Friesen found it necessary to read lists of verbal messages to which informants would perform appropriate movements. After a sufficient number of informants had been interviewed so that no new emblems appeared, elicited emblems were compared. To avoid contamination of the sample due to invention, only those emblems with meanings which were similar across all performances were used in the third step. Here a new group of informants were shown performances and evaluated each emblem according to whether it was an invention, a pantomime/charade, or a gesture they observed in daily life. They also gave meanings for each emblem. Through such "back translation," validity could be assured.

This methodology has been used in constructing an American dictionary. Subjects were white middle class males. Fifty percent of the emblems identified overlapped with those of Saitz and Cervenka (1972). The nonoverlap appeared to be related to regional differences and to the 11 year time difference between the two studies. In addition to analyzing American emblems, this methodology has been used with urban Japanese, the South Fore, Iranians, and Israelis living in the U.S. for less than a year. So far, emblems are known to give insult, directions, replies, affect, and to comment on one's physical state and appearance. Certainly this controlled type of study needs to be repeated while varying age, sex, region, social class, and ethnic background (Johnson, Ekman and Friesen, 1975). Ekman (1976) suggests that knowledge of cultural emblems might be very useful in critical situations when help-giving personnel do not speak their receivers' language. Contexts such as hospitals and classrooms immediately become obvious.

There are numerous studies which describe or analyze an entire gestural system of a particular culture. One of the most noteworthy and well known is that of Efron (1972). His efforts were originally directed to counter the claim that body movement is determined by racial descent and that ethnic groups, particularly Jews, could be universally identified by their nonverbal behavior. The introduction to his book contains an excellent critique and review of those who supported the genetic view. As Efron makes clear, any such claim must first prove that an individual under study belongs to a uniform racial type and, secondly, any trait indicative of race must be shown to be an exclusive characteristic of all individuals of that group. Neither of these stipulations has ever been fulfilled. It was Efron's specific intention to find out whether gestures of traditional Eastern European Jews and South Italians differed from those of their more assimilated counterparts and, thus, whether environment molded behavior. Using a diverse methodology, he both observed and filmed natural spontaneous interaction and used the trained observation skills of a well known artist. Altogether he observed 2,810 subjects, produced 5,000 feet of film, and 2,000 sketches.

Green (1971) urges institutions to employ nonverbal concepts in dialogues so that students learn to speak a foreign language as native "movers." He suggests that language teachers ask kinesic researchers to provide them with further high quality crosscultural material that can be responsibly used in the classroom.

Bodily Contact

"The patterning of direct tactile communication may be considered as one of the early and most significant social inventions. . . early tactile experiences provide the basis for transformation into learned symbolic contact and participating in social order" (Frank, 1957).

Cultures differ in prescriptions surrounding covering, exposing, and decorating the skin; the nature of tactile experiences sought after, avoided, and how these are to be endured; the public and private use of touch in self-communication; how symbolic experiences become tactile surrogates; the establishment of tactile thresholds; and how one relates to the severing of tactile experiences (Frank, 1957). The majority of these issues were explored by Williams (1966) when he analyzed tactile experiences of the Borneo Dunsun. Particular postures, gestures and some linguistic structures served as touch surrogates. Dunsun women used both dress and status as markers indicating what touch was permitted or restricted. There were complex systems of rules governing the approach, striking, and leaving of others, as well as for contact with land and sacred objects. The cultural patterning of touch in face-to-face interaction varies enormously; many such cultural norms are documented by LaBarre (1947). Montague's massive review of the role of touch in human communication (1971) attends not only to the prescriptions identified by Frank, but to varieties of culture-specific behaviors.

The work of Jourard and Rubin (1968) examining body accessibility and self-disclosure has been the impetus for a number of cultural investigations. Jourard wanted to find out what body parts of white American male and female students were touched by mothers, fathers, same-sex friends and opposite-sex friends. He discovered, overall, that females were more accessible to touch than were males, and that opposite-sex friends and mothers did the most touching. Touch and self-disclosure seem to be intimacy signals; Jourard's data indicated that both sexes would reveal more of themselves to females than to males. This type of study has been replaced with Israeli and Japanese students.

In the Israeli study, single male students evidenced greater body accessibility and engaged more in active touch than did females (Lomranz and Shapira, 1974). Other studies (Barn-lund, 1975; Elzinger, 1975) demonstrating the intercultural reliability of Jourard's methodology have looked at Japanese patterns of touch. The results of both are consistent: single women students were more involved in touching and being touched than were Japanese male students. While members of both Japanese and American culture seemed to be involved in touch most with opposite-sex friends and least with fathers, the degrees were very different. The avoidance of the father was much greater in Japan, while Americans tended to engage in much more contact with the opposite sex. Generally, Americans were involved in twice as much physical contact as were Japanese. While Americans evidenced more conscious, public touch display, the Japanese tended to tolerate crowding and public touching by strangers better than did Americans. Both cultures agreed on which bodily parts were open and forbidden to touch by others; in both cultures the desire to initiate touch and to be touched seemed to grow and diminish together.

Spatial Behavior

Intercultural interests in spatial behavior have been concentrated around three issues: differences in personal interaction distance, the choice of seating position, and the influence of architecture upon human behavior.

PERSONAL SPACE

Since Hall (1959) began to bring the concept of proxemics into public awareness, the notion that culture defines the size of the spatial bubble within which humans move has become a familiar part of educational and cultural training programs. It has also been subject of much experimental research. The majority of studies attempting to validate many of Hall's anecdotal descriptions have concentrated on documenting specific distances that different cultures employ in face-to-face interaction. However, some focus on cultural groups in a molar sense and others relate interpersonal distance to such situational variables as status, topic of conversation, or level of acquaintance within a cultural framework.

One of the earliest studies that experimentally verified some of Hall's descriptions was that begun by Watson (Watson, 1970; Watson and Graves, 1973). Through his proxemic inventory, conducted with foreign and American students and using Hall's labels, Watson identified Arabs, Latin Americans, and Southern Europeans as "contact" cultures and Asians, Indians, Pakistanis, and Northern Europeans as "non contact" cultures. Although contact has come to refer mainly to physical contact, Hall intended "contact culture" to indicate interaction in a much more immediate and overall sense than "non contact." In the former, people faced each other more directly, stood closer, touched more, had more eye contact, and talked louder.

Watson did not claim that the same immediacy cues were consistent for an entire culture. Moreover, he allowed that immediacy cues within different cultural systems may have different relationships to each other. For example, Watson (1970) reported that Arabs told him that the angle of presentation did not matter as long as eye contact was held, while Northern Europeans reported that the angle of presentation and eye contact should go together. A number of other studies followed that attempted to identify spatial norms without paying major regard to situational variables. Without reporting socioeconomic class or level of acquaintance, Willis (1966) found that blacks greeted blacks at greater distances than whites greeted each other, and that whites greeted blacks at greater distances than they greeted other whites. In natural observations of people standing side by side watching animals at zoos, Baxter (1970) found that blacks stood furthest apart, whites at an intermediary distance, and Mexican Americans stood closest together.

Three other studies have continued to illustrate that the label "American" must be subdivided in the examination of the proxemic behavior of black Americans. All three gathered data from such natural settings as the street, classrooms, and schoolyards. Looking at behavior of blacks, Puerto Ricans, Italians and Chinese in New York City, Jones (1971) observed conversational distance. Only those who were judged by physical appearance to belong to the desired ethnic group and who were not approaching or leaving, were not focused on a third party, not hampered by physical barriers, and not engaged in any instrumental activity were observed. Hall's proxemic notational system was used. Results indicated that regardless of culture, women used a more direct axis than did men. Eighty percent of all subjects observed stood between 1.5 and 2 feet apart, so there was no significant difference in the interpersonal distance between cultures. Jones suggested that the noise level and crowded conditions on the street may have overridden cultural differences. Looking at distancing of black and white elementary school students, Jones and Aiello (1973) again found that girls employed a more direct axis than did boys, especially in the fifth grade. In earlier grades, black children stood closer together than white children; this disappeared by the fifth grade. Black children also seemed to use less direct axis than did white children (Aiello and Jones, 1971). With regard to Watson's comments about the interrelationship of nonvariables, Jones and Aiello hypothesized that, for females, eye contact and direct axis may be a subset of variables that go together. They also suggested that while both axis and spatial behavior are learned early in life, only axis is affected by subcultural differences in the later elementary years. Again looking at children, Lomizanz et al. (1975) found that in Israeli born middle class three to seven-year-olds, younger aged peers kept the least distance from each other and all ages kept less distance from girls.

Forston and Larson (1968) found that when involved in discussions, Latin Americans sat further apart than North Americans. This contradicts what would be expected based on "generally" accepted knowledge about personal space. The dyads were, however, having a political discussion. Aiello and Jones (1971) have remarked that Latin Americans have been reported to sit further apart when engaged in serious discussions than when engaged in more social interaction. Forston and Larson suggested that context and whether or not subjects are speaking their native tongue may affect interpersonal distance.

Varying the language spoken, Sussman (1977) found that when using their native tongue to discuss a neutral topic, same-sex dyads of Japanese sat further apart than did Americans, and that both these groups sat further apart than Venezuelans. When speaking English, Japanese males sat closer together, while Venezuelan women and men sat further apart than they had when speaking their native language.

It is also true that any results are affected by such molar categories "Latin" and "North" American. In examining the touch and distance norms of the specific cultures of Costa Rica, Panama, and Colombia, Shuter (1976) found very significant differences. He used data from natural observation of two persons engaged in face-to-face interaction. He noted sex, axis, contact and distance. Results indicated that, regardless of culture, women used more direct axis, were more tactile, and had a more varied contact repertoire than did men. There appeared a progressive decline in the frequency of contact from Central to South America. The most extreme differences existed between Costa Ricans and Colombians, with the former standing closer, having a more direct axis, and touching more than did Colombians. Impressionistic data also suggested that Colombians gestured less than Costa Ricans. Generally, Shuter claimed that Costa Rica has a more highly involved culture than does Colombia.

While some of these studies provide information that is verified in repetition, it is clear that cultural differences and similarities may be masked when using only geographic distinctions or when ignoring both dynamic and static situational variables. As basic research progresses and the need to implement research results in educational programs becomes increasingly real, it is no longer adequate to continue to accept the very broad categories that were once the focus of proxemic investigation.

A study varying the political inclinations of interactants found that residents of Little Italy in New York City used smaller interaction distances with others who, via a flag symbol, indicated their conservative opinions than with those wearing a peace sign (Thayer and Alban, 1972). In a study which explored the relationship of distance to physical constraints, Mazur (1977) found that male strangers in Morocco, Spain, the U.S. and France tended to sit at the extreme ends of park benches even though the benches were of different shape and length.

A very sophisticated and seemingly accurate photogrammetric technique has been used by Scherer (1974), who took pictures of black and white grade school children conversing in schoolyards. While he held sex and race constant, he did not control the conversational content because he assumed that the children were in an area that reinforced play behavior and related topics of conversation. His findings indicated that sociial class, not culture, was the definitive variable determining distance. Lower class children stood further apart than did those of the middle class. Aiello and Jones (1971) have also found that lower class Puerto Rican and black children stood closer together than did their middle class counterparts.

SEATING

Based upon research with American subjects, specific relationships between seating and attitudes have consistently emerged. Close interpersonal seating, forward lean, direct orientation toward the other, and the amount of eye contact relate to liking of the other. It is not clear how seating distance is related to status. Research does indicate, however, that the timing of who sits down first and how long it takes to be seated or unseated is linked to status. Leaders often seem to gravitate to head positions at a table, and several studies have shown that, in actuality and in the perception of others, those seated closer to a dominant figure were also hierarchically closer (Delong, 1970a, 1970b). Condon and Kurata (1974: 83) provide one instance of intracultural verification of these results. They reported that the order of seating in Japanese formal or semiformal affairs is structured according to the vertical. The most important person sits with his or her back to the "kamiza" (literally, "the upper place") at one end of a rectangular table. Those of the nearest ranking sit at the right and left of this "head" position and those of lower rank sit, in order, further away from this position. The lowest place is the "shimaza" ("the low place"). It is nearest to the door and at the opposite end of the table from the highest ranking person.

Choosing a seat by another person relates to perceived qualities of that other, especially in the area of attitude similarity. This finding held up intraculturally in work that Brislin (1974) did with Micronesians. Elkin (1945) has warned that those responsible for assigning seats (classroom teachers) must be aware that cultural taboos may exist against being close to particular others.

Both Sommer (1968) and Ingham (1974) have explored intracultural perceptions about intimacy and seating. Sommer asked members of five cultures (American, English, Swedish, Dutch, and Pakistani) to rate the intimacy of a dyadic arrangement at a table on a 1 (intimate) to 7 (distant) scale. Results were as follows: side by side, 1.6; right angle, 2.6; close opposite, 3.4; and diagonal, 5.1. The ratings of Americans, Swedish, and English were exactly the same; the Pakistanis rated the opposite pattern more distant than did the others, though it was rated as third. A comment from a Pakistani informant throws light on this rating:

> Pakistanis are always on the same side of the fence, we sit opposite one another when we want to settle certain issues. . . group eating is generally done on the floor when people sit in rows side by side rather than opposing each other. [Sommer, 1968: 111]

Kuriki (1974) has taken the study of seating preference into the context of Tokyo snack shops. He charted the seating arrangements within four shops and asked clientele what kind of interaction was desired or to be avoided upon entering. Results indicated that regular customers had favorite seats, that the presence of others affected seat choice, and that the intention to have eye contact with others was also a determinant. Those who desired eye contact preferred counter seating, while those who wanted to avoid eye contact sat at tables. In addition, the comfort of the seats and the motivation of rest and relaxation was important in seat choice. Most of what we know about seating patterns and preferences is drawn from a Western data base. Consistent results are beginning to be interculturally verified. Such verification is important because seating is a particularly useful unobtrusive measure of interpersonal relationships.

ARCHITECTURE

Some of the more intriguing comments concerning intercultural aspects of architectural space relate to the design of cities and of houses. Hall (1959, 1966) provides a good deal of data about both these areas. He identifies European and Japanese patterns of organizing public and private space. There appear to be two major European patterns—the "radiating star" of France and Spain, and the "grid," which originated in Asia Minor and carried to England. In the former system, streets and subway lines meet at major intersections, thus bringing activities together; the latter pattern tends to separate activities. Both systems give names to streets. The Japanese system emphasizes the concept of center and intersections rather than streets are named (Hall, 1966: 106, 146, 150).

While Europeans and Westerners emphasize edges and boundaries, the Japanese are inclined to attend to space between objects. This edge versus inner space contrast is visible in the design and use of private homes. Westerners and Europeans tend to arrange furniture around the fixed outside walls of a room and leave the center relatively bare. Different activities are separated by walls. Interior walls of traditional

Japanese homes are semifixed; center space is utilized and total rooms are multipurpose (Hall, 1966: 150-154; Condon and Kurata, 1974: 77).

Bochner (1975) and Mead (1971) discuss the cultural ramifications that can accompany changes in vernacular house form. For Bochner, the house provides the setting in which cultural life styles are expressed. It is his thesis that "there is a direct link between the built environment and culture in the sense that the form of the built environment can be disruptive or supportive of life style and values of inhabitants" (1975). For him, "house form" refers to the layout of internal spaces and the relationship of dwellings to each other. This form is constructed very specifically in relationship to such variables as privacy, male and female relationships, and norm enforcement. Bochner presents line drawings of traditional homes of six cultures and hypothesizes what changes in values and behavior would have to occur if family members were to live in Western style housing. For example, the Navajo hogan reflects a nomadic life style. It faces East, thus incorporating the culture's spiritual values into its design. The inhabitants sleep together around the fireplace; there is little individual privacy. Bochner hypothesizes that the traditional Navajo culture would not survive a move into a Western-built structure. According to Hall (1966: 163-164), by examining different proxemic patterns,

> it is possible to reveal hidden culture frames that determine the structure of a people's perceptual world. Perceiving the world differently leads to differential definitions of what constitutes crowded living, different interpersonal relations, and a different approach to both local and international politics.

This review is by no means complete. Most obviously absent is a discussion of efforts focused around the facial expression of emotion and around paralinguistics. Is the expression of ear similarly expressed in all cultures; relying on facial expression, can we know what another intends though we share no common language? The universality of facial expression of emotion is a well known and long debated topic. A related issue concerns whether innate determinism or the strength of learning is responsible for facial display. Future research and application must make use of the understanding that there appear to be two frameworks through which to view facial expression. On the system level, behaviors are context free and there are abstract, genetically determined rules that control display. On the performance level, contextual, cultural, and psychological factors are involved in competent display.

Interest in paralinguistics has centered around several recurring themes. Evaluative reactions to accented speech and judgments about a speaker's social status and personality from paralinguistic cues have also been topics of investigation. An overview of results of this subcomponent provides specific information about the prestige ratings of various accents, about cultural stereotypes (Ortego, 1969; Ryan and Carranza, 1975; Miller, 1975), and about cultural misinterpretation of speech melody and rhythm (Adams, 1964).

There is also information that suggests that culture plays a large part in the categorization of judgments about paralinguistic cues and about how attributions are made. While having American and German listeners rate personality traits from content-filtered speech, it appeared that listeners were most attentive to voice cues which reinforced traits they perceived the speaker to have. For Americans, the trait was sociability; for Germans it was aggressiveness. The authors suggest that a listener uses an implicit theory of personality to assign traits that "go with" competence perceived to be necessary for a particular culture (Scherer, 1972).

Japanese and American college students seem to base their perception of social status on very different criteria. Japanese who were not fluent in English based perceptions of American English speakers on fluency and vocal quality, while Americans based judgments on sentence structure and vocabulary. As illustration, an American speaker who spoke slowly, did not enunciate clearly, but used a large number of polysyllabic words was perceived to be of an upper status by American raters and of a lower status by Japanese (Ellis, 1969).

In a related study exploring attribution of affective meaning by first and second language speakers, it appeared that students for whom English was a second language relied more on content for judgment, while native speakers relied more on intonation (Soloman and Ali, 1975). Certainly this is related to difference in familiarity with subtle aspects of language competence, which are very difficult to master. The subtle paralinguistic cues of rate, pitch, volume and rhythm used by native speakers to convey affective and other information on the "relationship" level are often the main source of communication problems for the second language learner because he or she misplaces and misperceives such cues.

Any attempt at active intervention designed to systematically identify nonverbal behavior patterns is plagued by the presence of experimenter expectancy effects, particularly those that are conveyed via the nonverbal channel. It is a generally accepted premise of social science research that particular cues from an experimenter's mood or demeanor, usually conveyed without awareness on the nonverbal channel, can influence the results obtained from human subjects (Rosenthal, 1966; Sattler, 1970).

The experimenter's behavior can convey both cognitive and affective information. While visual cues seem to influence feelings, paralinguistic cues manipulate cognitive input. The potential for these effects is especially high if subjects are apprehensive about their self-concept and presentation (Finklestein, 1976). The variable of proximity and thus of sensory involvement between experimenter and subject may be of more consequence in determining reactivity than is the mode of observation (Smith, McPhail and Pickers, 1975). "The ability to influence others depends on the extent to which one can reach them through their [sensory] receptors. Increased access increases the chances of influence. So control is dependent upon proximity" (Melbin, 1972: 21).

While the degree of sensory involvement may be a determining variable, no reliable ethnographic or experimental information yet exists for predicting sensory thresholds for specific cultural groups. In attempts to identify thresholds, such static variables as age, sex, and status must be accounted for. Sensory requirements of a subject may change when the experimenter is not of his or her native culture. Until more is known about intercultural variation, the ideal research paradigm involves experimenters and subjects who share cultural membership.

Philosophically, how is it possible to control or account for a system's effects on the investigation of itself? Certainly one answer lies in the use of unobtrusive measures; reliable ethnographic data combined with "meta" analyses could be an essential approach. The unconscious nature of nonverbal behavior combined with the tendency of people to believe that such behaviors convey "real" meaning create, in the nonverbal channel, powerful influences on the intercultural experimental paradigm.

SUMMARY AND CONCLUSION

It appears that data on nonverbal behavior patterns across cultures needs to be developed on two levels. First, on the culture-specific level, we learn about the functions and meanings of particular behaviors. These data must begin to be collected within more realistic frameworks. Pragmatically, interactions do not occur between "a Latin American" and "an American" within a contextual vacuum. Rather, each belongs to a very specific cultural group; each is of a particular sex, age, status, and role relationship. Actors are more or less acquainted with each other, they have particular feelings about each other, they engage in one of numerous social or task discussions, they do so in a particular place, and they are bound by culturally determined display rules. While this sounds very rudimentary, it is only recently that intercultural nonverbal research efforts have begun to take such considerations into account.

Second, on a more theoretical level, we discover how nonverbal behaviors function in the total communication process. For example, the concept of display rules is a useful way of examining the communicative function of nonverbal behavior, it is necessary to have a specific description of an action as well as knowledge of the options or range of expressive choices from which the action was chosen. In other words, knowledge about what was done takes on meaning from behaviors that could have been but were not performed. While options exist idiosyncratically, they also exist culturally.

Theoretically, it is through contrast arising in the cultural approach that the form and function of behavioral systems can best be identified. Pragmatically, the study of culturally variant aspects of nonverbal behavior is no longer relegated to the identification of quaint customs. There is need for knowledge that can be responsibly applied to interpersonal situations made critical by their intercultural component.

NOTES

1. Communicative acts may be understood as "those acts which are clearly and consciously intended by the sender." Informative behaviors are "those acts which have some decoded meaning in that such acts elicit similar interpretations in some set of observers" (Ekman and Friesen, 1969: 55). The "communication involves the creation of meaning" definition would, of course, encompass both the communicative and informative labels.

2. I used the following definition of code: "if a set of behaviors will be considered to constitute a code, it must be demonstrated both that the behaviors are known and used by the group; that is, used by at least two persons who emit (encode) the behavior to stand for the agreed-on referent and take (decode) the emitted behavior of the other to stand for the agreed-on referent" (Wiener, DeVoe, Rubinow and Geller, 1972: 204). These referents may exist as nonverbalized yet shared assumptions and they may exist on the culture-specific content level and on a more abstract process (thoughts about how communication should work) level.

3. This serves, of course, an interpersonal survival function. As a metaphorical example, one of the more dangerous feats to attempt is to begin to analyze how to ride a bike or drive a car while in the process of riding or driving.

4. Apparently, Desmond Morris is also engaged in research which focuses on the geographical distribution of gestures. He and others are looking at batons and emblems in England, France, and Italy. In particular he is looking at motor replacements for "yes" and "no" in North and South Italy (Argyle, 1975).

REFERENCES

ADAMS, J.B. (1964) "On expressive communication in an Egyptian village," pp. 272-273 in D. Hymes (ed.), *Language in Culture and Society: A Reader in Linguistics and Anthropology.* New York: Harper & Row.

AIELLO, J.R. and JONES, S.E. (1971) "Field study of the proxemic behavior of young school children in three subcultural groups." *Journal of Personality and Social Psychology* 19: 351-356.

ARGYLE, M. (1975) *Bodily Communication.* New York: International Universities Press.

BAILY, F.L. (1942) "Navajo motor habits." *American Anthropologist* 44, 2 (April-June): 210-234.

BARNLUND, D. (1975) *The Public and Private Self in Japan and the U.S.* Tokyo: Simul Press, pp. 91-113.

BATESON, G. (1953) "Why do Frenchmen." *ETC: A Review of General Semantics* 10, 2 (Winter): 127-380.

BAXTER, J. (1970) "Interpersonal spacing in natural settings." *Sociometry* 33: 444-456.

BEFU, H. (1975) "Konnichiwa." Essay read at meeting of Japan Society, San Francisco, April.

BLACK, H. (1969) "Race and sex factors influencing the correct and erroneous perceptions of emotion." Proceedings of 77th meeting of American Psychological Association, 4: 363-364.

BOAS, F., EFRON, D. and FOLEY, J.P. (1936) "A comparative investigation of gestural behavior patterns in racial groups living in different as well as similar environmental conditions." *Psychological Bulletin* 33: 760.

BOCHNER, S. (1975) "The house form as a cornerstone of culture," pp. 9-20 in R. Brislin (ed.), *Topics in Culture Learning*, vol. 3. Honolulu: East-West Center.

BOND, M. and SHIRAISHI, D. (1974) "Effect of body lean and status of interviewer on nonverbal behavior of Japanese interviewees." *International Journal of Psychology*, 9, 2: 117-128.

BOND, M. and SUATA, Y. (1976) "Proxemics and observational anxiety in Japan: Verbal and nonverbal cognitive responses." *Psychologia—An International Journal of Psychology in the Orient*, XIX, 3.

BOUCHER, J. (1974) "Display rules and facial affective behavior: A theoretical discussion and suggestions for research," pp. 87-102 in R. Brislin (ed.), *Topics in Cultural Learning*, vol. 2. Honolulu: East-West Center.

BRAULT, G.J. (1963) "Kinesics and the classroom: Some typical French gestures." *French Review*, 36, 4 (February): 374-382.

BREWER, W.D. (1951) "Patterns of gesture among Levantine Arabs." *American Anthropologist*, 53 (April): 232-237.

BRISLIN, R. (1974) "Seating as a measure of behavior: You are where you sit," pp. 103-118 in R. Brislin (ed.), *Topics in Culture Learning*, vol. 2. Honolulu: East-West Center.

CANFIELD, L.D. (1968) "Spanish with a flourish." AATSP Cultural Unit 1.

COLLETT, P. (1971) "Training Englishmen in the nonverbal behavior of Arabs: An experiment on intercultural communication." *International Journal of Psychology*, 6: 209-215.

CONDON. E.C. (1973) "Nonverbal communication." Reference Pamphlet on Intercultural Communication #4, Series C. New Jersey: Rutgers University.

CONDON, J. and KURATA, K. (1974) *In Search of What's Japanese About Japan.* Tokyo: Shufunotomo.

COOK, M. (1970) "Experiments on orientation and proxemics." *Human Relations*, 23: 61-76.

COOKE, B.J. (1972) "Nonverbal communication among Afro-Americans: An initial classification," pp. 32-64 in T. Kochman (ed.), *Rappin' and Stylin' Out: Communication in Urban Black America,* Urbana: Univ. of Illinois Press.

CRITCHLEY, M. (1975) *The Silent Language.* London: Butterworths.

CUCELOGLU, D.M. (1970) "Perception of faces in three different cultures." *Ergonomics*, 13: 93-100.

———— (1967) "A cross cultural study of communication via facial expressions." Urbana: Univ. of Illinois (Ph.D. dissertation).

DABBS, J.M., JR. (1969) "Similarity of gestures and interpersonal influence." Proceedings of the American Psychological Association, 4: 337-338.

DARWIN, C. (1872) *The Expression of Emotions in Man and Animals.* New York: Appleton.

DAY, R. (1970) "Kinesics and bilingualism: An experiment in nonverbal communication." *Pacific Speech,* 4, 2: 33-35.

DELONG, A.J. (1970a) "Dominance and territorial relations in a small group." *Environment and Behavior,* 2, 2: 170-191.

_____ (1970b) "Seating position and perceived characteristics of members of a small group." *Cornell Journal of Social Relations,* 5, 2: 134-151.

DICKEY, E.C. and KNOWLER, F.H. (1941) "A note on some ethnological differences in the recognition of simulated expressions of the environment." *American Journal of Sociology,* 47: 190-193.

DOOB, L. (1961) *Communication in Africa.* New Haven, Conn.: Yale Univ. Press.

EBERTS, E.N. (1972) "Social and personality correlates of personal space," in *Environmental Design: Research and Practice.* Proceedings of the EDRA III/ ARV III Conference. Los Angeles: University of California Press.

EDMAN, P. and FRIESEN, W. (1969) "The repertoire of nonverbal behavior— Categories, origins, usage and coding." *Semiotica,* 1, 1.

EFRON, D. (1972) *Gesture, Race and Culture.* T.A. Sebeok (ed.), Approaches to Semiotics #9. The Hague: Mouton.

EIBL-EIBESFELDT (1964) "Experimental criteria for distinguishing innate from culturally conditioned behavior," in F.S. Northrop and H.H. Livingston (eds.), *Cross Cultural Understanding: Epistemology in Anthropology.* New York: Harper & Row.

EKMAN, P. (1976) "Movements with precise meanings." *Journal of Communication,* 26, 3: 14-26.

_____ (1972a) "Preface to the 1972 edition," in D. Efron, *Gesture, Race and Culture.* The Hague: Mouton.

_____ (1972b) "Universals and cultural differences in facial expressions of emotion." Nebraska Symposium on Motivation, Lincoln: Univ. of Nebraska Press.

ELKIN, A.P. (1945) *The Australian Aborigine.* Sydney: Anges & Robertson.

ELLIS, D. (1969) "Japanese perception of Americans social status based on limited paralinguistic cues." *Pacific Speech,* 4, 1: 28-30.

ELLIS, H.D., DEREGOWSKI, J.B., and SHEPHERD, J.W. (1975) "Description of white and black faces by white and black subjects." *International Journal of Psychology,* 10: 119-123.

ELZINGA, R.H. (1975) "Nonverbal communication: Body accessibility among Japanese." *Psychologia,* 18: 205-211.

ENGERETSON, D. and FULLMER, D. (1970) "Cross cultural differences in territoriality: Interaction distances of native Japanese, Hawaiian Japanese and American Caucasians." *Journal of Cross-Cultural Psychology,* 3, 1: 261-269.

FINKELSTEIN, J. (1976) "Experimenter expectancy effects." *Journal of Communication,* 26, 3: 31-38.

FORSTON, R.F. and LARSON, C.U. (1968) "The dynamics of space: An experimental study in proxemic behavior among Latin Americans and North Americans." *Journal of Communication,* 18: 109-116.

FRANK, L.K. (1957) "Cultural patterning of tactile experiences." *Genetic Psychological Monographs,* 56: 209-225.

FRIESEN, W. (1972) "Cultural differences in facial expression in a social situation: An experimental test of the concept of display rules." San Francisco: University of California (Ph.D. dissertation).

FROIS-WHITTMAN, J. (1930) "The judgment of facial expression." *Journal of Experimental Psychology,* 13, 11: 113-151.
GOFFMAN, E. (1971) *Relations in Public.* London: Allen Lane.
GORDON, R.L. (1974) *Living in Latin America: A Case Study in Cross Cultural Communication.* Skokie, Ill.: National Textbook Company.
GRAHAM. J.A. and ARGYLE, M. (1975) "A cross cultural study of the communication of extra-verbal meaning by gestures." *International Journal of Psychology,* 10, 1: 57-67.
GRAHAM, J.A., RICCIBITTI, P., and ARGYLE, M. (1975) "A cross cultural study of the communication of emotion by facial and gestural cues." *Journal of Human Movement Studies,* 1: 68-77.
GREEN, J.R. (1971) "A focus report: Kinesics in the foreign language classroom." *Foreign Language Annals,* 5, 1: 62-68.
——— (1968) *A Gesture Inventory for the Teaching of Spanish.* Philadelphia: Chilton Books.
GROVE, C.L. (1976) "Nonverbal behavior, cross cultural context and the urban classroom teacher," in "Equal Opportunity Review," ERIC Clearinghouse, February.
HALL, E.T. (1976) *Beyond Culture.* Garden City, N.Y.: Doubleday/Anchor.
——— (1974) *Handbook for Proxemic Research* in S. Worth (ed.), Publication of the Society for the Anthropology of Visual Communication, Washington, D.C.
——— (1966) *The Hidden Dimension.* New York: Doubleday/Anchor.
——— (1959) *The Silent Language.* Greenwich, Conn.: Fawcett.
HALL, R.A., JR. (1966) *New Ways to Learn a Foreign Language.* New York: Bantam.
HAMALIAN, L. (1965) "Communication by gesture in the Middle East." *ETC: A Review of General Semantics,* 22, 1: 43-49.
HAYES, A.S. (1965) "New directions in foreign language teaching." *Modern Language Journal,* 49 (May): 281-293.
——— (1964) "Paralinguistics and kinesics: Pedagogical perspectives," pp. 146-190 in T.A. Sebok (ed.), *Approach to Semiotics.* The Hague: Mouton.
HAYES, F. (1941) "Gesture." *Encyclopedia Americana,* vol. 12.
HEWES, G. (1957) "The anthropology of posture." *Scientific American,* 196: 123-132.
——— (1955) "World distribution of certain postural habits." *American Anthropologist,* 52, 2: 231-244.
HOCKETT, C. (1964) "Scheduling," pp. 125-144 in F.S. Northrop and H.H. Livingston (eds.), *Cross Cultural Understanding: Epistemology in Anthropology.* New York: Harper & Row.
HUGHES, R.M. (1941) *The Gesture Language of the Hindu Dance.* New York: Columbia Univ. Press.
HYMES, D.H. (1971) "Competence and performance in linguistic theory," pp. 3-29 in R. Huxley and E. Ingram (eds.), *Language Acquisition: Models and Methods.* New York: Academic Press.
IKEGAMI, Y. (1971) "A stratificational analysis of hand gestures in Indian classical dancing." *Semiotica,* 4: 365-391.
INGHAM, R. (1974) "Preferences for seating arrangements in two countries." *International Journal of Psychology,* 9, 2: 105-115.
JAKOBSON, R. (1972) "Nonverbal signs for 'yes' and 'no'." *Language in Society,* 1, 1: 91-96.

JOHNSON, H.G., EKMAN, P., and FRIESEN, W. (1975) "Communicative body movements: American emblems." *Semiotica,* 15, 4: 335-353.

JOHNSON, K.R. (1971) "Black kinesics: Some nonverbal patterns in the black culture." *Florida Foreign Language Reporter,* 9, 1-2: 17-20, 57.

JONES, S.E. (1971) "A comparative proxemics analysis of dyadic interaction in selected subcultures of New York City." *Journal of Social Psychology,* 84: 35-44.

    and AIELLO, J.R. (1973) "Proxemic behavior of black and white first, third and fifth grade children." *Journal of Personality and Social Psychology,* 25, 1: 21-27.

JOURARD, S.M. (1966) "An exploratory study of body accessibility." *British Journal of Social and Clinical Psychology,* 5: 221-231.

    and RUBIN, J.E. (1968) "Self disclosure and touching: A study of two modes of interpersonal encounter and their interrelation." *Journal of Humanistic Psychology,* 8: 39-48.

KANY, C.E. (1960) *American-Spanish Euphemisms.* Berkeley: Univ. of California Press.

KAULFERS. W.V. (1932) "A handful of Spanish." *Education,* 52: 423-428.

KENDON, A. (1973) "The role of visible behavior in the organization of social interaction," pp. 29-74 in I. Vine and M. vonCranch (eds.), *Social Communication and Movement.* London: Academic Press.

    (1970) "Movement coordination in social interaction: Some examples described." *Acta Psychologica,* 32: 100-125.

    and FARBER, A. (1973) "A description of some human greetings," in R.P. Michael and J.A. Cook (eds.), *Comparative Ecology and Behavior of Primates.* London: Academic Press.

KEY, M.R. (1975) *Paralinguistics and Kinesics.* Metuchen, N.J.: Scarecrow Press.

KLEINFELD, J.S. (1974) "Effects of nonverbal warmth on the learning of Eskimo and white students." *Journal of Social Psychology,* 92: 3-9.

    (1973) "Effects of nonverbally communicated warmth on the intelligence test performance of Indian and Eskimo adolescents." *Journal of Social Psychology,* 91: 149-150.

KLINEBERG, O. (1940) *Social Psychology.* New York: Holt, Rinehart & Winston.

   _____ (1938) "Emotional expression in Chinese literature." *Journal of Abnormal and Social Psychology,* 33: 517-520.

   _____ (1935) *Race Differences.* New York: Harper & Row.

KURIKI, N. (1974) "Nonverbal communication in public interior space: A descriptive study of four Tokyo snack shops," in J. Condon (ed.), *Communication Patterns In and Out of Japan.* Tokyo: International Christian University.

LaBARRE, W. (1947) "The cultural basis of emotion and gesture." *Journal of Personality,* 16, 1: 49-68.

LEWIS, H. (1971) *Shame and Guilt in Neurosis.* New York: International Universities Press.

LITTLE, K.B. (1968) "Cultural variation in social schemata." *Journal of Personality and Social Psychology,* 10: 1-7.

LOMRANZ, J. and SHAPIRA, A. (1974) "Communication patterns of self discourse and touching behavior." *Journal of Psychology,* 88: 223-227.

   _____ CHORESH, N., and GIGAY, Y. (1975) "Children's perception of space as a function of age and sex." *Developmental Psychology,* 11, 5: 541-545.

MALLERY, G. (1881) "Sign language among North American Indians compared with that among other peoples and deaf mutes." Washington, D.C: Smithsonian

Institution, Bureau of Ethnology, pp. 263-552. Reprinted by Mouton, The Hague, 1972.

_____(1880) "Introduction to the study of sign language among the North American Indians: As illustrating the gesture speech on mankind." Washington, D.C.: Smithsonian Institute, Bureau of Ethnology.

MARSELLA, A.J., MURRAY, M.D., and GOLDEN, C. (1974) "Ethnic variations in the phenomenology of emotions/shame." *Journal of Cross Cultural Psychology,* 5, 3.

MATHAI, P. (1975) "Observed cultural differences in nonverbal communication between Americans and Indians." Paper presented at 1975 Conference on Cultural and Communication, Temple University, Philadelphia.

MAZUR, A. (1977) "Interpersonal spacing on public benches in 'contact' versus 'noncontact' cultures." *Journal of Social Psychology,* 101: 53-58.

McMAHON, E. (1976) "Nonverbal communication as a function of attribution in impression formation." *Communication Monographs,* 43: 287-294.

MEAD, M. (1971) "Cross cultural significance of space." *Ekistics.* 32, 191: 271-272.

MEGGITT, M. (1954) "Sign language among the Walbiri of central Australia." *Oceania.* 25, 1-2: 2-16.

MEHRABIAN, A. (1972) *Nonverbal Communication.* Chicago: Aldine-Atherton.

MELBIN, M. (1974) "Some issues in nonverbal communication." *Semiotica.* 10: 293-305.

_____(1972) *Alone and With Others: A Grammar of Interpersonal Behavior.* New York: Harper & Row.

MESSING, S. D. (1957) "The highland-plateau Amhara of Ethiopia." Philadelphia: University of Pennsylvania (Ph.D. dissertation).

MILLER, D. T. (1975) "The effect of dialect and ethnicity on communicator effectiveness." *Speech Monographs,* 42: 69-74.

MONTAGUE, A. (1971) *Touching: The Human Significance of the Skin.* New York: Columbia Univ. Press.

MORSBACH, H. (1973) "Aspects of nonverbal communication in Japan." *Journal of Nervous and Mental Disease,* 157, 4: 262-277.

NINE-CURT, J. (1974) "Nonverbal communication in Puerto Rico." Paper presented at the TESOL Convention, Denver, Colorado.

NOSTRAND, H. L. (1967) "Background data for the teaching of French, part A: la culture et la société francaise n XXe siecle." Seattle: Univ. of Washington Press.

OKAWA, H. (1974) "Bowing and expressive behavior of escalator girls and elevator girls in Tokyo department stores," in J. Condon (ed.), *Patterns of Communication In and Out of Japan.* Tokyo: International Christian University.

ORTEGO, P. D. (1969) "Some cultural implications of a Mexican-American border dialect of American English." *Studies in Linguistics,* 21: 77-84.

OSGOOD, C. (1966) "Dimensionality of the semantic space for communication via facial expressions." *Scandinavian Journal of Psychology,* 7: 1-30.

PEDERSEN, P. [ed.] (1974) "Cross-cultural psychology," in *Readings in Intercultural Communication,* vol 4. Pittsburgh: Society for Intercultural Education, Training and Research.

PHILLOT, D. C. (1907) "A note on sign, gesture, code and secret language, etc., among the Persians." *Royal Journal of the Asiatic Society of Bengal: Journal and Proceedings, N.S.,* 3, 9: 619-622. Calcutta.

POYATOS, F. (1976) *Man Beyond Words: Theory and Methodology of Nonverbal Communication.* Monograph #15, New York State English Council. Oswego, N.Y.: State University College at Oswego.

_____ (1970) "Kinésica del español actual." *Hispania,* 53: 444-452.

ROSENTHAL, R. (1966) *Experimenter Effects in Behavior Research.* New York: Appleton-Century Crofts.

RUBIN, J. (1976) "How to tell when someone is saying 'no'." pp. 61-65 in R. Brislin (ed.), *Topics in Culture Learning,* vol. 4. Honolulu: East-West Center.

RUDDEN, M. R. and FRANSDEN, K. D. "A Critical and empirical analysis of Albert Mehrabian's three dimensional framework for nonverbal communication." Unpublished paper, Department of Speech, Pennsylvania State University.

RYAN, E. B. and CARRANZA, M. A. (1975) "Evaluative reactions of adolescents toward speakers of standard English and Mexican American accented English." *Journal of Personality and Social Psychology,* 31, 5: 855-863.

SAITZ, R. L. and CERVENKA, E. (1962) *Columbian and North American Gestures: A Contrastive Inventory."* Bogota: Centro Colombo Americana. Republished as *Handbook of Gesture: Columbia and the U.S.* The Hague: Mouton.

SATTLER, J. M. (1970) "Racial 'experimenter effects' in experimentation, testing, interviewing and psychotherapy." *Psychological Bulletin,* 73: 137-160.

SCHEFLEN, A. (1968) "Human communication: behavioral programs and their integration in interaction." *Behavioral Science,* 13: 44-55.

_____ (1965) *Stream and Structure of Communicational Behavior.* Commonwealth of Pennsylvania: Eastern Psychiatric Institute.

SCHERER, K. R. (1972) "Judging personality from voice: A cross cultural approach to an old issue in interpersonal perception." *Journal of Personality,* 40: 191-210.

SCHERER, S. E. (1974) "Proxemic behavior of primary school children as a function of their socioeconomic class and subculture." *Journal of Personality and Social Psychology,* 29, 6: 800-805.

SCHNAPPER, M. (1975) "Nonverbal communication and the intercultural encounter." *The 1975 Annual Handbook for Group Facilitators,* pp. 155-159.

_____ (1969) "Your actions speak louder." *Volunteer Magazine:* 7-10.

SCOTT, H. L. (1893) "The sign language of the Plains Indians." pp. 206-220 in the Proceedings of the Third International Folk Lore Congress, Chicago.

SHAPIRO, J. G. (1968) "Responsiveness to facial and linguistic cues." *Journal of Communication,* 18: 11-17.

SHERZER, J. (1973) "Nonverbal and verbal deixis: The pointed lip gesture of the San Blas Cuna." *Language in Society,* 2, 1: 117-31.

SHIMODA, R., ARGYLE, M. and RICCI BITTI, P. (1975) "Intercultural recognition of emotional expressions," in M. Argyle, *Oxford University Department of Experimental Psychology-Programme on Social Interaction. Final Report to the Social Science Research Council,* September, 1970-August, 1975.

SCHUTER, R. (1976) "Proxemics and tactility in Latin America." *Journal of Communication,* 26, 3: 46-52.

SMITH, R. L., MCPHAIL, C., and PICKERS, R.G. (1975) "Reactivity to systematic observation with film: A field experiment." *Sociometry,* 3, 4: 536-550.

SOLOMON, D. and ALI, F.A. (1975) "Influence of verbal content and intonation on meaning attributions of first and second language speakers." *Journal of Social Psychology,* 95: 3-9.

STRIMPEL, S. (1975) "Gesticulation accompanying speech in English and Italian students" in M. Argyle (ed.), *Oxford University Department of Experimental Psychology. . . . Programme on Social Interaction.* Final Report to the Social Science Research Council, September, 1970-August 1975.

SUSSMAN, N. (1977) "Effect of sex, language and culture on interpersonal speaking distance." Lawrence: University of Kansas, Department of Psychology (Ph.D. dissertation).

THAYER, S. and ALBAN, L. (1972) "A field experiment on the effect of political and cultural factors on personal space," *Journal of Social Psychology*, 88, 267-272.

TRIANDIS, H. C. and LAMBERT, W. W. (1958) "A restatement and test of Schlosberg's theory of emotion within two kinds of subjects from Greece." *Journal of Abnormal and Social Psychology*, 56: 321-328.

TSOUTSOS, T. M. (1970) "A tentative gesture inventory for the teaching of French." New York: Queens College (Master's thesis).

TYLOR, E. B. (1818) "The gesture language," and "gesture language," and "word language," chapters II, III, and IV in P. Bohannon [ed.] (1964) *Researches into the Early History of Mankind and the Development of Civilization.* Chicago: Phoenix Books.

UEDA, K. (1974) "Sixteen ways to avoid saying 'no' in Japan: A survey of the function and frequency of Japanese patterns of declining requests," pp. 25-37 in J. Condon (ed.), *Communication Patterns In and Out of Japan.* Tokyo: International Christian University.

UNO, Y., KOIVUMAKI, J. H., and ROSENTHAL, R. (1972) "Unintended experimenter behavior as evaluated by Japanese and American observers." *Journal of Social Psychology*, 88: 91-106.

VINACKE, W. E. (1949) "The judgement of facial expressions by three national—racial groups in Hawaii. I. Caucasian faces." *Journal of Personality*, 17: 407-429.

_____ and FONG, R. W. (1955) "The judgement of facial expression by three national-social groups in Hawaii. II. Oriental faces." *Journal of Social Psychology*, 41: 185-195.

VIVAVRA, V. (1976) "Is Jakobson right?" *Semiotica*, 7, 2: 95-110.

WALKER, J. R. (1953) "The sign language of the Plains Indians of North America." *Chronicles of Oklahoma*, 31, 2: 168-177.

WASS, H. (1973) "Pupil evaluation of teacher message in three channels of communication." *Florida Journal of Education Research*, 15: 46-52.

WATSON, O. M. (1970) *Proxemic Behavior: A Cross Cultural Study.* The Hague: Mouton.

_____ and GRAVES, T.D. (1973) "Quantitative research in proxemic behavior." *American Anthropologist*, 25: 6-14.

WATZLAWICK, P., BEAVIN, J., and JACKSON, D. (1967) *The Pragmatics of Human Communication.* New York: W. W. Norton.

WIEMAN, J. M. (1977) "Explication and test of a model of communicative competence." *Human Communication Research*, 3, 3: 195-213.

WIENER, M., DEVOE, S., RUBINOW, S., and GELLER, J. (1972) "Nonverbal behavior and nonverbal communication." *Psychological Review*, 79, 3: 185-214.

WILDEN, A. (1972) "Analog and digital communication: On the relationship between negation, signification and the emergence of the discrete element." *Semiotica*, 6, 1: 50-82.

WILLIAMS, T. R. (1966) "Cultural structuring of tactile experiences in a Borneo society." *American Anthropologist*, 68: 27-39.

WILLIS, F. N., JR. (1966) "Initial speaking distance as a function of the speaker's relationship." *Psychonomic Science*, 5: 221-222.

WOLFGANG, A. (1977) "The silent language in the multicultural classroom," *Theory Into Practice,* 16.

PART III.

ISSUES IN INTERCULTURAL COMMUNICATION

Fundamental to the study of intercultural communication are the linkages between the broad concepts of communication and culture. Culture is problematic because the high degree of variance from one culture group to another creates communication problems. This points to an analysis of intercultural communication through the approach of similarities and differences. We tend to believe that the more similar two people or cultures are, the better they should communicate, whereas differences are hindrances to communication. Contemporary society is no longer in a state of isolation. People from every part of the world are in contact through advanced communication technology. Therefore, we need to develop an appreciation and respect for differences in language, attitudes, value systems and how we perceive and interpret the world. The goal is to develop mutual respect for ways of life and ideas different from our own.

The field of intercultural communication is still in the growing stage with issues ranging from definitional and methodological problems to relations between different cultures within one's own nation as well as across national boundaries. We need to grapple with the factors that enhance or hinder intercultural communication and search for ways to achieve effective human interaction. This section includes articles that discuss a few of these wide-ranging issues.

Sitaram and Haapanen place values at the base of a discussion of intercultural communication. They describe how values are communicated through verbal and nonverbal channels, the influence of our value system on how we communicate and with whom, and the difficulty of observing and measuring value systems. They outline two basic rules for better intercultural communication: the necessity of understanding others' values, and the ability to adapt one's communication in the face of difference, thereby generating respect and appreciation for diversity.

In the second selection, Newmark examines communication principles in international interaction setting, focusing specifically on diplomatic communication. She describes diplomatic negotiation as a communicative event and examines the particular factors that influence such communicative messages and strategies. The article thus begins to explore the interface between international relations and communication principles.

Hur discusses international communication through the media channels of telephone, mail and satellites. Relationships between domestic and international communication media are also examined. Hur demonstrates how international transaction factors such as trade, political relations and tourism affect international mail and telephone communication.

Stereotypes affect communication interactions because they form categories that preset one's judgements. In an interesting study, Alderton investigates five dimensions of the stereotyping process through which white Americans form opinions about the communication styles of both black and white Americans. The study reveals that whites have uniform and fairly rigidly held dissimilar views of white and black communicators. The author's findings also show a tendency for whites to use anticommunicative traits to describe blacks and traits conducive to communication to describe the characteristics of whites.

George Roberts, in the final essay, examines how values in Terramedia have retained their traditional basis and influence on behavior patterns despite the effects of modernization. In Northern Terramedia, the author traces this consistency to the widespread influence of Islam and its prescribed behavior rules. Roberts suggests that the wider range of values in Southern Terramedia is due to the influence of local ancestralism. The essay provides an interesting perspective on the notion of the role of values in changing societies.

9

THE ROLE OF VALUES IN INTERCULTURAL COMMUNICATION

K. S. SITARAM AND LAWRENCE W. HAAPANEN

Utah State University

The study of intercultural communication is a turning point in the development of communication theory. Until recently, we used to think of communication as a process involving just two elements: stimulus-response or sender-receiver. It was well known as the S-R process. We used to hypothesize that if the stimulus is powerful enough, it will elicit the desired response. In 1922, the Russian biologist Ivan Petvovich Pavlov tested this hypothesis in his experiments on dogs. Using food as stimulus, he elicited the response of salivation in the animal. He said:

> I had been working on the digestive glands. . . . Naturally I could not leave them without considering the so-called psychical stimulation of the salivary glands, i.e., the flow of saliva in the hungry animal or person at the sight of food or during talk about it or even at the thought of it. [Babkin, 1974]

One of Pavlov's associates, Snarksy, also worked on the project. Says Pavlov:

> Snarsky, on the other hand, undertook to analyse the internal mechanism of the stimulation from a subjective point of view, i.e., he assumed that the internal world of the dog — thoughts and desires — is analogous to ours. [Babkin, 1974]

Pavlov's concepts were applied to human communication. However, there was no occasion to test the hypothesis extensively on humans, particularly those of different cultures. In the 1950s and 1960s, several technically advanced cultures indirectly applied the hypothesis to less advanced cultures. They gave economic and other aids to the less developed cultures, hoping the latter would show gratitude and adopt the former's political thoughts. According to them, aid was the stimulus, and the response for it should have been acceptance of the political thoughts. In international negotiations, diplomats of the developed countries even communicated their intentions to the less developed ones. Content analyses of the media in the developed countries in the 1950s and 1960s would show that their coverage of the underdeveloped countries emphasized the same attitude, that is, that economic aid should result in the acceptance of the givers' political philosophy. But diplomats and the media alike failed to elicit the desired response. The diplomats then began asking: "where did we go wrong? how did we fail to communicate?"

Many scholars replied that a person must understand the culture of his audience, and that this should precede any attempt to communicate with them. Not only should the person know other cultures, but he should also know his own. A great interest then emerged in the study of intercultural communication. In the 1960s, many American and foreign universities began doing research and offering courses in the field. Both research and pedagogy emphasized the important role cultural values play in communication. But first of all, there was a need to study the nature of values.

The study of values is also comparatively new. During the past few decades, there have been many attempts to define values and compare those of different peoples. It has not been easy to explain the degree and causes of influence of cultural values on human beings. While many studies have shown that members of each culture believe in certain values which are unique to that culture, there have been few attempts to show how each of these values might affect communication. However, the "instinct" of all communication specialists says that there is a relationship between values and human interaction.

First of all, it is important to be aware of the studies and their findings on values per se. We shall discuss some studies dealing with cultural values, and then try to show their relationship to intercultural communication.

WHAT IS A VALUE?

A concept becomes a value to a people when they consider it as extremely desirable or undesirable. Values are thus positive or negative on the same continuum: while one people might consider a concept as most desirable, another might say it is most undesirable, and a third might not have a reaction. The first group welcomes the value, the second avoids it, while the third does not care one way or the other. Members of the first group might speak out in favor of the concept or belief in question; they might even try to impose it on others. The second group would of course do everything possible to fight what they perceived as the negative value.

For our purpose, a value will be defined as follows:

> Value seems to be the basis of all decisions that a person makes. It tells him how something ought to be and for what his life is worth living, worth fighting, and even worth dying. Since value is so important, it is also necessary to influence others to accept it as the only end state of life. Value thus becomes the standard for a person to judge his own and other's actions. [Sitaram and Cogdell, 1976: 163]

This definition underscores the importance of values in guiding human behavior toward oneself, toward others, and toward one's culture.

Discussion of values is not new. In the fourth century B.C., Aristotle mentioned the character of speaker or *ethos* as an important value that affected communication. At about the same time, the Buddha talked about too much greed as a negative value, and Confucius said that authoritarianism is necessary for the welfare of a society.

SYSTEMATIC STUDIES

Systematic studies of values are quite recent. A number of social scientists and philosophers have attempted to provide an explanation of human behavior under the general rubric of "values." One definition that has proven consistent with most of subsequent work is that offered by Kluckhohn (1951: 395), who defines a value as "a conception, explicit or implicit, distinctive of an individual or characteristic of a group, of the desirable which influences the selection from available modes, means, and ends of action." There has also been general agreement that because values are expressions of preference, they possess a hierarchical relationship to one another. As Kluckhohn (1951: 419) observes, "Certainly there is almost always a hierarchical notion to thinking about values: 'more beautiful than,' 'better than,' 'more appropriate than.' " This concept of hierarchy implies that values are arranged into systems in which they are "not simply distributed at random, but are instead interdependent, arranged in a pattern, and subject to reciprocal or mutual variation" (Williams, 1956: 385). The overall value system may be seen, in turn, as consisting of subsystems, depending on the type of value and its relationship to other values. Rokeach (1973) classifies some values as "instrumental," representing desirable modes of behavior, and other values as "terminal," representing desirable end-states of existence.

Several well known and widely used instruments have been developed to provide a means of measuring the relative importance of values and value orientations. The Allport-Vernon-Lindzey study of values (1951) was widely used for many years, and was designed to assess the relative importance of six classifications of values derived from Spranger's "types of men" (theoretical, economic, aesthetic, social, political, and religious). Morris (1956) developed an instrument known as the "ways to live" document, which embodies descriptions of 13 alternative life styles and requires each subject to rate each description on a Likert-type scale. Kluckhohn and Strodtbeck (1961) constructed an instrument designed to measure the extent to which each of five universal value orientations is reflected in human behavior. Rokeach (1973) provides a rank-ordering method for measuring the relative importance to a subject of 18 instrumental values and 18 terminal values, each one represented by a specific word or term. The Rokeach value survey has been used in a variety of studies in recent years, including crosscultural value studies (Rokeach, 1973; Feather, 1975).

In making comparative studies of cultural values, researchers typically measure the relative importance of selected values in different cultures. However, a value may be expressed in equivalent linguistic terms by persons in two different cultures and yet have different meanings for each. It can therefore be misleading to compare the relative importance placed on the value. As Feather (1975: 16) points out, "one can conceive of a value as an abstract structure involving an associative network which may take different forms for different individuals." If the individuals are members of different cultures, the degree of difference is likely to be even greater. Several approaches are possible in solving the problem of value comparability between cultures.

Triandis (1972) reports the results of both his own and Osgood's studies of values in different cultures (see also Osgood et al., 1975). Triandis measured the different associative meanings of values in four cultures: American, Greek, Indian, and Japanese. He selected 20 values. He then gave subjects a list of words representing antecedents and consequents that might be associated with each of the values, and had them choose the one antecedent and one consequent they would most associate with each value. The results revealed some degree of crosscultural compatibility in the associative meanings of the values: for every one of the 20 values, there were significant correlations in the chosen antecedents or consequents between at least two of the four cultures, and all of the cultures associated "morality," "proper behavior," and "good characteristics of the individual" as antecedents of their valued concepts. On the other hand, there were also numerous differences in the antecedents and consequents associated with each value, and in the relative importance placed on each value in the different cultures. In comparing his own approach with that of Osgood, Triandis reports that the associative meanings and the semantic differential judgments gathered by Osgood give overlapping results for only five of the 20 values. The antecendent-consequent method did provide a means, how-

ever, of distinguishing between values that were given the same
profiles on Osgood's semantic differential; for example, "freedom" and "power" elicited similar semantic differential profiles from Americans, but yielded different antecedents and
consequents.

Feather (1975) suggests another approach for determining
the "functional equivalence" of values in different cultures.
His premise is that if people in different cultures who agree on
the importance of certain values show similarities in related
behavior, the values would presumably be comparable in both
cultures. In a study of comparative value systems across
cultures, Feather found that students in Papua New Guinea
held a number of values significantly higher or lower than did
students in Australia. Feather attributed these differences to
the less affluent, developing society of Papua New Guinea
compared to the stable, more affluent society of Australia, as
well as to particular features of two cultures (e.g., the extended
family system and strong church influence in Papua New
Guinea).

Yet another approach to the study of values has been to
relate cultural values to the religious beliefs and practices of
the culture. Goff (1962), for example, studied the values of
Muslims in Iran. She found that Islamic philosophy has a pronounced effect on cultural values and that such specific values
as "spirituality," "brotherhood," and "respect for human
dignity" have great importance for Iranians. On the other
hand, she found little importance placed on such values as
"persistence," "dependability," "economic wisdom," and
efficiency," revealing the lack of a Muslim counterpart to the
so-called "Protestant ethic" of some Western societies.

In another part of the world, Appleton (1976-1977) found
that the people of Taiwan uniformly rank such values as
"religion," "faith," and "a happy afterlife" as least important,
even though a majority express a belief in God. He also noted a
tendency for the better educated to rank "inner harmony" and
a "meaningful life" the highest, which suggests that Tai-
wanese seek the means of achieving such goals outside the
boundaries of their religion.

VALUES AND COMMUNICATION

Studies conducted on the role of values in human behavior have revealed a number of ways in which values and communication are related. Much of the existing research supports two general propositions about that relationship.

Proposition 1: *Values are communicated, both explicitly and implicitly, through symbolic behavior.* Everything a person says and does is to some extent an individual expression of choice, but that does not mean that it necessarily expresses a value. As Scott (1965) points out, a person's behavior may reflect selfish motives, be subject to the constraints of the situation in which it occurs, or even result from impulse. However, much of our behavior does symbolize the values that we have learned through experience and acculturation. One way our behavior does this is through the verbalization of values. Williams (1956: 378) observes that "a great deal of verbalizing consists in the explicit avowal or disavowal of certain values," and Fallding (1965: 233) states that "values will scarcely consent to be born unless they are swaddled in verbalization."

Verbal expressions make it possible to emphasize specific values that are particularly important to the individual. The frequency with which a given value is mentioned and the strength of the language used to express it are both indications of its relative importance within the individual's value system (Jacob, Toune, and Watts, 1958). Several studies have been done to explore the degree to which certain values are expressed in writing or speaking by political figures. For example, Eckhart and White (1967) analyzed speeches by John F. Kennedy and Nikita Khrushchev and concluded that their stated values were positively correlated, but that each saw the other as lacking those values. Eckhart and White found this consistent with the "mirror-image hypothesis," which states that opposing nations will see themselves and their opponent as representing exactly the opposite values.

Values are often — perhaps usually — expressed to others through nonverbal behaviors that have come to symbolize them. The custom of exchanging gifts, for example, is an implicit expression of several possible values — generosity, respect, friendship, and so forth. Man uses social customs and rituals not only to communicate his values to others, but also to behave in the manner in which his values tell him he ought to behave. These nonverbal behaviors express values to others to the extent that they are recognized as symbolic in the community in which they are found.

It is when a person's behavior does not express to others recognizable values that it may become necessary to justify one's behavior more explicitly. The expression of values as justification for past or future action reveals a distinction between values and attitudes, since the latter may offer an explanation for one's actions but not a justification (Scott, 1965). As a person seeks to provide acceptable reasons for his actions, he may be pressed for additional reasons if the initial ones are not considered sufficient. Once that person reaches an "ultimate justification," beyond which no further justification is called for, he has expressed what for him is a value. If made to someone else, the justification must be based on common values in order to be accepted as legitimate. Such justifications must be explicit, and therefore usually verbal, since the need for the justifications arises out of the failure to symbolize values implicitly by the action being justified.

Proposition Two: *The way in which people communicate is influenced by the values they hold.* People's values will lead them to communicate in certain ways, because values will determine which ways of communicating are deemed more desirable than others. Whereas the first proposition emphasized the role of communication as a carrier of values, this second proposition emphasizes that communication behavior will be shaped by one's value system.

One illust. ion of this proposition is present in the process of interpei nal attraction. Studies by Precker (1953), Smith (1957), Newcomb (1963), and Scott (1965) show a relationship between value similarity and interpersonal attraction in dyads. In general, people tend to like other people whose values they perceive as similar to their own. For this to occur, people must get to know one another's values through communication. Then, the degree to which they seek further interpersonal relationship is influenced by perceived value similarity. Newcomb (1963) found in a study of students living in a group setting that there was no relationship between value similarity and mutual attraction in the second week of the study, but by the fourteenth week there was a highly significant relationship. On the other hand, the findings of Scott (1965), who studied fraternity and sorority members, indicate that value dissimilarity need not be a barrier to friendships if people are willing to show "tolerance for diversity."

People also tend to accord more credibility to communication sources whose values are perceived as being similar to their own. Hovland et al. (1953), found that a message on the practicality of atomic submarines was more persuasive for an American audience when attributed to American scientist Robert J. Oppenheimer than when attributed to the Soviet newspaper *Pravda*. Sometimes the degree of value similarity is selectively perceived, as Rokeach (1973) found in studying the value perceptions of Vladimir Lenin, Adolf Hitler, Norman Thomas, and Barry Goldwater among subjects with communist, fascist, socialist, and capitalist value orientations.

Giles and Powesland (1975) present a wealth of evidence that one's speech style is subject to the value judgments of others, and that such factors as interpersonal attraction and source credibility are influenced by the speech style of a communicator. One's regional accent has been found to communicate an impression of one's honesty, reliability, generosity, and so forth. In some cases subjects have been more favorably disposed toward speech styles that are different from their own, depending on the relative prestige value of the accent or dialect.

Finally, Starck (1973) reports that certain types of communication sources (e.g., interpersonal) are considered more important than others in providing information useful in achieving value-directed goals. Doob's (1961) analysis of communication in Africa also suggests that cultural values will become associated with certain traditional channels of communication such as the "talking" drums of central Africa. Both studies support the conclusion that values will lead people to prefer certain sources and channels of communication that symbolize their values or provide information useful in attaining their values.

MEASUREMENT OF VALUES

In spite of so many studies why is it difficult to measure correlation between values and communication and arrive at universally acceptable inferences? Scientists cannot *measure* values, since values are not accessible to clinical experimentation. It is not possible to *observe* values per se. Then what can we measure and observe? We can measure and observe *customs* of a people. For example, when a girl comes of age in many Asian and African cultures, her parents begin looking for a young man to marry her. Whatever the reasons be, the custom is for the parents or guardians to look for a husband for their girl. Customarily, the girl does not look for her own husband. Many stories have been told of how arranged marriages destroyed lives of young persons. In the west, people have criticized the eastern custom of arranging marriages. Anyway, we can observe the custom. Using good methodology, we can even measure the intensity with which a custom is observed in a culture. From custom we can go a step down to locate why it is expected of the parents to arrange the marriage of their sons/daughters and of the young persons to accept the decision of their elders. In other words, with some efforts, we can find out the *expectation* on which a custom or several customs are based. With more efforts we can even locate the *belief* on which an expectation or several expectations are based. Finally, with great efforts we can locate the value on which all the beliefs, expectations, and customs are based. But it is not easy to locate the basic value of a culture unless we observe its customs, expectations, and beliefs. Such observations and efforts take a long time.

Clearly, a value does not exist alone. It is a part of the overall value system of a culture. Often customs, beliefs, and expectations are confused with values. "Our values are different from our parents," is what the young persons say many times. A serious study of value systems would show that the differences are really the customs or expectations or beliefs, and not values. Values seldom change. However, beliefs based on a value might change. But *basic* beliefs, or values, remain the same. Beliefs are nothing but manifestations of values. They are ways a person or a generation interprets his/its values.

Communication of a person or a people is one such manifestation or interpretation. We interpret our values in the ideas we communicate. A strong voice in favor of freedom of expression on radio or an editorial in support of freedom of information in a newspaper is physical evidence of the journalist's belief in the value of individuality. That value forces the journalist to speak out in favor of his belief in the freedoms.

To give another example, blind belief in one's own values forces one to look down at others who do not accept the same values. When a person believes in individuality and another in the individual's responsibility, the chances are that the two cannot communicate very well.

When a person strongly believes in his right to say what he wants to say and know what he wants to know, he might think the others who do not share the same belief are stupid. When we talk about others who do not have the same freedoms we have, we pity them or even look at them contemptuously. The others might not even know that they do not have the freedoms. They might not seek our pity. They might scorn us who selfishly talk about our own freedoms while forgetting our responsibilities to others.

VALUES AND COGNITIVE DISSONANCE

For a person, believing in his/her own cultural values is a highly satisfying act. When a person believes in his own value he is rewarded by his people. Therefore the right thing to do is to speak out in favor of one's own cultural values and receive the recognition. Not believing and not speaking out is undesirable, leaving that person open to ridicule by his/her people. Belief is in consonance, while disbelief is in dissonance. What would a person do when he secretly feels that his cultural values are no good? He would probably find a way of showing his belief by trying to rationalize that the value is the best. He tries to convince himself that what he is doing is right. Then he is recognized and revered by his people.

Rationalizing in favor of one's own values is to practice cognitive dissonance as explained by Leon Festinger. There are others who run away from their own people and join those whose values are in consonance with their personal values.

VALUES AND INTERCULTURAL COMMUNICATION

Differences in values create gaps in communication and could even cause noncommunication. Values, then, are the most important variables in intercultural communication. The problem that arises with the difference in values is that we tend to use our own values as the standard when judging others. We tend to assume that our value system is best, an assumption that causes us to make value judgments of others. Such an attitude is *ethnocentrism*. A careful study of communication at interpersonal level as well as via the media shows that most communication is ethnocentric. Most news stories in today's newspaper on other cultures and countries are ethnocentric. Analyses of contents of newspapers around the world would certainly show ethnocentrism of their reporters and editors.

Ethnocentrism is not limited only to news stories on mass media. Even the lessons we teach in our schools and colleges are ethnocentric. We always imply that our culture and country are the greatest. While there is nothing wrong with being proud of our culture and country, it is not right to imply that others are inferior. Our textbooks in social sciences and humanities contain plenty of ethnocentric information. Even the references and bibliographies are works from our own culture and country. We ignore the works of others with the reason: "other books are not very good."

What is the solution to the problem of ethnocentrism? Is there any way we can communicate better interculturally? Herskovits (1973) suggests one solution. He says the opposite of ethnocentrism is *cultural relativism*. It is the study of the values of others within the framework of that culture rather than in comparison with our own values. It is not easy to practice cultural relativism. We are born and brought up in an ethnocentric world. The practice of cultural relativism should begin at a very early age. We have to teach our youngsters to practice it. They should learn that each value or custom is developed by its people to make their life easy and meaningful. Each value system is meant to establish order in its own society. Instead of doing "comparative studies" of others, we should study others as they are. Then, we need not look at other ways of speaking as "accent" and our way as standard speech.

Perhaps even cultural relativism is not the ultimate answer. Because each culture has something to offer to the world, it is necessary to locate that something in each culture. Effective communication is needed about what each culture can contribute to the rest of the world. That communication should be free of ethnocentrism as well as relativism. The communicator should be able to point out the best aspect of a culture so others could borrow it and enrich themselves. The purpose of intercultural communication should be to help each participant share his/her experience with another so each could enrich the lives of other persons. When sharing expands from the individual to the entire culture, then intercultural communication would have achieved the ultimate goal of all human interaction.

THE TWO RULES

When members of different value systems interact, such communication becomes intercultural. While it would not be hard for members of the same value system to understand each other's values, it may not be so for those of different systems. Therefore the first rule of intercultural communication is that each participant should understand the other's values. That understanding should precede any attempts to communicate interculturally. Because communicative techniques are manifestations of one's own values, the participants communicate differently. The second rule is that each should adapt his/her communication to the other's values. Adaptation implies respect for the other value system. Without such respect one cannot adapt his/her communicative behavior to the other system. Adaptation should be an on-going act. A person should know the art of constant adaptation to other cultures.

REFERENCES

ALLPORT, G. W., VERNON, P. E., and LINDZEY, G. (1951) *Study of Values: Manual of Directions for the Study of Values.* Cambridge, Mass.: Harvard Univ. Press.

APPLETON, S. (1976-1977) "Survey research on Taiwan." *Public Opinion Quarterly,* 40 (Winter): 468-481.

BABKIN, B. P. (1974) *Pavlov: A Biography.* Chicago: Univ. of Chicago Press.

DOOB, L. W. (1961) *Communication in Africa: A Search for Boundaries.* New Haven; Yale Univ. Press.

ECKHARDT, W., and WHITE R. K. (1967) "A test of the mirror-image hypothesis: Kennedy and Krushchev." *Journal of Conflict Resolution,* 11 (September): 325-332.

FALLDING, H. (1965) "A proposal for the empirical study of values." *American Sociological Review,* 30 (April): 223-233.

FEATHER, N. T. (1975) *Values in Education and Society.* New York: Free Press.

GILES, H., and POWESLAND, P. F. (1975) *Speech Style and Social Evaluation.* London: Academic Press.

GOFF, R. M. (1962) "Psychology and intercultural interaction." *Journal of Social Psychology,* 58 (December): 235-240.

HERSKOVITS, M. J. (1973) *Cultural Relativism: Perspectives in Cultural Pluralism.* New York: Random House.

HOVLAND, C. I., JANIS, I. L. and KELLEY, H. H. (1953) *Communication and Persuasion: Psychological Studies of Opinion Change.* New Haven, Conn: Yale Univ. Press.

JACOB, P. E., TEUNE, H., and WATTS, T. (1968) "Values, leadership and development: A four-nation study." *Social Science Information,* 7 (April): 49-92.

KLUCKHOHN, C. (1951) "Values and value-orientations in the theory of action" in T. Parsons and E. Shils (ed.), *Toward a General Theory of Action.* Cambridge, Mass.: Harvard Univ. Press.

KLUCKHOHN, F., and STRODTBECK, F. L. (1961) *Variations in Value Orientations.* Evanston, Ill.: Row, Peterson.

MORRIS, C. (1956) *Varieties of Human Value.* Chicago: Univ. of Chicago Press.

NEWCOMB, T. M. (1963) "Stabilities underlying changes in interpersonal attraction." *Journal of Abnormal and Social Psychology,* 66 (April): 376-386.

OSGOOD, C., MAY, W. H. and MIRON, M. S. (1975) *Cross-cultural Universals of Affective Meaning.* Urbana: Univ. of Illinois Press.

PRECKER, J. A. (1953) "The automorphic process in the attribution of values." *Journal of Personality,* 21 (March): 356-363.

ROKEACH, M. (1973) *The Nature of Human Values.* New York: Free Press.

SITARAM, K. S., and COGDELL, R. T. (1976) *Foundations of Intercultural Communication.* Columbus, Ohio: Charles E. Merrill.

SCOTT, W. A. (1965) *Values and Organizations: A Study of Fraternities and Sororities.* Chicago: Rand McNally.

SMITH, A. J. (1957) "Similarity of values and its relation to acceptance and the projection of similarity." *Journal of Psychology,* 43: 251-260.

STARCK, K. (1973) "Values and information source preference." *Journal of Communication,* 23 (March): 74-85.

TRIANDIS, H. C. (1972) *The Analysis of Subjective Culture.* New York: John Wiley & Sons.

WILLIAMS, R. M. (1956) *American Society: A Sociological Interpretation.* New York: Alfred A. Knopf.

10

INTERNATIONAL COMMUNICATION AND ITS MEDIA: A CROSS-NATIONAL STUDY

K. KYOON HUR

University of Texas at Austin

Through an examination of the world picture of international communication, Cherry (1971) noted that in the past the nations of the world have been deprived of communication with others through lack of means of communication; "their means, such as have existed, have been utterly inadequate to assist them to resolve their mutual involvements in stable ways, however much they may have wished to do so" (Cherry, 1971: 88). In recent years, however, others observed that the development of communication technologies, such as intercontinental submarine cables and communication satellites, has opened new channels for international communication (Fischer and Merrill, 1970; Gerbner et al., 1973). With this seemingly contrasting picture of international communication, an examination of the present status of international communication, particularly in relations with the new communication means, is especially urgent.

A number of studies have analyzed international communication at the national level through the examination of various communication media, including mail (Deutsch, 1956, 1964; Dupree, 1968; Frey, 1973), telephone (Cherry, 1971), newspaper (Schramm, 1960, 1964), and television (Thompson, 1971; UNESCO, 1974). In the public media, studies have typically faced analytic difficulties, primarily because of inherent measurement problems. As a result, the inflow of news items or broadcast programs has only been approximated

AUTHOR'S NOTE: *The study presented here is based upon a part of the author's doctoral dissertation, directed by Glenn Starlin, at the University of Oregon.*

and some hypotheses based on such data have been made. Among them, notable findings were: (1) the inflow of information and informational materials between countries is governed to a considerable extent by "the ownership of long-distance telecommunication facilities, the concentration of technology, wealth, and power" (Schramm, 1964: 58-59), and (2) the extent of inflow of television materials is largely influenced by four factors: economic wealth, population size, number of television sets, and exports' share of the gross national product (UNESCO, 1974: 53-54). In the private-type media (e.g., mail and telephone), on the other hand, the international communication picture has been more accurately and quantitatively documented, mainly due to the availability of data on these media communications. Some of the hypotheses suggested in this area were: (1) "advanced countries tend to send more mail than they receive" (Deutsch, 1964: 79); (2) certain nations tend to "specialize" in international communication (Frey, 1973: 353); and (3) "international traffic, both transportation and communication, is determined by trade and political relations, coupled of course with geography, rather than by technology" (Cherry, 1971: 93). The present study attempts to examine international communication in a macroquantitative context. Accordingly, the operational definition of international communication utilized here is limited to "two-way communication," using such devices as mail, telephone, and communication satellite.[1]

No study has compared these different international communication media, or examined the influence of communication satellites. In addition, the relationship between international communication and trade has not been empirically tested.[2] The data generated by such investigation might provide information concerning the following questions: How do the peoples and nations of the world utilize communication means, either new or old, for international communication? Is there variation in the use of specific media of international communication? What are the relationships among international communication media, and between international communication media and domestic communication media?

What is the relationship between international communication and international trade? The theoretic import of these questions provides the impetus for the study described herein.

The study has three specific objectives: (1) to examine, in a comparative cross-national setting, international communication through three specific media — mail, telephone, and communication satellite, (2) to ascertain what relationships exist among these media, and between international communication media and domestic communication media, and (3) to determine the relationship between international communication and international trade.

METHODS

The "nation" was chosen as the unit of analysis. Nations were chosen if they appeared on lists from the following sources: (1) UNESCO Statistical Yearbook, 1972-1974, (2) International Telecommunication Union (ITU) Telecommunication Statistics, 1972, and (3) Communications Satellite Corporation (COMSAT) Annual Report (1972-1974), or ITU Report on Space Communication (1972-1974). The final sample, which was severely limited by the availability of data, totaled 45 countries (see Appendix I).

In order to assess the relationships described above, operational definitions and measurement criteria for the three international communication media indicators were established, and are presented below:

1. International mail: the total number of foreign mail items sent and received across national boundaries.
2. International telephone: the total number of telephone calls sent and received acrosss national boundaries.
3. International satellite communication: the total number of voice-grade half-circuit channels linked between a country's earth station(s) and communication satellite(s).[3]

Measures for domestic communication media were imported from the common communication measures used in this type of research: domestic mail per capita, telephones per 1,000 population, radio receivers per 1,000 population, television

receivers per 1,000 population, and daily newspaper circulation per 1,000 population. It should be noted here that some of
these media, such as radio, television, and newspaper, cannot
be labeled "domestic communication" in a strict sense, since
they are used to a certain extent for global information. Our
attempt here is to see the domestic media situation with regard
to international communication. To ascertain what relationships exist among these media, various bodies of data collected
from the above-mentioned sources were tested against 45
countries, using the Pearson product-moment correlation technique.

The relationship between international communication and
international trade was ascertained by correlating international
communication and trade. Due to the limited use of communication satellites,[4] a total "international communication score"
for each nation was computed using international mail and
telephone calls. Both were weighted by the country's population in order to make the data more comparable for countries of
vastly different size, and combined, with each given equal
weight, into a total "international communication score."
International trade was determined by summing the total
amount of exports and imports, and also weighted this sum in
accordance with the national population.

It should be pointed out here that there were two inherent
problems with the national-level aggregate data used in this
study. First, certain variables in the study contained missing-
data values. For this problem, the study utilized pairwise
deletion of missing data in its correlation analyses that would
produce coefficients based on a different number of cases. This
method has "the advantage of utilizing as much of the data as
possible in the computation of each coefficient" (Nie et al.,
1975).[5] The unit of analysis was reported for each coefficient.
Second, the data collected for each variable reflected, in some
instances, a wide range of variations as well as high skewness
and kurtosis of the distributions. To alleviate this problem, the
study sought transformations of the data which would comple-
ment the assumption of linearity in correlational analysis. All
of the measures were examined on standardized Z scores, using
mean and standard deviation methods, for their skewness and

kurtosis. Those variables with high skewness and kurtosis were then logarithmically transformed to minimize skewness and kurtosis. They were the measures for international telephone and international trade; the raw data were used otherwise.

FINDINGS AND DISCUSSION

International Communication Volume

Figure 10.1 shows international rankings of selected "advanced" and "developing" nations[6] for international communication indicators. All indicators were translated to 1 to 100 scale to facilitate comparison and to permit visual display.

As expected, national differences based on amount of international communication are detected. An inspection of the data reveals great variation among national units in all of the three indicators. In fact, the variations in national levels are so great that the following description is illustrative for the international communication situation: a Barbados person receives and/or sends 69 mail items a year across his national boundaries, while an Indonesian does so only 0.2 mail item during the same period; in the same manner, a Swiss talks to someone in another country on the phone six times a year, while in India one out of 2,000 people may have an opportunity to talk to someone in another country on the phone during the same period.

Overall, the more developed Western European countries engage in a substantial degree of international communication by both mail and telephone: Belgium, Denmark, Finland, France, West Germany, Italy, the Netherlands, Norway, Spain, Sweden, Switzerland, and Great Britain. Switzerland surpasses every other nation in this category, except for Barbados, with mail. There are also other nations which show a high degree of international postal and telephone communication, including Australia, Barbados, Canada, Israel, Jamaica, Lebanon, New Zealand, and Singapore. These nations, as Frey (1973) suggests, have such significant political or economic ties with another country (such as the United States or Great Britain) that an unusually high volume of international

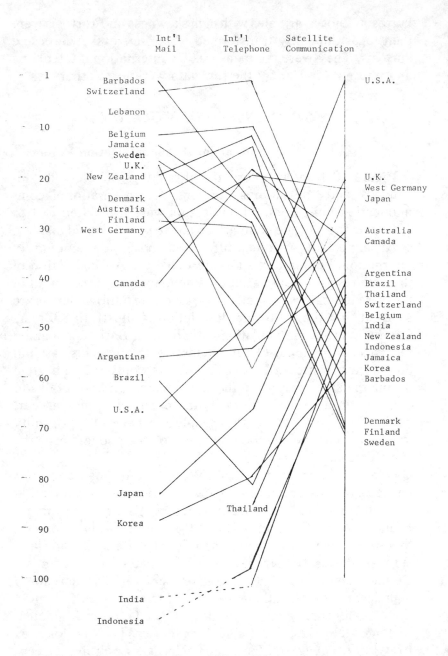

Figure 10.1: International Rankings of Selected Nations for International Communication Indicators

communication occurs. There is also more use of international mail and telephone in those countries whose geographical location is far from other parts of the world (such as Australia, Jamaica, and New Zealand). Surprisingly, in contrast, Japan and the United States exhibit a relatively low amount of international communication by both mail and telephone. This is feasible for the United States, whose self-supporting economy and independent political power is so great that more communication occurs domestically than internationally. For Japan, however, reasons are not readily understood.

International satellite communication is generally restricted to those nations possessing industrial and commercial power, including Australia, Canada, France, West Germany, Italy, Japan, Spain, Great Britain, and the United States. However, many developing countries in Asia and South America (such as Argentina, Brazil, Philippines, and Thailand) show a relatively high degree of communication satellite use when contrasted with such developed countries as Belgium, Denmark, Finland, Norway, Sweden, and Switzerland. This indicates that the technology of communication satellites has not quite appealed to those countries whose international communication routes are already well established with other existing communication means, such as mail and telephone.

International Communication Media Relations

As a conceptual scheme for relationships among international communication media, it is hypothesized that a new medium would depend on an old one for national use of international communication. That is, (1) the use of telephone for international communication will be influenced by international postal communication, and (2) the use of communication satellites will be affected by both international postal and telephone communication.

Tests of these hypotheses show that international telephone is well correlated with international mail ($r = .697, p < .001, N = 32$), supporting the first hypothesis. International satellite communication, on the other hand, correlates negatively with mail (r = −.151, N = 40) and telephone (r = −.003, N = 36). Neither correlation is significant, however. Subsequently, multiple regression of international satellite communication on international mail and telephone has not been pursued further. In other words, the existing means of international communication, such as mail and telephone, have little bearing upon national use of communication satellites for international communication.

International Communication and Domestic Communication

Table 10.1 shows the correlation matrix for domestic communication media and international communication. As has been well-demonstrated in other research, various national communication media are closely correlated with each other. These results are particularly consistent with the hypothesis suggested by Frey (1973: 359) that there is a clear correlation between a nation's relative development of its mass media (radio, cinema, and a composite print-television index) and its domestic communications (mail, telephones, and telegrams).

For the relationships between domestic communication media and international communications, international mail is weakly correlated with most of the domestic communication media (no relationship with radio), while both international telephone and satellite communications are relatively well correlated with most of the domestic communication indicators. The newspaper is weakly correlated with the communication satellite. Among various national communication indicators, radio plays a peculiar function in relation to international communication media. It is not related with international mail, somewhat weakly correlated with international telephone, but strongly correlated with satellite communication. Inspection of the data reveals that radio, unlike any other domestic communication indicators, has a peculiar distribution pattern across national units. There are not many variations in radio sets within a certain cluster of countries, but rather between the clusters of countries. For instance, the spread of radio sets is almost perfect within a group of highly advanced countries

Table 10.1: Intercorrelation Matrix for Domestic Communication Media and International Communication

	Telephones per 1,000 population	Radio sets per 1,000 population	Television sets per 1,000 pop.	Newspaper Circulation per 1,000	Int'l mail	Int'l telephone	Satellite communication
Domestic mail per capita	.914 (N=42)	.747 (N=42)	.914 (N=43)	.760 (N=39)	.258 (N=40)	.547 (N=43)	.600 (N=43)
Telephones		.736 (N=43)	.927 (N=44)	.833 (N=41)	.287 (N=39)	.642 (N=44)	.471 (N=44)
Radio			.802 (N=44)	.571 (N=40)	(.081)* (N=39)	.370 (N=44)	.846 (N=44)
Television				.839 (N=41)	.298** (N=40)	.610 (N=45)	.540 (N=45)
Newspaper				—	.327 (N=36)	.556 (N=41)	.258** (N=41)

Note: Correlation coefficients are insignificant and shown in parentheses.

**Correlation coefficients are significant at .05 level. Otherwise, all correlations are significant at .001 level.

including Britain, Canada, France, West Germany, Japan, and the United States, thus creating little variation in radio among these countries. But this level of radio diffusion is quite different from one found in such a group of countries as Columbia, India, Indonesia, Kenya, Korea, Nigeria, Peru, Senegal, and Thailand. Satellite communication follows a pattern similar to radio, and that is why the two are highly correlated to each other.

The relationships reported here provide two opposing hypotheses for the international communication situation. First, international postal communication seems independent from the general national communications situation: domestic mail and international mail are two different things, operating on two different dimensions. Second, in contrast, the availability or development of national communication media has a bearing on international telephone and satellite communication. Modern electronic communication media such as telephone, radio, and television, appear to have a more important bearing. Whether these national communication indicators are reliable for predicting international communication will be discussed further on.

International Communication and International Trade

Before attempting to find out determinants of international communication, the relationship between international communication and international trade is ascertained. Both international mail and telephone are significantly related to international trade, with correlations of .651 ($p < .001$, N = 40) and .878 ($p < .001$, N = 36) respectively. International communication, taking combined scores of both international mail and telephone, correlates significantly with trade ($r = .729$, $p < .001$, N = 32). This suggests that the trade activities of a nation have significant effects on international communication for that nation: the greater the amount of exports and imports of a country, the greater the external communication by that nation with others, and the greater the magnitude of that relationship.

In contrast, international trade has little bearing on international satellite communication ($r = .095$, $p < .05$, $N = 45$). This, along with the relationships between satellite communication and international mail and telephone, suggests that national use of communication satellites is not influenced by the existing international transaction routes including mail, telephone, and trade traffic.

Determinants of International Communication

Using all the variables described above as predictors of each international communication measure, a linear multiple regression was made for each of the international communication media.[7] Its results, including beta weights from the equation predicting each variable and multiple correlation coefficients, are reported in Table 10.2.

Table 10.2: Determinants of International Communication

	Int'l Mail		Int'l Telephone		Satellite Comm.	
	Beta Weight	F-value[1]	Beta Weight	F-value[2]	Beta Weight	F-value[2]
Domestic mail per capita					.697	12.045
Telephones per 1,000 pop.			(.344)	(1.682)		
Radio sets per 1,000 pop.					.983	45.146
Newspaper cir. per 1,000 pop.			−.319	3.458	−.260	2.853
International mail			.250	4.278		
International telephone	.605	4.278			(+.245)	(2.044)
International trade	(.514)	(2.104)	.644	10.578		
R^2	.493		.800		.800	

Notes: Significant level of F values are:1. $F = 2.41$, $p = .05$, $df = 7, 24$
2. $F = 2.38$, $p = .05$, $df = 8, 23$

Regressors whose parameters proved insignificant are shown in parentheses. See Note 9.

For international mail communication, international telephone is an only significant predictor. International trade has some effects on international mail, but its significant F-value ($F = 2.104$) falls a little below the required value ($F = 2.41$) at the .05 level. Taken together, however, these two variables account for 49 percent of the variance in international mail scores ($R^2 = .493$). Had the entire set of variables been used, 59 percent of the variance would have been accounted for. This indicates that general communication indicators are not reliable predictors for international mail communication; rather, international mail is relatively well-associated with other international transaction factors, such as have been identified here— international telephone communication and international trade. As the beta weights indicate, an increase in international mail goes hand in hand with increases in international telephone and international trade.

International telephone communication is a direct function of domestic telephones, international mail communication, and international trade; newspaper measures have an inverse effect on international telephone. Together they account for 80 percent of the variance in international telephone scores ($R^2 = .800$). The addition of other variables would have increased the variance to .83, a small increase in the variance account. The beta weights in this criterion indicate that with increases in three factors—the amount of both imports and exports, the foreign mail items, and the number of telephones—international telephone calls increase. On the other hand, more newspaper circulation within a country dampens international telephone communication of that nation with others. While the newspaper's dampening effect on international telephone communication needs further investigation and explanation, most domestic communication indicators have little apparent effect on international telephone communication. This suggests a substantial revision of the relationships depicted in the correlation matrix for domestic communication media and international communication. Only the availability of telephones has a direct effect; the remaining is determined by international mail and trade.

Satellite communication results most directly from radio, followed by domestic mail. More domestic mail items and more radios increase the use of communication satellites for international communication. For reasons not readily understood, telephone and television have little effect on satellite communication despite the fact that they are related to domestic mail and radio. Although not significant, international telephone communication plays an inhibiting role for satellite communication. All this suggests that there are few common characteristics among the predictors for satellite communication. The only visible trend is that it is not influenced by international communication means, but rather commonly available domestic communication means such as mail and radio. It appears that factors such as technology and economic development are other reliable indicators of a nation's satellite communication.[8] This needs long-term investigation, since the use of communication satellites has been limited, due to a slow diffusion of the satellite technology.

SUMMARY

An attempt has been made in this paper to examine international communication through three specific media—mail, telephone, and communication satellite—and to uncover other communication media variables that affect international communication through an examination of the relationships of international communication measures to domestic communication media and international trade measures. The study reveals great variation among national units in all international communication indicators. However, no clear distinction between advanced countries and developing countries is found in international mail and telephone communication. Unlike other socioeconomic indicators, including national communication indices, these international communication indicators are not affected by systematic development factors, once suggested by Lerner (1963). They are rather affected by international trade and by each other. This suggests that there are different international transaction factors which would determine international mail and telephone communication, such as trade, political relations, and tourism. On the other hand, international satellite communication reveals no clear determining factors; it follows the general scheme of communications developmental factors to a certain extent, but not to a systematic extent. But the study indicates clearly that satellite communication is not influenced by the existing international communication routes. This is suspected to be a temporary phenomenon. When the technology of communication satellites is adopted and utilized more widely by nations international satellite communication would follow the patterns of international mail and telephone communication. Possible extension of this research would attempt to specify the exact nature of communication satellites in international communication. While such an investigation should be carried out on a long-term basis, the analysis of international communication and its media by using multiple regression of various international communication media on those independent variables explored in this paper should provide impetus for another study.

NOTES

1. Harms (1973) argues that the telephone and the communication satellite are the important related items of technology for the study of intercultural communication, because they are two-way communication devices and the central concern in intercultural communication is with two-way communication between members of different communities. He further argues that radio and television are one-way devices and are of secondary importance to intercultural communication.

2. Deutsch (1956) suggested that there might be some correlations between the excess of mail which a country habitually receives from abroad and its position of an "importer" (rather than as an "exporter") of other kinds of communication. This hypothesis has not been verified by further research, however. On the other hand, Cherry (1971: 90) proposed the positive relationship between international communication and trade by noting the fact that Britain's gross revenue from her communication services (telephone, telex, and telegraphs combined) with France, the Netherlands, Belgium, West Germany, Norway, Sweden, and the United States bears a fairly constant ratio to her trade values with each of these countries.

3. The measure here does not indicate the volume of satellite communication, but the channel capacity carrying the message via communication satellite(s). The voice-grade channel provides service for voice, record, data, telephoto, facsimile, and others. The unit of measurement for this channel is available in the "half-circuit" which is a two-way communication path between one earth station and a satellite (Communications Satellite Corporation, 1972: 3).

4. Preliminary findings of this study indicated that satellite communication is a relatively minor form of international communication at present.

5. Under the circumstances that data are missing consistently across a certain cluster of countries (i.e., developing nations in Africa and Asia), the pairwise deletion method has the disadvantage of producing coefficients which are based on different subpopulations. An inspection of our data reveals that such is not the case. Missing data is randomly spread among national units.

6. Distinction between advanced and developing countries is made based on the United Nation's definiton that an "underdeveloped" country is one with less than three hundred dollars per capita.

7. No one of our variables is a perfect linear function of the others. That is not to say, however, that relationships among the regressors are not sometimes strong. There is rather a problem of multicollinearity; but this is not a violation of assumption. Parameter estimates are not inconsistent; rather, they are relatively inefficient in the sense that they have large standard errors of estimate. Multicollinearity, then, makes it difficult to reject hypotheses only because parameter estimates are statistically insignificant. As a result, some variables with low F values are retained in Table 10.2.

8. In his doctoral dissertation, the author has found three multiple-indicator factors that determine satellite communication of nation-states: socioeconomic factor (economy, technology, urbanization, and education), domestic communication factor, such as presented in this paper, and international trade. However, international trade showed an inverse effect on satellite communication (Hur, 1975).

REFERENCES

CHERRY, C. (1971) *World Communication: Threat or Promise?* New York: John Wiley.

Communications Satellite Corporation (1972) "COMSAT Annual Report to the President and Congress." Washington, D.C.: COMSAT.

DEUTSCH, K.W. (1964) "Transaction flows as indicators of political cohesion," in P. Jacob and J.V. Toscano (eds.) *The Integration of Political Communities.* Philadelphia: Lippincott.

———(1956) "International communication: The media and flows." *Public Opinion Quarterly* (Spring).

DUPREE, J.D. (1968) "International communication: View from a window on the world." Unpublished Ph.D. dissertation, University of North Carolina.

FISCHER, H.D. and MERRILL, J.C. [eds.] (1970) *International Communication.* New York: Hasting House.

FREY, F.W. (1973) "Communication and development," in Ithiel de Sola Pool et al., (eds.) *Handbook of Communication.* Chicago: Rand McNally.

GERBNER, G., GROSS, L.B., and MELODY, W.H. [eds.] (1973) *Communications Technology and Social Policy.* New York: John Wiley.

HARMS, L.S. (1973) *Intercultural Communication.* New York: Harper & Row.

HUR, K. (1975) "A cross-national study of satellite communication." Unpublished Ph.D. dissertation, University of Oregon.

International Telecommunication Union (1972-1974) "Eleventh, Twelfth, and Thirteenth Reports on Telecommunication and the Peaceful Uses of Outer Space." Geneva: ITV.

LERNER, D. (1963) "Toward a communication theory of modernization," in Lucian W. Pye (ed.) *Communications and Political Development.* Princeton, N.J.: Princeton Univ. Press.

NIE, N. et al., (1975) *Statistical Package for the Social Sciences* (2nd ed.) New York: McGraw-Hill.

SCHRAMM, W. (1964) *Mass Media and National Development.* Stanford, Conn.: Stanford Univ. Press.

———(1960) *One Day in the World's Press.* Stanford, Conn.: Stanford Univ. Press.

THOMPSON, M.E. (1971) "A study of international television programming within the structure of global communications." Unpublished Ph.D. dissertation. University of Wisconsin.

———NORDENSTRENG, K. and VARIS, T., *Television Traffic—A One-Way Street?* Paris: UNESCO.

APPENDIX I
LIST OF NATIONS

Argentina
Australia
Barbados
Belgium
Brazil
Canada
Chile
China (Nationalist-Taiwan)
Columbia
Denmark
Finland
France
Germany (West)
Greece
India
Indonesia
Ireland
Israel
Italy
Ivory Coast
Jamaica
Japan
Kenya

Korea (South)
Kuwait
Lebanon
Mexico
Netherlands
New Zealand
Nigeria
Norway
Pakistan
Peru
Philippines
Senegal
Singapore
Spain
Sweden
Switzerland
Tanzania
Thailand
Uganda
United Kingdom
United States
Venezuela

11

AN ANALYSIS OF DIPLOMATIC COMMUNICATION

EILEEN NEWMARK

State University of New York at Buffalo

An analysis of past developments in the study of international communication presents the scope of the field as its major problem. Included within this broad area are events and phenomenon such as: diplomatic negotiations, trade regulations, the work of agencies such as UNESCO, USIA, Voice of America, Radio Moscow, foreign exchange students, and missionaries. Each of these is a representative symbol of one part of international communication transactions. One definition of international communication states:

> International communication comprises those transactions taking place either across national boundaries or else within a national actor but affecting the ecology within which international transactions take place. [Merritt, 1972: 12]

International communication has become "all behaviors by one actor of which another actor could be aware" (Bobrow, 1972: 41). A more systematic approach views the field in dual levels. The formal level incorporates diplomatic communications, trade and military agreements, the work of the United Nations and related agencies, and institutions such as Radio Moscow and USIA. At this level we are dealing with interactions that affect the political, economic, and defense policies of other nations. The people and institutions engaging in such interaction are competing for influence over the minds of the international audience. The informal level includes tourism, foreign student exchange, nongovernmental organizations involved in voluntary services, aid programs, and missionaries. Interaction at this level is organized by the participants for their own purposes. The areas have unclear boundaries due to the difficulty of separating political from nonpolitical events. However, this structure provides us with a grasp of the complexity of levels that operate within the international system. This paper will focus on diplomatic communication as one significant area in international communication at the formal level.

The lack of literature by communication scholars relating to diplomatic communication points to the need for the development of sensitive conceptual schemes. The emphasis of the study for communicationists has mainly been in the realm of signals—language and visual images. Several scholars including Oliver (1952), Davison (1975), and Newman (1975) have discussed language and speech in diplomatic relations. They have suggested that such variables as ambiguity in language, selective perception, selective factual presentation, and technical vocabulary are important factors in an analysis of verbal messages utilized in diplomatic settings. A limited amount of work has examined the rhetorical dimensions of political situations (Heisy, 1970) including: United Nations diplomatic speeches (Prosser, 1970), small group analysis of conference behaviors (Bales, 1970), and the structuring of diplomatic reporting (Davison, 1975). Perhaps the most useful work has emerged from the area of conflict resolution through communication. For communicationists conflict is associated with attitudes that determine perceptions and behaviors (Jandt, 1973: 2). Burton's work in controlled communication and conflict analyzes elements of the conflict situation and the variables necessary to keep communication effective. Burton (1967), Doob (1900), and Deutsch (1968), theorists in conflict resolution, maintain that stereotypes and mistrust prove inefficient for communicative strategies, as is the use of power and threat in attempting to reach resolution. Each of these perspectives offer an approach with certain applicable principles. However, analytical studies are needed that will take a holistic exploration of communication principles in international interaction settings.

Diplomatic negotiations are particularly suited to such an explication of communication principles. Linkages between nations are frequently defined in the diplomatic sphere. Within current communication theory there are no models that adequately embrace the special characteristics of diplomatic communication. One way to view the inadequacies more clearly is to identify the specific conditions and factors which impinge on diplomatic interactions.

The three major factors which influence the communicative messages and strategies of diplomats are policy limitations, cultural variables, and the process and context of diplomatic negotiations. Diplomats are at the center of international communication as symbolic and political representatives of nations, responsible for promoting national interests through peaceful channels. They are the crucial links between the formulation and implementation of foreign policy, serving as the verbal and nonverbal mouthpiece, maintaining the two-way communication link. Within a diplomat's purview is the responsibility for public relations for his/her government, gathering information to assess the other nation's positions, and effectively delivering messages. Respect for his/her nation is intertwined with the power and prestige he/she holds. The messages communicated, the attitudes presented, and the means used to achieve purposes are shaped and limited by the foreign policy of the representative nation. In this sense, the diplomat is restricted in his/her directives for action, flexibility, and input into the foreign policy process. The representational nature of the diplomatic role places special constraints on the communicative interaction which I have termed policy limitations. The diplomatic framework does not invite policy alternatives since the priority is to achieve what is in the best interests of the representative nation without significant change in one's own position. We see the diplomat in a restricted position due to these imposed conditions.

The art of diplomacy requires accurate judgment of the situation and behavior of others and the ability to employ effective communication strategies. Diplomats need to be aware of the cultural determinants that affect human behavior. Hall (1966: 35) asserts that it is impossible for man to divest himself of his own culture, for it has penetrated to the roots of his nervous system and determines his perception of the world.

Individuals are often unaware how their perception is influenced by their immersion in one particular cultural setting. This issue has been addressed by several scholars in the field of communication as a significant element in communication between people of different cultural backgrounds (Porter, 1972; Stewart, 1971; Hall, 1966; Fischer, 1972). Crucial links in the process of mounting conflict are failures in perception, distorted images, and conflicting attitudes and values. The perceptions and images diplomats hold of each other and their respective nations are significant to their interaction, since they partly determine how they behave. National stereotypes frequently enter the diplomatic communication setting as a result of selective perception and interpretation. Information is sought after that is consonant with the stereotypes and attitudes already held. Accurate information is often denied which leads to impairment of a diplomat's judgment and accurate assessment of events. These variables are closely tied to our cultural patterns and affect the transfer of meaning in communication (Condon and Yousef, 1975; Sitaram and Cogdell, 1976; Holsti, 1965). Sensitivity to cultural differences in interpretation of events, approaches to conflict, and knowledge of what is valuable to others is important to deft negotiation.

Diplomatic negotiations are important communicative events. Communication principles merge here with the process of negotiation, language usage, the image of the diplomat, and the context. Charged with the responsibility of achieving a peaceful solution in the best interests of his/her nation, the diplomat needs to be skillful in the processes of negotiation. They need to figure out the most promising strategy for themselves with an eye toward the strategy of the other side. In effect,

> Genuine negotiations. . .are. . .games (and debates) with a joint venture of discovery and a mutual campaign of education toward a mutual appreciation and adjustment of the perceptions and preferences of several or all parties concerned. [Deutsch, 1968: 131]

In the initial stages of negotiation, the diplomat needs to discover as much as s/he can about the other nation's position. This information stage is important to persuade others to accept alternative positions. Negotiations move in a step-by-step procedure that incorporates limited concessions from each side, with different factors dominating at different stages.

Communication approaches to conflict resolution emphasize that within conflict there are alterable components: the perceptions of the external conditions, the selection of goals and assessment of values, and the means in relation to the assessment of the cost of the conflict (Burton, 1967: 50). Resolution then emerges out of proper analysis. What is needed is deliberate conveying of information that is accurate, procedures to ensure that messages sent are received accurately, and that the conflicting parties are able to evaluate their values and, if necessary, be willing to change their goals and modify their interests. The forms of communication (direct, indirect, visual, verbal) play a role in how the communication is received. Additionally, if the setting is one of fear of security it will affect the openness and trust of the negotiations.

The diplomatic tools of negotiation include: persuasion, the threat of force, and compromise. Influence through propaganda and mass media, cultural and educational exchanges is also involved in a more comprehensive nature. With these tools diplomats attempt to influence other nations and try to evince change without much change in their own positions. The language used by the diplomat is one important factor in moving through the stages of negotiation. Modes of expression, choice of words, and postures taken will change depending on the emphasis needed. Diplomats inherently use indirect verbal communication within a power framework. Diplomatic language entails cautious phrasing, ambiguity, use of a technical vocabulary, and facts to present one's case. The ambiguous nature of the language allows for flexibility and a middle ground position, while its technicalities allow further exploration and adjustment in positions (Oliver, 1952: 172-173). Cautious phrasing provides escape clauses from positions taken. Facts are chosen to deal with issues and can be selectively interpreted. Further manipulation of the issues and other diplomats is communicated through threats, bargains, and misinformation. Theoretically, for communication to be effective in conflict negotiation, there needs to be a check on perceptions and a flexibility to change. However, what we find is that the diplomatic situation calls for manipulation of the communication environment to achieve the foreign policy directives of his/her respective nation. Effectiveness then takes on a distinctly different meaning. Effective communication strategies address the specific issues at hand. Diplomats need maneuverability, a way to save face and generally approach the situation with an "all or nothing" viewpoint.

Another factor used for persuasion entails the image of the diplomat. The greater the prestige s/he holds, the more influence s/he will be able to exert. The relationship between the acts of an individual and the effects of those acts depends on the image maintained. The image can be changed quite quickly depending on role management and the consistency of information presented. Skillful diplncessions.

Negotiating processes in the diplomatic setting are concerned with changing the images and perceptions they hold of each other and the situation. Diplomats must simultaneously use the skills and tools available to them to impress the other side with their force, to advance compromise, and to be effectively persuasive (Morganthau, 1967: 521). This involves the idea of risk of self and risk of ideology. The tactics used will depend on how this risk is distributed among the negotiators. The political process is "one of mutual modification of images through feedback and communication" (Boulding, 1961: 98). One practical approach is to encourage restatement of the problem to find out exactly what the other side is saying, determine how the other side can be convinced of the truth of one's own views, consider their images of reality, and assess the amount of room built into the image they are presenting (Deutsch, 1968: 131). This process encourages feedback and clarification. The results of the negotiating process can bring about withdrawal or avoidance, reconciliation or compromise. Reconciliation is achieved when there is flexibility in images and values bringing convergence of positions. Flexibility depends on the level of importance the particular issue has for respective nations. In the compromise position, nations have been able to accommodate differences and will settle for less than they originally sought.

Two additional factors influence the approach and outcome of diplomatic negotiations. One is the context of the negotiations. These contexts vary from United Nations Security Council debates to international conferences (i.e., Law of the Sea conference), bilateral agreements, technical exchange agreements, and alliances of all types. Each of these contexts represent a different kind of communicative image, language, and policy alternative position. Within the context of the negotiations is the other significant factor—the aspect of time. Most conflicts, when viewed interpersonally, involve personal investment and the desire to come to resolution. In the world of international relations, conflict is continuous. It has a historical sense to it. What may be resolved at this point in history may be reversed in another administration. Therefore, there is little personal commitment to resolution. The pressure to reach an agreement does not have the same type of urgency we witness in interpersonal levels. The diplomat needs a posture of discourse with time to maneuver and change that will not cause embarrassment to the nation changing position. In interpersonal conflict the individuals are willing to confront each other directly on the issues, while room for adequate discourse can come after the issues are on the table. Therefore, the sense of urgency becomes distorted in the diplomatic negotiations. Although the diplomat needs to be aware of appropriate timing for issues, the concept takes on a larger connotation of timelessness.

This paper has discussed diplomatic negotiation as a communicative event and described the factors which affect the diplomatic setting. What I have outlined is a conception of the structure and processes of communication phenomena that occur in the social setting of diplomatic negotiation. The special characteristics of diplomatic communication do not fit existing communication theories and models. We need to have ethnographic studies to obtain information and formulate generalizations and hypotheses. Analytical research studies are needed to explore the relationship of communication principles in international interaction settings. Full exposition of the linkages between nations through communication will be possible only if we have a more precise understanding of policy

limitations, decision-making factors in foreign policy, the role
of personality and image for diplomats and their respective
nations in expressing power, prestige, and credibility, the
representational nature of the diplomatic role, cultural determinants of behavior and conflict resolution methods. The
subject matter is difficult to access because of limitations of
secrecy and security. These are the problem areas and the
issues in need of attention to further develop this area of communication. As has been demonstrated, the linkages exist and
are important for a better understanding of the processes of
international relations.

REFERENCES

BALES, R. (1970) "How people interact in conferences," in K. Sereno and C.D.
  Mortenson (eds.) *Foundations of Communication Theory.* New York: Harper &
  Row.
BARNA, L. (1972) "Stumbling blocks in interpersonal intercultural communication,"
  in L. Samovar and R. Porter (eds.) *Intercultural Communication: A Reader.*
  Belmont, Cal.: Wadsworth.
BOBROW, D. (1972) "Transfer of meaning across national boundaries," in R. Merritt
  (ed.) *Communication in International Politics.* Chicago: Univ. of Illinois Press.
BOULDING, K. (1961) *The Image.* Ann Arbor: Univ. of Michigan Press.
BURTON, J. (1967) *Communication and Conflict.* New York: Free Press.
CONDON, J. and YOUSEF, F. (1975) Introduction to intercultural communication.
  New York: Bobbs-Merrill.
DAVISON, W.P. (1975) "Diplomatic reporting: rules of the game" *Journal of Com-
  munication,* 25, 4 (Autumn).
DEUTSCH, K. (1968) *The Analysis of International Relations.* Englewood Cliffs,
  N.J.: Prentice-Hall.
DOOLITTLE, R.J. (1976) "Orientations to communication and conflict," in R.
  Applebaum and R. Hart (eds.) *MODCOM Series.* Chicago: Science Research
  Associates.
FISCHER, O.H. (1972) *Public Policy and the Behavioral Sciences.* Bloomington:
  Indiana Univ. Press.
HALL, E. (1966) *The Hidden Dimension.* New York: Doubleday.
  _____(1959) *The Silent Language.* New York: Doubleday.
HARMS, L.S. (1973) *Intercultural Communication.* New York: Harper & Row.
HEISEY, D.R. (1970) "The rhetoric of the Arab-Israeli conflict." *Quarterly Journal
  of Speech.*
HOLSTI, O. (1965) "Perceptions of time, perceptions of alternatives and patterns of
  communication as factors in crisis decision-making." *Peace Research Society
  Papers III.* Chicago Conference.
JANDT, F.E. (1973) *Conflict Resolution Through Communication.* New York:
  Harper & Row.

MERRITT, R. (1972) *Communication in International Politics.* Chicago: Univ. of Illinois Press.

MORGANTHAU, H. (1967) *Politics Among Nations.* New York: Alfred Knopf.

NEWMAN, R. (November 1975) "Communication pathologies of intelligence systems." *Speech Monographs,* 42, 4.

OLIVER, R. (1952) "Speech in international affairs." *Quarterly Journal of Speech.*

PORTER, R. (1972) "An overview of intercultural communication," in L. Samovar and R. Porter (eds.) *Intercultural Communication: A Reader.* California: Wadsworth.

PROSSER, M. [ed.] (1970) *Sow the Wind, Reap the Whirlwind: Heads of State Address the United Nations.* New York: William Morrow.

SAMOVAR, L. and PORTER, R. [eds.] (1972) *Intercultural Communication: A Reader.* Belmont, Cal.: Wadsworth Publishing Co.

SITARAM, K.S. and COGDELL, R. (1976) *Foundations of Intercultural Communication.* Columbus, Ohio: Charles E. Merrill.

SERENO, K. and MORTENSEN, C.D. (1970) *Foundations of Communication Theory.* New York: Harper & Row.

STEWART, E. (1971) *American Cultural Patterns: A Cross Cultural Perspective.* Pittsburgh, Penn.: SIETAR.

12

FIVE DIMENSIONS IN RACIAL-BASED COMMUNICATION STEREOTYPES

STEVEN M. ALDERTON

Indiana University

Stereotypes affect human behavior, especially interracial communication, for they determine perception of and subsequent interaction with stimuli. Research supports the view that the stereotyping of an ethnic group has a pervasive influence on communication. More specifically, stereotypes about how an ethnic group communicates (communicator style) may predetermine the outcome of interracial communication. Rich (1974: 61) found empirical support for the existence of communication stereotypes. She concludes: "the stereotypes Blacks hold of White communicators are so negative that, with the influence of selective perception reinforcing these negative views, productive interracial communication is rendered difficult, if not impossible, at times." The present study investigates five dimensions of communication stereotypes.

RATIONALE

Ethnic stereotypes are operationally defined as favorable or unfavorable, irrationally formulated, generalizations varying in the intensity (degree of favorableness), uniformity, and rigidity with which they are maintained. This definition includes the following five dimensions of the stereotyping process: (a) labels representing the *content* of the generalization; (b) *uniformity* or the extent to which an individual's stereotypes

AUTHOR'S NOTE: *This manuscript is based on the author's M.A. thesis directed by Raymond G. Smith at Indiana University. The author acknowledges J. Jeffery Auer, Rita Naremore, and Larry Miller for suggestions and evaluations contributing to this study.*

are in agreement with the responses of others; (c) *direction* or favorability of the stereotypes; (d) *intensity* of the response (degree of favorableness); and (e) *rigidity* with which ethnic stereotypes are maintained.[1]

Researchers have used various methods to investigate the dimensions of stereotypes. The content, uniformity, and polarity of ethnic stereotypes were studied by means of the Katz and Braly (1933) methodology. Essentially, this simple device requires subjects to choose the characteristics they feel best describe an ethnic group. Ratings are made on adjective checklists. Gilbert (1951), Karlins et al. (1969), and Maykovitch (1971) have used this technique to study, among other things, changes in the "image" White Americans hold about the personality of Black Americans and Whites over a period of years. Ogawa (1971) and Rich (1974) used Katz and Braly checklists to investigate communication stereotypes. The research supports the conclusion that White America's 1933 "*Saturday Evening Post* image" of Blacks as "superstitious," "lazy," and "happy-go-lucky" changed to a "picture" of the "argumentative," "impulsive," and "aggressive" Black of the 1970s, while the 1933 White self-image of "intelligent," "industrious," and "progressive" was retained over a 40-year period.

In addition to content, uniformity, and polarity, Gardner et al. (1968) developed a Stereotype Differential to study intensity, a fourth dimension of stereotyping. This technique requires individuals to rate ethnic groups on a series of bipolar adjectival scales. Though Gardner et al., found that the stereotypic "picture" gained from scale ratings was similar to the "image" generated by the Katz and Braly checklist, the Stereotype Differential allows subjects to rate the *extent* to which stereotypic traits are applicable.

The rigidity with which stereotypes are held, a fifth dimension of stereotyping, has been explored by asking individuals to respond to material which confirms or contradicts a stereotypic "image." Gardner and Taylor (1969) used controlled videotaped messages to assess the maintenance of expected stereotypic "pictures." They concluded that outside information, discrepant or anticipated, can affect the rigidity of stereotypes.

This information may come from an individual who is representative of an ethnic group (outgroup) and/or from peer pressure (ingroup).

Except for two studies, the previous research included investigations into varying dimensions of stereotypes held about the overall personality of an ethnic group. Ogawa (1971) and Rich (1974), however, used Katz and Braly checklists to identify, respectively, the content and uniformity of the stereotypes White Americans hold about Black communicators and the content and uniformity of the stereotypes Black Americans hold about the communication style of Whites. Neither of these studies examined the polarity, intensity, and rigidity of communication stereotypes, nor did the subjects rate their own ethnic group's communication style. In order to more thoroughly investigate the role of communication stereotypes in interracial communication, five dimensions of these stereotypes should be studied. Five research questions, therefore, have been posed:

1. What are the similarities and dissimilarities between the "pictures" that White Americans hold about the communication styles of Black Americans and themselves?
2. Do Whites agree upon a standardization or uniform "image" of the speech of Black Americans and White communicators?
3. Do White Americans have a favorable or unfavorable "image" of the communication of an outgroup (Blacks) and an ingroup (Whites)?
4. How intensely do Whites maintain stereotypes about Black communicators and themselves?
5. How rigidly held is the White "image" of the communication style of Black Americans and White Americans when individuals are confronted by messages which either confirm or contradict the expected "image?"

A preliminary descriptive study was conducted to answer the first four research questions pertaining to the content, uniformity, polarity, and intensity of communication stereotypes. On the basis of the findings in the initial investigation, an experiment was designed to answer the fifth question about stereotyping.

PRELIMINARY METHOD AND RESULTS

Katz and Braly (1933) checklists and Stereotype Differentials (Gardner et al., 1968) were designed to include many of the traits identified by Ogawa (1971) and Rich (1974) as being most characteristic of the communication of Black Americans. Preliminary research determined polar adjectives of the 18 traits (Table 12.1). One hundred and twenty White undergraduates enrolled in Public Speaking and Interpersonal Communication classes at Indiana University during the Spring term of 1975 served as pretest subjects. They rated the concepts "Speech Traits of White Americans" and "Speech Traits of Black Americans" on 18, seven-point Stereotype Differential scales. Additionally, they chose the five adjectives most characteristics of each group from adjective checklists. Sixty-one of the students were males and 59 were females. The data from these pretest questionnaires provided information about the content, uniformity, direction, and intensity of the communication stereotypes held about Blacks and Whites. As the coefficient of reliability was .81 (Cronbach's Alpha) the measure was considered reliable for the purpose of this study.

The operationally defined content of a group's communication stereotypes is the list of traits consensually chosen as most characteristic of a group's speech (Table 12.2). In the present study, Black communicators were attributed a "potent/defiant image" as characterized by the traits of "showy," "temperamental," "arrogant," and "fault-finding." White Americans perceived themselves as having the "all-American image" of "progressive," "responsive," and "intelligent." In addition to this favorable self-description, White subjects characterized Whites with the "Watergate image" of "concealing." Though certain similarities existed in the overall characterization of Blacks and Whites, the number of dissimilarities between these two "pictures" indicates that the subjects have a unique stereotypic "image" of each group's communication.

The degree to which the subjects uniformly agreed upon the communication stereotypes, as revealed by the Katz and Braly (1933) method, was strong enough to conclude that stereo-

Table 12.1 Bipolar Traits Used in Stereotype Differentials and Checklists

Positive traits	Negative traits
Agreeable	Quarrelsome
Calm	Temperamental
Active	Inactive
Straightforward	Evasive
Tolerant	Fault-finding
Sensitive	Insensitive
Modest	Showy
Obedient	Disobedient
Friendly	Hostile
Open	Closed
Responsive	Resistant
Intelligent	Ignorant
Progressive	Backward
Humble	Boastful
Unpretentious	Arrogant
Individualistic	Unindividualistic
Peace-loving	Belligerent
Revealing	Concealing

typing occurred. The least number of traits which accounted for 50% of the checklist responses were determined. If there were perfect agreement, 2.5 traits would receive 50% of the ratings. Perfect disagreement or change would mean that 18 traits accounted for half of the votes. Approximately 7.75 traits, therefore, should receive half of the selections if a group is stereotyped. For the concept "Speech Traits of Black Americans," 7.24 of the 36 adjectives received 50% of the responses on the checklists, while 8.22 adjectives accounted for 50% of the total pretest responses to the concept "Speech Traits of Black Americans." In short, stereotyping occurred. Further, because fewer traits were used to characterize Blacks, the "picture" of Black communicators was more standardized than the "image" of White communicators.

Neither Whites nor Blacks were attributed an entirely positive or negative set of traits (Table 12.2). Analysis of the polarity of these traits, however, suggests that the unfavorable adjectives assigned to Blacks are characteristics that deter

Table 12.2: Content of the Traits Agreed upon as Being Most Characteristic of a Group's Communicator Style

"Speech Traits of Black Americans" (Concept 1)

Trait	percent	Polarity
Showy	10.1	−
Active	7.6	−
Boastful	7.3	−
Temperamental	6.3	−
Individualistic	6.0	+
Straightforward	6.0	+
Arrogant	5.6	−
Fault-finding	4.6	−
	53.5	

"Speech Traits of White Americans" (Concept 2)

Trait	percent	Polarity
Individualistic	7.1	+
Progressive	6.6	+
Active	6.5	+
Concealing	5.8	−
Straightforward	5.7	+
Intelligent	5.7	+
Friendly	5.7	+
Boastful	4.9	−
Responsive	4.7	+
	52.5	

positive interpersonal interaction (e.g., "showy," "boastful," "temperamental," "arrogant," and "fault-finding"), but the favorable traits assigned to Whites are characteristics that facilitate communication (e.g., "intelligent," "friendly," "straightforward," "responsive," and "progressive"). There is a tendency, therefore, for Whites to use anti-communicative traits to describe Blacks, while characterizing the White ingroup with traits conducive to communication.

The t-statistics,[2] values reflecting the polarity of the ratings on the Stereotype Differential scales, were employed to determine the intensity of communication stereotypes. These values suggest that the subjects, for the most part, chose the same traits to describe the communication of Blacks and Whites on the bipolar scales as they did on the stereotype checklists. The only bipolar semantic differential scale highly rated on its positive end for the concept "Speech Traits of Black Americans" was "active-inactive," whereas Blacks were highly ranked on the negative traits of "showy," "temperamental," "boastful," "arrogant," "fault-finding," and "belligerent." The ratings for the concept "Speech Traits of White Americans" were highly polarized on the "friendly," "intelligent," "progressive," and "active" ends of the scales, while White Americans were polarized strongly toward the negative ends of the scales "boastful-humble," "showy-modest," and "fault-finding-tolerant" (see Appendix A). This investigation further substantiates the White American "potent/defiant image" of Blacks and rather splendid "all-American self-picture."

EXPERIMENTAL DESIGN AND RESULTS

In order to test for stereotype rigidity, 52 of the pretest subjects listened to four audio-taped stimulus messages that were generally based upon the content, uniformity, direction, and intensity of the pretest responses. A bidialectal Black speaker recorded each of the interviews representing the following four conditions: (1) a Black speaker portraying in his communication the stereotypes anticipated by White listeners; (2) a Black speaker conveying the opposite of anticipated stereotypic traits; (3) a White communicator speaking in a manner expected by White listeners; and (4) a White speaker presenting an anti-stereotyped message. After each of the four groups ($N = 13$ in each group) listened to one of the audio-taped messages, the subjects completed a questionnaire identical to the pretest. In addition, the subjects answered a question about the race of the interviewee in order to be certain that his perceived race was consistent with the design. A control group ($N = 12$) completed the questionnaire twice during the four-week period but did not listen to a stereotyped message. Further, a validity test ($N = 10$) required subjects to choose from a list of 36 adjectives those five traits they felt best characterized the communication of the interviewee. Results of the validity test indicated that at least 50% of the students selected four out of the five stereotypic "images" developed in the messages, while there was total agreement on the race of each interviewee.

The topic of the messages was desegregation of public schools and the use of forced busing. Each message included similarly constructed arguments. The speaker, posing as an interviewee, was introduced as a member of a busing committee. The content of these interviews was general enough so as to convey attitudes which could potentially be expressed by either Blacks or Whites.

Stereotypic traits were developed within the messages by either direct or indirect methods. The trait "active," for example, was represented in the message by the interviewee's direct reference to himself as highly-motivated and involved with the committee, while "active" was indirectly conveyed by the use of a fast and energetic speaking style. The "inactive" interviewee was noncommittal and disinterested in the issue of desegregation, while this interviewee spoke in a slow and monotonous fashion. In addition, the follow-up questions by the interviewer served to reinforce the "image" of the interviewee (Table 12.3).

Table 12.3: Examples of Stereotypic Traits Developed Within Wording of Interviews

Trait		Dialogue
"Active"	Q.	"What is the purpose of your committee?"
	A.	"I'm involved in an organization which objects to the busing of children for the purpose of desegregating schools in New York."
"Inactive"	Q.	"What is the purpose of your committee?"
	A.	"We're sort of concerned (um) with busing and desegregation."
"Evasive"	Q.	"Why did the Supreme Court decide that segregated schools are unconstitutional?"
	A.	"Most of the reasons are obvious."
	Q.	"Could you get to the point? Which reasons are obvious?"

A bidialectal Black American recorded the four stimulus messages. This individual portrayed the stereotyped "images" of a group's communication by varying his vocal inflections, rate of speaking, and so on, and through the wording of the dialogue, while at the same time the interviewee was perceived as either a White American or a Black American by the use of dialectal variations. Because one person recorded all of the interviewee portions of the dialogues, the vocal qualities (pitch, range, rhythm, tempo, articulation, pronunciation, and so forth) and vocalizations (characterizers, qualifiers, and segregates) were greatly controlled.

In order to determine the influence of the anticipated or discrepant messages upon the stereotype rigidity of the four treatment groups, the pretest and posttest responses to the appropriate concept were compared with a two-factor ANOVA. Since none of the scales were correlated, an analysis of variance was computed for each of the 18 scales (see Appendix B).

The F test results for each of the 18 scales suggest that the messages affected responses to certain scales, but the scales affected were not the most rigidly held stereotypic traits. Inspection of the findings reveals that the race of the speaker significantly affected reactions to the bipolar scales of "quarrelsome-agreeable," "peace-loving-belligerent," "unpretentious-arrogant," "ignorant-intelligent," "disobedient-obedient," and "friendly-hostile," while the type of message significantly affected responses to the scales of "temperamental-calm," "nonindividualistic-individualistic, " "unpretentious-arrogant," and "friendly-hostile" (see Appendix B). This finding can be interpreted in three ways. First, the subjects reacted to the "defiant/active image" portrayed by the speaker in stereotyped messages and/or the "passivity" of the speaker in the anti-stereotyped messages. This assumption, however, cannot be verified because the statistical analysis does not indicate which ends of the scales were rated differently by the treatment groups. Second, those scales rated differently by the groups were not, for the most part, scales which included traits that comprised the anticipated or contradictory "images." The second interpretation is supported by the fact that only three of the 10 stereotypic traits used in the stimulus messages received significantly different ratings. Third, a percentage of the change in ratings between pretest and posttest may be attributed to a weakening of stereotypic "pictures" over a period of time or to the reactive effect of retaking the test. Nevertheless, race of speaker and type of message affected the maintenance of certain communication stereotypes. Few of the affected stereotypes, however, were those traits most often attributed to the communication of Black Americans and White Americans.

DISCUSSION AND CONCLUSIONS

Ogawa (1971) and Rich (1974) concluded that the "image" one has of the communication of another group influences interracial interaction. Also, as Wilmot (1975) contends, "Each person's view of himself affects his as well as his partner's behavior." Thus, interracial behavior will be affected by the perceptions of a friendly ingroup and a defiant outgroup.

More importantly, if the stereotypes about a group's communication, as supported by the conclusions of this study, are uniformly held, they tend to be favorable for an ingroup and unfavorable for an outgroup. They characterize an outgroup with traits that deter communication and an ingroup with traits that facilitate communication. They are rigidly held because of support from mass media, selective perception, or because there is a "kernel of truth" in the generalization. It is doubtful that brief encounters with members of such a group will significantly diminish one's stereotypic "image" and, subsequently, allow for interracial communication.

Stereotyping most likely affects that interracial interaction occurring prior to the initiation of authentic interpersonal communication. Miller and Steinberg (1975) delineated and explicated three levels for analyzing interaction: cultural, sociological, and psychological. Communication resulting from expectations based upon cultural norms and values or an individual's membership in a social group is termed noninterpersonal communication. This type of behavior is not based upon perceptions of an individual's uniqueness. It is only at the psychological level that individuals respond to each other's personality and, therefore, initiate interpersonal communication. Since much of initial interracial interaction is based upon cultural or sociological information, stereotypes that one holds about an ethnic group amplify the superficialities that are evident in contacts governed by cultural or sociological expectations. Hence, stereotypes may preclude the interaction from advancing to the psychological or interpersonal level. One method for overcoming the barriers posed by stereotypic "images" is interracial encounters where confrontation and frankness about ethnic stereotypes ought to help foster communication based on perception of individuals.

The actual impact of stereotypes about a group's communicator style upon interracial interaction is unknown. Future research could include investigations of the influence of face-to-face interracial confrontation upon the dimensions of stereotyping. Also, because stereotyping is a two-way process, the five dimensions of the communication stereotypes Blacks hold about White Americans should be explicated.

NOTES

1. Four of the five dimensions were defined and studied by Edwards (1940) in an examination of political stereotypes. The fifth dimension, rigidity, was not included in the Edwards study.

2. The t-statistic, $(X-u/s)N$, is not to be confused with the t distribution. This index of polarity, developed by Gardner and Kirby at the University of Western Ontario, is used to evaluate the intensity with which a group attributes certain characteristics to another group by considering both deviations of mean ratings from neutrality ($X-u$) and agreement in ratings. The original computer program could not be used, thus a comparable SPSS program calculated the t-statistics. The SPSS program, however, did not determine the significance of the t-statistics.

REFERENCES

EDWARDS, A.L. (1940) "Four dimensions in political stereotypes." *Journal of Abnormal and Social Psychology,* 35: 566-572.

GARDNER, R.C. and KIRBY, D.M. (1971) "Ethnic stereotypes: A computer program for their analysis by assessing polarization of semantic differential ratings." *Research Bulletin,* 172: 1-2.

GARDNER, R.C. and TAYLOR, D.M. (1969) "Ethnic stereotypes: Meaningfulness in ethnic-group labels." *Canadian Journal of Behavioral Science,* 1: 182-192.

GARDNER, R.C., WONNACOTT, E.J., and TAYLOR, D.M. (1968) "Ethnic stereotypes: A factor analytic investigation." *Canadian Journal of Psychology,* 22: 35-44.

GILBERT, G.M. (1951) "Stereotype persistence and change among college students." *Journal of Abnormal and Social Psychology,* 46: 245-254.

KARLINS, M., COFFMAN, T.L., and WALTERS, G. (1969) "On the fading of social stereotypes: Studies in three generations of college students." *Journal of Personality and Social Psychology,* 13: 1-16.

KATZ, D. and BRALY, K. (1933) "Racial stereotypes in one hundred college students." *Journal of Abnormal and Social Psychology,* 28: 280-290.

MAYKOVITCH, M.K. (1971) "Changes in racial stereotypes among college students." *Human Relations,* 24: 371-386.

MILLER, G.R. and STEINBERG, M. (1975) *Between People.* Chicago: Science Research Associates.

OGAWA, D. (1971) "Small group communication stereotypes of Black Americans." *Journal of Black Studies,* 1: 273-281.

RICH, A.L. (1974) *Interracial Communication.* New York: Harper & Row.

WILMOT, W.W. (1975) *Dyadic Communication: A Transactional Perspective.* Reading, Mass.: Addison-Wesley.

APPENDIX A
T-Statistics for the Degree of Polarization of
Responses to Each Scale for Both Concepts

Speech Traits of Black Americans (Concept 1)

Rank	Scales	Mean	Variance	t	Frequency		
	Rated on Positive Ends						
	− +				1-3	4	5-7
P1	Inactive-Active	5.35	1.77	+11.13	.09	.19	.73
P2	Backward-Progressive	4.37	1.97	+ 3.38	.26	.24	.50
P3	Evasive-Straightforward	4.47	2.84	+ 3.08	.35	.14	.50
P4	Insensitive-Sensitive	4.35	2.80	+ 2.28	.33	.19	.47
P5	Ignorant-Intelligent	4.21	1.16	+ 1.68	.26	.35	.37
P6	Concealing-Revealing	4.17	2.70	+ 1.16	.40	.16	.32
P7	Closed-Open	4.15	2.86	+ .96	.41	.19	.40
P8	Individualistic-Nonindividualistic	4.15	3.98	+ .86	.44	.92	.47
P9	Quarrelsome-Agreeable	4.00	2.14	+ .06	.38	.25	.37
	Rated on Negative Ends						
N1	Showy-Modest	2.37	1.26	−15.77	.86	.10	.04
N2	Temperamental-Calm	2.80	1.56	−10.45	.78	.11	.11
N3	Boastful-Humble	2.80	1.85	− 9.60	.74	.16	.11
N4	Arrogant-Unpretentious	2.95	1.68	− 8.75	.69	.20	.11
N5	Fault-finding-Tolerant	3.03	1.84	− 7.79	.70	.17	.13
N6	Belligerent-Peace-Loving	3.27	1.36	− 6.83	.64	.23	.13
N7	Resistant-Responsive	3.51	2.05	− 3.68	.57	.18	.24
N8	Disobedient-Obedient	3.70	1.10	− 3.12	.39	.47	.14
N9	Quarrelsome-Agreeable	3.60	1.90	− 3.10	.52	.23	.24

Speech Traits of White Americans (Concept 2)

Rank	Scales	Mean	Variance	t	Frequency		
	Rated on Positive Ends						
	− +				1-3	4	5-7
P1	Hostile-Friendly	5.17	1.02	+12.70	.04	.22	.74
P2	Ignorant-Intelligent	5.07	1.09	+11.19	.83	.20	.71
P3	Backward-Progressive	5.30	1.81	+10.63	.10	.16	.74
P4	Inactive-Active	5.07	1.86	+ 8.60	.15	.13	.72
P5	Nonindividualistic-Individualistic	4.75	3.14	+ 4.60	.31	.07	.62
P6	Resistant-Responsive	4.60	2.04	+ 4.60	.24	.16	.60
P7	Disobedient-Obedient	4.41	1.10	+ 4.30	.14	.43	.43
P8	Insensitive-Sensitive	4.50	2.18	+ 3.76	.27	.13	.55
P9	Belligerant-Peace-loving	4.30	1.35	+ 2.83	.22	.34	.43
P10	Quarrelsome-Agreeable	4.30	1.75	+ 2.47	.28	.26	.46

P11	Closed-Open	4.19	2.17	+ 1.42	.35	.19	.46
P12	Evasive-Straightforward	4.06	2.68	+ .44	.47	.07	.46
	Rated on Negative Ends						
N1	Boastful-Humble	3.10	1.50	− 8.03	.67	.21	.12
N2	Showy-Modest	3.30	1.56	− 6.06	.67	.12	.21
N3	Fault-finding-Tolerant	3.22	1.99	+ 6.00	.63	.17	.20
N4	Arrogant-Unpretentious	3.50	1.04	− 5.37	.53	.31	.17
N5	Temperamental-Calm	3.69	1.52	− 2.72	.56	.15	.29
N6	Concealing-Revealing	3.67	2.28	− 2.35	.58	.09	.33

APPENDIX B
Two-Factor ANOVA of Each of Eighteen Scales

Scale	Main Effects (F Ratio)		
	Race (A)	Message (B)	AXB
Quarrelsome-Agreeable	9.64**	3.21	3.60
Revealing-Concealing	1.22	1.96	1.31
Temperamental-Calm	2.58	4.11*	.31
Peace-loving-Belligerant	5.65*	2.01	*4.13*
Active-Inactive	2.32	3.34	1.77
Nonindividualistic-Individualistic	1.06	4.16	1.27
Unpretentious-Arrogant	5.61*	4.05	.45
Straightforward-Evasive	.23	.09	2.57
Fault-finding-Tolerant	.75	.01	.02
Humble-Boastful	.71	1.24	.60
Insensitive-Sensitive	1.36	1.25	.56
Progressive-Backward	.38	.46	.10
Modest-Showy	2.81	2.03	.01
Ignorant-Intelligent	4.95*	.00	.18
Open-Closed	.40	1.32	1.76
Resistant-Responsive	3.40	.80	.90
Disobedient-Obedient	9.68**	3.27	.05
Friendly-Hostile	4.49*	4.29*	.88

p .05
**p .01

13

TERRAMEDIAN VALUE SYSTEMS AND THEIR SIGNIFICANCE

GEORGE O. ROBERTS

University of California, Irvine

Value systems are universal phenomena which are prominent features of all societies and cultures. They may be limited or comprehensive, essentially rational or mainly emotional; nevertheless, value systems—in relation to their specific cultures and societies—define the goals that are worth pursuing and, in turn, the behavioral patterns and attitudes which ought to be encouraged and safe-guarded (see Parsons, 1967: 8-9). Value systems also provide continuity in that they relate past achievements and practices to present situations and aspirations, and to future goals (Armstrong, 1971). Although inevitably subject to change, value systems generally assume an aura of sanctity which results in attempts to preserve them from the "destructive" tendencies of change.

Several important distinctions must be made before one can properly understand the values of a given culture. First, one must determine what the values of a people are by examining what the people themselves pronounce them to be—their stated ideals and beliefs; and second, what people do—what values are implied by their behavior. Furthermore, one must make a distinction between the traditional values of long standing, and those whose recent adoption might have replaced or integrated themselves into the old, traditional package of values. Finally, one must understand that the values of one culture which are not shared by another culture are not

AUTHOR'S NOTE: *Grateful acknowledgement is expressed to Professor Austin J. Shelton for his contribution and assistance, including the design of the figures.*

necessarily superior or inferior; in short, one cannot use the values of one culture to make judgments about the "goodness" or "badness" of the values or behavior of people of a different culture (Arensberg and Kimball, 1965; Warwick, 1973). Such cultural relativism, of course, applies primarily to values, not necessarily to technology (Foster, 1962; Preston, 1971; Beckford, 1972). Whether the most beautiful woman is fat or slender, or whether one's traditional God is the true God or not, are relative matters and cannot be determined outside the culture. But whether a certain medical method of one culture works better to end or reduce infant mortality than another method is something quite different, and is not subject to cultural relativism at all.

TERRAMEDIAN VALUES

Despite the invasion of modernization, Terramedia (i.e., Africa and the Middle East) has managed to retain—for better or worse—many values which date far into its past, and which continue to be influential in the thought patterns and behavior of the majority of its inhabitants. It is particularly important, consequently, to analyze the nature of the principal traditional values so as to understand the extent of their influence; to weigh their significance to people who wish to hold onto cherished values, even as they simultaneously endeavor to modernize and reap some of the benefits available in less traditional societies. For the purposes of this analysis, a traditional society might be defined as one in which the social organization and culture (the behavior and heritage of the people of the society) are determined by custom and tradition and are accordingly resistant to innovation and other change. Values, of course, are important clues to the degree of traditionalism which one might discover in any society.

Throughout Terramedia there are certain areas in which values coincide; at the same time, there are values which, because of peculiar responses to the challenge of living in different environments, are unique to certain regions. A meaningful analysis must take these historical and ecological differences into account, including the necessity of distin-

quishing the Northern Muslim sector from the Southern sub-
Saharan sector of Terramedia.

As in most, if not all societies, Terramedian groups have
always recognized the importance of the family as the basic
unit of socialization; the process whereby a person is made into
an effective participant in inevitable human interactions.
Unlike "westernized" societies, however, Terramedia has
always made certain unique emphases in living. Marriage, for
example, continues in most cases to be regarded as a contract
between families rather than between consenting individuals
(which does not mean, of course, that the marrying couple have
no say in the matter). This attitude results in a high value being
placed on the extended, consanguine family rather than on the
nuclear, conjugal family. To illustrate the similarities of
extended families in the Northern (Middle East) and Southern
(sub-Sahara) sectors of Terramedia, we might briefly examine
the structure of the Arabic Bedouin family and that of the
Nsukka Igbo family of Eastern Nigeria. The Bedouin family is
designated by the word *ahl,* meaning "kin," which is reckoned
strictly (see Figure 13.1: *Arab Extended Family*). In the *ahl,*
EGO (a Latin word meaning "self" used in kinship charts to
enable the reader to place himself in the charter structure in
order to better understand the relationships) reckons his kin
according to the following criteria:

1. *Blood*: his kin are "blood" relatives.

2. *Patrilinealism*: his kin are male relatives in the line of his
father, not in the line of his mother.

3. *Three Generations Vertically*: he counts his kin for only
three generations in the past and three in the future; therefore
his father's *ahl* differs from his own *ahl*, and his son's *ahl*
differs from his own *ahl*, and accordingly he, his father, and his
son have rights and obligations to slightly varying groups of
people. The "family" more extensively considered includes
the clan, or *qawm,* which comprises all those who possess
blood relationship because of descent from the same fore-
father. Bedouin were, and are, largely endogamous in their
marriage-system, which means that they practised "inside-
marriage" or marriage within a clan or kin-group—a practice
varying from the exogamy of sub-Saharan Africa.

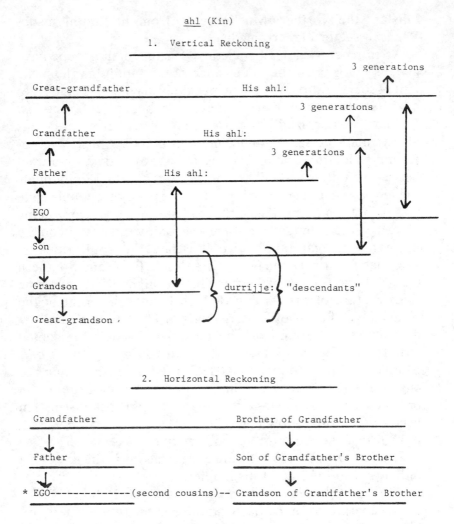

* This is the most distant relationship within the *ahl,* generally, although among some peoples it is extended by one generation.

Figure 13.1: Arabic Extended Family

The Nsukka Igbo family similarly is an extended family (see Figure 13.2), and is centered particularly on the *umunna,* or patrilineage. Differing slightly from Igbo family structures in general, the northern Nsukka Igbo family also has a larger unit which might be called "clan" in English, and in Igbo is *ukwu*

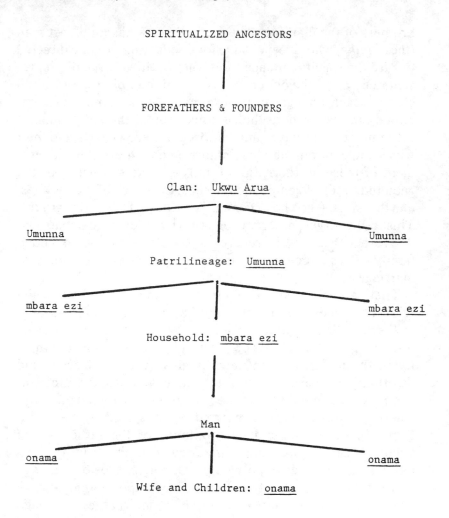

SPIRITUALIZED ANCESTORS

FOREFATHERS & FOUNDERS

Clan: Ukwu Arua

Umunna   Umunna

Patrilineage: Umunna

mbara ezi   mbara ezi

Household: mbara ezi

Man

onama   onama

Wife and Children: onama

Figure 13.2: Northern Igbo Extended Family

arua. (Shelton, 1971). Unlike the *ahl* of the Bedouin, the Igbo kin-group is reckoned broadly, although blood relationship and patrilineality are the major determinants. Belonging to the extended family or *umunna* are the living members; the ancestors, and the unborn, all the descendants of the sons or brothers of the clan founder. Each lineage has an eldest man (the *okpube*) who is responsible for conducting worship directed toward the specific lineage forefathers, who are usually represented by a small wooden status, small mud pillars, or sacred stones. Each lineage, in turn, consists of a number of compound families or households consisting of the eldest man of the family and his wives and children, his grown sons and their wives and children, and his unmarried daughters. The government of these northern Igbo family-societies consists of the gathered heads of compound families, the heads of the lineages, and the *onyisi* (the "head person" or eldest of the entire group). This results in gerontocracy, or a rule by elders who debate and derive a consensus in regard to problems of the extended family. These societies practise exogamy as their form of marriage.

There are other aspects of family organization which, while relevant at one time in most societies, remain prominent only in Terramedia and some other Third World societies. There is, for example, an emphasis on patriarchy (the vesting of authority in the male), and on patrilineality (tracing descent and determining inheritance through male ancestors). A consequence of such emphasis has been a preference for patrilocality whereby the residence of married persons tends to be established in the compound or proximity of the father of the husband (see Figure 13.3: *Patrilocality*). There is, furthermore, an acceptance of polygyny as the ideal type of marriage relationship, in contrast to the emphasis upon monogamy in "westernized" societies. It should be noted that, even though Islam prescribes that a man have up to four wives, the permissiveness entailed in adding a limitless number of "slave wives or concubines" parallels the nonrestrictive polygyny which prevails in non-Muslim oriented societies.

With the high value placed upon procreation along with the stress on patriarchy, offspring are considered to be the property of the male line (McCall, 1974: 280-284). Accordingly, if a divorce should occur—relatively easy to obtain by the male, but usually much more complicated and difficult for a female to obtain—the child becomes the responsibility of the husband's family. There is a modification of this provided by the *Shari'a*

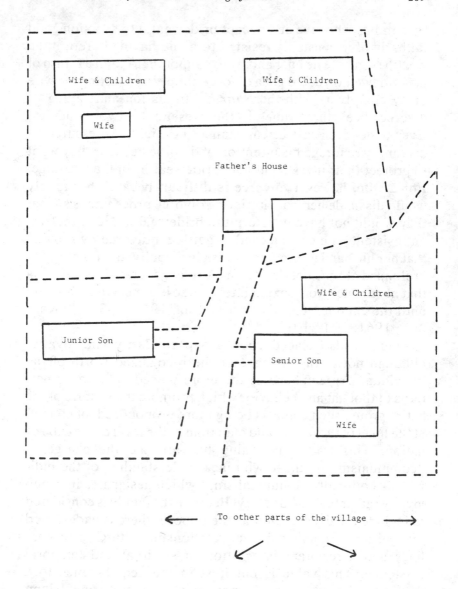

Figure 13.3: Patrilocality

(the comprehensive code of proper conduct for Muslims) whereby the child of divorced parents can be cared for by the mother until the age of nine—with the financial support of the father—after which the child becomes the sole concern of the father (Schacht, 1964: 161-174). Because marriage is arranged by families who give and accept bridewealth to sanction good faith, divorce is usually resisted to avoid having to return the wealth or gifts. The husband, who cannot then claim a return of his bridewealth, could get a divorce simply by evicting the wife or by complying with the *Shari'a* stipulation and saying "I divorce thee" three times in the presence of two witnesses. Even under such easy circumstances he might be pressured by his family to forego his intention of divorce because they want to protect their investment (the bridewealth) in the marriage. For a wife, however, divorce is difficult because her family would dissuade her from initiating divorce proceedings so that they would not have to return the bridewealth. Nevertheless, an insistent wife can succeed in getting a divorce by proving that her husband is impotent, or is chronically ill, or is guilty of prolonged absence or desertion. A final general observation is that abstinence from sexual intercourse is expected of mothers until the child is weaned (Trimingham, 1959: 163-178; Kadduri, 1961: 304-310).

Value is also placed upon group solidarity and loyalty, although not at the expense of the recognized worth of the individual. An emphasis is therefore placed upon those patterns of thought and behavior which promote the welfare of the entire group; such empasis being more pronounced, of course, at the level of the family and clan than at the level of the tribe or nation. This traditional value has aroused the charge of "communism" by those who lack understanding of the indigenous notion of "communalism," which designates in-group loyalty rather than an ideology. Because the family is considered to include the dead as well as the unborn, there is widespread recognition of man's spiritual relationship with God or godlings and a resultant integration of spiritual and temporal existence. This value is manifest in the acquiescence to a theocratic imprint upon human existence, featuring Islam, Cyclism, and Animism in varying degrees of importance throughout Terramedia.

THE THEOCRACY OF ISLAM

The term "theocracy" refers to prescriptions and proscriptions which derive from religious or spiritual force, and are concerned not only with the immediately relevant matter of religious behavior, but with temporal and secular affairs as well.

The center of Islamic influence is in the northern sector of Terramedia, especially in the proximity of the holy cities of Mecca and Medina in Saudi Arabia. It is to be noted, however, that prior to the emergence of Islam in 622 A.D., other religions — particularly Judaism and Christianity — had begun in the same general area, and people there had also supported a variety of religious beliefs which included animism (Yinger, 1957: 51-60). Some of these religions have remained fairly prominent, such as Christianity in Ethiopia and Lebanon, and Judaism in Israel. Nonetheless, it is Islam, and the resulting comprehensive *Shari'a*, which is the most influential determinant of values and human thought and conduct today. This influence, noticeable as far back as the seventh century in northern Terramedia, has even spread southward into West, Central, and East Africa.

Islam means "Submission" or "Act of Submitting" (i.e., to God), and is related to the verb *aslama,* "to submit." (Watt, 1962; Anderson, 1959). A *Muslim* is one who submits (to God), a believer and practitioner of the faith of Islam. As a religion, Islam consists of a set of beliefs and a number of expected behaviors. In the holy book, the *Qur'an,* this is made clear:

> In the name of Allah, the Compassionate, the Merciful. . . . Allah has promised those who have faith and do good works forgiveness and a rich reward. As for those who disbelieve and deny our revelations, they shall become the heirs of hell.

The Belief System of Islam

Among the very important religious beliefs in Islam are the following: (1) The *Oneness of God.* Sura IV, Verse 51, of the Qu'ran reads, "Truly God forgiveth not the giving of partners to Him; other than this will He forgive to whom He pleases, but whosoever gives a partner to God has conceived a monstrous sin." (2) The *Omnipotence of God.* While an Arabic proverb makes clear that "the beginning of wisdom is the fear of God," the following declaration is made in Sura II, Verse 256 of the Qu'ran: "There is no God but He, the Living, the Self-subsistent. Neither slumber nor sleep seize Him. To Him belongs whatsoever is in the Heavens and in the Earth. . . . He knows what is present with men and what shall befall them, and they comprehend nothing of His knowledge save what He wills them to understand." (3) *Human Existence after death,* implicit in the notion of the *Last Judgement.* Sura XXVIII, verse 88 reads: "Call not on any other God but Allah; there is no other God but He. Everything shall perish except His being. To Him belongs the rule and to Him shall you be brought back for judgement." (4) The *Qu'ran is the Word of God,* Who is merciful and compassionate and furnished the revelations for man's salvation. Thus, as a prefix to every chapter of the Qu'ran, but one, is the acknowledgment, *bismi'llah ir-rahman ir-rahim* ("In the Name of God, the Compassionate One, the Merciful"). (5) *Muhammad was the final Prophet.* It is believed that God's message was given to Abraham, but the people fell into idolatry; then it was given to Moses as the Pentateuch, but the Hebrews thought they were a chosen people, even after David had been given the Psalms; God's message was then given to Jesus as the Gospels, but the Christians deified Jesus; finally, God gave his message to Muhammad, as the Qu'ran or Recitation. (6) Therefore, *Islam is a world religion,* not intended merely for the Arabs, but for all mankind.

Expected Behavior in Islam

Islamic belief and practice are centered around the *'Ibadat* (acts of devotion) and the *Shari'a* (the law). The acts of devotion are mandatory for membership in the *umma* (body of believers) who belong to a "world" distinct from that to which infidels and non-believers belong. An acceptance of Muhammad as the last and most accurate carrier of the intentions of the one God, Allah, forms the basic bond of unity among members of the *umma.* Of course, with room within the *umma* for all and sundry — subject to their compliance with the

Shari'a — it is permissible to encourage the conversion of non-believers by force, to tolerate, temporarily, their "wrong beliefs," or even to impose such direct pressure as poll taxes or other forms of discrimination against nonbelievers. Indeed, at times the *jihad* (holy war) has been used as a means of extending the membership of the *umma.*

The *'Ibadat* (acts of devotion) stipulates the following categories of actions, commonly referred to as the "pillars of Islam" because they are basic to being a Muslim (a believer of Islam):

1. *Shahada,* or Creed, the fundamental profession of a Muslim's faith. This is a simple statement containing the core elements of the belief system: *la ilaha illa'llah muhammadun rasulu'llah* ("there is but one God; Muhammad is the Apostle of God").
2. *Salah,* or ritual prayers to be spoken five times daily — at sunrise, noon, mid-afternoon, sunset, and at night before retiring. They must be recited with pure intention and cleansed body while facing the holy city of Mecca, Saudi Arabia.
3. Giving of Alms (*zakat*) in support of the poor and needy, in the amount of one-fortieth of one's income. *Sadaqat* (free-will offerings above the minimum) is laudable as extra good works.
4. *Sawm* or fasting, consisting of complete abstinence from food and drink during the hours of daylight, is required during *Ramadan* (the ninth month of the lunar year).
5. Pilgrimage (*hajj*), entailing a visit to, and participation in the rituals, at the *Kaaba* (shrine in Mecca) must be made at least once in one's lifetime, if health and financial resources permit.

The *Jihad* or "holy war," is thought by some to be a sixth pillar. In support of this viewpoint, reference is made to *Sura* II, verses 186 ff. of the Qu'ran: "Fight in the way of God against those who fight against you, but do not commit aggression. . . . Slay them wheresoever you find them, and expel them from whence they have expelled you. . . . Fight against them until sedition is no more and allegiance is rendered to God alone."

The *Shari'a* is Muslim law in general, and prescribes the practical dimensions of Islam. It is concerned not only with the nature of man's relationship with God, but also with marriage and family life, contractual obligations, property and inheritance, penal law, judicial organization and procedure, and international relations. Through the centuries, Islam has so effectively diffused the theorcracy of the Shari'a that one can easily agree with Professor Anderson's observation (1959: 3) that "to the Muslim there is indeed an ethical quality in every action, characterized by *qubh (ugliness, unsuitability) on the one hand, or husn* (beauty, suitability) on the other. . . . Thus all human actions are subsumed under five categories": those which are required by God and are thus obligatory upon all believers; recommended actions; legally and morally indifferent actions; those which are disapproved but not forbidden; and actions prohibited by God.

The *Shari'a* is Muslim law in general, and prescribes the practical dimensions of Islam. It is concerned not only with the nature of man's relationship with God, but also with marriage and family life, contractual obligations, property and inheritance, penal law, judicial organization and procedure, and international relations. Through the centuries, Islam has so effectively diffused the theocracy of the Shari'a that one can easily agree with Professor Anderson's observation (1959: 3) that "to thc Muslim there is indeed an ethical quality in every action, characterized by *qubh* (ugliness, unsuitability) on the one hand, or *husn* (beauty, suitability) on the other. . . . Thus all human actions are subsumed under five categories": those which are required by God and are thus obligatory upon all believers; recommended actions; legally and morally indifferent actions; those which are disapproved but not forbidden; and actions prohibited by God.

The Shari'a is rather comprehensive and complex, and its interpretation has been the task of scholars and jurists through the centuries. Because of inherent contradications in the basic sources, there emerged four prominent "schools of law" — *Hanafi, Maliki, Shafii,* and *Hanbali* — which have differed in their interpretations of specific prescriptions and proscriptions. It suffices to note, however, that through the Shari'a all possible questions which might face man in his spiritual and temporal affairs are provided for or answered.

The Shari'a is based on several sources, the primary one being the Qu'ran. Other sources are the *hadith* or anecdotes about the personal behavior and utterances of Muhammad; the *qiyas* or conclusions drawn from analogical reasoning; and the *ijma* or consensus derived from the discussions of Islamic scholars (the *'ulema*).

One might, in conclusion, summarize the major values or notions about values in Muslim societies into the following propositions:

1. God is best, superior in all respects, and ultimately determines everything except man's sinfulness.

2. The human soul is superior to the body, hence matters of the soul are superior to material or temporal affairs.

3. Islam as a religion is the guide and criterion for judging behavior.

4. The community in which individuals or groups hold membership is all-important in the temporal sphere of human activity. This can be divided, as it were, into the religious community of believers (*umma*); the blood community of the extended family or clan; and the political community which modern nationalism has evoked, such as *ujamaa* (from *ijma*— consensus) villages in Tanzania.

5. Tradition is a very important criterion for judging the worth of behavior and things in general. This, too, can be subdivided into actual Islamic tradition of the faith, and tribal or ethnic traditions. The latter can be perceived from such Arabic proverbs as (a) "Your grandfather's enemy will never be your friend." (b) "A jinn you know is better than a person you don't know." (c) "They took the camel to school, and now he wants fried eggs."

6. Change can be good, especially if it is developed without violating the Shari'a, and if it can be justified by analogical reasoning, the *hadith,* and by consensus of the learned (*ijma*).

7. A sense of guilt at wrong-doing, rather than shame alone, tends to guide human behavior at the individual level. Accordingly, the individual feels a sense of righteousness if he is a good Muslim and is law-abiding in the total sense of the word "law."

VALUES OF AFRICAN, NON-MUSLIM IMPERATIVES

Unlike northern Terramedia where the theocracy of Islam minimized the importance of nontheological values, southern Terramedia—especially Black Africa—has retained its evolving and additive value systems in prominence. These can be examined under the following major categories:

1. *Spiritual Force.* By observing natural phenomena, one comes to understand early in life that there are many forces which one is powerless to control. One is relatively powerless against hurricanes, floods, lightning, earthquakes, and other natural catastrophes. Even persistent and diligent research has yet to save man from his relative powerlessness in regard to aging, disease, and morbidity. The African, therefore, has always considered it rational to recognize the power invested in natural and social phenomena. Traditionally, he has maintained a profound appreciation of the immensity of the power of those spiritual forces which can *cause* or *end* hurricanes, which *cast* the lightning, *cause* people to be born and to die, and *strengthen* the spirits of warriors and soldiers in armies. Indeed, Spiritual Force, often personified as the High God or Gods, as godlings or tutelary spirits or other beings, ultimately is believed to determine all that happens. Causality is not accidental, but is intentional, particularly that causality which otherwise would not be readily explainable by simple inference or logical reasoning. Thus, no chance exists, for accidents can be explained—if one uses the proper explanatory methods—as results of intentions.

The High God, the major possessor of spiritual force, is tremendous and powerful. If He wills it, a child will be born, a person will die, drought will parch the earth, the people will have an abundant harvest, and so forth. God (*Chukwu* among the Igbo, *Olodumare* among the Yoruba, and *Ngewoh* among the Mende) is so powerful the He can do what He pleases. If He wants to kill you, He will do it, and you cannot stop Him. But perhaps you can placate Him by making a sacrificial offering to Him, to demonstrate that you duly appreciate His power and omnipotence. If your offering is satisfactory and is received by Him, the illness or calamity will be lifted from you. Knowing that God becomes provoked and that He possesses such power, you will regularly propitiate Him, worship Him, offering Him food and blood sacrifices and libations of palm wine, praising Him publicly and in a loud, clear voice—if you are at all intelligent. In this manner you can have greater peace of mind and, perhaps, avoid His wrath. Group antagonism (traditionalist versus Muslim), as well as the supremacy of God, is expressed in the following Yoruba verse (Beier and Gbadamosi 1959: 26):

> The Muslims are still lying.
> They say: "We are fasting for God every year."
> One day *Eshu* (High God's Inspector-General) went to them and said:
> "Why do you fast for God?
> Do you believe that God is dead?
> Or do you believe that He is ill?
> Or perhaps sad?
> *Oludumare* (High God) is never ill,
> And He can never be sad.
> We shall never hear of His death,
> Unless the liars lie."

Spiritual force is possessed not only by the High God, but is diffused, although it is never weakened by the process. Force is diffused to somewhat weaker spirits than the High God—to godlings who guard farmlands, dwellings, sources of water, sacred groves and hills; who are responsible for the fertility of women and livestock, and who are simply related to other lesser spirits. These godlings, like the High God, can bring devastation upon a group or an individual, and therefore must be "fed," praised, "housed" in a shrine, and in general kept in a nonaggressive attitude. Spiritual force is diffused also to certain human beings, such as blacksmiths who make objects of iron, to shrine priests who direct the worship of the gods, to healers, sorcerers, rain-makers and rain-stoppers, to magicians, diviners, members of animal societies, and to witches. As Father Placide Tempels has said (Bantu Philosophy, 1959: 59),

> Any simple skill . . . is shot through and through with this dynamic conception of beings. . . . Coppersmiths and blacksmiths think that they

will not be able to smelt the ore, thereby changing the nature of the material treated, unless they dutifully appeal to a higher force which can dominate the vital force of the "earth" which they claim thus to change into metal.

Spiritual force is diffused also to amulets and charms, which protect the wearer against persons and beings wishing to do him harm. In fact, almost anything can be invested with spiritual force. Perhaps more important is the fact that spiritual power is diffused directly to human beings in one peculiar manner: the human soul is of the same basic substance as the creative spirit (usually the High God), and this soul is said to "belong" to God. Consequently, when God wants a child to be born, He permits a man's sperm to fertilize a woman's ovum, to "bring the baby to life"; and when God wants His "soul" back, the person will die. The creative God's role in directly creating each new child is clearly illustrated by the Yoruba:

> *Obatala* (God) who turns blood into children:
> I have only one cloth to dye with blue indigo;
> I have only one headtie to die with red camwood,
> But I know that you keep twenty or thirty children for me,
> Whom I shall bear.

Spiritual force is power, spiritual power; it is neither good nor bad in itself. Indeed, spiritual power is so great that it transcends ordinary human value judgments. It does not matter whether God is good or evil; what counts is whether He has enough power to have His own way and do as He pleases. It is man's task to avoid the negative exercise of such power, not to make judgments about its essential goodness or evil (Bewkes et al., 1963, and Bellah, 1973).

2. *Ancestralism and Cyclism.* Ancestralism refers to the set of beliefs and behaviors characterized by the spiritualization of the dead ancestors and the worship of them by the living. It is normally accompanied by veneration of the elders and by gerontocracy (rule by elders) in democratic societies, or by belief that the King or Chief is the living representative of the ancestors in the monarchy (see Figure 13. 4). The First Men, or the founding fathers of the clan or tribe, received spiritual force from God(s). Although dead, they are spiritualized and

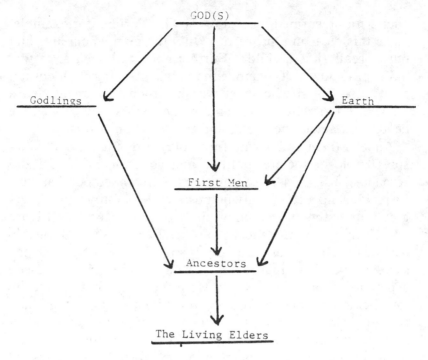

Figure 13.4: Gerontocracy

participate in Divine Force; they are even mythicized so that they sanction certain religious behavior of the living, or certain social practices currently in effect. Among the Malagasy, for example (Mannoni, 1964: 50, 60), "it is said that the dead are the sole and inexhaustible source of all good things: life, happiness, peace and, above all, fertility. . . . The word for 'child' appears frequently in the names of Malagasy tribes, and ultimately it is only the dead who are to the Malagasy what adults are to European children." There is a similar view in other parts of Africa where it is felt that one's ancestors have the ear of God.

Becoming an ancestor, as a rule, requires a bit more than merely dying. One must die in adulthood, must have had living offspring, and must have been buried "properly" in accordance with prescribed funeral rites. The Yoruba, for example, make this clear in a proverb: "Only the man whom his child buries really has a child." Furthermore, although ancestors have spirit-power, it is among their own offspring or blood-kin; so it is their kin who must worship them. There is also a recognition of categories among ancestors—the collective dead, the named ancestors, and the titled ancestors.

Ancestralism and divine force play a dominant and wide-spread role in societal politics and government (Ajayi and Ayandele, 1974: 34-35). Traditional African temporal authority resided most commonly in the extended family and village-group, or in the elected chieftaincy or monarchy (see Figure 13.5). In every instance, there was a close relationship between such temporal authority and divine sanction. In the system of divine kingship, for example, the king possessed supernatural sanctions which were inherited or acquired by "medicine" or magic. If the king himself did not possess supernatural sanctions, the kingship was either supernaturally endowed, or rule as such was by divine sanction. The king or chief symbolized the kingdom or chiefdom, and his physical well-being was linked closely with the "health" of the domain. The king was believed to *own* the domain, including the people in it, and like God he diffused some of his power by delegating authority to others—legislative authority to chiefs and sub-chiefs, judicial authority to chiefs and village heads, military authority to chiefs and specialist warriors, and religious authority to shrine priests. When the king manifested signs of illness, impotency or insanity, this would be construed as a weakening of his derived spiritual force, and he would normally be ritually executed by a group delegated to this task, so that a "fresh" king could be named and the health of the domain restored or maintained.

The ancestors possess spiritual power and can be appealed to by the living children because they are "closer" to God and, as spiritualized beings, they possess greater powers than do any of the living. Among those "children" closest to the ancestors are the elders, or the King or Chief, or both. The ancestors, furthermore, do not as a rule remain spiritualized in

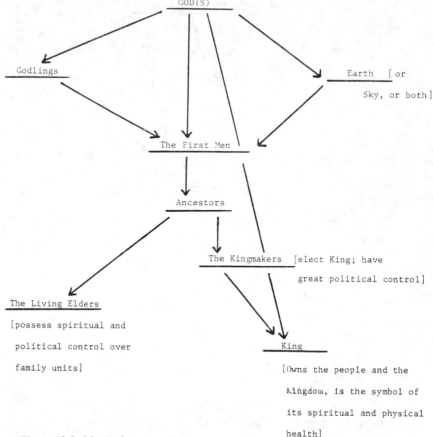

Figure 13.5: Monarchy

Heaven or some dim never-never land of the dead; they also are reincarnated as the notion of cyclism portrays (see Figure 13. 6).

Cyclism, or the sharing of spiritual forces, refers to the belief that the pattern of human existence is cyclic, or circular: one is born, dies, and is reborn. The inference is that (Abraham, 1962: 51) a human being is an "incapsulated spirit, and not an animated body. . . . Living men too were essentially spirit, even if encased in flesh for a time." Things which exist derive, in most instances, from the High God, Who shares His divine force with His creatures. Indeed, as has been argued by Mabona (1964: 158-162), the sacred character of all things

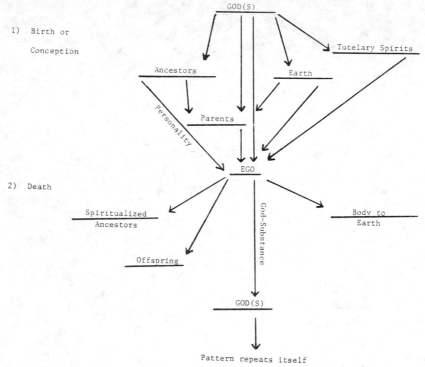

Figure 13.6: Cyclism

seemingly increases with the degree of dynamism or energy
which a thing manifests in its own order—that is, with the
degree of participation of the thing in vital or spiritual force.
The creatures involved in the cycle of human existence include the founders of one's clan or tribal group, or of the human
race; the founders of one's social group, or those ancestors who
migrated to the group's present location and established the
existing lineage; the ancestors in the order of time down to the
most recent dead of one's people; and one's own elders and
parents. From this line one derives his bodily features and
personality, which are in part those of a reincarnated ancestor.
It is not uncommon in many African villages to hear a small
child being addressed as "Grandmother" or "Father of my
Father's Mother." The created beings also commonly include
Earth, which is often spiritualized and personified as a god,
from whom one derives his actual flesh, and who aided one's

mother in conceiving—for it is in the actual earth that plants grow; earth sustains life, like a mother who feeds her children. Creatures also include godlings and tutelary spirits who sometimes transmit one's shadow or wraith (which among some peoples is believed to take the shape of a particular totemic animal), and who otherwise are responsible for one's general well-being. When the individual dies, the process is reversed and one's God-substance is taken back by God: his body is returned to the earth; unless the proper spiritual forces are asked for their help, one's shadow might roam about on earth as a ghost until it is properly sent—through appropriate rituals—to the spirit-world; and one's life is transmitted to one's children. The whole process, accordingly, consists of a vast cycle of birth and death and endless rebirth.

3. *Communalism.* The group is seen as more important than the individual; hence the value placed upon the community of residence or identity. The community is made up of families and clans, and it is from these groups that the individual gains his rights from, as well as his responsibility to, the community of membership. Through family membership, and by extension membership in a community, the individual acquires a reliable form of "social security" which negates the need to depend on outsiders. This "benefit" carries with it, however, a reciprocal responsibility for such involvement as the community well-being would demand. This spirit of communality has been formalized in Tanzania as *Ujamaa*—similar to the notion of "African socialism," "Arab socialism." and "Guided Democracy" being articulated in other parts of Terramedia. There is ample evidence of "westernized" young people who, in choosing to scorn traditional attitudes and expectations of communalism and behave as "other-directed" individualists, tragically fall to their doom (Chambers, 1969; Herskovits, 1962; Rustow, 1971).

Several important values derive from the stress upon the community. Dependence, for example, becomes a positive virtue because, in fact, one is dependent upon the community and upon the Gods. The Malagasy, for instance, feels a sense of inferiority only when the bonds of his dependence upon the dead ancestors are threatened; when his security is challenged he is not particularly concerned with technically solving the problem, but with avoiding any feeling that his ancestors might abandon him. The Malagasy wants to belong to his family and social group and to his dead ancestors; he wants to be able to depend upon them, because they can solve all problems (Mannoni, 1964: 40-49). Similarly, the Tswana proverb asserts that "one's parent is one's god." Arising from this dependence is respectful behavior toward elders as the only proper behavior for children and young people. The priority given to custom, furthermore, derives from this emphasis upon communalism and ancestralism. The group, after all, has maintained the group wisdom and enculturated its members with it—just as it was transmitted by the elders who, thereby, remain the source of wisdom and truth. The elders are the ones with the knowledge to teach about the ancestors, the High God, and other sources of wisdom and power. Therefore, it is commonly held—and this is widely true of human societies in general—that what was good enough for the forefathers has to be good enough for the descendants.

In traditional African societies there was a sharing of values. All the people of the community partook of the same value system, believed in the same things and beings, participated in the same destiny, and (by means of myths, stories, and proverbs) indicated their support of specific rituals and a common lifestyle. There tended to be relatively little privacy, and he who spent too much time alone was soon suspected of engaging in evil practices such as sorcery or witchcraft, or simply the plotting of evil against others. There was, therefore, an emphasis upon conformity, and because of the rather public nature of one's life, *shame* rather than *guilt* tended to be the major stimulus to proper, approved behavior on the individual level (Caplan, 1955; Ross and Wheeler, 1971). Let us take the example of a villager's failure to give a daily offering to the ancestors, especially where it is considered that person's duty to perform the ritual act. If he would fail simply out of forgetfulness, he would feel little more than temporary fear that the ancestors will be insulted or angry at him until he placates them with apologies and extra offerings; if he deliberately fails in his duty, he is in a state of defiance, and can become frightened should sudden illness or an accident befall him or his loved ones, in which case he might repent—usually he would, or the society would sooner or later learn the cause of its new troubles and "solve" the problem by him. If he is publicly shown to be remiss in his duties, he will tend to feel ashamed of himself, because people will gossip unfavorably about him, indicating that he is "different," that he does not "belong," or even that he is accursed. In a public society, of course, shame works well as a deterrant to immorality and lawbreaking; but in societies which emphasize privacy and individualism, as in westernized societies, it is perhaps more proper for the individual to be inculcated with a sense of guilt over any actual or potential wrong he might commit (Giddens, 1972: 89-140; Nisbet, 1965: 137-152).

4. *Rationality.* Arising from the foregoing and related to all of the values in varying degree is the stress upon rationality— the notion that a human being's reason is superior to his emotions, and that performance of human actions according to right reason is the best behavior (Davidson, 1952: 117-190). Accordingly, it is reasonable for a person to share in spiritual force, for example, beyond what he possesses as his normal human quota. God can do whatever He pleases, because He possesses infinite power, so the human being's liberty of action is restricted accordingly; but a person can, nevertheless, increase his dynamism. A rational man wants to be protected by the strongest spiritual forces so that he cannot, for example, be victimized by lesser spiritual forces. To acquire such protection, one must make payment in the form of sacrifices to the strongest spiritual forces, since one does not get a good thing for nothing. Once this powerful protection is acquired, one would be foolish to forsake it or change it. Dependence, consequently, is rationally sanctioned, because it is intelligent to recognize one's own limitations and to seek strength from God, the ancestors, and from one's social group. Similarly, he who deviates from the behavioral norms of the society is irrational, unless the society possesses certain attitudes which provide flexibility in the normally rigid patterns of custom. Furthermore, it is considered always rational to do those things which have proved proper and practical in the past. "My father

told me that" or "our forefathers did it this way" are sayings which commonly give the strongest support to custom and illustrate one's reasonableness within one's society.

The widespread emphasis in sub-Sahara Africa (southern Terramedia) upon gnomic literature, particularly proverbs, illustrates the high status accorded rationality in African scales of values. Proverbs themselves are intellectual forms, often structured with a high degree of skill at figurative language, and their content itself stresses the prudent, the reasonable, and the intelligent, while their tone ranges from the very serious to the ironic and satirical. A Fulla proverb asserts that "it is a wise father who does not acknowledge every misdeed of his child," whereas from the Mende comes the warning that "in a court of fowls a cockroach should expect no justice." "A man who brings home ant-infested wood," says the Igbo proverb, cautioning prudence, "should not be angry if he is visited by lizards." And, about reasonable limitations being put upon sharing—despite the proverb, "he who gives is he who gets"—"it is good to send wine to the monkeys, but who will return the pot?"

CONCLUSION

In northern Terramedia (the Middle East), one observes a high degree of consistency in values because of the widespread effects of Islam—the submission of mankind to God—which furnished a predetermined belief system and a set of approved behavior patterns (Heggoy, 1975: 149-160). In southern Terramedia (Black Africa), on the other hand, there is a much wider range of values and value systems reflective of the influence of localized and limited ancestralism. Nevertheless, one can draw some conclusions which are generally true for Terramedia as a whole. Spiritual force, throughout, is valued highly because of its inherent power; men accordingly want to share in it, to increase their own dynamism. Along with ancestralism, divinity as viewed by men results in a widespread sense of dependence, which is considered to be proper and thus good: dependence upon one's ancestors, subordination to one's living elders and to the community, and belief in the traditional wisdom of the group. The community itself is a source of good things, possessing power and transmitting power to the individual, and acting as the safeguard of custom. Such values are good in themselves, or were good in themselves, so long as conditions remain the same as when such behaviors and attitudes developed. But, fortunately or unfortunately, conditions have never remained the same given the reality and inevitability of socio-cultural change. Increasingly, the older traditional values have been challenged by systematic acculturation, whether planned for or unanticipated. Only time will tell how well Terramedia can absorb these continuing incursions upon its cherished values, and still keep intact its characteristic of changing, yet enduring, traditionalism (Coulson, 1964; Mbiti, 1969; Nelson, 1973).

REFERENCES

ABRAHAM, W. E. (1962) *The Mind of Africa.* Chicago: Univ. of Chicago Press.

AJAYI, J.F.A. and AYANDELE, E. A. (1974) "Emerging themes in religious history," *Journal of African Studies* (Spring).

ANDERSON, J.N.D. (1959) *Islamic Law in the Modern World.* New York: New York Univ. Press.

ARENSBERG, C. M. and KIMBALL, S. T. (1965) *Culture and Community.* New York: Harcourt, Brace & World.

ARMSTRONG, R. P. (1971) *The Affecting Presence.* Urbana: Univ. of Illinois Press.

BECKFORD, G. L. (1972) *Persistent Poverty.* New York: Oxford Univ. Press.

BEIER, U. and GBADAMOSI, B. (1959) *Yoruba Poetry.* Ibadan: Ministry of Education.

BELLAH, R. N. (1973) *Emile Durkheim on Morality and Society.* Chicago: Univ. of Chicago Press.

BEWKES, E. G. ET AL. (1963) *The Western Heritage of Faith and Reason.* New York: Harper & Row.

CAPLAN, G. (1955) *Emotional Problems of Early Childhood.* New York: Basic Books.

CHAMBERS, R. (1969) *Settlement Schemes in Tropical Africa.* New York: Praeger.

COULSON, N. J. (1964) *A History of Islamic Law.* Edinburgh: University Press.

DAVIDSON, R. F. (1952) *Philosophies Men Live By.* New York: Henry Holt.

FOSTER, G. M. (1962) *Traditional Cultures: and the Impact of Technological Change.* New York: Harper & Row.

GIDDENS, A. (1972) *Emile Durkheim: Selected Writings.* Cambridge, Mass.: Cambridge Univ. Press.

HEGGOY, A. A. (1975) "Arab education in colonial Algeria," *Journal of African Studies* (Summer).

HERSKOVITS, M. J. (1962) *The Human Factor in Changing Africa.* New York: Random House.

KHADDURI, M. (1961) *Islamic Jurisprudence.* Baltimore: Johns Hopkins Press.

MABONA, M. (1964) "African spirituality," *Presence Africaine,* 4.

MANNONI, O. (1964) *Prospero and Caliban.* New York: Praeger.

MBITI, J. S. (1969) *African Religions and Philosophy.* New York: Praeger.

McCALL, D. F. (1974) "Women in Gur myth and society," *Journal of African Studies* (Fall).

NELSON, C. (1973) *The Desert and the Sown.* Berkeley: University of California.

NISBET, R. A. (1965) *Emile Durkheim.* Englewood Cliffs, N.J.: Prentice-Hall.

PARSONS, T. (1967) *Sociological Theory and Modern Society.* New York: Free Press.

PRESTON, R. H. (1971) *Technology and Social Justice.* Valley Forge, Penn.: Judson Press.

ROSS, J. C. and WHEELER, R. H. (1971) *Black Belonging.* Westport, Conn.: Greenwood.

RUSTOW, D. A. (1971) *Middle Eastern Political Systems.* Englewood Cliffs, NJ.: Prentice-Hall.

SCHACHT, J. (1964) An Introduction to Islamic Law. London: Oxford Univ. Press.

SHELTON, A. J. (1971) *The Igbo-Igala Borderland.* Albany: State Univ. of New York Press.

TEMPELS, P. (1959) *Bantu Philosophy.* Paris: Collection Presence Africaine.

TRIMINGHAM, J. S. (1959) *Islam in West Africa.* London: Oxford Univ. Press.

WARWICK, D. P. and OSHERSON, S. (1973) *Comparative Research Methods.* Englewood Cliffs, N.J.: Prentice-Hall.

WATT, W. M. (1962) *Islamic Philosophy and Theology.* Edinburgh: Edinburgh Univ. Press.

YINGER, J. M. (1957) *Religion, Society and the Individual.* New York: Macmillan Company.

PART IV.
GENERAL PROBLEMS WITH DATA

Despite the growing preponderance of literature on intercultural interactions and relations, there is still need for scholars to advance new ways to collect and treat data. How to collect and analyze intercultural data continues to be a tantalizing question for most researchers. Although data acquisition can be complicated in any research venture, the intercultural communicationist faces problems compounded by culture.

In this section our authors advance innovative approaches and analysis to intercultural data. Tyler, Hall, and Taylor tackle the problem of general data acquisition in a comprehensive essay. Their review of the possible approaches to conducting intercultural research provides useful evaluations of the methods. Discussing strategies in data acquisition, they continue a line of thinking started in Part One by Stanley E. Jones' "Emic and Etic Considerations in Intercultural Communication." Tyler, Hall, and Taylor conclude that the solution might be an etic approach which is then developed into emic evaluations when applied. Significantly, their essay leads us into an extension of methodological frames beyond one way of thinking.

The second essay by Robert Shuter is a pioneer effort for intercultural communicationists. What Shuter does is to examine the use of still photography as a data collection method in intercultural research. Shuter's treatment of intercultural data has general implications for communication research. Since photographs freeze a moment in time while recording numerous interactions, they are useful for in-depth observational studies. They may be employed in an unobtrusive manner for greater reliability. Shuter warns that validity and reliability are better ensured through the recording of customary patterns of intercultural communications.

Njoku Awa's penetrating analysis of ethnocentric bias in development research demonstrates how intercultural researchers can misconstrue information from people in different cultures. Western values cannot be properly utilized in judging the values and life styles of other people. Awa would, of course, argue that the reverse is also true. Cultural considerations are necessary "in designing investigations which cross cultural frontiers."

Finally, Tzeng and Landis develop a multidimensional scaling methodology for crosscultural research in communications. With insight into miscommunication caused by cultural characteristics, they develop a far-reaching approach to obtain information regarding cultural roles, social environments and situations. Using the multidimensional scaling method, they found similarities between cultures that seemed to have little in common when casually considered. This section seeks to advance the intercultural field by providing substantive approaches to data collection and analysis.

14

INTERCULTURAL COMMUNICATION DATA ACQUISITION

V. LYNN TYLER
PEGGY HALL
JAMES S. TAYLOR

Brigham Young University

The development of methods for acquiring data on intercultural communication necessitates research that focuses on *inter-* (between) rather than cross- (one-way) cultural communication. "We must investigate people . . . communication situations . . . *between* members of different cultures." (Porter and Samovar, 1973: 7). This investigation should include:

1. Relevant and specific information which will enhance people's understanding of people—their challenges and needs—through an assessment of the role (both *how* and *why*) culture plays in influencing communicative behavior. As Hall (Denver Center for Research in Education; 1976-1977: 41) asserts: "Culture is communication,"—implying that messages depend on how people think, move, solve problems, organize systems, and interact. Or, to quote Porter and Samovar (1973: 4) again: "Intercultural communication occurs whenever meaning is attributed to behavior coming from another culture." One challenge, of course, comes in defining cultures as they interrelate—especially in communicative patterns.
2. A flexible theoretical framework into which investigations can be applied. Without such a theory or structure, the acquisition of data serves the limited purpose of curiosity.

AUTHOR'S NOTE: *The authors wish to acknowledge Richard Brislin of the Culture Learning Institute, Honolulu, Hawaii; David Hoopes of the Regional Council for International Education, University of Pittsburgh; Robert Kaplan, University of Southern California; Alfred Smith, University of Texas at Austin; John L. Sorenson, Brigham Young University; Edward C. Stewart, University of Southern California; and Gordon Whiting, Brigham Young University.*

3. A way of accounting for significant factors or components of on-going intercultural exchanges. This can be accomplished by extending applicable existing theories of communication and rhetoric (or providing more applicable frameworks) to specific intercultural situations.
4. A multiple-theory approach, which will not discard an intercultural communications system simply because it fails to solve *all* problems or to explain everything; instead, an approach is required to integrate a variety of theories and draw applicable conclusions from any or all of these.
5. The eventual development of diverse methods for teaching and improving intercultural communication skills, which will be accessible to all concerned.
6. An adequate means of validation for evaluation of any intercultural communicative encounter (Porter and Samovar, 1973: 6).

USE OF GENERALIZATION IN RESEARCH

In any research situation a certain degree of generalization must occur. As Triandis (1972: 5) points out: "If we are to study interpersonal attitudes, we must first learn much that is general about attitudes, regardless of culture, and how these attitudes are related to interpersonal interactions."

One aim of intercultural communication research should be to develop general laws which predict best, with the least risk of misunderstanding. In organizing data, it is certainly much easier to fit them around a "few dozen basic dimensions than around several hundred different opinions, attitudes, values, and behaviors" (Bass, 1971: 304).

On the other hand, researchers should heed Nida's (1977) caution that often differences within any individual culture are as great as the differences between cultures. Knowing when and how to apply these generalizations in gathering intercultural research data is a significant challenge for any intercultural communicator.

The purpose of this article is not to provide an in-depth analysis of each of the methods of data acquisition in intercultural communication; obviously, a proper study of each subject could require volumes. The statements given here are to provide intercultural communication researchers with an outline of possible approaches to conducting research, questionnaires, strategies in data acquisition, suggested methods of validation, and a look at future perspectives.

METHODS OF ACQUIRING DATA

Survey Method

Probably the most commonly known method of acquiring data on intercultural communication is the survey/interview method, such as is used in public opinion polls. Gallup (1976: 133) conducted a recent world-wide survey based on 10,000 interviews, which covered representative samples from "every significant segment of society." The interviews were conducted in the subjects' homes and in their particular language. The interview included more than 100 questions, which were very carefully translated to "mean the same" in every culture. Gallup officials insist that the range of error of the poll is relatively small, despite the seemingly small number of people who were questioned. This assertion may be valid if, as it is claimed, adequate sampling techniques were used. The question is how equivalent are the sampling techniques from culture to culture? What does "mean the same" mean? And how can we be sure we have "representative" samples from all cultures?

There appears to be little concern as to whether statistical groups represented "real groups" or just individuals accidently sharing certain social characteristics. Validation of individuals' answers requires much care. For instance, are they necessarily telling the truth, or are they giving responses which are more "proper and convenient," rather than factual? There is also the question of determining whether the interviewees interpreted the questions correctly.

Another major concern is the fact that the survey method only captures isolated individuals of the culture. As Beltran (1976: 121) notes: "It is these interactive relationships which may 'speak' for society, rather than the electronically accumulated independent and 'destructed' behaviors of its components."

Other problems encountered in the survey/interview approach are the high refusal rate of individuals to respond, difficult access to female or other respondents in some cultures, the weighted data to compensate for the low cooperation (which may cause the data to be fallacious), incomplete and out-dated census data, and interference from government ideology (Hwang, 1973: 1-2).

In addition to statistical problems, cultural problems also crop up in the interview. People in distinct cultures respond in different ways. Even in "objective tests" one person may answer by analogy or a story, another by a quantitative response, still another by a philosophical reply. The problem comes in drawing equivalencies among these replies.

The researcher should also realize that similar answers to the same questions do not necessarily reflect similar salience or significance for these questions in different countries. The responses may have been motivated by entirely different causes (Bogart, 1973: 102-103).

The interviewer must also guard against imposing his own frame of reference and thought patterns onto those he is interviewing (Fisher, 1973: 157). Successful interviewing cannot even be guaranteed by employing people from the same geographical area who can speak the same language. Particularly among illiterates, there is a great deal of suspicion of the more educated of their fellow countrymen. For these reasons the method requires particular care in its application.

Questionnaires

Perhaps the most successful of the various questionnaire types is the Q-Sort Questionnaire. This particular procedure uses interviews of persons from two different cultures, and from their responses a questionnaire is devised. The various culture characteristics derived from the interview are transformed into example statements, which illustrate the principle being researched. These statements are then given to representatives of the two cultures, who arrange them into three groups: whether they agree with the statement, whether they disagree with the statement, or whether they cannot decide. After the participants have arranged the statements into three groups, they are then asked to arrange the "agree" group into three more groups—strongly agree, moderately agree, slightly agree —and do the same with the "disagree" statements. Thus, they end up with seven different categories. The responses are then compared between the two cultures (Barney, 1974: 4). The Q-Sort Questionnaire has been found to be in some ways superior to most other approaches; however, inconsistencies between responses given in the interviews and those given in the questionnaire can occur. The division into seven categories also poses some problems, with subjects being unable to draw such fine distinctions.

Another type of questionnaire similar to the Q-Sort is the rank-order approach. In this approach the subjects arrange a given number of concepts in rank. This could create problems across cultures because of differing value systems. Not all cultures rank "1 as high and 10 as low." In the Iranian culture, for example, 10 often indicates top rank, and 1 indicates lowest rank. Another drawback to this approach is that only a limited number of concepts can be used, unless open-end designs are provided.

Subjects have also been asked to distribute 100 points among a given number of values. Results of this approach show that most of the values receive no points, while those which are considered "essential" receive several points and those considered "important" receive some points. This system seems to provide more valid results, but the instructions are often confusing to subjects, or many have difficulty ensuring that the total adds up to exactly 100 points (Triandis, 1972: 81).

The "Behavioral Item" asks subjects if they have ever engaged in certain kinds of behavior. An advantage to this approach is that it avoids the abstract use of attitudes which are particularly confusing to different-thinking or uneducated people. Subjects are also not required to differentiate between so many levels of agreement or disagreement (Chu, 1972: 309). (See references for much greater detail on these methods.)

Content Analysis

Beltran (1976: 121-122) suggests another method of data acquisition known as "content analysis." This approach attempts to "describe objectively, systematically, and quantitatively, the manifest content of communications." This includes the characteristics of the content, its form and rhetoric.

This type of analysis, however, because it concentrates on the purely descriptive nature of the content, often fails to account for the communication effects which are latent in the immediate and overt form of the message. Though this method provides a quantitative expression of the data, it doesn't give the feeling of having touched the deeper information structures.

Holsti (1968: 596-692) in his article on content analysis discusses the major trends in the development of this method, and surveys current research in which content analysis has been employed. In the latter part of his article he discusses the various problems of sampling, reliability, and validity. Other sources on content analysis include Sinclair and Coulthard's *Toward an Analysis of Discourse* (1975), and John R. Searle's *Speech Acts* (1970).

Experimental Method

True Experimental Methods test for cause-and-effect relationships by exposing at least one experimental group to one or more treatment conditions and comparing the results with one or more control groups not receiving the treatment. A Quasi-Experimental Method simply approximates the conditions of the true experiment in a setting that does not allow the control or manipulation of all relevant variables. The researcher using this method must obviously account for the compromises and limitations inherent in this method (Pace, 1975: 8). Cole and Scribner (1974) in their text *Culture and Thought*, illustrate the application and validation cautions required for the use of experimental methodology as this could be used in varied cultural settings. Those desiring to apply any of the many experimental approaches to communicate would do well to assess their recommendations.

Projective Techniques

Holtzman et al. (1975) use a series of projective techniques in their cross-cultural study of American and Mexican children. The Holtzman Inkblot Technique extended the Rorschach method to 45 match inkblots of various colors, forms, and shading nuances. Inquiry and objective scoring criteria were standardized, so that the results had greater reliability.

Holtzman used a longitudinal method along with a cross-sectional method in observing the same group of children over a period of six years. He studies three basic groups: the first group from grades 1 to 6, the second group from grades 4 to 9 (in conjunction with group one, grades 4 to 6), and the third group from grades 7 to 12 (in conjunction with group two, grades 7 to 9).

Other projective techniques included:

1. Human figure drawing.
2. Wechsler Intelligence Scale for Children (WISC), based on vocabulary and block design.
3. Time estimation—subjects estimate the duration of one minute without external cues.
4. Object-Sorting Test (OST)—subjects sort 60 items of various material, color, shape, size, and content into groups.
5. Conceptual Styles Test (CST)—subjects group two of three line-drawings together based according to analytical, relational, or inferential response.
6. Free Word-Association—subjects say the first word that comes to mind when they hear each stimulus word.

STRATEGIES IN DATA ACQUISITION

The above methods can be applied in any of a number of ways, depending on the focus and intent of the research project. Outlined below is a list of strategies which the researcher should consider before beginning research.

Emic-Etic Approaches

A general concern among intercultural and cross-cultural researchers has been whether to use an "emic" or "etic" approach. The *emic* approach generally takes into account what the people of that culture themselves value as meaningful and important, while the etic approach attempts to make generalizations across cultures that take into account all human behavior (Brislin, 1976a: 215). The emic approach is the one generally used in ethnographic analysis, with the specific culture as the basic unit of measurement. Problems with this kind of research are: (1) it does not allow for comparable research, and (2) it encourages bias in coding and observation. To combat that bias, Hwang (1973: 5-6) suggests that a team of investigators be used so that intercoder reliability can be used as a check. He also points out that researchers should not rely solely on public observation, but should study private communication behaviors as well. He also suggests the cautious use of audio and video tapes, films, and photographs for additional accuracy.

On the other hand, if one approaches research from an etic point-of-view, he runs the risk of missing important aspects of phenomena due to emphasis on generalizations.

The pseudo-etic approach is used quite extensively. This is really an emic approach developed in a Western culture and translated into other cultures. The fallacy of this approach is the assumed equivalency between Western cultural theories, upon which the instruments are based, and those of other cultures. Theories are based on cultural conditions, which obviously vary.

A possible solution to the emic-etic dilemma is to start with a somewhat universal construct which can then be developed into emic evaluations (Triandis, 1972: 40-41). Another possibility is to select specific domains or "themes" in several cultures, sample a variety of concepts within each domain, and discover the attributes that are appropriate to it in determining how people categorize experience with respect to that domain in different cultures (Triandis, 1972: 20).

Inductive and Deductive Approaches

Many researchers in intercultural communication utilize a deductive approach, where they attempt to prove a hypothesis, either valid or invalid, based on the data obtained. Some have used an inductive approach, where they observe the actions and reactions of their subjects to certain concepts or behaviors, and form conclusions based on these somewhat subjective data. Triandis (1972) and Fuglesang (1972) both provide several examples of these approaches.

Unobtrusive Measures

Webb et al. (1966) discusses unobtrusive measures methods in his research. Their approach is measuring results by observation rather than by the attitude/opinion approach; their assumption being that measuring conditions directly rather than measuring how people think conditions are is a more valid approach. These procedures are just beginning to be validated. Webb's text remains a good source for data-gathering, using this method.

Formal and Informal Channel

Smith (1973) notes distinctions between formal and informal channels and the various functions these serve in research situations. He points out that formal channels are generally used with larger groups with more general rules, while informal channels are used with smaller, more homogeneous groups having more specific rules. However, there is a "continuing switching back and forth among channels" which follows a standardized sequence. Informal channels are first used for exploration purposes, to diagnose a situation in determining what actions or products would be successful. Then this hypothesis is confirmed and legitimatized through the form channels of the system.

> Informal channels are used for exploration whereas the formal channels are used for validation and legitimatization. In these sequences the function of the formal channel is to reduce the alternatives, to reduce the variety of possible behavior. The formal channels serve to bring situations back to a standard, through some regularity. The function of the informal channel is to increase the variety. That is why they are used when the formal is too reducing, too restrictive. When the formal channels lead to a run-around, we return to informal channels to open things up again. [Smith, 1973: 4)]

Intercultural communications researchers should be aware of the various formal and informal channels in the areas in which they are conducting research.

Applied Communication

Fuglesang (1972: 11-12) advocates more of an applied communication methodology, which focuses on the researcher's awareness of the conceptual literacy, pictorial or visual, literacy, and authority concept of the culture he is working with. In order to achieve this awareness the researcher must be able to fully "integrate" himself into the internal communication system operating in that culture.

Fuglesang (1976: 11-12) points out the importance of defining and understanding the conceptual and logic patterns of both cultures, for without a proper understanding of these patterns people will miss entirely the meaning of the message. If the farmers, for example, have not been taught to understand the relative relationships between output of crops, input of fertilizers and foods, and area of plot, they could completely miss the message of "agricultural extension."

People may also have to be taught pictorial literacy (Fuglesang, 1972: 61-62). There is an assumption that pictures or other visuals are some kind of intercultural language which everyone understands, but this assumption is fallacious. People have to learn to read pictures, just as they have to learn to read pages in a book. This fact is often overlooked, since education in reading pictures is an informal process, which goes on autonomously in most developed societies. This process must be learned, however, in societies where there are no or very few pictures.

The concept of authority of power/influence is another area of importance in intercultural communication. In the modern industrial society, authority is delegated downwards in a hierarchical system. A person derives his authority from his position rather than from his personal characteristics. In the village community, or even in broad societies, authority may be derived more from the person himself rather than from the system (Fuglesang, 1972: 37-38). It is to the communicator's greatest advantage to establish rapport with the authority figure in the society or community. Having an understanding that authority may be derived from personality rather than position is vital to the communicator in establishing his contacts.

The intercultural communication researcher will also want to utilize the various sources of information in the society to their fullest extent. These may include education systems, adult-literacy program, agriculture and public health services, as well as traditional media forms, such as touring companies of traditional actors, the market women, local comedians, story-tellers and singers (Fuglesang, 1972: 40). Through these media opportunities the researcher and communicator will be better able to observe communicative interactions among individuals in an intercultural setting.

Study of the Relationship Between Language and Culture

A study of "the language" of a culture often results in the surfacing of significant revelations about the culture in which the language develops. Language also serves a key role in intercultural communication through the use of translations, interpretations, and intercultural writing (Tyler, 1972: 1-4).

Understanding the connotative (cultural setting) meanings of words is often more significant in communication than understanding their denotative (dictionary) meanings. For example, nutrition educators in many parts of Zambia were baffled by the people's refusal to eat cassava leaves, which are high in protein, until they realized the negative connotative meaning of cassava leaves being "poor man's food" (Fuglesang, 1972: 60).

Through studying both verbal and nonverbal language we can often discover how people of a culture organize experience. Word association experiments have been conducted for establishing similarities and norms developed in different linguistic communities. Controlled word associations have been used for studying cultural differences in the meanings of words. (Szalay and Fisher, n.d.). Osgood's (1964) *semantic differential* is one of the most widely used instruments for the measurement of selective connotative meanings. Cross-cultural analyses of these differentials are performed to point up cultural similarities and differences in representative language groups (Triandis, 1972: 182-183).

Kaplan discusses the study of language convergencies and divergencies as language interactions and as interpreted cultural relationships. He argues that "there must take place over time some basic changes in cultural perceptions of which language is merely the reflection (Kaplan, 1976: 4). The emergence of a *lingua franca* (universal language) in the fields of science and technology has stimulated a new outlook on language: the possibility of certain uses of language being described as "acultural." Language, Kaplan (1976: 24) asserts, is in fact, the key to intercultural understanding. "An understanding of the role of language in human interactions may constitute a key to significantly new directions in foreign policy development."

SOURCES OF DATA

Secondary Sources

James Becker (1972) has compiled an excellent list of available reading for those interested in intercultural communication. Possible data and information can be obtained by simply studying a variety of significant literature of the culture, as well as secondary sources written by other observers. The following list includes those categories mentioned by Becker among others:

1. Psychological and/or sociological novels or stories by the "great minds" of a people (e.g., Shaw, Balzac, DeMaupassant, Thomas Mann, Cervantes). These are best read in the original if at all possible;
2. discussions/analyses of a culture by bicultural writers (e.g., Sania Hamady, *Temperament and Character of the Arabs,* 1960; Salvador de Madariaga, *The Genius of Spain; Englishmen, Frenchmen, Spaniards,* 1937);
3. documentary material drawn from direct communication with the people and selected by persons with behavior science training (e.g., Oscar Lewis, *Children of Sanchez,* 1961; Jurgen Neven-du-Mont, *After Hitler: A Report on Today's West Germans,* 1970).
4. personal experiences/observations by discerning foreigners who have had long residence in a country (e.g., James Michener, *Iberia: Spanish Travels and Reflections,* 1968);
5. organized/analytical views by other trained and discerning observers (e.g., Paul Crane, *Korean Patterns,* 1967);

6. surveys of historical development and/or contemporary products of a culture (e.g., Gilbert Freyre, *The Masters and the Slaves* (Brazil, 1964). [Becker, 1972].

Tertiary Sources

The following anthologies, handbooks, documentary sources, and bibliographies can be of tremendous help to intercultural communication researchers. We suggest just a few:

1. Documentary materials from governmental training programs (e.g., Kohls' work on cross-cultural studies—International Training Assessment Program on "Cross-Cultural Interviewing: The Importance of Societal Differences"—put out by the American University Development Education and Training Research Institute; CRE research reports on Improving Cross-Cultural Training and Measurement of Cross-Cultural Learning, 1973);
2. handbooks on anthropology, sociology, psychology, cross-cultural psychology, communication, cross-cultural communication (available in any large library);
3. journals on cross-cultural research (e.g., *Journal of Cross-Cultural Psychology: The Bridge*);
4. bibliographical references (e.g., Bibliography on *International and Intercultural Communication*; Seelye and Tyler, *Intercultural Communicator Resources,* 1977);
5. Experiential Learning Aids and Culturgrams, covering 57 areas of the world (available at the Language and Intercultural Research Center Brigham Young University).

Use of Computer Files

Naroll et al. (1976) published a manual on *Worldwide Theory Testing* which delineates the necessary procedures for a rigorous culture study through use of the Human Relations Area Files [HRAF] Probability Sample. It is suggested that through use of the HRAF files, "you can do a more rigorous study more cheaply and easily than otherwise." The Sample has two shortcomings: (1) it comprises only 60 societies, so for some study purposes it is too small; and (2) for studies of traits that are rarely reported, an individually tailored sample may be needed—a sample of societies with reports on those traits. However, if a person does decide to use another sample, he can still follow the procedures offered in the manual for a pilot study or a tentative study. A rigorous study would take approximately 10 to 20 more hours of work per society. He would have to supply his own data quality control codes, unit focus codes, regional codes, bibliographic quality codes, and diffusion alignments (all of these codes are explained in the manual). In addition, he would have to supply the HRAF researchers with a list of societal names for the "deviant case search printout."

The second part of the manual provides instructions on how to formulate testable theories and measure theoretical variables from ethnographic materials. Part III describes how to analyze the data and interpret the results of the study. The manual also provides appendixes, supplying special technical data and coded data for more than 1,100 ethnographic sources.

The manual describes the various levels of rigor for conducting a rigorous study. These include background information sections, pilot study sections for trying out concepts cross-culturally to see if they work, tentative study sections which serve as intermediates between pilot and rigorous studies (they take approximately twice as long as pilot studies but substantiate reliability of testing instruments), and the rigorous study section which should take about two to three years, working half-time. There is also a section marked special solutions to special problems. This section provides information of how one might use other people's measures. This would save one the time of having to work out a good measure that someone else has already worked out for a particular variable (Naroll, 1976: 1-4).

Naroll's text is an excellent source for cross-cultural research. However, very little has yet been done in intercultural communication. One system being developed is the Intercultural Communication Data Bank (ICDB). This is a data-gathering application system which is based on intercultural survey questionnaires from many selected countries. The ICDB is now in the pilot stage of development, but anticipates the eventual full computerization of unlimited application (Brigham Young University Language and Intercultural Research Center).

METHODS OF VALIDATION

Once the intercultural data have been obtained, there must be some means of validation for the data to carry any significance. As was mentioned, one of the major criticisms of many of the methods was the lack of interrelationship validation. It should be noted that validation of information in the field of intercultural communication research is extremely difficult because of the many variables involved. Problems of this sort will be discussed further, after reviewing some ways of validating acquired data.

Verifying Informant Information

In verifying informant information one can cross-check for accuracy with other reliable informants. The wider the sample, the more reliable the information. The internal self-consistency of replies can also be checked. This can be done by simply restating the question or response in a different form. The informant can also be asked to give a retrospective account, often correcting his own misinformation by reflectively restating what he has already said or written (Fisher, 1973: 157).

Verifying Questionnaires

The administration of several locally developed (with native help) questionnaires, as opposed to just one to culturally diverse groups, can often bring more reliable results (Triandis, 1972: 82). It is important to establish equivalency in test conditions and experimenters. Where this is not possible, it is then best to vary both the conditions of administration and the type of experimenter in a systematic fashion in order to determine the effects of these shifts in conditions on the observed results (Triandis, 1972: 54).

In validating underlying themes and values in a culture, check for frequency. "If the same theme appears in different tasks, under different instructions, or in response to different stimuli, it often is more important than if it does not" (Triandis, p. 82)

In devising a questionnaire, it is essential that questions be worded simply and clearly, usually avoiding politically sensitive areas, providing for open-ended and short-answer responses, along with culturally appropriate restricted-choice responses. These responses can then be compared and checked with other culturally aware people for validity. Responses on questionnaires should usually be cross-validated with responses given in private interviews. The more sophisticated methods of validation are reviewed in extensive detail in the various handbook sources and in Triandis', *Analysis of Subjective Culture* (1972).

PROBLEMS IN VERIFICATION

Translation Problems

In many cross-cultural studies, validation is often lost due to ineffective or inaccurate translation. Unfortunately, many translations are what might be called "dictionary translations," where words are translated from a dictionary; however, the translations themselves do not have the correct meaning for the persons for whom the text was intended (Sechrest, 1972: 44).

The reliability and validity testing of an instrument is often lost when it is translated and adapted for a foreign culture, because it is often impossible to fully translate certain concepts into another language (Hwang, 1973: 3-4).[1]

Non-Quantitative Measures

Many research methods lack validity because many researchers today are using nonquantitative techniques of message analysis or are trying out semi-quantitative procedures (Beltran, 1976: 128).

Environmental Influences

The fact that the same environmental unit provides different inputs to different persons, or even different inputs to the *same* person if his behavior changes, causes problems in validating data. Also, human behavior is affected by many variables. It is practically impossible to isolate any one of these for research purposes. Rather, what is required is a flexible consolidation of techniques (Hall, 1977: 100).

Pointing out these problems in no way implies that validation in intercultural communication research is impossible. These problems have been given as cautions which researchers should be aware of and try to avoid in their work.

IMPLICATIONS FOR FURTHER RESEARCH

What does all this lead to? As was mentioned earlier, intercultural communication research must focus within a specific framework. There must be an effective systematic framework which will guide the acquisition and categorization of the data as well as its validation. Hall (1977: 13) points out the necessity of models in communication research, for the purpose of the model is to enable the user to do a better job in handling the enormous complexity of life. One may well ask, however, what is a model? Models serve different functions in varying circumstances. They are purposeful abstractions of systems—whether it be a language system, a mathematical system, and cultural system, whatever—and thus provide a means of forming rules and generalizations about that system. As noted before, research must include a certain amount of generalization; this we do through the use of models. "Without a model which can account for the broad features of the social and economic system and the factors which govern it, such norms, sanctions, roles, hierarchies, resources, and technologies, a theory of communication is meaningless" (Beltran, 1976: 118).

Application of Models

In intercultural communication anthropologists, sociologists, psychologists, and some linguists have attempted to devise culture models in order to define certain general characteristics about culture (see Hall 1977; Poyatos, 1976). The problem in the past, however, is that researchers have studied only those things people could or would talk to them about and failed to capture the "culture patterns that make life meaningful and really differentiate one group from another" (Hall,

1977: 14). Hall likens this to a linguistic model, consisting of strictly vocabulary but lacking the syntactic or phonemic rules which define the relationships between the different elements of the vocabulary. A model must not only enumerate the various parts of the system, but also show applicable relationships and operations among the parts. Such a comprehensive model for intercultural communication has yet to be developed.

The Language and Intercultural Research Center at Brigham Young University has been devising several preliminary models, forerunners to more comprehensive ones. These include the following:

1. *Unique Encounters*, which map a people of a culture by answering 85 questions under the following categories: (1) people classification, (2) people description, (3) human interaction and activity, (4) values, attitudes, and beliefs, (5) cultural arts and leisure, and (6) communication.
2. *PASTEL* (Patterns of Style, Thoughts, Emotions, and Living), which seek to uncover mis-cues (miscommunications)—which are offensive and missed-cues (noncommunications)—which are unclear, ambiguous, or meaningless. This is done through an analysis of verbal, paraverbal, nonverbal, paranormal and other message modifiers.
3. *ICCI* (Intercultural Communicative Indicators) which propose culture-specific relationships between various communicative indicators. By inserting intercultural communication data into this model, the communicator eventually will be able to determine where communication stops and why.

Synthesis of Models

A major criticism of intercultural communication research is that thus far there has been no—or, at best, very little—synthesis of models and methodologies. Anthropologists, psychologists, linguists, and so on, all conduct research according to their own methodologies, but this makes any attempt to draw interrelated conclusions extremely difficult, if not impossible. What is needed is more integration and interaction among intercultural communication researchers and the various methodologies as outlined in this article. As yet there is no such comprehensive methodology.[2] Intercultural applications have yet to be made. Only recently have scientists and researchers been coming together for integrative study. The "State of the Art" report of the Society for Intercultural Education, Training, and Research (forthcoming) is such an attempt to integrate these several disciplines (see also the forthcoming *Handbook of Cross-Cultural Psychology*, 1978).[3] The interdisciplinary field of Intercultural Communication is only now beginning to gain recognition in the eyes of those who should be most concerned. Perhaps the greatest enemy of intercultural understanding is its own illusion that communication is taking place between cultures, when in actuality what we have is miscommunication. Verification is essential when miscommunication has taken place. The task is to determine when it is taking place, and to help make the necessary adjustments.

CONCLUSION

The intent of this article has been to outline various methods, strategies, and source materials being used in intercultural communication data acquisition. Integration among the different disciplines and methodologies still is practically nonexistent.

As Edward De Bono (1976: 15) states: "Most people are aware of only one deliberate way of using the mind, and that way is the vertical way which includes logical thinking. . . . There is, however, a different way of using the mind. You cannot dig a hole in a different place by digging the same hole deeper. Vertical thinking digs the same hole deeper; lateral thinking is concerned with digging a hole in another place."

Researchers are so caught up with their own vertical ways of thinking and methodologies that they fail to recognize the possibilities of integrating several methodologies into one. This is the purpose of the ICCI (Intercultural Communicative Indicators) Model—to incorporate the methodologies of language, culture, interaction, and communication research into one. But, as Edward Stewart (1974) comments: "In all developing areas of learning, new or renovated ideas and methods are exciting and unsettling at the same time. They flourish with promise and uncertainty simultaneously."

NOTES

1. For a more extensive discussion of these problems, see Tyler (1977) and Brislin (1976b).

2. We suggest the reader see Hildebrand and Laing's *Prediction Analysis of Cross Classifications,* which seems to suggest a step in this direction of a more comprehensive synthesis of methodologies in research.

3. Harry Triandis is senior editor, along with six section editors: William Lambert, Walter Lonner, Alastair Heron, Richard Brislin, John Berry, and Juris Draguns. The *Handbook* is scheduled to appear in five volumes, and will be published in 1978 by Allyn & Bacon.

REFERENCES

BARNETT, G. A. (1974) "Social systems homophily as a function of communication." Paper presented at the Intercultural Division of the International Communication Association Convention, New Orleans, April.

BARNEY, R. D. and SMITH, C. N. (1974) "A Q-sort comparison of Mexican and American values." Paper presented at the International-Intercultural Division of the Speech Communication Association at the Annual Convention in Chicago, Ill., December.

BASS, B. M. (1971) "The American advisor abroad." *Journal of Applied Behavior Science,* 7: 285-308.

BECKER, J. M. (1972) "World studies perspectives." Unpublished manuscript from the World Studies Program, Social Studies Development Center, Indiana University, August.

BELTRAN, L. R. (1976) "Alien premises, objects, and methods in Latin American communication research." *Communication Research,* (April) 3: 107-134.

BERRIEN, K. F. (n.d.) "A super-ego for cross-cultural research," *Intercultural Communication: A Reader* in L. Samovar and R. Porter (eds.), Belmont, Cal.: Wadsworth.

BOGART, L. (1973) "Is there a world public opinion?" in M. Prosser (ed.) *Intercommunication Among Nations and Peoples.* New York: Harper & Row.

BRISLIN, R. W. (1976a) "Comparative research methodology: cross-cultural studies." *International Journal of Psychology,* II, 3: 215-229.

———(1976b) *Translation: Applications and Research.* New York: John Wiley/Halsted. (Copies of this paper are available from: The East-West Center, 1777 East-West Road, Honolulu, Hawaii 96822.)

——— and CHARLES, J. (1977) "Research on cross-cultural interaction." Paper presented at the International SIETAR Conference in Chicago.

——— LONNER, W. J. and THORNDIKE, R. M. (1973) *Cross-Cultural Research Methods.* New York: John Wiley.

Center for Research and Education [CRE] (1973) "Improving cross-cultural training." Denver: Center for Research and Education, 2010 17th Ave., 80206.

———(1973) "Measurement of cross-cultural learning." Denver: Center for Research and Education, 2010 E. 17th Ave., 80206.

CHU, G. C. (1972) "Problems of cross-cultural communication research," in L. A. Samovar and R. E. Porter (eds.), *Intercultural Communication: A Reader.* Belmont, Cal.: Wadsworth.

COLE, M. and SCRIBNER, S. (1974) *Culture and Thought: A Psychological Introduction.* New York: John Wiley.

CRANE, P. (1967) *Korean Patterns.* Seoul, Korea: Hollym.

CRAWFORD, R. W. (1965) "Cultural change and communications in Morocco." *Human Organization,* 24 (Spring): 73-77.

De BONO, E. (1976) *New Think: The Use of Latest Thinking in the Generation of New Ideas.* New York: Avon.
de MADARIAGA, S. (1937) *The Genius of Spain; Englishmen, Frenchmen, Spaniards.* London: Oxford University Press.
Denver Center for Research in Education (1976-1977) "Reviews: Beyond culture, the hidden dimension, the silent language." Bridge, (Winter): 41-42.
ETZIONI, A. (1977) "Public affairs." *Human Behavior* (March): 10.
FISHER, H. (1973) "Interviewing cross-culturally." *Intercommunication Among Nations and Peoples* in M. H. Prosser (ed.), New York: Harper & Row.
FISHMAN, J. (1967) "Review of J. Hertzler: A sociology of language." *Language,* 43: 586-604.
FREYRE, G. (1964) *The Masters and the Slaves.* (S. Putnam, trans.) Abridged from the 2nd English language edition (rev.). New York: Knopf.
FUGLESANG, A. (1972) *Applied Communication in Developing Countries: Ideas and Observations.* Uppsala, Sweden: Borgstroms Trycker, AB, Motala.
GALLUP, G. H. (1976) "What mankind thinks about itself." *Reader's Digest* (October): 132-136.
HALL, E. T. (1977) *Beyond Culture.* Garden City, N.Y.: Anchor/Doubleday.
HAMADY, S. (1960) *Temperament and Character of the Arabs,* New York: Twayne Publishers.
HILDEBRAND, D. and LAING, J. (1977) *Prediction Analysis of Cross Classifications.* New York: Wiley Interscience.
HOLSTI, O. R. (1968) "Content analysis." *The Handbook of Social Psychology.* Addison-Wesley.
HOLTZMAN, W. H., DIAZ-GUERRERO, and SHAW, J. D. (1975) *Personality Development in Two Cultures.* Austin: Univ. of Texas Press.
HOOPES, D. S. (1973) "Problems in intercultural communications research and training." Paper presented at the annual Conference of the International Communication Association, Montreal, April.
HWANG, J. C. (1973) "Problems of intercultural communication research." Paper presented at the International Communication Conference, Montreal, April.
JAIN, N. C., PROSSER, M. H. and MILLER, M. H. (1974) *Intercultural Communication: Proceedings of the Speech Communication Association Summer Conference.* New York: Speech Communication Association.
Journal of Cross-Cultural Psychology (n.d.) The Bridge. Bellingham, Wash.: Center for Cross-Cultural Research, Department of Psychology, Western Washington State College.
KAPLAN, R. (1977) Interview with V. Lynn Tyler at Language and Intercultural Research Center, Brigham Young University, January.
_____ and BIRNBAUM, H. (1976) "Language: Bridge and barrier to cross-cultural understanding." (unpublished manuscript)
KOHLS, R. (n.d.) "Cross-cultural interviewing: The importance of societal differences." (unpublished manuscript).
LEWIS, O. (1961) *Children of Sanchez.* New York: Random House.
LONNER, W. J. (1978) "The search for psychological universals." *Handbook of Cross-Cultural Psychology,* in H. C. Triandis (ed.), Beverly Hills, Cal.: Sage Publications.
MAYERS, M. K., RICHARDS, L. C. and WEBBER, R. (1972) *Reshaping Evangelical Higher Education.* Grand Rapids, Mich.: Zondervan.
MICHENER, J. (1968) *Iberia: Spanish Travels.* New York: Random House.

NARROLL, R., MICHNIK, G. L. and NAROLL, F. (1976) *Worldwide Theory Testing.* New Haven, Conn.: Human Relations Area Files.
NEVEN-du-MONT, J. (1970) *After Hitler: A Report on Today's West Germans.* New York: Pantheon.
NIDA, E. (1977) Personal correspondence with V. Lynn Tyler, Language and Intercultural Research Center, Brigham Young University, January.
OSGOOD, C. E. (1964) *Semantic Differential.* Reprinted from *American Anthropologist,* 66, (Part 2, June).
PACE, W., PETERSON, B. and BOREN, R. (1975) *Communication Behavior and Experiments: A Scientific Approach.* Cal.: Wadsworth.
PEDERSEN, P., LONNER, W. and DRAGUNS, J. (1975) *Counseling Across Cultures.* Honolulu: Univ. Press of Hawaii.
PORTER, R. E. and SAMOVAR, L. A. (1976) *Intercultural Communication: A Reader.* (second edition) Cal.: Wadsworth.
_____(1973) *Readings in Intercultural Communication: Complete Volume III,* in D. S. Hoopes (ed.), The Intercultural Communications Network of the Regional Council for International Education.
POYATOS, F. (1976) "Analysis of a culture through its culturemes: theory and method." pp. 265-274 in A. Rapoport (ed.), *The Mutual Interaction of People and Their Built Environment,* The Hague: Mouton.
SEARLE, J. R. (1970) *Speech Acts.* London: Cambridge University Press.
SECHREST, L., FAY, T. L. and ZAIDI, S. M. H. (1972) "Problems of translation in cross-cultural research." *Journal of Cross-Cultural Psychology,* 3 (March): 41-56.
SEELYE, N. H. and TYLER, V. L. (1977) *Intercultural Communicator Resources.* Brigham Young University, Language and Intercultural Research Center; in conjunction with the Bilingual Education Department of the Illinois Office of Education.
SINCLAIR, J. M. and COULTHARD, R. M. (1975) *Toward an Analysis of Discourse.* London: Oxford University Press.
SMITH. A. G. (1973) "Communication in pluralistic systems." Paper presented at International Communication Association Annual Conference, Montreal, April.
Society for Intercultural Education |SIETAR| (n.d.) "State of the Art." series of reports in process. Washington, D.C.: Georgetown University.
STEWART, E. C. (1974) "Definition and process observation of intercultural communication," in N. C. Jain, M. H. Prosser, and M. H. Miller (eds.), *Intercultural Communication: Proceedings of Speech Communication Association Summer Conference X.* New York: Speech Communication Association.
SZALAY, L. B. and FISHER, G. H. (n.d.) *Communication Overseas.* Washington, D.C.: Foreign Service Institute, Department of State.
TRIANDIS, H. C. (1972) *The Analysis of Subjective Culture.* New York: Wiley/ Interscience.
TYLER, V. L. (1977) "Intercultural writing, translation, and interpretation." paper presented at the International SIETAR Conference in Chicago.
WEBB, E., CAMPBELL, D., SCHWARTZ, R. and SECHREST, L. (1966) *Unobtrusive Measures: Nonreaction Research in the Social Sciences.* Chicago: Rand McNally.
U.S. News and World Report (1977) "What people around the world say." (January 24): 66-67.

15

STILL PHOTOGRAPHY: AN APPROACH
TO INTERCULTURAL COMMUNICATION

ROBERT SHUTER

Marquette University

In 1859, Darwin demonstrated that still photography could be used to systematically explore nonverbal communication. Convinced that photos capture the "most evanescent and fleeting facial expressions," Darwin relied on photography to investigate emotional expression in human beings and animals (Darwin, 1859: 74). In addition to Darwin's early study, other researchers, notably Mead and Macgregor (1951), Gesell (1934), and Collier (1957), have utilized photography in examining human interaction. Except for these classic investigations, social scientists have made very limited use of still photography in conducting communication research. Intercultural communication could be profitably examined using still photography.

Essentially, still photographs have been employed as stimulus material in laboratory experiments on perception and nonverbal communication. Researchers have used facial photos, for example, to test whether the face is a source of information for such traits as age, intelligence, and emotional stability (Pittenger and Shaw, 1975; Pinter, 1918: 137; Gosciewski, 1975: 600). Similarly, to determine how individuals interpret body postures, experimenters have had subjects rate postural photographs (Mehrabian, 1967: 248). In these types of studies, the subjects' responses serve as research data: the photos are merely a tool to elicit information from the individuals being examined.

As stimulus material, a photograph is most effective; however, it can be used in many different ways by communication researchers. These multiple uses become apparent after the investigator realizes that photos often contain a great deal of information that can be systematically analyzed and measured. This wealth of communication data is frequently unseen by the untrained observer; nevertheless, it can be scientifically evaluated once a researcher learns to read the language of still photographs.[1]

PHOTO LANGUAGE: ANALYZING VISUAL COMMUNICATION DATA

In an extensive study of photography, Byers (1964: 11), a noted behavioral photographer, concluded that most individuals view "still photography as a tool to illustrate concrete objects or convey abstract feelings rather than a subject for close and critical attention." With this orientation, it is not surprising that observers frequently do not notice significant communication data in a photo, data that can be perceived if the observer carefully scrutinizes the recorded artifacts and people. For example, consider what a person may discover about interaction by examining a wide-angle photograph of an international airport.

At first glance, the observer would probably notice the animate and inanimate objects in the picture: people, food, counters, chairs, and video units. On closer examination, sociometric data can be gleaned from the photograph.[2] For example, individuals may be seated with members of the same race; similarly, conversants may have segregated themselves on the basis of gender. Age clustering would also become apparent: are middle-aged individuals sitting with young people; with whom are the elderly seated? After many people in the photo are identified, accomplished by showing the print to knowledgeable informants, patterns should become visible, particularly those based on cultural membership.

Certainly, conclusive sociometric findings cannot be derived from one photograph. To gather more definitive data, an analysis must be made of airport photos taken at the same time of day over a period of at least a week. With this type of research design, discussed in detail later in the paper, the investigator can identify customary sociometric patterns.

In addition, the airport photograph most likely contains substantial information about nonverbal communication. An investigator interested in proxemics, for instance, can measure the distance at which the recorded communicators interacted.[3] After noting the proxemic patterns of numerous photographed dyads (certainly possible with many prints), the researcher can statistically correlate distance with the sex, race, and age of the interactants. In fact, it is argued in a following section that still photography, if used judiciously, can improve proxemic research.

Information about the interactants' kinesic behavior, notably posture, gesture, eye contact, and facial expression, may also be contained in the airport photograph. Using Birdwhistell's (1970: 147-153) system of kinesic analysis, a researcher, for example, can systematically examine the gesture and stance of photographed interactants. Basic eye contact patterns may also be identified in the still photograph (Mead and Byers, 1967). However, to accurately measure kinesic behavior, numerous closeup photos are needed. These can be secured through a microphotography study.

In processing additional communication data in the airport print, an observer can count the members in photographed groups, examine and categorize each group's network arrangement, and explore the impact of furniture placement on sociometric patterns. Finally, the written stimuli in the photo —advertisements, posters, and announcements—can also be analyzed. Though seemingly unimportant, this material often contains information about the airport.

Evidently, one photograph can contain substantial communication data. In fact, since a photo freezes a moment in time—recording objects, events, and interactions too numerous to perceive at the scene—an observer often has more information available to him through a photograph than was available at the scene itself. Moreover, because a photograph can be examined repeatedly, the verbal and nonverbal stimuli captured in a print arc readily analyzed, measured, and compared.

Having explored the potential research significance of a photo, two important questions still remain: what types of communication studies can be conducted with photography? How can a researcher ensure that these investigations are valid and reliable?

RESEARCHING SOCIAL INTERACTION THROUGH MACRO AND MICRO PHOTOGRAPHY STUDIES

A macro and a micro investigation are two types of communication studies that can be conducted with still photography. In a macrophotograpy study, the researcher trains his camera on a setting—student union, classroom, tavern—to discover how people interact. Interested in recording information about many communication variables, the investigator in this type of study takes numerous wide angle photographs of the chosen setting. Exploratory in nature, the macrophotography study can produce substantial communication data, capable of being categorized, measured, and analyzed.

In a microphotography study, the camera is used to record information about a selected communication variable, be it gesture, posture, facial expression, or the like. To conduct this type of study, the researcher chooses one or more conversants who are engaging in the selected behavior and photographs them. If the microphotography study is conducted properly, the recorded communication behavior can be analyzed in detail.

To ensure the validity and reliability of micro and macro investigations, the camera must record customary patterns of interaction, not idiosyncratic behavior. According to Collier (1967: 33-45) an expert on behavioral photography, customary communication can be recorded through saturation as well as time and motion photography. To utilize these photography methods, a researcher must take numerous pictures (saturation photography) of a selected setting or conversant(s) for a specified time interval, be it five minutes or a half hour (time and motion photography). This process should be repeated each day for a certain period of time (i.e., a week, a month)— the final component of time and motion photography. With a long-term, multipictorial record of human communication, the researcher, according to Collier (1967: 36), can be reasonably certain that the photographs contain customary interaction patterns.

Although time-consuming, saturation and time and motion photography can be readily employed in macro and micro investigations. For example, to investigate sociometric behavior in a hospital, Rotman (1964) photographed a hospital cafeteria at fifteen-minute intervals every day for one month. After comparing each day's photographs, Rotman was able to identify cliques, determine the extent of black/white contact, and isolate other sociometric patterns. In contrast, this investigator conducted a microphotography study of distance patterns by photographing German, Italian, and American dyads over a four-month period during selected morning, afternoon, and evening hours (Shuter, 1977: 197-206). With these photos, the distance between recorded interactants was measured.

In addition to the preceding studies, other macro and micro communication investigations can be conducted with saturation and time and motion photography. In the following sections, several possible photography studies are explored in detail.

The Micro-Investigation:
Using Still Photography in Proxemic and Kinesic Research

Still photography can be used productively in many types of kinesic studies. For example, to record interactants' eye contact patterns in the subjects' natural habitat—an investigation rarely undertaken in the past—a researcher should take continuous closeup photos of selected dyads for a specified period of time. With the assistance of several camerapersons who can utilize a telephoto lens, a dyad can be photographed unobtrusively from many angles—an effective strategy for recording eye contact between interactants. In examining the prints, gaze patterns can be measured, traced, and compared frame by frame—a difficult and arduous task with film and videotape.

Like eye-contact research, few reported studies on gesture, posture, and facial expression have been conducted in the field, despite Birdwhistell's (1970) cogent plea for this type of exploration. By taking numerous closeup photos of paired interactants from several angles (photography techniques detailed in the preceding paragraph), an investigator, for example, can record gesticulation in the field and subsequently categorize the photographed gestures in terms of type and frequency of appearance.[4] Similarly, with saturation and time and motion photography, photographs of posture and facial expression can be gathered in the field and later analyzed frame by frame.

In terms of proxemic experimentation, still photography can increase the accuracy of this type of research. Instead of estimating the distance between conversants, the imprecise method utilized in reported proxemic field studies, an investigator can surreptitiously photograph selected conversants and then accurately measure the recorded distance with extraordinary precision (Shuter, 1976a). Utilizing techniques developed in aerial photography, interpersonal distance in a photograph can often be measured to the nearest half-inch.[5]

Finally, still photography can be used effectively in laboratory research on proxemics and kinesics. In fact, since laboratory subjects are photographed unobtrusively with relative ease, saturation and time and motion photography can often be employed more easily in this setting than in the field. However, field investigations are worth the additional effort, for the camera may record the conversants natural interaction patterns —behaviors often missing in laboratory photographs.

The Macro-Investigation: Still Photography in Organizational and Ethnographic Research

Identifying and analyzing communication patterns in an organization is frequently a difficult task. Presently, this type of study is conducted primarily through survey, direct observation, and interview. While these tools provide the organizational researcher with valuable data, they do not permanently record the ebb and flow of human interaction; only a camera can capture this. If used properly, still photography can enrich data collection in an organizational study.

In deciding what to photograph in a selected organization, the researcher should focus his attention on one or more organizational settings in which there is a relatively high degree of interaction. The schoolyard, halls, and classrooms, for example, are ideal locations for recording valuable information about communication in an educational institution. Similarly, saturation and time and motion photography of a prison yard, inmate cafeteria, and recreational facilities can provide the investigator with significant data about prisoner interaction. Finally, to record horizontal and vertical communication in a large corporation, photographs can be taken of the coffee area in several offices, meetings of corporate personnel, and the building cafeteria.

Though still photography has been used rarely in reported studies on organizational communication, photo methods have been systematically employed in ethnographic research.[6] In this type of study, communication patterns of a culture or subculture are examined through photographs of neighborhood hangouts, nuclear families, festive and solemn gatherings, community institutions like churches and supermarkets, and other settings. As demonstrated in Collier (1957: 843-844) and Mead's (1967: 189-208) ethnographic investigations, photographs are a rich source of interactional data; the recorded information need only be categorized, measured, and compared.

CONCLUSION

Still photography is an exciting alternative research strategy; its potential uses in intercultural communication are limited only by the research background and creativity of the investigator. Certainly, those who have a sophisticated understanding of photography and behavioral research should be able to utilize the medium to its fullest extent. However, with a basic awareness of camera techniques, a fundamental knowledge of the scientific method, and a moderate degree of resourcefulness, the communication researcher can use still photography in a variety of productive ways.

NOTES

1. For incisive discussions on scientifically evaluating information in still photographs see Byers (1964: 78-84), Collier (1967), Mead (1963: 166-184), Mead and Byers (1967).
2. An interesting discussion on sociometry and photography can be found in Byers (1966: 27-31).
3. For insight into measuring the distance between photographed interactants, see Shuter (1977: 4).
4. An exploratory photography study of gesture patterns among Jews and Wasps was conducted by this investigator. See Shuter (1976b).
5. For an interesting discussion of the use of aerial photography in behavioral research, see Collier (1967: 17-25).
6. Ethnographic studies conducted with still photography include, among others, Collier (1957: 843-859), Goldschmidt and Edgerton (1961: 26-47), Hall (1966), Mead and Macgregor (1951).

REFERENCES

BIRDWHISTELL, R. (1970) *Kinesics and Context.* Philadelphia: Univ. of Pennsylvania Press.
BYERS, P. (1966) "Cameras don't take pictures." *The Columbia University Forum,* IX, 1: 27-31.
_____ (1964) "Still photography in the systematic recording and analysis of behavioral data." *Human Organization,* 23, 1: 78-84.
COLLIER, J. (1967) *Visual Anthropology.* New York: Holt, Rinehart, & Winston.
_____ (1957) "Photography in anthropology: A report on two experiments." *American Anthroplogist,* 59, 5: 843-859.
DARWIN, C. (1859) *The Expression of Emotion in Man and Animals.* New York: Appleton.
GESELL, A. (1934) *An Atlas of Infant Behavior.* New Haven, Conn.: Yale Univ. Press.
GOLDSCHMIDT, W. and EDGERTON, E. (1961) "A picture technique for the study of values." *American Anthropologist,* 63: 26-47.
GOSCIEWSKI, W. (1975) "Photo counseling." *Personnel and Guidance Journal,* 53, 8 (April): 600-604.
HALL, E. (1966) *The Hidden Dimension.* New York: Doubleday.
MEAD, M. (1963) "Anthroplogy and the camera." Pp. 166-184 in *Encyclopedia of Photography.* Little Falls, N.J.: Career Institute.
_____ and Byers P. (1967) *The Small Conference.* The Hague: Mouton.
MEAD, M. and MACGREGOR F. C. (1951) *Growth and Culture: A Photographic Study of Balinese Childhood.* New York: Putnam.
MEHRABIAN, A. (1967) "The inference of attitudes from the posture, orientation, and distance of a communicator." *Journal of Consultation Psychology,* 32, 3 (1967): 296-308.

PINTNER, R. (1918) "Intelligence as estimated from photographs." *Psychological Review,* 25: 137-142.

PITTENGER, J. and SHAW R. (1975) "Perception of relative and absolute age in facial photographs." Perception and Psychophysics, 18, 2: 137-143.

ROTMAN, A. (1964) "The value of photographic technique in plotting sociometric interaction." Paper presented at the annual meeting of the Southwestern Anthroplogical Association, San Francisco.

SHUTER, R. (1977) "A field study of nonverbal behavior in Germany, Italy, and the United States." *Communication Monographs,* 44; 4: 197-206.

———— (1976a) "Proxemics and tactility in Latin America." *Journal of Communication,* 26 (Summer): 46-52.

———— (1976b) "Gestures, proxemics, and tactility among Jews and Wasps." Unpublished manuscript, Marquette University.

16.

ETHNOCENTRIC BIAS IN DEVELOPMENT RESEARCH

NJOKU E. AWA

Cornell University

Ethnocentrism may be defined as "the emotional attitude that one's own race, nation, or culture is superior to all others" (Webster's New World Dictionary, 1966: 499). Originated by Sumner (1907) in his book, *Folkways,* the term is used to denote the tendency of most people to use their own beliefs, values, mores, practices, and so on, "as a standard for judging others" (Hoult, 1969: 122). There are few areas, academic or otherwise, in which ethnocentrism has found as much expression as in the area of development research.

In this chapter an attempt is made to pull together some of the major charges of ethnocentric bias in development research in the hope that knowledge of these will aid reconceptualization of both the theoretical paradigms and the measurement instruments used in such research. Greater emphasis is placed on problems of conceptualization than on those related to statistical tests, for, as some writers have noted, when wrong questions are asked, no amount of statistical wizardry, "no amount of interpretative ingenuity at a later stage" will enable a researcher to reach his or her objectives (Newcomb, 1966:2).

This chapter is divided into three parts: definition of development, methodological bias is crosscultural (development) research, and linguistic problems in such research. But perhaps it is better to begin by clarifying some terminology that the reader will encounter in the chapter. First, some terms (e.g., development research, crosscultural research, and intercultural research) are used interchangeably in the text. Most of the studies done by behavioral and social scientists under the rubric of development research are essentially crosscultural in nature, involving crosscultural and cross-national comparisons. Second, most of the countries of Africa, Asia, and Latin America that have not met the United Nations' criteria for "development status" will be variously referred to as the Third World, developing nations, or low-technology cultures.

DEFINITION OF DEVELOPMENT

In recent years much discussion has revolved around the definition or precise meaning of the term "development." No scholar or discipline has offered a definition acceptable to others. Furthermore, like a great mountain peak that is described differently by viewers from different vantage points, development (or modernization, as it is termed by some), is viewed differently by each of the social science disciplines. For example, economists see it as a planned expansion of a nation's economy (Sloan and Zurcher, 1970) while sociologists and social anthropologists view it as the process of "differentiation" that characterizes modern societies (Weiner, 1966: 3). Some disciplines, notably psychology, concentrate on such individual or personality variables as self-reliance and achievement motivation; others, such as political science, focus primarily on how governments develop a capacity to innovate change, to respond to the demands of the populace, and to adapt to conflict situations.

Two definitions, one of development, the other of modernization, seem to offer a common notion of what the process involves. Development, according to Caplow and Finsterbusch (1964), is the process by which a society improves its "control of the environment" by means of increasingly sophisticated technologies applied by increasingly "complex organizations." Modernization, in Black's (1966: 7) words, "may be defined as the process by which historically evolved institutions are adapted to the rapidly changing functions that reflect the unprecedented increase in man's knowledge, permitting control over his environment," that accompanied the scientific revolution. Both of these definitions emphasize man's ability to shape the forces of his environment to suit his purpose.

However, other definitions, and especially that of Rogers (1969), distinguish between development, which is viewed as social system change, calling for a macroanalytic approach, and modernization, which is viewed as individual level change, involving a microanalytic procedure. These definitions are to some extent empirical, since they are designed to aid research conceptualization and choice of unit of analysis. However, the purpose of the distinction between development and modernization is somewhat compromised by Roger's (1969: 7) claim that the former term is interchangeable with differentiation, integration, or adaptation, the latter with adoption, acculturation, or learning.

Complicating these definitional and terminological problems are the more parochial terms used in describing social change in Third World countries. Among these are Europeanization, Westernization, and Christianization, terms which are more deterministic, albeit more precise, than the "umbrella" or euphemistic terms—development and modernization.

A question may be raised as to the significance of this discussion for development research, since each investigator has a preferred definition for his work. This is precisely the point: definitions vary critically from one investigation to another "and even within the confines of a single study" (Frey, 1973: 340). Apart from the effect of this on reliability, there is the danger of misdirecting the focus of an inquiry when problems are vaguely defined. As Caplan and Nelson (1973: 200) have shown, what is done in a research is determined by the way the problem is defined. And since problem definitions are based on researchers' assumptions about the "causes of the problem and where they lie," if development is defined as Westernization, then it would be logical to proceed by measuring the extent to which a non-Western culture has assimilated Western traits, values, practices, and so on.

In sum, the preponderance of evidence on development research seems to buttress the claims that (1) social scientists have no precise meaning for "development" or "modernization" and (2) both the instruments and the yardsticks used in development research are parochial. For example, Frey (1973) views as highly ambiguous the meaning that different disciplines attach to development, and Seers (1970) thinks that social scientists have not found a precise meaning for the word, outside the web of fantasy they have woven around it.

Also, several critics view as highly ethnocentric the core features of the shift from traditionalism to modernity—GNP per capita, literacy, percentage of the active population in agricultural occupations, and so forth (Golding, 1974). The argument is that in general, social and qualitative advances made in low-technology nations are slighted with impunity because such advances do "not fit on a dollars-and-cents yardstick" (Rogers, 1976: 124-125). And it is Rogers' contention that because of the deterministic character of current definitions of development, investigators tend to forget the earlier achievements of such older centers of civilization as India, China, Persia, and Egypt, and the fact that these countries' rich cultures had provided the foundation for the development of Western cultures. Futher, since these old cultures are currently poor in a material sense, their earlier contributions to the enhancement of social justice and art are no longer conceived as development.

METHODOLOGICAL BIAS IN DEVELOPMENT RESEARCH

It is not possible here to discuss or analyze all the evidence bearing on methodological bias in development research. Instead, selected evidence on theory and value biases are presented together with the effect of these on data interpretation.

Theory Bias

Social science research on national development has been dominated by three theoretical approaches. These are the *index theory,* the *differentiation theory,* and the *diffusion theory* (Elliott and Golding, 1974). Each of these is briefly reviewed for exemplification.

1. *Index Theory:* The index theory states that indices such as GNP, percentage of adults literate, percentage of adult population in argicultural occupations, and so on, are a

composite evidence of modernity or development. Under this approach, socioeconomic development is measured in strictly quantifiable terms. So are the indicators of communication development—number of radios, television sets, daily newspapers, telephones, and the like—which are essentially manifestations of the Western industrial acquisitive emphasis.

Admittedly, these material artifacts are somewhat indicative of real wealth.[1] But they are superficial, mainly quantitative measures of development. For example, education measured in terms of number enrolled in schools does not include the system of cultural transmission by which moral and technical education is acquired in less industrialized nations. Similarly, measuring mass communication by the number of radio and television sets owned is a poor way to determine media exposure. By this standard, in countries such as those in Africa where villagers constantly congregate in a radio or television owner's house to listen to or view media programs, only the owner can be counted as participating in media products. And clearly these "measures" are not a total assessment of modernity, since they do not touch qualitative differences among nation states.

2. *Differentiation Theory:* Differentiation theory describes modernization as the "emergence of role-segmentation, institutional differentiation, and the adoption of new values appropriate to such changes" (Elliott and Golding, 1974: 232). Under the assumptions of this theory, low-technology cultures are seen as having simple social structures and little (if any) orientation toward role specificity. Furthermore, in these cultures human relations are said to be particularistic, rather than universalistic, as is the case in high-technology cultures. To modernize, these (low-technology) countries would have to bring their beliefs, values, and practices in line with those of the more industrialized (modern) countries.

Studies based on this theory have tended to emphasize the role of the media in depicting the advantages of "modern" values and also in catalyzing the "characterological transformation" of traditional people (Lerner, 1964). Empathy, the inner mechanism which enables modernizing men to function efficiently in changing societies, is viewed as a distinguishing characteristic of the "modern" man. The implication is that the more empathic individuals there are in a society, the more modern the society is bound to be. Consequently, in order to accelerate the modernization process, and by implication the spread of empathy among the polity, it is necessary to use the mass media which, as history attests, "disciplined Western man in those empathic skills which spell modernity" (Lerner, 1964: 54).

Some writers have questioned the validity of the assumptions of the theory. For example, Elliott and Golding (1974) have raised the seemingly rhetorical but clearly testable question: To what extent are the concepts of role-specificity and institutional differentiation the exclusive characteristics of "modern" societies, as distinct from a mythology they cherish? Given the pervasive influence of culture on human symbolic behavior, it is likely that cultures which are markedly different from one another can perceive and define a term, say role-segmentation, in markedly different ways (cultural relativism).

Assuming, for purposes of argument, that many of the phenomena of research interest to social scientists are culturally related, why would their measurement assume cultural universalism? Projective questions based on Western socialization experience have been used in testing empathy in the Middle East (Lerner, 1964) and in India (Rao, 1966), among other non-Western cultures. One of the typical questions in these studies requires respondents to name some of the things they would do if they were made the head of their government. Yet anyone with basic knowledge of social conditions in these cultures knows that the man in the street simply does not become a president or a premier. Nor does he allow such a fantasy to form a dominant part of his intrapersonal communication.

The Western man, by contrast, allows his imagination to run wild. He pictures himself as a university president or the head ∙f a major corporation or even president or prime minister of his country. His greater willingness to engage in this kind of ∙ntasy than his non-Western counterpart derives from both ∙s socialization experience and the probability of his assuming such roles. This is hardly the case in many a Third World culture. In the Middle East, for example, Lerner (1964) found that some of his projective, Western-oriented questions were judged as baffling, others simply impious.

3. *Diffusion Theory:* Diffusion theory deals mainly with the process through which externally or exogenously induced change is incorporated into the belief and response patterns of those adopting the change. Originated by Western scientists, the theory has been used in the United States in myriad investigations. Among these are studies focusing on the spread and adoption of (1) educational innovations (Mort and Cornell, 1941), (2) hybrid seed corn (Ryan and Gross, 1943), (3) new drugs (Coleman et al., 1958), and (4) rumor (Dodd, 1958: 9).

In the drug study, certain personality and subgroup characteristics were found to be related to innovativeness: among them, gregariousness, cosmopoliteness, and high exposure levels to the media, including special-interest publications. In the hybrid seed study, as in the drug inquiry, it was "found that the media and commercial sources bring first news of an innovation, but that colleagues, friends, and trusted professional sources are required to 'legitimize' decisions" (Katz, 1963: 86).

Based on these and similar findings, a typology of the adoption process was developed, showing the movement of an innovation from awareness of its existence to adoption. In the 1960s this typology was used in applied social research to explain behavioral change in agricultural and economic development in the Third World.

Thus, early investigations found that Third World villagers were, like their rural counterparts in "modern" societies, conservative and markedly less neoteric than city dwellers. Unlike their "modern" counterparts, however, these villagers were largely illiterate and severely limited in their opportunities for print media exposure. Furthermore, the assumptions underlying the construction and application of the diffusion theory—such as, for example, "bigger is better" and "more productivity, more cash flow"—did not hold in the majority of Third World areas.

Also, experience from Western studies had demonstrated the unimportance of situational and structural variables in diffusion-adoption research. Consequently, when similar studies were made in Third World countries, no attempt was made to incorporate variables not already identified in Western studies. Thus, villagers, functioning under constrictive sociopolitical and economic structures and lacking the privilege of education and of print media exposure, were made the focus of adoption research. They were asked the type of questions that Western doctors, farmers, and educators had been asked in the early investigations. It was this methodological bias—measuring adoption scores in Third World communities with concepts that are of limited salience to the respondents—that signaled the demise of the classical diffusion model in crosscultural research.

In recent years, scholars interested in development research have grown increasingly sensitive to the continued use of Western theoretical paradigms in crosscultural investigations (see Rogers, 1976). Many of them seem to concur with Rogers (1975b: 31) that "as definitions of development, and actual development programs, stress equality of distribution, popular participation in decentralized activities, self-development, etc., the concepts and methods of diffusion inquiry must change appropriately." Rogers' admonition is even more compelling when some other aspects of Third World cultures are considered.

For example, there are places in Africa where economic and political expediency has combined with colonial legacies to limit media exposure. In Nigeria, 90% of the newspapers, "private and government, are printed in English using a literary style. Poorly educated persons are but marginal members of the audience of the print media, while farmers who are literate only in the vernacular are permanently excluded" (Awa, 1976: 12). It is obvious, then, why Alao (1971) found that literacy in English was by far a more powerful predictor of knowledge and adoption of innovations than literacy in the respondent's mother tongue.

It seems that the real impediment to adoption, and even to awareness of innovations, lies not in the traditionalism of farmers per se, but in the social structure. There are reasons to buttress this view. First, politicians in most Third World nations are notoriously insensitive to the plight of subsistence farmers. The demands of these farmers for rural electrification and for the development of viable transportation and economic infrastructures are never heeded. Second, small farmers have difficulty obtaining credit from government and private agencies. Yet in India, Nigeria, and elsewhere in the Third World, production credit is graciously granted to large (commercial) farmers, despite the fact that it is the large farmer, not the small one, who has shown a tendency to default (Mellor, 1976; Awa, 1976). Finally, except where a villager has kinship ties with urbanites, there is little chance for contact with urban inhabitants and such other influential but unsung agents of change as itinerant salesmen.

These are some of the social and structural barriers that small farmers must overcome in order to meet the assumptions of the diffusion paradigm. It is becoming increasingly evident that in Third World countries it is the system, that is, the institutional framework of development—not the individual small farmer (the so-called laggard or late adopter)—that ought mainly to change.

In a summary of structural impediments created by the inordinate exercise of power by the dominant classes in Latin America, Beltran (1976) notes that in one community, Colombians who were located in key economic and political positions wielded so much power and influence that they could, if they chose, use communication channels as deterrents of institutional change. Evidence from other investigations—for example Echavarria (1967) on Brazil and Grunig (1968) on Colombia—provides support for Esman's (1969) position on the need for changing those institutions of the Third World which seem stubbornly committed to the status quo.

What crosscultural investigators need today is a modified theory of development, a new set of analytical preconceptions about Third World cultures, their politics and peoples. As Myrdal (1973: 89) has shown, research tools and master models forged in the West (and for Western inquiries) cannot, without considerable modification, serve the research needs of investigators working in other cultures.

Value Bias

Values are defined as "feelings about what is good or bad, desirable or undesirable, or about what should or should not exist" (Bertrand 1967: 86). Values are a primary determinant of human action or inaction, including decisions affecting research. Admittedly, values have a role to play in social research, because they aid the researcher in choosing topics that are socially relevant. But there is always the danger of an investigator's allowing his personal and cultural bias to influence his choice of topics and the outcome of his investigation. Selltiz et al. (1976: 53) have written about this danger: "Scientists are . . . human; they would like their research findings to come out in a way that conforms to the way they think the world is, or that fits with the particular theory they have put forward or to which they subscribe, or, at least, that is consistent with findings they have reported earlier."

The question has often been raised: What guarantee is there that researchers would not allow their wishes and values to intrude into the conduct and the results of their inquiries? (Selltiz et al., 1976: Smith, 1975). There are actually no safeguards, as such, except through a self-conscious effort to minimize the influence of one's values on one's research. Thus, as Keniston (1965: 12) says, the most truly scientific approach to minimizing value biases in research is by a persistent effort to clarify one's own motivations and preconceptions. Keniston goes on to indicate that "the most objective students of society are those whose own values are most clearly stated, not those who claim that 'as scientists' they have no values."

But evidence from national and cross-national inquiries shows that choice of research topics and the procedure adopted in researching the topics are influenced, to a great degree, by value bias. Caplan and Nelson (1973) found this to be true of the majority of the psychological studies they analyzed from published reports. According to these researchers, "certain groups within society become continually stigmatized as problem groups (e.g., migratory workers . . . blacks, the poor) because they are visible and accessible, but, most especially, because they are vulnerable to the social scientist" (1973:

207). Similarly, nonachieving lower income children who are both identifiable and accessible as a research population are generally selected over "greedy," profit-motivated slum land-lords. This is practically echoed in Dervin's (1970) summary of poverty-related inquiries: "Establishment-oriented" social scientists appear to have carefully excluded the "establishment" in studies designed to understand poverty and its syndrome.

At the intercultural level, the practice is to use Western middle-class values and life-style as yardsticks for judging the appropriateness of the values and the life-styles of "emergent" non-Western cultures (Elliott and Golding, 1974). One of these values, the acquisition instinct of Western man, is supposed to be portrayed by the media which show the modernizing personality "what opportunities exist for using new commodities such as electricity, refrigeration, or automotive transportation" (Pool, 1966: 99). In fact, Pool talks about the media's potential to undermine "traditional values" and to introduce new kinds of music and political beliefs in a modernizing milieu.

This is why attitudinal and value changes are regarded by some investigators as prerequisites to creating a modern society (see Weiner, 1966). Also, it is for this reason that researchers are reluctant to investigate the potential of traditional media—the talking drum, the town crier, and the like—in accelerating development. The problem is compounded by the intellectual outlook of Third World intelligentsia, who are themselves products of Western education and who often are eager to demonstrate their ability to do things the "Western way." Thus, lack of intellectual independence on the part of these scholars is at least in part responsible for the perpetuation of some value biases in development research.

THE INFLUENCE OF LANGUAGE ON CROSSCULTURAL RESEARCH

Human experience the world over is shared in a symbolic manner, the most common symbol systems being the verbal and the nonverbal modes. Language is a bond that binds a culture together. The moral and ethical rules of a culture are institutionalized by language. So are the prejudices, values judgments, and stereotypes that govern cultural behavior.

The focus of this section is on how distinct language features, as well as the value orientations and judgments underlying linguistic codes, can influence the conceptualization, conduct, and analysis of crosscultural research. Whorf (1956: 212-214) posits two propositions regarding language. The first maintains that the world (reality) is perceived and experienced differently in distinct language communities. The second holds that the language of a community helps to shape the cognitive structure of its native speakers. The first proposition is often regarded as a "weak" version of the linguistic relativity hypothesis, while the second one is viewed as a "strong," rather determined pronouncement. Among contemporary writers on the subject there is little doubt or controversy about the relative validity of the weak version of the Whorfian hypothesis.

There are, of course, differences in the syntactical, phonological, and other features of different languages, and there is some evidence that these differences influence perception (Carroll and Casagrande, 1958). There is support also for the contention that these differences relate to distinctive aspects of the cultures in which the different languages are spoken. Thus, it is generally accepted that language is a guide to thought and behavior (Slobin, 1971), but is not, as the deterministic version of the Whorfian hypothesis suggests, a rigid and an inescapable constraint on cognitive processes. Endorsing the weak version of the Whorfian hypothesis, however, Cole and Scribner (1974: 59) add that language has a "filtering effect" on perception and that this is greatest in such areas as social roles, ideology, and theoretical work, "where concepts largely acquire their meanings through their being embedded" in culture-specific, explanatory verbal networks.

If language affects perception, and if language can predispose an investigator to emphasize certain distinctions and minimize others, then it should be clear that a researcher's language can influence his conceptualization of crosscultural research problems. In some cases, language may function as a barrier to a researcher's perception of different conditons in the culture under study: The problems which his culture guides him to see may in reality be insignificant or irrelevant. And as noted by Rogers (1969: 366), the assumptions about human behavior that a researcher may hold are "so implicit that it is difficult to bring them to the surface when (one is) faced with a culture where human behavior changes may result from vastly different stimuli."

In many cases, the research concepts and theoretical terminology that have been transplanted by crosscultural investigators are inappropriate for foreign research populations: such terms as "laggards," "opinion-leaders," and "homophily" may be used to describe behaviors with meanings very different from those inferred by the researcher. And it is for this and similar reasons that a growing number of Third World intelligentsia are beginning to question the "honesty" of some crosscultural investigators. Sharma (1971: 4), for example, laments that:

> For decades, using cultural variables to disguise their ideologies, apologists for imperialism have been describing the Indian peasantry (and the peasantry of other developing societies) by reference to such characteristics as ineptitude, passivity, lethargy, religiousity, traditionalism, lack of the Protestant ethic, etc. In a few short years, however, the peasants of India have transcended their "cultural milieu" to make a major breakthrough in productivity [*that is, the dramatic success achieved by the Indian peasantry in adapting to the Green Revolution technology*]. [emphasis added]

Sharma thinks it is a mistake, possibly an ideological camouflage, to seek the causes of India's underdevelopment in the cultural traits of its peasantry to the exclusion of variables dealing with structural constraints and with institutional frameworks that favor the status quo.

As mentioned earlier, language affects choice of research problems, the way the problems are defined, and the way that variables selected for the research are operationalized. In Africa, competence in cognitive behavior, otherwise known as intelligence, has been studied by a number of Western scholars, using the Western conceptual system (Berry and Dasen, 1974). Some of these studies have been of great value in advancing our knowledge of ecocultural and other factors affecting the cognitive capacity of people from distinct language and subcultural communities. However, others tend to remind the reader of the substance of Wober's (1969) question as to whether the aim of crosscultural study of intelligence is to discover how non-Western respondents can play Western tricks.

Especially in crosscultural tests of intelligence, language is apt to pose a formidable problem. Berry (1965) notes that in Temne, Sierra Leone, there are no words for many of the geometric shapes that are so easily visually recognized and designated in Western languages. In a study of Southern Nigerians, Wober (1966: 126-127) found that terms such as "square," "diagonal," "hexagon," and so on do not exist in Ibo and Edo languages, the mother tongues of the majority of his respondents. Based on his findings, Wober concluded that "while Western languages may be shown to use a great number of metaphors referring to the sense of vision, perhaps in excess of other sensory metaphors, it remains to be seen . . . with which senses African languages prefer to illustrate (or sing of) their experience."

In another study, this time in South Africa, Biesheuvel (1974) found differences in cognitive behavior (test performance) between Bantu and European communities in South Africa, with the Bantu showing greater prowess in the verbal and auditory spheres and lesser ability than Europeans in tackling spatial problems. Biesheuvel attributed these differences to ecocultural factors, among them, child-rearing methods, parental outlook, and the nature of the stimulus value of the environment; that is, the kinds of skills that a culture "encourages" its members to develop. Based on his findings, Biesheuvel concluded that an indication of the power of mind, measures of cognitive ability are comparable only with homogeneous cultures.

Apart from the inherent bias in the methods and variables used in crosscultural measurement of intelligence, there is the danger that where concepts are described in a circumlocutory manner, some members of the research population will respond to irrelevant aspects of the stimuli. In Ibo and Edo (Nigeria) for example, it will probably take one or two long sentences to define "hexagon"or similar geometric designs. Yet no amount of lexical definition of alien concepts can guarantee meaning equivalence and absence of semantic errors when difficult terms are translated.

Several investigators, among them, Wober (1969), Vernon (1969), and Berry and Dasen (1974), have written pointedly about the cultural relativity of cognition and about the fact that non-Western modes of thought often are unamenable to Western tests. Their argument is summed up in Vernon's (1969: 10) words: "We (Western scholars) tend to evaluate the intelligence of other ethnic groups on the same criteria, though it would surely be more psychologically sound to recognize that such groups required, and stimulate, the growth of different mental as well as physical skills for coping with their particular environments, i.e., that they possess different intelligences."Some of these investigators are urging the adoption of an emic (culture-specific) approach, which involves the rejection of "assumed psychological universals" across cultures (Berry and Dasen, 1974). To do this, concepts used in measuring cognitive competence in a given culture would have to come from that culture. And such concepts would have to be operationalized by reference to symbols that are relevant and salient to the culture.

There are other areas in which the influence of language has been discovered. Consider, for example, the situation where a researcher, unaware of what is acceptable and what is not acceptable in an alien culture, incorporates into his questionnaire words that are taboo in that culture. For one thing, data elicited by taboo terms are apt to be misleading. For another, taboo words tend to impede communication during interviews, because they violate modesty codes and alienate respondents who view such violation as evidence of maladjustment.

In some cultures, family planning ideas are taboo, especially among rural populations and the urban poor (Rogers, 1973). As an externally stimulated change process, family planning communication involves the use of foreign symbols, and some of these symbols are often part of the group of terms that are used only in private communication in some cultures. Complicating the problems created by oral (taboo) communication are the subtle ones arising from cultural variations in kinesic and proxemic codes.

CONCLUSION

This chapter has attempted to pull together some of the biases implicit in the theories, methodologies, and language used in crosscultural research. As a composite of selected biases in intercultural and intracultural inquiries, it is not an exhaustive overview of ethnocentric and other problems in crosscultural research. As other critics have shown, e.g., Skinner (1953)

> Science is a willingness to accept facts even when they are opposed to wishes. Experiments do not always come out as one expects, but the facts must stand and the expectations fall.

Crosscultural investigators must recognize that cultures differ in the way they perceive and handle social, economic, and political problems, and that this and similar considerations must be taken into account in designing investigations which cross cultural frontiers.

NOTE

1. In most of the Third World, where hire-purchase privileges are extended but to a select few, and where television, radio, and similar possessions are bought largely on a "cash-and-carry" basis, these indicators do indeed constitute evidence of wealth.

REFERENCES

ALAO, J. A. (1971) "Community structure and modernization of agriculture: An analysis of factors influencing the adaption of farm practices among Nigerian farmers." Unpublished Ph.D. Thesis, Cornell University, Ithaca, N.Y.

AWA, N. E. (1976) "Methodological bias in diffusion research: Some lessons from Nigeria." Paper presented to the International Communication Association Conference, Portland, Oregon, April.

BELTRAN, S., L. R. (1976) "Alien premises, objects, and methods in Latin American communication research," in E. M. Rogers (ed.), *Communication and Development: Critical Perspectives.* Beverly Hills, Cal.: Sage Publications.

BERRY, J. W. (1965) "A study of Temne and Eskimo visual perception." Preliminary Report, No. 28. Psychological Laboratory, University of Edinburgh.

_____and DASEN, P. R. [eds.] (1974) *Culture and Cognition: Readings in Crosscultural Psychology.* London: Methuen.
BERTRAND, A. L. (1967) *Basic Sociology: An Introduction to Theory and Method.* New York: Appleton-Century-Crofts.
BIESHEUVAL, S. (1974) "The nature of intelligence: Some practical implications of its measurement," in J. W. Berry and P. R. Dasen (eds.), *Culture and Cognition: Readings in Cross-Cultural Psychology.* London: Methuen.
_____(1943) *African Intelligence.* Johannesburg: South African Institute of Race Relations.
BLACK, C. E. (1966) *The Dynamics of Modernization: A Study in Comparative History.* New York: Harper & Row.
CAPLAN, N. and NELSON, S. (1973) "On being useful: The nature and consequences of psychological research on social problems." *American Psychologist,* 28, 3 (March).
CAPLOW, T. and FINSTERBUSCH, K. (1964) "Development rank: A new method of rating national development." Unpublished paper, Bureau of Applied Social Research, Columbia University, 1964. (Quoted in Rogers, 1969: 9)
CARROLL, J. B. and CASAGRANDE, J. B. (1958) "The function of language classification." Pp. 18-31 in E. E. Maccoby et al. (eds.), *Readings in Social Psychology.* New York: Holt, Rinehart & Winston.
COLE, M. and SCRIBNER, S. (1974) *Culture and Thought.* New York: John Wiley.
COLEMAN, J. S., MENZEL, H. and KATZ, E. (1958) "Social processes in physicians' adoption of a new drug." *Journal of Chronic Diseases,* 8: 1-19.
DERVIN, B. (1970) "The communication of the American urban poor: A summary of research and suggestions for future research." Project CUP #12, Dept. of Communication, Michigan State University, East Lansing, Michigan, September.
DODD, S. C. (1958) "Formulas for spreading opinions." *Public Opinion Quarterly,* 22, g: 537-554.
ELLIOTT, P. and GOLDING, P. (1974) "Mass communication and social change." in E. de Kadt and G. Williams (eds.), *Sociology and Development.* London: Tavistock.
ESMAN, M. (1969) "Institution building as a guide to action," in D. W. Thomas and J. G. Fender (eds.), *Proceedings: Conference on Institution Building and Technical Assistance,* Wash., D.C., Dec. 4-5. (Committee on Institutional Cooperation and the Agency for International Development, Wash., D.C.)
FREY, F. (1973) "Communication and development," in I. de Sola Pool and W. Schramm et al. (eds.), *Handbook of Communication.* Chicago: Rand McNally.
GOLDING, P. (1974) "Media role in national development: Critique of a theoretical orthodoxy." *Journal of Communication,* 24, 3 (Summer): 39-53.
GRUNIG, J. (1968) "Communication and the economic decision process of Colombian farmers." Land Tenure Center Report. Madison: University of Wisconsin.
HOULT, T. F. (1969) *Dictionary of Modern Sociology.* Totowa, N. J.: Littlefield, Adams.
KATZ, E. (1963) "The diffusion of new ideas and practices," in W. Schramm (ed.) *The Science of Human Communication.* New York: Basic Books.
KENISTON, K. (1965) *The Uncommitted: Alienated Youth in American Society.* New York: Harcourt.
LERNER, D. (1964) *The Passing of Traditional Society: Modernizing the Middle East.* New York: Free Press.
_____and SCHRAMM, W. [eds.] (1967) *Communication and Change in the Developing Countries.* Honolulu: East-West Center Press.

MARTINS ECHAVARRIA, T. (1967) "Difusáo de novas practicas agricolas e Adocáo por pequeños agricultores de Guaracai." Sao Paulo, Brazil: Piracicaba. (Mimeo)

MELLOR, J. W. (1976) *The New Economics of Growth: A Strategy for India and the Developing World.* Ithaca, N.Y.: Cornell Univ. Press.

MORT, P. R. and CORNELL, F. G. (1941) *American Schools in Transition.* N.Y.: Teachers College, Columbia University.

MYRDAL, G. (1973) "The beam in our eyes," in D. P. Warwick (ed.), *Comparative Research Methods.* Englewood Cliffs, N.J.: Prentice Hall.

NEWCOMB, T. M. (1966) "The interdependence of social-psychological theory and methods: A brief overview," P. 2 in L. Festinger and D. Katz (eds.), *Research Methods in the Behavioral Sciences,* New York: Holt, Rinehart & Winston.

POOL, I. de S. (1966) "Communication and development," in M. Weiner (ed.), *Modernization: The Dynamics of Growth.* New York: Basic Books.

RAO, Y. V. (1966) *Communication and Development.* Minneapolis: Univ. of Minnesota Press.

ROGERS, E. M. [ed.] (1976) *Communication and Development: Critical Perspectives.* Beverly Hills, Cal.: Sage Publications.

———(1975a) "The anthropology of modernization and the modernization of anthropology." *Reviews in Anthropology,* 2: 345-358.

———(1975b) "Innovation in organizations: New research approaches." Paper presented to the American Political Science Association, San Francisco, September 2-5.

———(1973) "Communications strategies for family planning in developing countries." Paper presented at the Population Association of America, New Orleans, April 26-28.

———(1969) *Modernization Among Peasants: The Impact of Communication.* New York: Free Press.

RYAN, B. and GROSS, N. (1943) "The diffusion of hybrid seed corn in two Iowa communities." *Rural Sociology,* 8: 15-24.

SEERS, D. (1970) "The meaning of development." Conference of the Society for International Development, on the theme, "Challenges to Prevalent Ideas on Developmental," New Delhi, November 14-17, 1969. Agricultural Development Council, 630 Fifth Avenue, New York.

———(1969) "The meaning of development." Paper presented at the Eleventh World Conference of the Society for International Development. New Delhi, November 14-17.

SELLTIZ, C., WRIGHTSMAN, L. S. and COOK. S. W. (1976) *Research Methods in Social Relations.* New York: Holt, Rinehart & Winston.

SHARMA, H. (1971) "Green revolution in India: A prelude to a red one?" Revised version of a paper presented at the Conference on "Asia in the '70s: Problems and Prospects." Carleton University. Ottawa, Canada, November 12-13.

SKINNER, B. F. (1953) *Science and Human Behavior.* New York: MacMillan

SLOAN, H. S. and ZURCHER, A. J. (1970) *Dictionary of Economics.* New York: Barnes & Noble Books.

SLOBIN, D. I. (1971) *Psycholinguistics,* Glenview, Ill.: Scott, Foresman.

SMITH, H. W. (1975) *Strategies of Social Research: The Methodological Imagination.* Englewood Cliffs, N.J.: Prentice-Hall.

SUMNER, W. G. (1907) *Folkways: A Study of the Sociological Importance of Usages, Manners, Customs, Mores and Morals,* Boston, Mass.: Ginn.

VERNON, P. E. (1969) *Intelligence and Cultural Environment.* London: Methuen.
WEINER, M. [ed.] (1966) *Modernization: The Dynamics of Growth.* New York: Basic Books.
WHORF, B. L. (1956) *Language, Thought and Reality.* Boston: MIT Press.
WOBER, J. M. (1966) "Psychological factors in the adjustment to industrial life among employees of a firm in South Nigeria." Unpublished doctorial dissertation, University of Edinburgh.
WOBER, M. (1969) "Distinguishing centri-cultural tests and research." *Perception, Mot. Skills,* 28.
_____(1966) "Sensotypes," *Journal of Social Psychology,* 70:181-189.

17

A MULTIDIMENSIONAL SCALING METHODOLOGY FOR CROSSCULTURAL RESEARCH IN COMMUNICATIONS

OLIVER C.S. TZENG
DAN LANDIS

Indiana-Purdue University at Indianapolis

In its simplest form, the process of communication involves two persons, one of whom, P, emits some set of signs to the other, O. In forming the message, P encodes a set of desires or statements. Such encoding may be verbal, as in speech or the written word, or nonverbal, as in body movements or facial expressions. O decodes the sense data in such a way as to produce an approximation of P's desires. This process, which occurs many millions of times each day, is, within relatively homogeneous groups, a rather marvelously accurate and efficient exchange. As the characteristics of P and O diverge, the process becomes less and less accurate. In its extreme, it leads to a veritible Tower of Babel, where misunderstandings abound. Triandis (1976) has termed the communication exchange as on where both parties come to have isomorphic attributions about the psychological state of the other—i.e., coming

AUTHOR'S NOTE: *The research presented here was supported by the following grants: NSF and NIH grants to the Center for Comparative Psycholinguistics at the University of Illinois (Charles E. Osgood, Principal Investigator); NSF Grants to Dan Landis for the series of studies entitled "Studies in Subjective Culture." Portions of this chapter were presented at the 1977 meetings of the Society for Intercultural Education, Training and Research, Chicago, January, 1977. Questions about this work may be addressed to either author at: Department of Psychology, Purdue University School of Science at Indianapolis, 1201 E. 38th Street, Indianapolis, IN 46205 USA.*

to think as the other does. But how does this process come about and—when it does—how can we know it?

It would seem reasonable to suggest that the process of isomorphic attribution is facilitated when both P and O share common viewpoints about social behavior—norms, values, roles, and so on. These aspects of "subjective culture" are communicated in verbal terms. Osgood and his colleagues have demonstrated through an impressive corpus of research (Osgood et al., 1975) that verbal concepts carry affective connotations (the dimensions of which transcend boundaries of language, nationality, and culture). Thus, the statement of the aspects of subjective culture imply certain affective loadings. If we could determine when P and O share affective meanings of verbal concepts, it should be possible to predict low levels of miscommunication—even in the face of similar surface cultural characteristics. However, as in most things, the statement of the solution is a good deal simpler than the solution itself. This chapter is concerned with specifying an analytical method of determining the amount of such sharing.

Formally, the method described and illustrated here has a parentage based on attempts to determine the significance in differences in factor patterns of communication variables. Historically, the problem was focused on determining change over time when the variables and the population remained identical—as in tracing age—but related changes in cognitive abilities. Beginning in the early 1960s, the focus shifted somewhat to a concern for identifying different factor structures between subgroups of a larger population. This approach, called points-of-view analysis (Tucker and Messick, 1963), is a direct forerunner of the method used in this chapter.

Even more recently, the focus has shifted once again to determining similarity between groups differing in certain characteristics (e.g., language, culture). At the same time, it is recognized that the variables could no longer remain fully identical, if the populations were allowed to vary in cultural characteristics. That is, while variables might be functionally equivalent, the methodology for obtaining the data might vary considerably. With such functional identity assured, comparisons across cultural groups become both reasonable and feasible.

Before we turn to the specific approach being presented, it is necessary to consider a center aspect of crosscultural research. Crosscultural research has been a major concern among many disciplines. Psychology, anthropology, and sociology all have equally illustrious backgrounds and history. Although they have used different approaches to examine the same or similar problems, the efforts on interdisciplinary cooperation has been a new trend in recent years. In essence, contemporary crosscultural research has both humanistic and scientific interest (Rohner, 1977). It focuses on an understanding of the nature of the human condition and the commonalities and significant differences among men. The general laws or principles of human behavior are then to be established to account for and/or predict individual actions and group behavior both within and across cultures. Furthermore, due to the emergence of the contemporary one-world community in which individuals as well as nations are no longer self-sufficient and isolable, crosscultural research is especially necessary.

Rohner (1977) proposes three major reasons or rationales to characterize the interest of behavioral scientists in crosscultural research. The first is to test for the level of generality of a theory or proposition to all mankind. A second reason is to be able to test for the effects of more extreme behavior that can be found normally within any single society. That is, for a given culture, acceptable behavior alternatives are often set within some restricted ranges. Those individuals who behave beyond these limits are considered deviant, and negative sanctions are often placed against them. A third rationale is to be able to systematically vary factors that cannot be varied within a single population or cultural system. This, in theory, is to use the adult culture as an experimental treatment for individual subjects. Life experiences and backgrounds would then be used to differentiate intercultural similarities and differences.

The above issues seem to relate quite closely to the three types of crosscultural research distinguished by Sechrest (1977). In the context of crosscultural communication research, the focus is more on understanding the cultures themselves and communication processes involved in social interactions. This is because of the fact that in the present one-or-no world situation, social interactions or communication processes are an intrinsic part of daily activities from the interpersonal to the international level. Before we discuss the measurement issues in crosscultural communication research, let us address some basic concepts associated with the terms *communication* and *cultures*.

According to Holsti (1968), all communication is composed of six basic elements: (1) a source or sender, (2) the encoding process of the sender, (3) a message from the sender's encoding process, (4) a channel of communicating or transmitting, (5) a recipient of the message, and (6) the decoding process of the recipient. It is clear that all these elements would have effects, to various degrees, on the consequence of any interpersonal communication. On the other hand, at the level of crosscultural communication, the interactions among these six elements would become more complicated since individuals have different cultural backgrounds and life experiences. Therefore, any variables directly or indirectly associated with the encoding and decoding process should be included in the research domain of crosscultural communications.

There are two aspects of culture which should be differentiated in crosscultural research. The first aspect is the objective culture, which contains such social indicators as names (concepts) of things—ethnicity, sex, age, education, economic background, living conditions, occupations, crime, drug addiction, and so on. These objective indicators are stages or behaviors of people in a given society which can be directly observed. The other aspect is the subjective culture, which contains such social indicators as feeling, believing, conceiving, judging, hoping, fearing, intending, meaning, and so on. These subjective indicators are the mental states of members of a culture which cannot be directly observed. Both objective and subjective cultures have simultaneous effects on interpersonal relationships and communications. However, in the process of generating (encoding) and understanding (decoding) input and output messages, subjective cultures will necessarily play a more dominant role (Osgood, 1962; Tzeng, 1977b). Therefore, in communication research at both interpersonal and intercultural levels, the emphasis should also be on the investigation of the characteristics of subjective cultures.

MEASUREMENT OF SUBJECTIVE CULTURE

In social psychology, subjective cultures have been the major research focus in recent years. Three most promising theoretical frameworks for such research are: (1) Osgood's mediation theory of meaning and human cognition, (2) Triandis's model of the antecedents and consequents of subjective cultures, and (3) the general psychological principles of intercultural behavior (Tzeng, 1977b). In the assessment of the relationship between a limited portion of social structures (i.e., black and white subcultures of three social classes) and six psychological subjective indicators (i.e., stereotypes, behavioral intentions, role perceptions, job perceptions, perceived antecedents, and consequents of behaviors), Triandis (1976) has demonstrated the sophistication and applicability of the above theories and other psychological measurement procedures for intersubcultural (group) relations as well as international comparisons in other objectives as well as subjective indicator domains.

In the context of intercultural communications, the above theories and related procedures seem readily applicable. However, methodologies in multidimensional scaling in quantitative psychology also seem quite relevant. For example, Tzeng and Osgood (1976) have developed a crosscultural research methodology for evaluation of denotative semantic components in predicting the affective attribution of any concept domain. The model was applied to Osgood et al. (1965), data on 11 time-unit terms from 23 language/culture communities with very interesting results. However, for interpersonal and intercultural communication research, we feel another newly developed multidimensional scaling technique, called Three-Mode Multidimensional Scaling with Points-of-View solutions (3M-POV), seems to have more general applications. The presentation and illustration of such a model is the objective of this chapter.

SIMILARITY JUDGMENTS AND STANDARD
MULTIDIMENSIONAL SCALING

Tzeng (1975) has argued that in the process of human perceptions and cognition, three major variables are involved: (1) the unique characteristics of individuals' processing the information (individual differences in both subjective and objective indicators, e.g., physical, emotional, social, and economical), (2) characteristics of the objects or stimuli of perception and judgment (signs or assigns of events, messages, names), and (3) the meaning systems (or sets of psychosemantic criteria) used by the individual in making judgment. Therefore, each message in communication should have its meaning to each individual due to the idiosyncracies of individual learning and life experiences. For facilitating interpersonal as well as intercultural communications, an understanding of how other people perceive interpreting or decoding) the messages (or objects) is extremely important. With this regard, the semantic differential developed by Osgood et al. (1957), seems to be the most powerful technique. It can be used to measure effectively not only affective (connotative) but also nonaffective (denotative) meaning systems of any homogeneous concept domain (Osgood, et al., 1975; Tzeng, 1977a).

It should be noted that the ratings of a group of concepts on each SD or SD-type scale (i.e., a prespecified attribute or continuum) are in the realm of unidimensional measurement. On the other hand, for the same set of stimuli, we can also ask subjects to compare their global similarities and differences without the restriction of any particular criterion. From such global similarity ratings, the structural relationships among all objects or concepts under investigation can then be investigated. The procedure involved in such investigation is known as multidimensional scaling in quantitative psychology. Briefly, this method can be illustrated as follows: from a preselected set of n concepts (e.g., stimuli or objects) within an intercultural communication domain, we can construct $n(n-1)/2$ nonredundant pairs between all objects and have a group of individuals (subjects) to rate each pair on a nine-point similarity or dissimilarity (distance) scale. The corresponding values used in this rating are 1 through 9, with 1 standing for extremely similar, 9 for extremely dissimilar, and the values in between for intermediate degrees of similarity. For example, the concept pair between *My Teacher* and *My Boss* may be given a scale value 1 for extremely similar:

MY TEACHER/MY BOSS

Extremely similar ①　2　3　4　5　6　7　8　9　Extremely dissimilar

From ratings of all n objects a square, symmetric data matrix can be obtained for each subject as in Figure 17.1. Entries (Sij) represent the similarity judgments between all pairs of objects with the diagonal entries being zeros, (identical property of each object when compared with itself), while off-diagonal entries are from 1 to 9. These responses are considered as psychological distances between all objects in a multidimen-

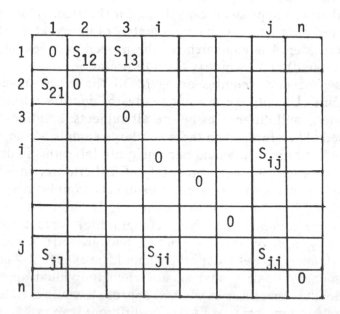

Figure 17.1: Similarity Matrix of a Subject

sional object space. The procedure, employed in standard (metric) MDS, will include the following four steps: (1) these psychological interobject distances are transformed into geometrical distances. This is equivalent to representing each object as a point in a geometrical space (e.g, this is known as an additive constant problem in MDS). (2) All points of objects are characterized as vectors in the space with respect to a common origin set at the centroid of all points. This is the issue of converting interpoint geometrical distances to intervector scale products in a real, Euclidean space. (3) The vector space will be decomposed to yield a set of parsimonious dimensions which can maximally account for the entire interobject distances. (4) A "private perceptual structure" (i.e, the object configuration matrix) will be obtained to characterize each resultant dimension in terms of its relationship with the object vectors in the space.

It should be noted that the last two steps are identical to the general procedures employed in factor analysis. While step 3 is equivalent to the procedures, solving for the eigenvalues and characteristic vectors of the input matrix of intervector scalar products, step 4 is equivalent to the procedure, seeking the final (rotated) factors matrix for interpretation.

This procedure requires doing MDS for every subject's judgments. Usually we are not ready to identify individual similarities and differences before all subjects' solutions are obtained. Therefore, when there is a large sample of subjects involved in ratings, it would become quite laborious in doing MDS for each of them separately. Furthermore, in some psychological scaling research, all subjects samples may not necessarily be distinctive in judgments. In fact, if subjects share some common objective (demographic) characteristics (same sex, age, or social economic background), some response homogeneities among them should be expected. Therefore, separate scaling analysis for each individual appears statistically unnecessary. An ideal approach would then be to just analyze representative data for different response homogeneous subgroups or types of individuals.

This chapter presents a model that will not only resolve the above difficulty inherent in standard MDS but also provide complete information that is usually not available in any single, more advanced MDS technique. Detailed discussion on this will be made after the model is illustrated with an empirical data in the next section.

DESCRIPTION OF 3M-POV

Data

As stated before, given a set of n stimuli which may represent terms or concepts in intercultural interactions, we can ask subjects from different cultural populations to make similarity judgments among all possible $(n(n-1)/2)$ pairs of stimuli. The ratings will result in a data matrix of three modes (in Figure 17.2) in accordance with n objects by n objects by N subjects. This data matrix is the input to the present 3M-POV model.

Semantic Description of the Model

The mathematical model, called Three-Mode Multidimensional Scaling with Points-of-View solutions (3M-POV), is rather complicated, involving factor analytic procedures, hierarchical clustering and standard multidimensional scaling analyses. Those readers who are interested in such theoretical development are referred to Tzeng and Landis (1977a). For the present chapter, only the semantic scheme is presented (as in Figure 17.2) to illustrate the formats (matrices) of resultant solutions when the 3M-POV computer program is applied to such data. Detailed procedural instructions in application of the program can be found in a monograph by Tzeng and Landis (1977b).

The following five types of solutions are standard results from five successive runs of the program for any three-mode input matrix (either similarity ratings, distance matrix, or scalar products matrix).

Object Mode Solution

This is to obtain a group common-object space solution— matrix A of n objects by p dimensions as given in Figure 17.2-

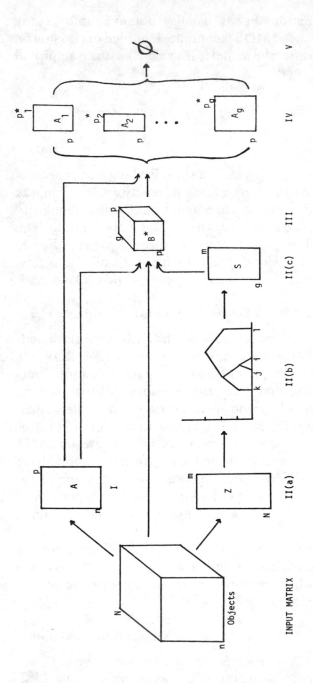

INPUT MATRIX

I   II(a)   II(b)   II(c)   III   IV   V

*Five major outputs, to be obtained include: I. group common object matrix A; II(a). subject coefficient matrix Z; II(b). hierarchical clustering of subjects; II(c). ideal individual coefficients matrix S; III. ideal individual core matrix B; IV. private object configurations A_g; and V. coefficients of congruence among all private configurations ϕ.

Figure 17.2: Semantic Scheme of 3M-POV Model*

I—by decomposing the n by n interobject cross-products computed across all individuals. Since this solution is equivalent to the factor matrix in factor analysis, an orthogonal, varimax, rotation scheme (Kaiser, 1958) was also built in the program so that the resultant p dimensions can be rotated to some meaningful orientation. Psychologically, the resultant dimensions are commonly interpreted in the MDS literature as "average individual's perceptual structure of objects" in similarity ratings. However, Tzeng and Osgood (1976) warn that this structure does not automatically recapture the basic implicit criteria or meaning components actually employed by subjects in discriminating objects.

Subject Mode Solutions

This step is equivalent to solving for the subject matrix in factor analysis by decomposing the N by N intersubject cross-products which are computed across all *n* by *n* interobject variables. The resultant subject coefficients in matrix Z of order N (subjects) by m (dimensions), as in Figure 17.2-II(a), would indicate the intersubject homogeneities and/or heterogeneities in pair-wise similarity ratings of all objects.

When the subject coefficients matrix appear to be completely simple (i.e., each subject vector is salient on only one dimension and has null or close to zero projections on remaining dimensions), each resultant dimension would indicate that the vector termini of salient individuals are closely clustered together as compared with the dispersion of the entire vector termini in the space. Such a cluster could then be interpreted as a homogeneous subject type, sharing a similar point of view in judgments. However, in the practice of most psychological measurements, the distributional characteristics of subject vectors are rarely simple under either orthogonal or oblique rotations. Identification of individual homogeneities should therefore depend upon the actual orientation of the individual vector termini in the space. A common way to accomplish this, as frequently employed in the literature, is to determine the closeness of subject vectors in pair-wise plots across all m dimensions. But such a procedure becomes cumbersome and subject to possible perceptual errors on the part of the investigators when the subjects' vectors are located in a space of more than three dimensions.

Hierarchical clustering of subjects: In order to avoid possible difficulties inherent in subjective observations of pairwise factor plots, an objective procedure and a computer program developed by Tzeng and May (1976) has been employed. In essence, this procedure performs the following: (1) In the retained m dimensional subject space, intersubject Euclidean distances are first computed yielding an N x N distances matrix.(2) A revised Johnson's hierarchical clustering of individuals is then performed on this matrix based on a "centroid" approximation method. That is, at each level of clustering two object notes, the centroid of these two member vectors in the space will be used to represent the location of such a new "vector." Its relationships with all outside (non-member) nodes are then obtained by averaging distances of the two member nodes with all other subjects. (3) After the hierarchical (reversed) tree is constructed, a post hoc treatment is finally conducted to evaluate all trientry relationships in the tree. As a result, as given in Figure 17.2-II(b), among any three nodes at all levels, which are under a common least upper node, the node (subject) in the middle is always closest to the outside node. Therefore, the entire intersubject relationships in the m dimensional space are parsimoniously represented by a meaningful structure of a hierarchical tree.

Idealized individuals and their projections: On the basis of some criterion boundary of intersubject distances, subjects clustered together under some node will be identified as an "idealized individual" in the m dimensional space. Let us assume that there are a total of g idealized individuals isolated and each contains different numbers of individual member vectors. Each ideal individual's vector in the space can then be located precisely at the centroid of the cluster, by averaging the coefficients of all member individuals on m axes as shown in Figure 17.2-II(c). As a result, the original individual factor coefficients matrix Z of N by m can be reduced to a smaller matrix S of g by m, which is referred to as the idealized individual coefficients matrix. Finally, such a new coefficients matrix will further be rotated to some simple structure, signifying a clearer pattern of idealized individual vectors in the person space.

Derivation of Idealized Individual Private Configurations

In correspondence to the (rotated) common object space matrix A (Figure 17.2-I), the present model can yield the following two types of results for each subject cluster:

Idealized Individual Core Matrix. As indicated in Figure 17.2-III, this is a p x p x g three-mode matrix corresponding to p x p final object dimensions for all g idealized individuals. The entries represent the intercorrelations among all p group common dimensions. Idealized individual differences can therefore be inferred in terms of their deviations in patterning such interdimensional correlations. It should be noted, however, such inferences become quite difficult when the two other mode matrices (i.e, group common object matrix A and idealized individual coefficients matrix Z) are of more than three dimensions, and the rotated p x p core matrices for all g ideal individuals contain no obvious patterns of intercorrelations among the object dimensions.

Private Object Configurations: This step is to solve for private perceptual structures for each idealized individual by the following three steps: (1) decompose each ideal subject's core matrix B of p x p for its eigenvalues which can be used in determining the number of dimensions in each private object space; (2) transform the group common object space matrix A into an idealized individual private space matrix (Ag) (Figure 17.2-IV) by the eigenvectors which correspond to some significant roots retained; and (3) submit the obtained idealized individual private configurations to some rotational scheme for interpretation. In sort, the present stage will provide standard multidimensional scaling results for all idealized individual ratings separately.

Cross-Idealized Individual
Comparisons on Private Configurations.

The resultant private object configurations of all g idealized individuals will be evaluated for their agreement by coefficients of congruence (ϕ) as indicated in Figure 17.2-V (Tucker and Messick, 1951 cf., Harman, 1967). Psychologically, this stage of analysis will provide objective, detailed information about ideal individual differences with respect to concept attributions in similarity ratings.

ANALYSIS OF AN ILLUSTRATIVE SET OF DATA

Material

The data used for this illustration were from Osgood's crosscultural research conducted at the Center for Comparative Psycholinguistics at the University of Illinois. A brief orientation to this research is necessary (Osgood, 1962, 1971; Osgood, et al., 1975). In compiling an Atlas of Affective Meaning, subsets of 40 subjects in each of some 28 cultures rated subsets of some 620 translation-equivalent concepts against 13 culturally indigenous, but functionally equivalent semantic differential scales: four each for Evaluation (E), Potency (P), and Activity (A) and one for Familiarity. The concept profiles are expressed by the three factor composite scores (means of 40 subjects across four scales on each factor). In order to make manageable the analysis of similarities and differences, about 50 categories, such as Months and Seasons, Color Terms, Emotions, and Occupations, were devised for the concepts in the Atlas. For all such categories various standardized analytic procedures were devised, and computation of an interconcept distance matrix within each culture was one of them.

In this study, 22 concepts in the Atlas Kinship category for the 28 language/culture communities described in Table 17.1 were used. There were 19 kinships: aunt, bride, bridegroom, brother, cousin, daughter, father, father-in-law, grandfather, grandmother, husband, mother, mother-in-law, relatives, sister, son, uncle, wife, and I-myself (ego). Added to this set were

Table 17.1: General Indices and Two-Letter Key for 28 Language/Culture Communities

Key	Location, Language	Site of Location	Language Family	Colleagues in the Field
FR	France, French	Paris, Strasbourg	Indo-European (Romance)	Abraham A. Moles, Francoise Enel
BF	Belgium, Flemish	Brussels	Indo-European (Iranic)	Herbert Rigaux; Robert Hogenraad
ND	Metherlands, Dutch	Amsterdam	Indo-European (Germanic)	Mathilda Jansen, A.J. Smolenaars
GG	Germany (West), German	Munster	Indo-European (Germanic)	Suitbert Ertel
SW	Sweden, Swedish	Uppsala	Indo-European (Germanic)	Ulf Himmelstrand
AEw	United States, American English	Illinois State (White Subjects)	Indo-European (Germanic)	Center for Comparative Psycho-linguistics
AEb	United States, American English	Trenton, Chicago (Black Subjects)	Indo-European (Germanic)	Dan Landis; James E. Savage; Tulsi B. Saral
YC	Yucatan (Mexico), Spanish (Mayan)	Ticul, Chablekal, Kom Chiem	Indo-European (Romance)	Victor M. Castillo-Vales
MS	Mexico, Spanish	Mexico City	Indo-European (Romance)	Rogelio Dian-Guerrero
CS	Costa Rica, Spanish	San Jose, Liberia, C. Quesada	Indo-European (Romance)	Flora Rodriguez
BP	Brazil, Portuguese	Sao Paulo	Indo-European (Romance)	Sylvia T. Maurer-Lane
HM	Hungary, Magyar	Budapest	Finno-Ugric	Jeno Putnoky
YS	Yogoslavia, Serbo-Croatian	Belgrade	Indo-European (Slavic)	Djordje Kostic; Tomislav Tomekovic
IT	Italy, Italian	Padova	Indo-European (Romance)	Giovanni d'Arcais
GK	Greece, Greek	Athens	Indo-European (Greek)	Vasso Vassiliou
IH	Hebrew, Israel	Hebrew, Israel	Hebrew	
TK	Turkey, Turkish	Istanbul	Altiac	Beglan B. Togrol
LA	Lebanon, Arabic	Beirut	Afro-Asiatic (Semitic)	Lutfy N. Diab; Levon Melikian
IF	Iran, Farsi	Tehran	Indo-European	Tehran Research Unit (U. of Ill.)

Table 17.1: General Indices and Two-Letter Key for 28 Language/Culture Communities (cont.)

Key	Location, Language	Site of Location	Language Family	Colleagues in the Field
AD	Afghanistan, Dari	Kabul	Indo-European (Iranic)	Noor Almad Shaker
AP	Afghanistan, Pashtu	Kabub, Kandahar	Indo-European (Iranic)	Noor Ahmad Shaker
DH	Delhi (India), Hindi	Delhi	Indo-European (Indic)	Krishna Rastogi; Ladli C. Singh
CB	Calcutta (India), Bengali	Calcutta	Indo-European (Indic)	Rhea Das; Alokananda Mitter
MK	Mysore (India), Kannada	Mysore City, Bangalore	Dravidian	A. Shanmugan; B. Kuppuswamy
MM	Malaysia, Maley	Kuala Lumpar	Malgyo-Polynesian	Jerry Boucher
TH	Thailand, Thai	Bangkok	Kadai	Jantorn Rufener; W. Wichiarjote
HC	Hong Kong, Cantonese	Hong Kong	Sino-Tibetan	Anita K. Li; Brian M. Young
JP	Japan, Japanese	Tokyo	Japanese	M. Asai; Y. Tanaka; Y. Iwanatsu

three common nouns, individualized—person and friend—and generalized—most people.

For each community, standard composite factor scores of the 22 Kincepts on E, P, and A were first transformed into indigenous interconcept distances in the Euclidean affective space, yielding a 22 x 22 (kinship by kinship) symmetric distance matrix. After each indigenous distance matrix was converted to the scalar products between all kinship vectors in the space, a three-mode (22 x 22 x 28) data matrix was generated to represent the data from an intercultural communication research. The analytic results through the 3M-POV procedures developed in this article are summarized below.

Determination of Dimensions

For both the culture and concept modes, principal components analyses for cross-products among variables in each mode (i.e., culture or kincept) across the other modes were obtained. For the culture mode, the first 10 characteristic roots are as follows: 12,743, 3,041, 2,042, 1,374 1,115, 1,029, 730, 617, and 558. Root one is considerably larger (44% of the sum of squares) than the remaining roots, reflecting the group average factor obtained when cross-products were analyzed. The differences among successive roots indicate that a break occurs between the fourth and fifth roots. Thus the first four factors, accounting for 68% of the total sum of squares, were retained for subsequent analysis. For the concept mode, the first 10 roots are: 14,233; 5,503; 2,682; 1,268; 963; 777; 508; 471; 441; and 424. A decision was made to retain the first six dimensions, accounting essentially for 87% of the total sum of squares.

Identification of Idealized Cultures

The first four characteristic vectors in the culture space were used as the initial solution of the cultural vector configurations. The 28 x 28 intercultural Euclidean distance matrix was computed from this retained culture space and submitted to the Tzeng-May hierarchical clustering procedure.

The resultant tree diagram is given in Figure 17.3. When level 13 (with a criterion distance of .19) was set as the cut-off for accepting clusterings of homogeneous cultural subgroups, 13 subtrees, including six combination clusters and seven unique cultures, emerged. If more restricted cut-off levels were employed, Costa Rican (CS), French (FR), and Italian (IT) would also be excluded from their respective combination clusters. This indicates that they are also potentially unique in affect attribution to kinship conceptions.

As indicated in the method section, the communities within each cluster are considered as members of an "idealized culture"(i.e., culture type), therefore, the centroid of each cluster is considered to be the location of each idealized culture in the "viewpoint" space. Projections for each idealized culture on all four viewpoint dimensions were then obtained by averaging the coordinates of the cultures in each cluster on each dimension. Orthogonal rotations were then carried out for this idealized culture factor configuration, yielding a simple structure of the idealized cultural space as given in Table 17.2.

Table 17.2: Rotated Factor Coefficients of 13 Idealized Cultures

Ideal Culture	Dimension				Culture Members
	1	2	3	4	
I	.23*	.65*	−.07	.11	BE
II	.05	−.11	−.07	.56*	FR, IT
III	−.16	.28*	−.02	.45*	HC
IV	.16	−.33	.24*	.10	MS
V	.00	−.12	.42*	−.05	IH
VI	−.03	.00	.23*	.00	SW,MM, CB
VII	−.04	.02	.12	.10	GG, AP, MK, IF, HM, BF, ND
VIII	.09	.03	.02	−.02	BP, AD
IX	.12	−.10	.11	.08	TH, TK, JP, AE, CS
X	.04	.33*	.14	.02	LA, DH
XI	.09	.23*	.57*	4m.09	GK
XII	.48*	.04	−.09	−.02	YC
XIII	71.*	−.06	−.04	.00	YS

*Salient coefficient with an absolute value greater than .20.

It is apparent that each of the four viewpoint dimensions tends to be defined by a unique subset of idealized cultures: Dimension 1 is specifically dominated by YS (Yugoslavia, Idealized Culture XIII) and YC (Yucatan, Idealized Culture XII) with salient loadings .71 and .48 respectively; Dimension 2 by BE (Black American English, Idealized Culture I); Dimension 3 by GK (Greece Greek, Idealized Culture XI), and Dimension 4 by FR (French), IT (Italian, Idealized Culture II), and also by HC (Hong Kong Chinese, Idealized Culture III). It is interesting to note that these seven cultures

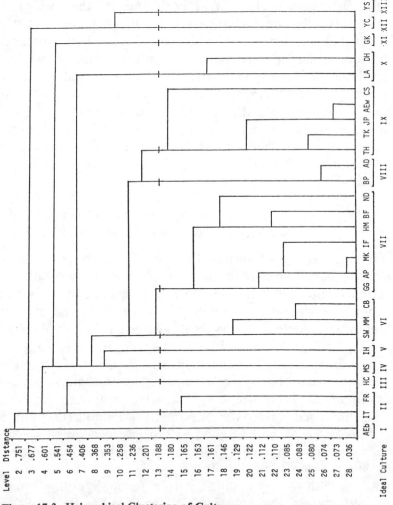

Figure 17.3: Heirarchical Clustering of Cultures

are the most unique in the space, as shown in Figure 17.3, being farthest away from the other clusters.

The fact that, except for FR, IT, LA (Lebanese Arabic) and DH (Delhi Hindi) (Idealized Cultures II and X), other four combination clusters (Idealized Cultures VI-IX) have loadings less than .24 on all four dimensions, indicates that their 17-member culture vectors are less dispersed around the origin of the crosscultural common space. As shown in Figure 17.3, these four combination clusters meet together in the center of the tree at clustering level 11 (d = .24) prior to their connection with other unique clusters at both ends of the tree. This suggests that they have relatively lower affect attribution to the 22 kinships. Examination of all indigenous input distance matrices in the Atlas confirm the fact that these 17 member cultures have indeed the smallest means and standard deviations across all 22 Kinships (means between 1.2 and 1.9 with medial equal to 1.6 and standard deviations between .56 and .96 with median equal to .76), whereas the seven unique cultures and Idealized Culture II (FR and IT) have means greater than 1.9 (median = 2.1) and standard deviations greater than .96 (median = 1.03).

Group Concept Factor Loadings and Semantic Components of Kinship Terms

The first six characteristic vectors of interconcept scalar-products corresponding to the retained roots were rotated by Varimax criterion. This yielded a simple structure of group common concept space (Table 17.3) which can be directly interpreted as potential universals shared by the sample of 28 language/culture communities. However, in order to get a clearer characterization of the results, it seems important to take into account the role of meaning in human categorizing of kinship terms. Therefore, the denotative component analysis of kinships used in the Atlas of Affective Meaning (Osgood, et al., 1975; Tzeng and Osgood, 1976) were adapted in this study. As given in Table 17.4, the eight kinship components and their systems are as follows:

(1) Sex (with trinary codings, +/0/− for male/either/female respectively. For example, UNCLE is coded +, RELATIVE

A Multidimensional Scaling Methodology For Crosscultural Research 303

Table 17.3: Rotated Group Common Concept Matrix

Concept		1	2	3	4	5	6
1	AUNT	−.09	−.24*	−.16*	.09	−.10	.01
2	BRIDE	.71*	.04	−.23*	−.16*	−.02	−.04
3	BRIDEGROOM	.11	−.03	.06	−.30*	−.09	.05
4	BROTHER	−.26*	.19	−.03	−.06	.02	−.16*
5	COUSIN	.11	−.55*	−.04	−.26*	−.08	.01
6	DAUGHTER	.08	−.03	−.23*	.08	.47*	−.04
7	FATHER	−.02	−.06	.52*	−.01	−.19*	−.26*
8	FATHER-IN-LAW	.01	.13	.23*	.05	−.04	.47*
9	GRANDFATHER	.08	−.04	.27*	.58*	.01	.06
10	GRANDMOTHER	.05	−.01	−.25*	.60*	−.11	.04
11	HUSBAND	.11	.49*	.04	−.10	−.14	.01
12	MOTHER	.23*	−.01	.10	.04	−.19*	−.47*
13	MOTHER-IN-LAW	.08	.03	.00	−.08	−.20*	.58*
14	RELATIVES	−.36*	−.15*	−.18*	.05	−.13	−.02
15	SISTER	−.07	−.04	−.41*	.00	−.02	−.11
16	SON	.01	−.05	.33*	−.09	.55*	.07
17	UNCLE	−.10	−.23*	.22*	−.01	−.08	−.03
18	WIFE	−.01	−.01	−.05	.03	.50*	−.00
19	PERSON	−.16	.38*	−.08	.00	−.09	.03
20	MOST PEOPLE	−.22*	−.20*	−.08	−.15	−.12	.15*
21	FRIEND	−.08	.11	.06	−.05	−.07	−.27*
22	I (MYSELF)	−.31*	.27*	−.11	−.23*	−.08	−.07

*Salient loadings

is coded 0, and WIFE is coded −); (2) Generation (with +/0/− codings for grandparental/parental/ego generations); (3) Typical age (with +/0/− for old/middle/young); (4) Lineality (with +/00/− for direct/irrelevant/non-linear); (5) Nuclearity (with +/00/− for nuclear family/irrelevant/non-nuclear family); (6) Consanguinity (with +/00/− for blood related/unrelated/by law); (7) Specificity with +/00/− for particular person/irrelevant /more-than-one persons); and (8) Maritality (with+/0/− for must be/must have been/indefinite). Note that the symbol 00 represents irrelevance or nondifferentiation of a component for a given concept. For example, the concept BRIDE is 00 on components Generation, Consanquinity, and Specificity because it can refer to all three

Table 17.4: Semantic Codings of Kincept Components*

Concepts (AE) (BE)	Sex (m/e/f)	Gen (gp/p/e)	Age (o/m/y)	Lin (d/i/n)	Nuc (n/i/n)	Sang (b/u/l)	Spec (y/i/n)	Mar (m/m/i)
AUNT (Auntie)	−	0	0	−	−	−	−	−
BRIDE (Fool)	−	00	−	−	+	00	00	+
BRIDEGROOM (Sucker)	+	00	−	−	+	00	00	+
BROTHER (Bro)	+	−	−	−	+	+	−	−
COUSIN (Cuz)	0	−	−	−	−	+	−	−
DAUGHTER (Little Queen)	−	00	0	+	+	+	00	0
FATHER (Old Man)	+	0	0	+	+	+	+	0
FATHER-IN-LAW (Fir Law)	+	0	0	−	−	−	00	0
GRANDFATHER (Grandpa)	+	+	+	+	+	+	−	0
GRANDMOTHER (Nan)	−	+	+	+	+	+	−	0
HUSBAND (Old Man)	+	00	0	−	+	−	00	+
MOTHER (Mamma)	−	0	0	+	+	+	+	0
MOTHER-IN-LAW (Old Nag)	−	00	0	−	−	−	00	0
RELATIVES (Kin Folks)	0	00	00	−	+	00	−	−
SISTERS (Sisters)	−	−	−	−	+	+	00	−
SON (Little King)	+	00	0	+	+	+	−	−
UNCLE (Unc)	+	0	0	−	−	+	00	+
WIFE (Old Lady)	−	00	0	−	+	−	−	−
PERSON (A Head)	0	00	00		00	0	00	−
MOST PEOPLE (The Happening Things)	0	00	00	−	−	0	−	−

304

Table 17.4: Semantic Codings of Kincept Components* (cont.)

Concepts (AE)	(BE)	Sex (m/e/f)	Gen (gp/p/e)	Age (o/m/y)	Lin (d/i/n)	Nue (n/i/n)	Sang (b/u/l)	Spec (y/i/n)	Mar (m/m/i)
FRIEND (My Man)		0	–	–	–	–	0	–	–
EGO (May Damny)		+	–	–	+	+	+	+	–

*This table is from Osgoods et al's Atlas of Affective Meaning. The codings, with some modifications, are based on the following categorizations:

1. Sex (male/either/female: +/0/−)
2. Generation (grandparent/parent/ego: +/0/−)
3. Typical Age (old/middle/young: +/0/−)
4. Lineality (direct/irrelevant/non: +/00/−. Note: nested in consanguine)
5. Nuclearity (nuc. family/irrelevant/non/nuc: +/00/−)
6. Consanguinity (blood rel./unrelated/-by law: +/0/−)
7. Specificity (particular person/irrelevant/more-than-one persons: +/00/−)
8. Maritality (must be/must have been/indefinite: +/0/−)

305

generations, either blood or by-law relationship, and one or many persons.

Since the codings of all 22 kinships are objective indicators of each concept it seems helpful to compare the codings of all concepts salient on each concept dimension across all eight denotative components (features). For the present identification of concept factors, however, only the features having a consistent pattern of codings from all concepts on either or both polarities of a concept dimension will be reported as in Table 17.5.

Dimension 1 is dominated by bride and mother in the positive pole and relative, ego, brother, and most people on the negative pole. Given the fact that the respondents were unmarried, teen-age boys, the concepts relative, brother, and most people may have been perceived as unmarried males. This seems to be supported by the characteristics of the positive pole which are -Sex (female) and +Maritality (married). The concepts salient on Dimension 2 are husband, person, ego on the positive pole and cousin, aunt, uncle, most people and relative on the negative pole. Such bipolarities are well differentiated by the underlying features of Nuclearity and Specificity.

The third dimension, defined by father, son, grandfather, father-in-law, and uncle on one hand and sister, grandmother, daughter, bride, relatives, and aunt on the other, is clearly defined by a single Sex component with +Sex for the positive pole and −Sex for the negative pole. The fourth factor, comprising grandmother, grandfather versus bridegroom, cousin, ego, and bride seem to separate the grandparental generation from ego generation and also old people from younger people. Both features, Generation and Age, are confounded for this concept factor, interestingly enough.

For the fifth dimension, concepts salient on the positive pole, son and daughter (with the exception of wife), and −Generation, −Age, and −Maritality, whereas concepts salient on the negative pole, mother-in-law, mother and father, are ⁰Generation, ⁰Age, and ⁰Maritality. Since all these concepts tend to be +Nuclearity and +Lineality, this dimension may reflect a generational differentiation within the

Table 17.5: Salient Kinships on Cross-Cultural Common Concept Dimensions

Dimension I

		Sex	Mar
BRIDE	.71	−	+
MOTHER	.23	0	+
RELATIVES	−.36	0	−
EGO	−.31	+	−
BROTHER	−.26	+	−
MOST PEOPLE	−.22	0	−

Dimension II

		Nuc	Spe
HUSBAND	.49	+	00
PERSON	.38	00	−
EGO	.27	+	+
COUSIN	−.55	−	−
AUNT	−.24	−	−
UNCLE	−.23	−	−
MOST PEOPLE	−.20	−	−
RELATIVES	−.15	−	−

Dimension III

		Lin	SDx
FATHER	.52	+	+
SON	.33	−	+
GRANDFATHER	.27	+	+
FATHER-IN-LAW	.23	−	+
UNCLE	.22	−	+
SISTER	−.41	+	−
GRANDMOTHER	−.25	−	−
DAUGHTER	−.23	−	−
BRIDE	−.23	+	−
RELATIVES	−.18	+	00
AUNT	−.16	+	−

Dimension IV

		Gen	Age
GRANDMOTHER	.60	+	+
GRANDFATHER	.58	+	+
BRIDEGROOM	−.30	00	−
COUSIN	−.26	−	−
EGO	−.23	−	−
BRIDE	−.16	00	−

Dimension V

		Age	Mar	Nuc	Lin
SON	.55	0	−	+	+
WIFE	.50	0	+	−	+
DAUGHTER	.47	−	−	+	+
MOTHER-IN-LAW	−.20	0	+	−	−
MOTHER	−.19	0	+	+	+
FATHER	−.19	0	+	+	+

Dimension VI

		Con	Nue
MOTHER-IN-LAW	.58	−	−
FATHER-IN-LAW	.47	−	−
MOST PEOPLE	.15	0	−
MOTHER	−.47	+	+
FRIEND	−.27	0	−
FATHER	−.26	+	+
BROTHER	−.16	+	+

*Salient loadings whose absolute values are above .15 are reported in this table.

nuclear family. The last dimension may reflect a generational differentiation with the nuclear family. The last dimension, defined by mother-in-law, father-in-law, and most people versus mother, friend, father, and brother, seems to represent personalities presently having close or remote relationships with teen-aged boys. It is interesting to note that except for most people and friend, other salient concepts are well accounted for by two confounded semantic features, consanquinity and nuclearity.

Idealized Cultural Characteristic Matrices

On the bases of the resultant three-mode 6 x 6 x 4 (concept factors by concept factors by culture viewpoint dimensions) inner core matrix and idealized cultural factor coefficients S in Table 17.2, 13 two-mode characteristic matrices (B in Figure 17.2-III) were derived—one for each idealized culture with rows and columns corresponding to the six resultant dimensions of the object space. As stated before, entries in each matrix are "intercorrelations" among group common object dimensions for an ideal individual. A principal components analysis was applied to them separately. The distributions of their eigenvalues, given in Table 17.6, were then used to decide the number of object dimensions retained for each idealized cultural private space.

Conceptual Structures of Culture Types

The retained factor coefficients of kinship terms within each idealized cultural private space were rotated orthogonally via the varimax criterion, yielding 13 separate structures of idealized cultures. However, the results, reported in the present illustration as given in Table 17.7, include only five idealized cultures: I (BE), II (FR and IT), XI (GK), XIII (YS), and IX (TH, TK, JP, AE, and CS). This is based on the consideration that while each of the first four idealized cultures represents a separate viewpoint dimension in Table 17.2, the last one represents the five combination cultures (i.e., Idealized Cultures VI-X) which are close to the centroid of the viewpoint space. Evaluation of these five private conceptual structures

Table 17.6: Characteristic Roots of Core Matrices of the 13 Idealized Cultures

Idealized Culture	Dimension					
	1	2	3	4	5	6
I	30.96	8.19*	4.17	3.68	−1.17	−4.67
	(.75)a	(.20)	(.10)	(.09)	(−.03)	(−.11)
II	42.74	8.02	5.92*	1.12	.34	−2.53
	(.77)	(.14)	(.11)	(.02)	(.01)	(−.05)
III	29.60	7.92*	3.68	1.05	−0.83	−1.90
	(.75)	(.20)	(.09)	(.03)	(−.02)	(−.05
IV	34.21	10.95	6.76*	2.52	−0.05	−5.96
	(.71)	(.23)	(.14)	(.05)	(.00)	(−.12)
V	31.20	8.51	5.50*	2.37	−0.41	−2.33
	(.70)	(.19)	(.12)	(.05)	(−.01)	(−.05)
VI	17.63	4.06	3.11*	1.51	.09	.00
	(.67)	(.15)	(.12)	(.06)	(.01)	(.00)
VII	14.02	4.55	2.49*	1.22	.57	.18
	(.61)	(.20)	(.11)	(.05)	(.03)	(.01)
VIII	4.74	2.70	1.48*	.78	.58	−.17
	(.47)	(.27)	(.15)	(.08)	(.06)	(−.02)
IX	18.12	6.25	4.35*	1.76	.66	−.78
	(.60)	(.21)	(.15)	(.06)	(.02)	(−.03)
X	19.52	6.19*	2.61	1.98	1.15	−.72
	(.64)	(.20)	(.09)	(.06)	(.04)	(−.02
XI	4.382	16.38*	7.17	6.01	3.41	−.20
	(.57)	(.21)	(.09)	(.08)	(.04)	(.00)
XII	22.06	6.31*	3.68	1.49	.46	−1.19
	(.67)	(.19)	(.11)	(.05)	(.01)	(−.04)
XIII	37.07	10.67*	5.09	3.70	2.90	.88
	(.61)	(.18)	(.08)	(.06)	(.05)	(.02)

a Proportion of sum of squares accounted for by each dimension.
*Cut off point. This root and those above were retained.

seems enough to demonstrate the construct and utility of the present 3M-POV model.

Idealized culture I.: There are only two dimensions in the conceptual space of this culture type, which is represented by Black American English (BE). The first factor, comprising son, wife, daughter, and grandfather versus husband, person and mother-in-law, tends to differentiate kinships in terms of three denotative components: Age, Nuclearity and Consan-

Table 17.7: Salient Loadings of Five Idealized Cultural Private Configurations

Idealized Culture I: BE

Dimension 1		Age	Nuc	Con	Dimension 2		Lin	Con
SON (Little King)	.47	–	+	+	BROTHER (Bro)	.27	–	+
WIFE (Old Lady)	.41	0	+	–	FRIEND (My Man)	.26	+	0
DAUGHTER (Little Queen)	.39	–	+	+	MOTHER (Mamma)	.25	+	+
GRANDFATHER (Grandpa)	.24	+	–	+	FATHER (Old Man)	.25	+	+
HUSBAND (Old Man)	–.39	0	+	–	EGO (My Damny)	.17	+	+
PERSON (A Head)	–.26	00	00	0	GRANDFATHER (Grandpa)	.15	+	+
MOTHER-IN-LAW (Old Nag)	–.18	0	–	–	GRANDMOTHER (Nan)	.15	+	+
					MOTHER-IN-LAW (Old Nag)	–.49	–	–
					BRIDE (Fool)	–.38	–	00
					COUSIN (Cuz)	–.32	–	+
					FATHER-IN-LAW	–.27	–	–
					BRIDEGROOM (Sucker)	–.20	–	00

Idealized Individual II: FR and IT

Dimension 1		Age	Dimension 2		Sex	Age	Dimension 3		Con	Mar
EGO	.37	–	FATHER-IN-LAW	.36	0	0	MOTHER	.42	+	0
SON	.29	–	father	.34	0	0	FATHER	.37	+	0
BRIDEGROOM	.19	–	GRANDFATHER	.25	+	+	FRIEND	.23	0	–
BROTHER	.18	0	MOTHER-IN-LAW	.25	0	0	GRANDFATHER	.23	+	0
HUSBAND	.16	0	UNCLE	.18	0	0	MOTHER-IN-LAW	–.44	–	0
GRANDMOTHER	–.60	+	BRIDE	–.45	–	–	MOST PEOPLE	–.32	0	–
GRANDFATHER	–.46	+	DAUGHTER	–.41	+	+	COUSIN	–.28	+	–

Table 17.7: Salient Loadings of Five Idealized Cultural Private Configurations (cont.)

Continuation of preceding configuration

Dimension 1			Dimension 2				Dimension 3				
Term	Loading		Term	Loading	Sex	Cons	Term	Loading	Lin	Con	Nuc
AUNT	-.18	0	SISTER	-.29	+		RELATIVES	-.20	-	-	-
			WIFE	-.26	+	0	AUNT	-.18	-	-	-
							FATHER-IN-LAW	-.18	-	-	0

Idealized Culture IX: TH, TK, JP, AE, and CS

Dimension 1

Term	Loading		Term	Age	Gen
EGO	.34		FATHER	-	-
BRIDEGROOM	.23		UNCLE	-	00
SON	.20		MOTHER	-	00
BROTHER	.18		GRANDFATHER	-	-
GRANDMOTHER	-.61		DAUGHTER	+	+
GRANDFATHER	-.53		WIFE	+	+
			BRIDE	+	+
			SISTER	+	+

Dimension 2

Term	Loading	Sex	Cons
MOTHER-IN-LAW	.51	+	+
FATHER-IN-LAW	.23	+	+
MOST PEOPLE	.20	-	+
MOTHER	.17	+	+
FATHER	-.48	-	+
BRIDE	-.36	-	-
FRIENDS	-.32	00	00
	-.25	-	-

Dimension 3

Term	Loading	Lin	Con	Nuc
MOTHER-IN-LAW	.54	-	-	-
FATHER-IN-LAW	.40	-	-	+
MOST PEOPLE	.26	-	+	+
MOTHER	-.49	+	+	+
FATHER	-.27	+	+	-
BRIDE	-.24	-	00	+
FRIENDS	-.20	-	0	-

Idealized Culture XI: GK

Dimension 1

Term	Loading	Age	Gen
BRIDEGROOM	.27	-	00
EGO	.31	-	-
HUSBAND	.18	0	0
GRANDMOTHER	.60	+	+
GRANDFATHER	.56	+	+

Dimension 2

Term	Loading	Nue
SON	.51	+
WIFE	.43	+
DAUGHTER	.42	+
COUSIN	.23	-
HUSBAND	-.34	+
PERSON	-.27	00
MOTHER-IN-LAW	-.19	-

Table 17.7: Salient Loadings of Five Idealized Cultural Private Configurations (cont.)

	Dimension 3	Sex
BRIDE	.48	–
SISTER	.36	–
GRANDMOTHER	.19	–
DAUGHTER	.19	–
FATHER	-.46	+
SON	-.33	+
GRANDFATHER	-.28	+
FATHER-IN-LAW	-.23	+
UNCLE	-.20	+

	Dimension 4	Nuc	Con
MOTHER-IN-LAW	.56	–	–
FATHER-IN-LAW	.47	–	–
MOTHER	-.48	+	+
FATHER	-.30	+	+
EGO	-.27	+	+
BROTHER	-.15	–	+

Idealized Culture XIII: YS

	Dimension 1	Age	Lin	Con	Mar	Nuc
GRANDFATHER	.43	+	+	+	0	–
GRANDMOTHER	.39	+	+	+	0	–
FATHER	.26	0	+	+	0	+
MOTHER	.19	0	+	+	0	+
WIFE	-.37	0	–	–	+	+
SON	-.36	–	+	+	–	+
DAUGHTER	-.35	–	–	+	–	+
BRIDE	-.21	–	–	00	+	+
EGO	-.20	–	+	+	–	+

	Dimension 2	Lin	Con
MOTHER-IN-LAW	.58	–	–
FATHER-IN-LAW	.40	–	–
HUSBAND	.21	–	–
PERSON	.18	–	0
MOTHER	-.38	+	+
FATHER	-.34	+	+
FRIEND	-.20	–	–
SON	-.16	+	+

*Salient loadings whose absolute values exceed .15 are reported in this table.

guinity. It is reasonable that for teen-aged boys, the concepts salient on negative pole are rather remote. The second dimension has the leading kinships of mother-in-law, bride, cousin, father-in-law, bridegroom on the negative side and brother, friend, mother, father, ego, grandfather, and grandmother on the positive side. It is obvious that the concepts on the negative pole tend to reflect marital relationships, whereas the concepts on the positive pole tend to be +Lineality and +Consanquinity.

Idealized culture II.: The dimensions of Idealized Culture II, representing French (FR) and Italian (IT), are almost identical to three factors of the crosscultural common space. While Dimension 1, with salient kinships ego, son, bridegroom, brother, and husband versus grandmother, grandfather and aunt, is clearly characterized by Age (young versus old). The second dimension, dominated by father-in-law, father, grandfather, mother-in-law, and uncle verus bride, daughter, sister, and wife, is well accounted for by Sex and Age components. The third dimension is defined by mother-in-law, most people, cousin, relatives, aunt, father-in-law, versus mother, father, friend, and grandfather. It can be identified by Consanguinity for the positive pole (except friend) and by an indefinite marital status for the negative pole (except father and mother-in-law).

Idealized culture IX.: This idealized type represents three Asian member cultures: Thai (TH), Turkish (TK) and Japanese (JP), and two American groups: American English (AE) and Costa Ricans (CS). All three conceptual dimensions have maximal similarities to the crosscultural common factors. That is, dimension 1, dominated by ego, bridegroom, son, brother versus grandmother and grandfather, is well differentiated by Age (young versus old) and Generation (grandparental versus ego generation). Dimension 2, dominated by father, uncle, mother, and grandfather versus daughter, wife, bride, and sister seems to reflect kinship conceptual differences in Sex and possibly also in Consanguinity (blood related versus unrelated). Dimension 3, characterized by mother-in-law, father-in-law, and most people versus mother, father, bride, and friend seems to reflect a close or remote relationship among individuals in society. The fact that bride is also salient on this dimension may suggest its connotation of being a girl friend for the teenage male subjects. In addition, it is interesting to note that this dimension tends to associate with Lineality, Consanguinity, and Nuclearity.

Idealized culture XI.: This type is represented by a single-language/culture community, Greece (GK), which has salient loadings on two crosscultural viewpoint dimensions in Table 2. Dimension 1, dominated by grandmother and grandfather on one hand, and bridegroom and ego on the other, seems to be an Age and Generation differentiating factor. But the presence of husband on the "young" pole makes this factor distinct. Dimension 2, like the first dimension of BE, consists of the concepts husband, person, and mother-in-law versus son, wife, and daughter. The only differly a Sex determinating factor. Dimension 4, characterized by mother-in-law and father-in-law versus mother, father, ego and brother, is differentiated by Nuclearity and Consanguinity.

Idealized culture XIII.: The other single community, uniquely representing an idealized culture, is Yugoslavia (YS). The positive pole of the first factor, dominated by grandfather, grandmother, father, and mother, is +Age, +Lineality and +Consanguinity and ⁰Maritality, whereas the negative pole, dominated by wife, son, daughter, bride and ego, tends to be − Age, and +Nuclearity (possibly +Lineality also). The second dimension is a crosscultural common factor, characterizing personalities with a close or remote relationship with the young male subject. The Lineality and Consanguinity components seem also to play a discriminating role.

By way of summarizing the preceding results, it is obvious that five of the six crosscultural common structures of kinships in Table 17.5 (except dimension 1) are identifiable from at least two private configurations of the present five idealized cultures. Among them, four dimensions, III to VI, are most salient, being shared by most idealized cultures. On the other hand, it should be noted that although most dimensions in each private space can basically be accounted for by the group common space, some unique characterizations of these dimensions exist for subsets of idealized cultures. This suggests that for detailed information on crosscultural commonalities as well as idealized cultural uniquenesses, the present model would provide a promising objective course for further pursuits. However, detailed interpretation of the data presented above is beyond the scope of the present paper which is methodological in focus. Such interpretations and discussions can be found in Landis and Tzeng (Note 4) where a culturological analysis of the Black English data is made against the backdrop of the other 27 cultures.

CONCLUSIONS

This chapter has presented and illustrated a method for determining cultural similiarity and difference in a variety of domains. While we have confined ourselves to dealing with distance data on verbal concepts the method could be applied to nonsocial data, e.g., psychophysical scalings of color, shape, brightness, and so on. When the data are obtained from aspects of each culture's subjective social world, then we are close to specifying areas in which we can predict levels of communication ease. In such cases we will find ourselves with a most powerful tool which is not dependent on an anecdotal report for developing crosscultural training programs.

In some aspects the data presented here are surprising. We find similarities between cultures that seem, on the surface at least, to have little in common. In order to interpret such findings, we will need to obtain more detailed information on the cultures and the individuals from which the data are gathered. Other statistical technicals, such as canonical correlation and multiple discriminant function analysis, can then be applied to specify the interpretation of the "idealized" individuals or cultures. The interested reader may refer to Triandis (1976) for an illustration of the application of such methods.

It should be noted that in any social behavioral research, any particular methodology on strategy has its own strengths as well as weaknesses. Similarity ratings are no exception. There-fore, even though the present analytic model will provide detailed information for similarity ratings among a set of objects, the resultant solutions are usually not self-sufficient or complete for a simultaneous explanation of all six elements of communication components as addressed by Holsti (1968). Unfortunately, this is the fundamental limitation of the simi-larity rating procedure which emphasizes only global compar-isons of pair-wise object relationships.

Despite such a limitation, the resultant information derived from the present model would have significant utility in inte-grating and interpreting other information from the same subject populations and other measurement domains. For example, since the identification of idealized subjects (types) is based on response patterns in the subject mode, one can bypass the boundaries of subject demographic variables (e.g., sex, age, and status) for investigation of individual differences. That is, the resultant subject factor structure and hierarchical tree of intersubject distances can be used to probe not only the *differences* among the various groups as a whole, but also the *similarities* among *subgroups* of individuals across different cultures. In the situation of intercultural communications, such information seems especially desirable.

Similarily, in the concept mode, the interobject relation-ships and structures identified from both the group common and ideal subject specific spaces can be used to interpret and/or integrate information from the same or other research conditions and domains. This type of data is proved to be valuable in social, experimental, and cognitive psychology. Therefore, resultant factor structures of such communication variables as roles, social environments, situations, and mes-sages seem also indispensable for effective interpersonal interactions. The method presented in this chapter would seem to be a good means to obtain such information.

REFERENCES

HARMAN, H.H. (1967) *Modern Factor Analysis.* Chicago: Univ. of Chicago Press.
HOLSTI, O.R. (1968) "Content analysis," in The Handbook of Social Psychology. Reading, MA: Addison-Wesley.

foolproof—

KAISER, H.F. (1958) "The varimax criterion for analytic rotation in factor analysis." Psychometrika 23: 187-200.

LANDIS, D. and TZENG, O.C.S., (in preparation) The kinship space of black adolescents," chapter 3 in D. Landis, *The Black Affective World.*

[333] MAY, W.H, and MIRON, M.S. *(1975) Cross-cultural Universals of Affective Meaning Systems.* Urbana: Univ. of Illinois Press.

    (1971) "Exploration in semantic space: A personal diary." *Journal of Social Issues,* 27, 4: 5-64.

    (1962) "Studies on the generality of affective meaning systems." *American Psychologist,* 17: 10-28.

OSGOOD, C.E., SUCI, G.J. and TANNENBAUM, P.H. (1957) *The Measurement of Meaning.* Urbana: Univ. of Illinios Press.

ROHNER, R.P. (1977) "Why cross-cultural research," L.L. Adler (ed.), *Issues in Cross-Cultural Research.* Annals of the New York Academy of Sciences. New York: New York Academy of Sciences.

SECHREST, R. (1977) "On the need for experimentation in cross-cultural research," p. 285, 104-118 in L.L Adler (ed.), *Issues in Cross-Cultural Research.* Annals of the New York Academy of Sciences. New York: New York Academy of Sciences.

TRIANDIS, H.C. (1976) Variations in Black and White Perceptions of the Social Environment. Urbana: Univ. of Illinois press.

TUCKER, L.R. (1951) "A method for synthesis of factor analysis studies." Washington, D.C.: Department of the Army, Personnel Research Section Report, 984.

    and Messick, S. (1963) "An individual differences model for multi-dimensional scaling." *Psychometrika,* 28: 333-367.

TZENG, O.C.S. (1977a) "Differentiation of affective and denotative semantic subspaces," pp. 476-500 in L.L. Adler (ed.), *Issues in Cross-Cultural Research.* Annals of the New York Academy of Sciences. New York: New York Academy of Sciences.

    (1977b) "Comparison of subjective cultures among blacks and whites." *International Journal of Intergroup Relations,* 2.

    (1975) "Differentiation of affective and denotative meaning systems and their influence on personality ratings." *Journal of Personality and Social Psychology,* 1975, 32, 6: 978-988.

    and LANDIS, D. (1977a) "Three-mode multidimensional scaling with points of view solutions." *Multivariate Behavioral Research.*

   _____(1977b) "A computer program for three-mode multidimensional scaling for point-of-view solutions." Indiana/Purdue University at Indianapolis, Department of Psychology.

TZENG, O.C.S. and MAY, W.H. (1976) "A computer program for hierarchical clustering." Center for Comparative Psycholinguistics, University of Illinois at Urbana-Champaign.

TZENG, O.C.S. and OSGOOD, C.E. (1976) "Validity tests for comportial analyses of conceptual domains: A cross-cultural study in methodology." Behavioral Science, 21: 69-85.

PART V.

RESEARCH IN SPECIFIC CULTURES

The examination of intercultural communication phenomena as they occur in specific cultural settings provides us the opportunity to test and further advance our knowledge of the cultural basis of communication behavior. Preceding sections have explored theoretical and conceptual frameworks for analyzing intercultural communication, the methodological problems, and innovative approaches necessary for crosscultural research. For research to promote the development of theories in intercultural communication, we need to gather, record, and analyze communication principles and assumptions as they occur, and influence outcomes in different cultural environments.

Attention to specific cultural manifestations of intercultural communication has been the primary focus of contemporary researchers. It is here that we can uncover the basis of intercultural encounters. Most of the research in these areas has been through the investigations of anthropologists and social psychologists. As a by-product, some intercultural research was achieved. Continued research and data-base building are necessary to help delineate the boundaries and assumptions of intercultural communication.

In the first essay, Ogawa presents a comprehensive treatment of communication among Japanese-Americans in Honolulu. He views the centrality of the traditional Asian family structure as the point of departure for understanding Japanese-American communication behavior. Ogawa concludes that, despite the impact of modern urbanization and social mobility, the traditional family structure though modified in form by these forces, still remains a strong influence in shaping communication behaviors.

Vora and Vora examine mate-recruiting through the media in West Germany, India, and the United States. They identified five criteria for mate-recruiting to include, sociocultural, economic, physical traits, psychological attributes, and emotional factors. Though these criteria were universal, their evaluative aspect was culture specific, with different cultures placing different emphases on the criteria. Research in this area helps us to examine the concepts of homophily and heterophily as they apply to intercultural relations.

(3) Sanda is concerned with cultural self-comprehension in Black Africa. He utilizes African oral literature as an example of agreement in the philosophical and normative characteristics of African cultures that display unified cultural awareness. Sanda believes the dynamics of African interaction with the West and the dynamics of ethnicity to be the major factors impeding unification among Africans. Focusing particularly on the aspect of ethnicity, Sanda believes it can be either a unifying or splintering factor, depending on how government policy and educators use the image.

(4) Medicine's essay attempts to explain the significance of Lakota as a functional native-American language. It establishes the social contexts for Lakota usage and makes a case for assessing the rate of bilingualism among native Americans.

(5) In a forceful essay, Pennington examines the difficulty of communication between whites and blacks. She discusses the behavioral hindrances to interracial communication as variables of cultural differences in language, perception, nonverbal aspects, family structure, and racism as seen through prejudices, stereotypes, power struggles, and symbolic imperialism. Her central thesis is the need to develop systematic determination of how whites and blacks view the world and how these basic assumptions help us grasp the dynamics of culture and racism as they affect white/black communications. Improvement of interracial communication must account for the group and social dimensions of the problems as well as the interpersonal aspects.

18

COMMUNICATION CHARACTERISTICS OF ASIAN AMERICANS IN URBAN SETTINGS: THE CASE OF HONOLULU JAPANESE

DENNIS M. OGAWA

University of Hawaii

The traditional approach of analyzing Asian-American communication has centered on the Asian family and its effect on behaviors. Indeed, the Asian familial system stemming from ancient rural roots has been viewed as playing a dominant role in shaping the Asian-American personality. Filial piety, family honor, shame, "saving face," the traditional "Oriental attributes," have been integral components of Asian-American behaviors inculcated within the family and circumscribing social roles.

As the Asian-American family has been urbanized, however, one would expect that the influence of these "Oriental attributes" would undergo continual de-emphasis. Concepts which have defined individual behavior in the rural environment of Asia would become irrelevant, even dysfunctional, in the modernized urban centers of Los Angeles, New York, Seattle, or San Francisco. "Shame," "family honor," would seemingly become prohibitive anachronisms to modern generations of Asian-Americans "on the make." But in analyzing the contemporary experience of Honolulu's Japanese-American population, this is evidently not the case. Rural traditional patterns have not disappeared under the impact of social mobility and urbanization, but have become modified. Although not replications of the rural heritage, the traditional familial behaviors and values of the Asian-American continue to influence communication behavior among the ethnic group.

To explore the importance of this traditional familialism as a basis antecedent for understanding Japanese-American communication in Honolulu is the purpose of this chapter. Consequently, discussion will focus upon the traditional Japanese concept of *ie* "household" as it has evolved from rural Japan into the modern concept of the modified extended family, and the consideration of certain modal familial values as they continue to affect the communication of Island Japanese-Americans. From such an analysis it is hoped that the student of Asian-American communication will gain a viable perspective or cultural outlook from which to create hypotheses concerning the communication of Japanese-Americans in Hawaii's urban center of Honolulu. And in the process, the student might gain an insight into the communication of other Asian-Americans residing in various urban environments throughout the United States.

THE DEVELOPMENT OF A
MODIFIED EXTENDED FAMILY

The Japanese-Americans of modern Honolulu trace their family heritage to the Meiji world of eighteenth-century Japan. In ancient Japan the Japanese rural family was called *ie,* meaning "house." The *ie* was a residential unit which was comprised of not only the family of procreation, but a large array of members associated by kinship or affiliation. As a large social network of kin relations, the *ie* also was a critical economic unit, providing a stable agricultural work force in rural communities. Due to this economic function, the family was viewed as a corporate group, with property and land being shared communally rather than individually.

Survival in a constantly demanding environment meant that the individual's will and effort had to be funneled into a group consciousness. Familial communalism demanded the suppression of individualism to the needs of the corporate group. The suppression of individual desires and motivations was insured by a social system which clearly defined the individual's place within the family—a world view predicated on a vertical, hierarchical order of the universe. Every family member had a specific, delineated role of behavior differentiated by status and power. As Ruth Benedict observed in her study of Japanese culture, *The Chrysanthemum and the Sword,* (1946: 9), "hierarchy based on sex and generation and primogeniture are part and parcel of family life."

Extending from the family, the hierarchy of social order formed a comprehensive "natural law" of Japanese society. From the symbolization of language to the everyday routines of behavior and value beliefs, the Japanese world view was marked by the emphasis on social order. The individual understood that the "natural" hierarchy presupposed that some should govern and others should be governed—that authority and influence be rigidly inbred in the roles and statuses of the vertical arrangement of the world. In the following diagram of the Japanese hierarchy, each pairing is listed in relative order of importance, status, position and authority. The role on the left is dominant over the one on the right (Hilo and Himeno, 1957: 37).

kun-shin—Emperor and subject
fu-shi—father and child
fu-fu—husband and wife
cho-ya—elder and junior
shi-tei—teacher and pupil

Permeating this sense of hierarchy and order, was a feeling of obligation and adoration to one's place in the scheme of things. The child was taught not to begrudge his restrictions of status and position, but to emote a strong sense of *on*, obligation to family, community, teachers, and Emperor. The *ie* was idealized by ancestor worship into a quasi-religious deity, a symbol of social order and meaning.

These patterns of agrarian ruralism shaping the Japanese *ie* were designs of environmental influence characteristic of cultural developments in most rural areas. Although Ronald Dore (1958: 91), a Japan scholar, could accurately state that few societies "are as consciously aware of their family system as the Japanese," all societies have a common heritage of familial relations molded by agrarianism. Whether it be the Philippines, China, Korea, Portugal, nineteenth-century New

England or ancient Hawaii, similar rural folkways necessitated a
similar social ambience of cooperation and communalism as
found in Meiji Japan. The *ie*, viewed in crosscultural perspective, was simply a pattern of extended family relationships
evolving from the economic interdependencies of individuals
in agricultural, rural communities.

Since family members provided free labor to harvest the
crop, plow the fields, or maintain the household, large families
became common necessities in most rural establishments. The
extended family pattern developed where the grandparents,
parents, children, uncles, and aunts lived under the same roof.
And because the extended family could not survive alone, it
became economically and relationally interdependent with
other extended family units, comprising the rural village.

The perpetuation of this extended family pattern required
the successive generational enculturation of values and priorities conducive to cooperative interpersonal and interfamilial
relationships. Most important of these values was an emphasis
on affiliation. Individuals and families became implicitly
linked and dependent on one another through an emotional
bond of love, by a notion of duty and commonness of purpose
and the basic assumption that energy, property, affiliation, and
cooperation will be perpetually reciprocated. In the truest
sense, the agrarian family and community implicitly recognized the intuitive integrity of their world system as a meaningful organism of interrelated values, structures, and relationships.

The eminent German sociologist Ferdinand Tonnies in the
late nineteenth century described this rural family organism,
characteristic of the Japanese *ie*, as a component of what he
called *Gemeinschaft:* communication, kinship, neighborhood,
and friendship. There is an implicit spirit between individuals
in *Gemeinschaft,* basing human relationships on an affiliative
love. We may now establish the great main laws of Gemeinschaft (Tonnies, 1963: 48):

1. Relatives and married couples love each other or easily adjust
    themselves to each other. They speak together and think along similar
    lines. Likewise do neighbors and friends.
2. There is understanding between people who love each other.

3.   Those who love and understand each other remain and dwell together and organize their common life.

Within this Gemeinschaft of instinctual human bonds, within the *ie* of order and obligation, the young Japanese child ,matured into a man. And in the case of the Japanese immigrant, as he found his rural world upset by crop failure and economic stagnation, he became enticed by stories of opportunity across the sea. Most likely a younger son who would not feel the responsibility of ancestral inheritance, he responded by testing his ambitions against the resiliency of his character. Venturing to a foreign land — Brazil, Peru, the United States, or Hawaii— he would labor to earn wages which he thought would one day raise his standard of living in his ancestral village. But after several years he found himself unable or disinclined to return to his homeland. He sent for a wife and established a family in his new host society. As a father, he sought to instill in his children the same world views which he had been given as a child—the same values and behaviors which had defined his Gemeinschaft. But in most cases, the conditions in the new homeland were not conducive to the behaviors learned in the rural village he had left in Japan. The jungles of the Amazon, the deltas of Sacramento, and the backstreets of Honolulu demanded coping skills and values different from those in a small farming village in Hiroshima.

The most startling "social shock" the immigrant would encounter in many of his new host societies was the realization that the family organism, the spirit of *ie* with which he was so familiar, was challenged by an environment of expanding capitalism, urbanization, and industrialization. The Gemeinschaft bond of love underlying his world view and community relations was being threatened by the bludgeoning effects of modern Gesellschaft society. Tonnies distinguished Gesellschaft as an urban, highly individualized society based not on implicit love, but explicitly defined social contracts. And as the immigrant discovered in Hawaii, self-reliancy, the ability to exert self-will, not love, was the tempo of the Island plantation economy.

"In Gesellschaft," Tonnies wrote (1963: 77), "every person strives for that which is to his own advantage and he affirms the actions of others only in so far as and as long as they can further his interest." In such a system, the extended family is reduced to the nuclear of parents and children, serving as an enculturator of individualism and independence. Instead of affiliation, obligation, and dependency, the child must learn self-will, self-expression and self-achievement.

Gemeinschaft and Gesellschaft are archetypal forms on a continuum of social organization—a continuum arising from the conflict between technological and industrial advancements and the rural lifestyle. The extended family, valuing affiliation and obligation, bound by love, undergoes transformation as industrialization and urbanization prohibit its economic worth. To survive under the impact of an ever expanding Gesellschaft, the extended family system, now a sociocultural burden, gives way to the nuclear family. Values of dependency and affiliation give way to independence and self-aggrandizement. Intuitive books of love by necessity are supplanted by bonds of the social contract.

These tensions between the forces of Gesellschaft and Gemeinschaft reshaped the Japanese family as it was adapting to the Hawaiian environment. The immigrant and his family had naturally sought to recreate the implicit bonds linking the communities of the homeland—to transplant in toto the Gemeinschaft *ie*. But the need for modification became immediately apparent. The disorganization of plantation life, the general inability to purchase land and develop independent farming communities, the disorienting urban Gesellschaft of Honolulu, created a cultural setting far different from that of rural Japan. The world view designed to perpetuate a stable, landed peasantry was inadequate for the plantation and urban colonies of Japanese immigrant families.

Internally, the fragmented character of the first generation Issei family equally exacerbated the inability of the *ie* system to find duplication in Hawaii. The Issei couples were, after all, separated from their homeland kinship systems—the immigrant home became the domain of the nuclear, not extended family. There were no elderly grandparents, few uncles and aunts, brothers and sisters living under the same roof. The immigrant had come as a loner, and consequently the family he created in Hawaii did not represent the diverse *ie* pattern of Japan. "In Hawaii," a sociologist (Masuoka, 1936: 164) concluded in the pre-World War II era,

> the Japanese family system is undergoing changes. Immigration has resulted in the creation of conditions that tend to weaken moral bases of the family. The removal of the immigrants from their families and home communities meant that they left behind all the prestige which went with their family names. They left behind, too, the living symbols of land, house, family cemetery, and the village shrines which constantly reminded them of the love and affection of their illustrious forefathers. The economic system of Hawaii, with its money wages, has tended to undermine family solidarity. The presence of other people whose family systems have different moral bases has helped to weaken family sentiment among the Japanese.

The structural changes which the Japanese family would undergo in Hawaii, the impact of Gesellschaft on the nature of the *ie* system, can be seen in the birth rates, size, and urbanization of the Japanese family over the last 50 years. The simple extended family has been affected by modernization and nuclearization as economic, social, and cultural forces shaped the immigrant institution in this, now that direction. Prominent among the trends influencing the *ie* pattern has been the tendency toward a diminishing size of the procreating family and stabilizing birth rates in increasingly urban settings.

Actually, though, the early period of stabilization of the Japanese family coincided with a high birth rate. The peasant, extended family tradition of the Issei resulted in an initially high birth rate of the second generation, Nisei. The high fertility of the young Issei female population resulted in a rapid increase in births. In the years 1920-1921 the Japanese birth rate climbed to a level only exceeded by Part-Hawaiians. And in the period 1920-1937, the second generation catapulted from 39,127 to 113,289 (Johnson, 1972: 58).

The high birth rate in the 1920s resulted in the increased size of the family unit. By 1930 the size of the Japanese family in Hawaii had become larger than the equivalent unit in Japan— in plantations the average size of the Issei family was 5.4, a figure varying from island to island (Masuoka, 1940: 169). Thus the early period of settlement of the Japanese family, as with other birth rate and expanding family size. This pattern, similar to the rural family pattern in the "old country" would be tapered by a trend toward urbanization and the desire to improve the standard of living. Large families, necessary to the survival of a self-sufficient rural community of extended families, were economically unfeasible in a modern, socially progressing society. Large families meant larger costs, more expensive housing and less ability to save. As urbanization moved the Japanese family from plantation to town, the family size would abate.

The gradual urbanization of the Issei population corresponds with the movement away from the plantation in the 1920s. The plantation, with its closed economic system, undemocratic worker-employee relationship, and continually futile cycle of labor, was abandoned by large numbers of workers seeking alternative livelihoods, in Honolulu, small towns or on independent farms. Although 62,000 Japanese immigrants had entered the Islands between 1900 and 1922, the population of Japanese on the plantation had dropped from 31,000 to 17,000 (Fuchs, 1961: 120). More dramatically, the exodus of Japanese workers reduced their population on the plantation from 73.5% in 1902 to 18.8% in 1932 (Lind, 1969: 45).

The reduction of Japanese workers on the rural plantation meant a swelling of their numbers in urban centers. Though in 1900 only 10% of the Japanese population were living in Honolulu, this number had climbed to 22.4% in 1920 (Lind, 1967: 52). By 1930, one-third of the population of Honolulu was Japanese. Operating nearly 40% of the retail stores and influencing the composition of most blue-collar urban jobs, the Japanese filled the urban ghettos in areas such as Kalihi, Palama, Moiliili and Kakaako (Fuchs, 1961: 123).

The urbanization of the Japanese family has remained a significant trend since 1930. The population of Honolulu Japanese in 1960 was thirty-seven percent greater than their general Island proportion. In the smaller towns as well, Japanese have predominated. In 1960 forty-seven percent of

Hilo was Japanese and the ethnic group also comprised the majority of the populations of various small urban centers including Wahiawa, Waipahu, Wailuku, Honokaa, Lahaina, and Lihue (Lind, 1967: 52, 53).

The outcome of urbanization was a competitive spirit of social mobility. The immigrant family, without paternal protection, became keenly aware of the value of a rising standard of living. This in turn resulted in a decline of the early high birth rates and the subsequent reduction of family size. Especially the Nisei, trained to assimilate into an urban, competitive system, educated in birth control, and the economic advantages of smaller families, continued the trend.

Even in the early stages of the Issei experience, urban families were smaller than rural ones. In 1907, when the Japanese family was in its infancy, figures indicated that the rural family consisted of 3.6. members, while the urban family contained only 3.0 (Masuoka, 1940: 168). From 1930 to 1940 the birth rate of Japanese dropped substantially. In 1930, there were 1,112 Japanese children under five years of age per thousand women aged 20-44. By 1940 that number had tapered to 550.

Except for a post-World War II baby boom, a phenomenon characteristic of national trends, the Japanese birth rate continued to decline in the 1950s and 1960s. Indeed, the birth rate for the socially mobile Nisei generation was one of the lowest of any ethnic group in Hawaii (Horman, 1964: 2). And statistics in 1970 suggested a continuation of the reduction of birth rates and procreated family size—the younger Japanese, the third generation, Sansei, seem to be having continually smaller families (U.S. Department of Health, Education, and Welfare, 1974: 57).

Even though with the younger Sansei generation the procreating family has become increasingly nuclear in profile (the average Japanese household in 1960 was 4.1 persons, Johnson, 1972: 112), these nuclear families were linked, attitudinally and socially, with an extended kinship pattern. In other words, nuclear families of average household size are connected in the Japanese-American community in a modified extended-family network of relational dependencies and obligations. So as the

Gesellschaft reality or urban mobility and economic aggressiveness was reordering the internal structures of the Japanese
family, patterns of familial obligation and extended relations
were finding reexpression.

In her study of Japanese families in Honolulu, Colleen
Johnson investigated the familial identifications of a sample of
Nisei and Sansei and demonstrated the emergence of this
modified extended family. Johnson's results showed a progressively strong identification of succeeding generations—not
with the nuclear family, but with the extended familial network. So while 34% of the Nisei respondents felt their families
were nuclear in design, only 16% of the Sansei responded in a
like manner. In addition, 58% of the Sansei viewed their
families as a network of extended relationships, compared to
49% of the Nisei (1972: 115). Johnson (1972: 114) noticed
that in many cases, those interviewed even failed to mention
the nuclear family as part of their familial relations:

> In defining who constitutes their family (as opposed to "relatives") most
> respondents identified their immediate family as consisting of *their*
> *spouse and children, their own parents and siblings, and their families*
> *of procreation.* The recognition of the nuclear family to some respon-
> dents was so minimal that they neglected to include their own husband
> and children in listing their closest relationships.

What these results indicate is that progressively for the
Island Japanese family, as the birth rate and size of family has
stabilized in nearly typical urban patterns, the extended
relationships and identifications with kinship has for the
Sansei and Yonsei generations, intensified. This modified
extended family pattern, Johnson (1972: 109) suggests, is a
kinship model

> whereby nuclear families are bound together both through affectional
> ties and by choice. Although this family type does not resemble a
> corporate group sharing political and economic functions (as in
> primitive societies), it does preserve an emphasis on sentiment and
> sociability as well as mutual aid.

In part the psychological mechanisms behind the growth of a
modified extended family attitude is understood as a genera-

tional reaction to urbanization. For the Issei generation, without extended family relations, dependent on other immigrants, the identification was primarily with the Japanese ethnic community—in the alien world one gained strength through one's countrymen. But urbanization and the Gesellschaft pluralistic world were to weaken the ethnic bonds between the immigrant's progeny and the ethnic community. By the Sansei generation, the community would have little geographical integrity, few self-help services not provided for more effectively by state agencies, few means to express itself as a single ethnic group since ethnic assimilation and social mobility had undercut community identity. Granted that the Sansei identify as "Japanese" vis à vis other local ethnic groups. Granted that economic cooperation and cultural continuity of heritage as shared commonalities have a degree of relevancy to the young Japanese American. But these community ties are certainly not as solidifying as were the ties for the early immigrant community.

The waning community identifications have been overshadowed by an increasing family identification. While the ethnic group as a whole might not have much relevancy to Sansei lives, the ethnic family does have a significant impact. Uncles, aunts, cousins, nephews, nieces, grandparents, and even in some cases great-grandparents for the first time in the Japanese-American experience can play an effective role in creating cultural and psychological stability in the home. Even though the modified extended families do not live under the same roof, they are involved in relationships of extensive interdependency due to geographic propinquity. In Johnson's study, 75% of the Sansei respondents indicated that 30 or more of their relatives, compared with 53% of the Nisei respondents, lived on Oahu (1972: 111). Such kinship solidarity, geographically and attitudinally, implies that for the Sansei, familial values, behavioral influences and stuctural relationships are becoming more prominent as a source of identification and communication.

FAMILIAL VALUES AND THEIR AFFECT
ON COMMUNICATION

Due to the development of the modified extended family, traditional values of familialism continue to be inculcated in the present day Japanese-American experience. These values as they have been perpetuated in an urban setting remain to serve as determinants of Japanese-American behavior and communication. In particular, two broad tradition values can be examined as cultural forces shaping the interaction among the Japanese of Honolulu. First, the generations of Island Japanese have shored a common familial value toward filial piety and obligations in parent-child and sibling relationships. Second, family honor and image, the notion of the institution as an organic social whole, has been vigorously protected. Essentially, filial piety can be defined as the oath of empathy which links a person to the hierarchical order of the world. "Be loyal to thy land and be filial to thy parents" (Masuoka, 1936: 161), said the Japanese ethnical code. And the loyalty was engrained as an unquestioned emotional attachment to parents and siblings.

Filial piety was a Chinese Confucian concept transplanted into the Japanese conceptualization of *ie* and ancestral worship. Elders were to be respected, the authority of the *ie* was beyond reproach, the individual was committed, obligated to the family:

> The filial duty of a son is a continuous obligation as long as the family is in existence. It is handed down from one generation to another. "Fathers may not be fathers but sons must always be sons," and they must learn to be more pious than their fathers were to their forefathers. [Masuoka, 1936: 162]

Among Japanese-Americans, then, the deference shown parental authority, the acquiescence shown the parents through duty and compliance, are communication patterns stemming from filial piety which have been commonly affected. In essence, these patterns function to maintain familism as an organic unit. Indeed, the instance is rare of Japanese-Americans who cannot identify to some degree with the feeling of obligation and duty to family. Although the expression of individual desires and interests has perhaps increasingly modified the notion of absolute obedience, for the younger Sansei generation, the wishes of the family for even the Sansei are frequently the "last word" on the issue. Silent acquiescence to authority, an obedient submission of the individual for the "good of the family" are still cultural behaviors and attitudes functioning to maintain the integrity and cohesiveness of the Island Japanese family.

In addition to filial piety and obligation, another broad traditional value linking Japanese-Americans has been the notion of family honor and image. If the family is an important social and economic unit, an organic whole demanding obedience of its individual members, then the status of the family in the community is an imperative factor in behavior. The family must not be shamed. The individual must do nothing which reflects negatively on the image which the family projects to neighbors and friends. As Ruth Benedict (1946: 56) noted: "The Japanese learn . . . in their family experience that the greatest weight that can be given to a decision comes from the family conviction that it maintains the family honor."

Essentially, honor to the family organism involves the functions of several behavioral mechanisms creating communication patterns of self-restraint. Most prominent of these mechanisms is the use of *haji*, shame, to regulate individual behaviors. "What will others think of you?" "What will the neighbors say?" are behavioral injunctions reinforcing family honor and image.

This orientation of the Japanese individual as opposed to one of guilt or the self-appraisal of personal actions through conscience, is a more highly valued and effective tool of social conformity in the rural, Gemeinschaft community. In the Gesellschaft individual interest and will are supreme—what others think of you is really secondary to the establishment of mutually rewarding social contracts. In the Japanese Gemeinschaft world of relationships, implicit bonds of common purpose and mutual interdependency characterize social relationships instead of willfully designed explicit contracts. Consequently, the judgment of your peers and family, what

others think of you, is an important determinant reinforcing
bonds of love. If you fail to implicitly perpetuate the open
bonds of love and trust, then you irrevocably threaten your
position in the society—you are shamed.

The behavior of the individual with respect to the family
organism is also maintained through the cultural norms of
enryo. *Enryo* involves a complex of deference behaviors
helping to establish the perimeters of the individual's freedom.
Harry H.L. Kitano in his definitive study, *Japanese Americans*, (1969: 169), employed the concept of enryo to discuss
many of the self-restrained communication patterns of the
Japanese-American:

> *Enryo* helps to explain much of Japanese-American behavior. As with
> other norms, it had both a positive and negative effect on Japanese
> acculturation. For example, take observations of Japanese in situations
> as diverse as their hesitancy to speak out at meetings; their refusal of any
> invitation, especially the first time; their refusal of a second helping;
> their acceptance of a less desired object when given a free choice; their
> lack of verbal participation, especially in an integrated group; their
> refusal to ask questions; and their hesitancy in asking for a raise in
> salary—these may be based on *enryo*. The inscrutable face, the
> noncommittal answer, the behavioral reserve can often be traced to this
> norm so that the stereotype of the shy, reserved Japanese in ambiguous
> social situations is often an accurate one.

Highly sensitive to the feelings of others, reactive to the
opinions of peers and relatives, deferent to status and age, the
Japanese individual becomes hesitant to express himself
verbally: once the words have been said, they cannot be
retracted. The shame, the confrontation, the highly emotional
charge have already been released. The individual learns the
value and advantages of "keeping the mouth shut" when
necessary, demurely acquiescing in unpleasant situations and
kuchigotae suru na "don't answer back" in the face of
authority.

The values of filial piety and family honor have to varying
degrees and styles defined the cultural character of Hawaii's
Japanese. In no two families, for no two individuals are
communication behaviors, values, and world views identical.
But the modally shared values of family respect, obligation, the

sensitive regard for honor, image and status, and the intense personal identification with the familiy unit, often at the expense of individual self-action or open communication, are themes of the Japanese family which have touched all generations.

And these values have, to a large degree, superceded the structural urban changes of the nuclearized Japanese family. Though the family has become structurally attuned to Gesellschaft society, patterns of communication and other behaviors in step with a Gemeinschaft spirit of *ie,* especially on the familial level, have tenaciously survived. And this "survival" of *ie* patterns will be increasingly relevant to the Japanese-American modified extended family as the cultural transmission between generations become more coherent. As an enculturator of ethnic values, the Sansei family will have to deal less with the difficult social and cultural issues with which previous generations grappled. Language difficulties, value confrontations and adapting to multicultural inputs are concerns mostly irrelevant for Sansei. The culture of the Japanese-American, the fusion of a number of cultural elements in everday life-style and the promulgation of numerous highly ingrained values will be passed on with greater integrity for future generations.

Moreover, for the Sansei and their children, the greater emergence of grandparents as active transmitters will also enhance the ethnic integrity of the Japanese family and individual. Grandparents, especially in the extended family situation, are "caretakers of culture," passing on the cultural continuity of their world view to the grandchildren—a role perpetuated by many grandparents in the Sansei family. Significantly, Johnson's (1972: 186) study revealed that 60% of the Sansei respondents indicated that grandparents played an active, welcome part in family affairs.

This active role of a new generation of Nisei grandparents, the kinship solidarity between economically independent but emotionally affiliative nuclear families in a modified extended pattern, portend a continually strengthened ethnic communication among the Sansei and future generations. Family, not community will be the focus of Japanese-American ethnic identity and communication in a Hawaiian pluralistic society. And the basis of this family identity will be a maturing blend of dynamic Gesellshaft structures with a pervasive spirit of Gemeinschaft cultural commonalities.

CONCLUSION

As have been discussed, the determinants of Japanese-American communication in the urban setting of Honolulu have evolved from several familial values having traditional roots in the rural villages of Japan. Though perhaps in the Japanese-American experience other values have been adapted or lost in American acculturation, the values of filial piety and family honor appear to have remained vibrant in the human relations and communication patterns found within the Japanese ethnic group. Indeed, contrary to the general notion that urbanization has produced radical changes in cultural values and outlooks, as seen by the modified extended family of the Sansei, a spirit of Gemeinschaft continues to be generated, binding individuals with their families and families with their ethnic group.

More importantly, in providing insight into the general area of Asian-American communication, perhaps the case of Honolulu's Japanese-Americans also suggests an approach to the study of the communication of Chinese, Korean, Filipino, and other Asian groups found in urban settings. Perhaps the familial organism remains to function effectively within the Asian-American cultural matrix of today. And if such is the case, perhaps the humanism, the bond of affiliative relationships, the sense of tradition, and ethnic identification innate in the Gemeinschaft family will continue to provide meaning for Asian-Americans, counter-balancing the alienating, impersonal forces generated in a modern, technological society.

REFERENCES

BENEDICT, R. (1946) *The Chrysanthemum and the Sword.* Cleveland, Ohio: World.
DORE, R.P. (1958) *City Life in Japan: A Study of a Tokyo Ward.* Berkeley: Univ. of California Press.

FUCHS, L. (1961) *Hawaii Pono: A Social History.* New York: Harcourt, Brace & World.

HILO, M. and HIMENO, E. (1957) "Some characteristics of American and Japanese culture." *Social Process in Hawaii,* 21: 34-41.

HORMANN, B. (1964) "The contemporary family in Hawaii." Honolulu: Social Work Conference.

JOHNSON, C. (1972) "The Japanese American family and community in Honolulu: Generational continuities in ethnic affiliation." Unpublished Ph.D Thesis, Syracuse University, New York.

KITANO, H. (1969) *Japanese Americans: Evolution of a Subculture.* Englewood Cliffs, N.J.: Prentice Hall.

LIND, A.W. (1969) *Hawaii, the Last of the Magic Isles.* London: Oxford Univ. Press.

⎯⎯⎯ (1967) *Hawaii's People.* Honolulu: Univ. of Hawaii Press.

MASUOKA, J. (1940) "The structure of the Japanese family in Hawaii." *American Journal of Sociology,* 46, 2.

⎯⎯⎯ (1936) "Changing moral bases of the Japanese family in Hawaii." *Sociology and Social Research,* 21, 2.

TONNIES, F. (1963) *Gemeinschaft and Gesellschaft.* Charles Loomis (trans.) New York: Harper & Row.

United States Department of Health, Education and Welfare (1974) *A Study of Selected Socio-Economic Characteristics of Ethnic Minorities Based on the 1970 Census, Volume II: Asian Americans. Washington: United States Printing Office.*

19

A CROSSCULTURAL STUDY OF
MATE RECRUITING THROUGH MASS MEDIA

ERIKA VORA
JAY A. VORA

St. Cloud State University

This study deals with the recruitment of marital partners through advertisements in newspapers and magazines. It encompasses three cultures representing three nations, namely, India, the United States, and West Germany. The purpose of this study is (1) to develop patterns and a hierarchy of criteria used in mate recruiting in the above cultures; (2) to test the applicability of existing concepts of premarital relationships; (3) to develop a framework for understanding and explaining recruiting methods in the three cultures; and (4) to discuss the implications for crosscultural recruiting.

Marriage is an accepted social concept and norm in most cultures for a permanent relationship between a man and a woman. There are many stages of interaction between the mates before marriage. In Western societies, these premarital stages may be sequentially described as recruiting, followed by "casual dating, going steady, engaged to be engaged (pinned), and engaged" (Delora, 1963: 81-84). Courting or dating is not a generally accepted custom in India. The premarital stages in India consist of recruiting, betrothel, and engagement. The focus of this study is on the first premarital stage, that is, recruiting in the Western cultures of the United States and West Germany and the Eastern culture of India.

In Germany and the United States, prospective mates are introduced in schools, colleges, at work, at church, through one's interest or hobbies (playing tennis, swimming, skiing, and so on), through sociability networks (parties), as well as by chance contacts (traveling, public transportation, shopping, restaurants). In India, these sources of acquaintance are rare. Except for a slight chance when in college, the opportunities for getting acquainted with a person of the opposite sex are almost nonexistent. Usually, it is the family's responsibility to locate eligible mates and to introduce the potential mates after a familial match is considered acceptable (Goldstein, 1972: 38). Our study is limited to the recruiting of eligible mates through advertisements in newspapers and magazines rather than through the introductions described above. Although matrimonial advertisements are not traditional in either Germany, the United States, or India, they provide an excellent source of formally stated explicit descriptions of mate characteristics.

Mate selection has been studied in many Western countries, such as Denmark (Auken, 1964: 124), Finland (Haavio-Mannila, 1964: 155), France (Michel, 1964: 163), Sweden (Ramsoy, 1966: 773), as well as in such eastern countries as Japan (Blood, 1967: 3) and India (Chekki, 1968: 707). There are numerous studies in various stages of mate selection as well as on the total process of mate selection (Cavan, 1953; Waller and Hill, 1951; Kerckhoff and Davis, 1951). However, the studies on recruiting are few. Since recruiting sets boundaries on the pool of eligible and available potential mates for the selection process it is, we believe, of extreme importance to a successful selection of a marital partner.

METHODOLOGY

Matrimonial advertisements from nationally distributed newspapers and magazines in India, the United States, and West Germany were collected for this study. The sample size, the mates' median age ranges and the specific mass media sources are described in Table 19.1. The sample sizes varied from 306 to 402 male and female advertisers in each country. The advertisers in India were the youngest (in their 20s) of the three countries while those from the United States were the oldest (in their 40s).

For India, primary data were gathered from matrimonial advertisements published in *The Times of India* (October, 19,

Table 19.1: Sample Descriptions from Three Countries

Country	India		U.S.A.		West Germany	
Sex	Male	Female	Male	Female	Male	Female
Sample Size	148	158	185	210	230	172
Median Age	26-30	20-25	41-45	43-47	37-41	37-41
Source of Media	Times of India		*Horoscope* "Midnight"		*Brigitte* *Heim and Welt* *Die Welt* *Bielefelder Anzeigen* *Mindener Tageblatt* *Neue Westfaelische*	

26, 1975; November 9, 16, 1975). These included 148 male and 158 female mate seekers. The following descriptions of a sample of advertisements represent the degree of specificity in the content (*Times of India:* November 16, 1975):

> Educated parents invite matrimonial correspondence for their son, 26 years, 175 cm. Good personality. Chief Officer, Mercantile Navy, salary 3.000—Good Saraswat Brahmin girl should be educated, smart looking, good family. Contact with horoscope.

> Wanted most handsome Iyengar bridegroom—NonShetamarshana Gothram, highly qualified Class I Officer with four figure salary, below 28—for fair, beautiful girl, 19, well versed in Bharatha, Natyam, studying B.A. Reply with horoscope.

The American advertisements were taken from the magazine, *Horoscope* (May, 1977), and the leaflet "Midnight" (April 19, 1977). The following are two examples of the advertisements:

> Professional man, in his 40s, 185 lbs., down to earth, with beautiful home, seeking slender, warm gal, 25-35, sensitive, homeloving. Must relocate to him. [*Horoscope*: May, 1977].

> Tall, classy gal, 39, magnetic personality, full of life. She's a psychic artist and business woman. Wants to meet tall, modern, honest man who is working to help humanity. [*Horoscope*: May, 1977].

The German matrimonial advertisements were taken from the following magazines and newspapers: *Brigitte* (February

10, 24, 1977; January 27, 1977). Newspaper sources included such national papers as *Heim und Welt* (April, 1977) and *Die Welt* (April, 1977), as well as two newspapers from Westfalia, namely, *Bielefelder Anzeigen* (April, 1977) and *Mindener Tageblatt* (March 26, 1977; April 2, 1977). Examples of the German advertisements and their translations are as follows (*Heim und Welt*; April, 1977):

Junger Mann, 39 Jahre, 1,85 gr., schlank, dunkelblond, natuerlicher sportlicher Typ, ortsgebunden, Wohnung vorhanded, Beruf Techn. Angestellter, wuenscht auf diesem Wge ein nettes, liebes und anstaendiges Maedel zwecks Ehe kennenzulernen (Alter 25-35 Jahre).

Translation: Young man, 39 years, 1.85 m tall, slim, dark blond, natural, sporty type, region bound, with home, employed as a technician, would like to meet a nice, loving, and decent girl through this channel for marriage.

West Berlin, Wwe, 54 Jahre, 1,68 gross, blond, sehnt sich nach einem netten, lieben Partner.

Translation: West Berlin, widow, 54 years, 1,68 m tall, blond, longs for a nice, loving partner.

ANALYSIS AND FINDINGS

The data from the various newspapers and magazines were analyzed for content into two major categories: the self-descriptions of the mate seekers called the "proffered characteristics" and the "desired characteristics" prescribed by them. The data were further subcategorized into coded criteria such as age, height, attractiveness, education, caste or sub-caste, and so on. The coded criteria in these subcategories and their empirical descriptions in the data are summarized in Table 19.2.

The proffered characteristics of the male and female mate seekers from the three countries (India, the United States, and West Germany) are summarized in Table 19.3. The coded criteria are presented in the order of descending frequency. Any criteria with a percentage frequency of less than 12 percent were arbitrarily excluded from this list as being insignificant.

Table 19.2: Empirical Descriptions of Coded Criteria

Coded Criteria	Empirical Descriptions
Affectionate	Affectionate, loving, kind, trusting, understanding
Appearance	Mostly height, sometimes weight
Attractive	Good looking, beautiful, handsome
Education	BA, BS, MS, MSc, Phd, graduate, educated
Financial Security	Steady income; own home, property
Interests	Hobbies, music, travel
Natural	Natural, simple
Nice	Nice, likeable
Sporty	Sporty, athletic
Occupation	Government job, chemist, business man, technician, professional, teacher
Caste/Subcaste	Brahmin, Gotram
Subculture	Bavarian, Westfalian, Berliner

The characteristics desired from the mates in the three countries are summarized in descending order of their frequency (see Table 19.4). Any criteria with less than 8 percent frequency were excluded as being insignificant. This percentage was smaller than that for the proffered characteristics because the mate seekers were less explicit on the desired characteristics than the proffered characteristics. The norm seemed to be that of "selling your credentials" while encouraging a broad choice of applicants.

It should be noted that the proffered characteristics and the desired characteristics are not easily separable although they are presented in two separate tables. They are not independent of one another. In many cases a mate seeker gave his/her self-description on his/her age for example, and at the same time listed the desired age of the mate. In some cases the proffered characteristics implied desired characteristics such as subcaste, subculture, and even physical height, and age. Hence, the findings of this study were to be assessed with their totality in perspective. The findings for each individual country are discussed, followed by a crosscultural analysis of these findings.

Proffered and Desired Characteristics of Mates Recruited in India

Male and female advertisers described themselves in terms of being a certain age, educator, occupation, attractiveness,

Table 19.3: Proffered Qualities (in Descending Order) of Advertisers Based upon Frequency

Males

United Stated		India		West Germany	
Age	81%	Age	89%	Age	90%
Height/Wt.	71%	Education	77%	Height	64%
Occupation	40%	Occupation	57%	Occupation	40%
Financial Sec.	23%	Subcaste	45%	Subculture	31%
Interests	23%	Attractive	31%	Financial Sec.	29%
Attractive	19%	Financial Sec.		Sporty	18%
Nonsmoker/		(Income)	24%	Hair & Eye	
Nondrinker	14%			Color	14%
Retired	14%			Attractive	14%
				Slim	13%
(N = 185)		(N = 148)		(N = 230)	

Females

United States		India		West Germany	
Age	81%	Age	95%	Age	83%
Height/Wt.	57%	Education	68%	Hair & Eyes	32%
Marital Stat.		Attractive	39%	Subculture	31%
(Divorced/Wid.)	41%	Occupation	27%	Occupation	22%
Interests	38%			Marital Stat.	
Attractive	34%			(Div./Wid.)	22%
Hair & Eye				Attractive	16%
Color	25%			Children	12%
Financial Sec.	21%			Slim	12%
Occupation	14%				
Nonsmoker/					
Nondrinker	13%				
(N = 210)		(N = 158)		(N = 172)	

and subcaste group. They were looking for similar characteristics in their future mates. In addition, the females sought and the males offered financial security through steady income or ownership of some property. The males sought their mate to come from an influential family. Most of the above findings were supported by seven other empirical research studies (see Table 19.5). Their combined sample size represented 6,579 advertisements and covered six major Indian newspapers (published in English) from four large metropolitan centers.

Table 19.4: Desired Qualities in Descending Order (of Importance) Based upon Frequencies

Males

United States		India		West Germany	
Age	36%	Age	23%	Age	8%
Financial Sec.	17%	Occupation	20%		
Interests	17%	Education	18%		
Height/Wt.	11%	Subcaste	18%		
"One woman man"	8%	Financial Sec.	17%		
(N = 210)		(N =158)		(N = 172)	

Females

United States		India		West Germany	
Affectionate,		Education	43%	Loving, trust.,	
Loving, kind	38%	Attractive	34%	Understanding,	
Able to relocate	17%	Occupation	17%	Tolerant	22%
Attractive	17%	Same Caste	14%	Age	18%
Age	17%	Caste no bar	14%	Nice	18%
Slender	13%	Influential Family	10%	Children	17%
Interests	10%			Natural	14%
				Attractive	9%
(N = 185)		(N = 148)		(N = 230)	

Their patterns of criteria for seeking mates were essentially the same as the findings from our data.

Proffered and Desired Characteristics of Mates Recruited in the United States

The proffered and the desired characteristics of male mates were their age, appearance, financial security, and interests. In addition, the males described themselves in terms of their occupation, attractiveness, being nonsmokers/nondrinkers, and their retirement stage. The females, on the other hand, sought "a one woman man." The desired and proffered characteristics of women were their age, attractiveness, and interests. The most important desired characteristic of female mates was that they be affectionate in addition to being slender

Table 19.5: Proffered and Desired Characteristics of Matrimonial Mates in Seven Articles

The most proffered qualities described by

Males		Females	
Age	79.8%	Caste	81.9%
Occupation	77.0%	Age	79.8%
Caste	75.8%	Education	69.2%
Salary	48.2%	Attractive	55.1%
Education	40.9%	Occupation	24.4%
Attractive	17.3%		

The most desired qualities wanted from

Females		Males	
Attractive	64.3%	Same Caste	65.7%
Same Caste	63.5%	Occupation	63.0%
Education	44.8%	Income/Property	16.5%
Influential Family	33.4%	Education	14.4%
Employed	15.0%	Age	13.4%

SOURCE: See Reyes-Hocking (166:25-39) and Das (1964:151-159). Also see Agrawal (1964:107-112), Anand (1965:59-71), Chakrabarti (1974:142-143). Compare Gist (1953:481-495), Wiebe and Ramu (1971:111-120).

Table 19.6: Filtering Factors in Mate Recruiting

Filtering Factors	Criteria
Sociocultural	Subcaste, Subculture, Education
Economic	Occupation, Financial Security
Physical Traits	Age, Height, Weight, Hair and Eye Color
Psychological Factors	Interests, hobbies
Emotional Factors	Affectionate, Understanding

and able to relocate. The female advertisers, however, described their appearance (height and weight), hair and eye color, financial security, marital status (in terms of being divorced or widowed), occupation, and being nonsmoker/nondrinker. The financial security among female mate speakers, the non-smoking/nondrinking self-descriptions of males and females, and the men seeking affectionate women who are able to relocate may suggest uniqueness and trends in mate recruiting in the United States.

Proffered and Desired Characteristics
of Mates Recruited in West Germany

The male and female mate seekers in West Germany described themselves in terms of their age, height, occupation, subculture (region), hair and eye color, attractiveness, and being slim. In addition, the men described their financial security and being sporty (athletic). The women, on the other hand, described their marital status (widowed or divorced) and the fact that they had children.

The desired characteristics from the female mates were that they be affectionate, nice, natural, attractive, and of a certain age. The men welcomed women with children. The only characteristic that the women specifically desired of their mates was a certain age. However, the self-descriptions of both sexes imply that there are additional desirable characteristics such as height, slimness, and belonging to a certain regional culture.

Crosscultural Comparative Analysis

Are there any mate characteristics common to all the three cultures of India, the United States, and West Germany? Our findings indicated that the men and women advertising for mates in newspapers and magazines described their age, occupation, and attractiveness. In addition, men from all the three cultures described their financial security (see Figure 19.1 and 19.2). The only explicitly stated characteristic that women in all the countries desired of the sought mate was a certain age. Men in every culture looked for and explicitly stated that the sought mate be attractive. However, implicitly and explicitly, every culture considered age, attractiveness, occupation, and financial security (for men) as important in recruiting marital partners.

Are there any culture-specific mate characteristics in recruiting mates through newspapers and magazines (mass media)? The education levels of the mates were emphasized only in the Indian culture. Interests and hobbies as well as being nonsmoker/nondrinker were unique to the United States. Women with children, and men welcoming children were a

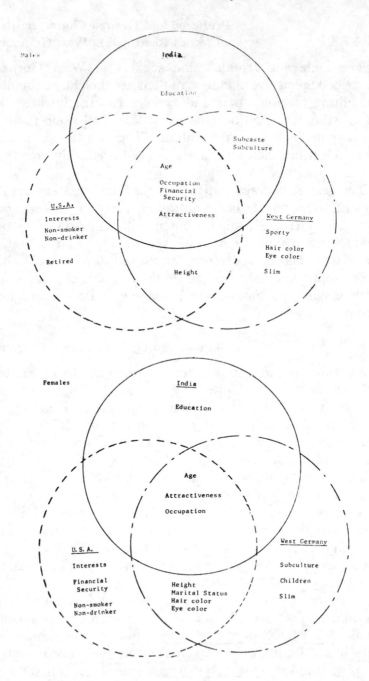

Figure 19.1: Proffered Characteristics of Mates in Three Cultures

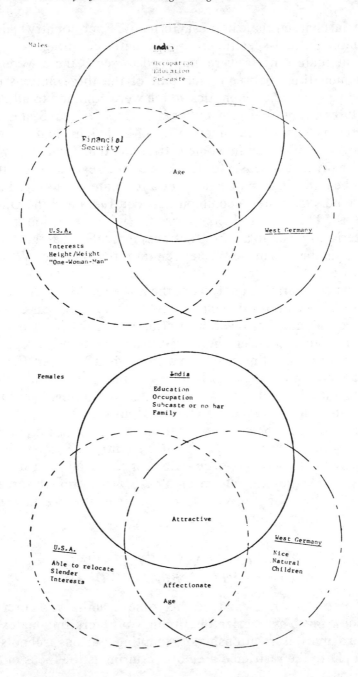

Figure 19.2: Desired Characteristics of Mates in Three Cultures

special characteristic in West Germany. Each country had one or more culture-specific criteria in mate recruiting.

The mate criteria were analyzed to see if there were any commonalities between each pair of the three nations (excluding those characteristics which were common to all three cultures). The Western cultures of the United States and Germany shared such mate criteria as height, hair and eye color, and affection in women. It seems that India and West Germany had subcaste for the former and regional subculture for the latter in common as criteria for mate recruiting. There were no such criteria common between India and the United States. These paired comparisons (with exclusion of the criteria common to all three nations) indicated that there were more similarities in the Western cultures than between Western and Eastern cultures.

The comparative analysis of the mate recruiting criteria in these three cultures indicated that (1) there were pan-cultural as well as culture-specific criteria, and (2) there was more commonality between the two Western cultures in terms of criteria in recruiting marital partners than between Eastern and Western cultures. It should be noted that although there were some pan-cultural criteria for mate recruiting, they do not have the same meaning in all these cultures. For example, what is considered a beautiful woman in one country may not be considered the same in the other two countries. The perception of what is a good age, occupation, or financial security may vary from culture to culture. In other words, while the criteria may be common across cultures, their evaluative measurement may be culture specific.

APPLICATIONS OF EXISTING CONCEPTUAL FRAMEWORKS

There does not exist at this time a unitary theoretical framework to synthesize the findings on recruiting mates for future marital relationships. Adapting various schools of thought to the restricted area of recruiting is the focus of this section.

Homogamy

Many research studies have supported homogamy as a factor in mate selection (Christensen, 1964). The concept of homogamy states that "like tends to attract like." (Sullivan, 1972: 11). Our findings indicated that attractive or "good looking" men and women sought the same qualities in their mates in all three cultures. Furthermore, mates with similar interests and hobbies were sought in the United States. "Nice" and likeable mates were sought in West Germany by individuals of similar qualities. Educated mates sought educated marital partners in India. These findings support the notion that the concept of homogamy is operating in the recruitment of mates.

Mating Gradient

The concept of the mating gradient refers to the tendency of males to marry down with regard to certain mate characteristics. Glick and Landau (1950: 517-529) found that males tend to marry younger females. Our findings supported the same concept in mate recruiting. However, the slope of the gradient varied between the three cultures. The desired age difference between marital partners was about 10 years in thee United States and about six years in West Germany and in India.

Endogamy

Marrying within a given group is called endogamy. The endogamous norms were operative in mate recruiting in India and West Germany. The Indian advertisers sought mates belonging to the same or similar caste and subcaste as their own. Chekki (1968: 707-711) reports on similar findings in mate selection and lends some support to our findings. An interesting (and unexpected) finding of this study was that the advertisers in West Germany advertised their region of residence (with its unique subculture). This implied a tendency toward endogamy within subcultures in West Germany. Michel's (1964: 143-176) study of mate selection in Norway lends some credibility to our findings. He states that some values and norms respected in each ethnic group or social class determine the acceptability or rejection of other choices (of mates). There was insufficient support for endogamy in mate recruiting in the United States. This may be an artifact of our data source.

Propinquity

Residential propinquity has been reported as a major factor in mate selection (Katz and Hill, 1958: 27-35). Burchinal (1960) suggested that the influence of residential propinquity may increase during the courtship process. Our findings do not tend to support this concept as a major factor in recruiting mates. Propinquity may become important as a by-product of the endogamous concept operating through Indian subcastes and West German regional subcultures, but it was not an explicit criterium in the matrimonial advertisements. In addition, men in the United States sought women who were able to relocate. The emphasis here was mobility rather than residential propinquity. These findings suggested that propinquity was not a major factor in the recruiting stage of mate selection. However, it may become more important as one progresses through various sequential stages of mate selection as suggested by Burchinal (1960).

The Structural-Functional Concept

Jacobson and Matheny (1962: 98-123) have described two ideal types of marriage systems: the closed and the open. Since the closed marriage system has a relatively stable and homogeneous social organization, it provides a convenient matrix from which functional relationships can be deduced. Hence, one develops function from structure. Open marriage systems have heterogenous and often mutually contradictory subsystems. Accordingly, in order to generate viable theoretical propositions concerning the social order, we should attempt to derive structure from function. Hence, it is important to determine the relative closeness or openness of marriage systems in a culture before applying the structural-functional concept.

In the closed marriage system, the criteria for the choice of a mate are minutely specified by impersonal norms, prescriptions, and proscriptions; the element of choice is minimized and the system predetermines boundaries. Our findings indicated that there is generally the same number of prescriptions and proscriptions in all three cultures under study. However, the boundaries were limited by subcastes in India and subcultures in West Germany. There were no such boundaries in the United States. The prescriptions or characteristics desired from males in West Germany were much fewer than in the other two cultures. Hence, one would describe India as having a relatively closed marriage system and West Germany as being in between the other two countries.

TOWARD CONCEPTUAL SYNTHESIS

"Modern mates expect to form a dyad whose members have been consciously fitted to order" (Jacobson and Matheny, 1962: 109). The findings of this study suggest that the process of filtering prospective marriage partners is dynamic (see Figure 19.3). The filtering process is achieved by recruiting a

Filtering in the Mate Seeking Process

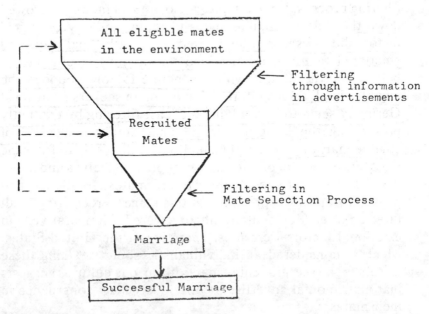

Figure 19.3: Filtering in the Mate Seeking Process

few selected mates from all the eligible ones in the environment. Further filtering of the recruited mates continues until a final decision on marrying a mate is made, which hopefully will lead to a successful marriage. It should be noted that the process is not flowing in one direction only, but loops back and can have more than one element operating at the same time. For example, recruiting may continue while the selection process goes on. If the recruiting has not been successful enough, one may go back to advertise more and reduce filtering factors.

Kerckhoff and Davis (1961) have recognized "filtering factors" in mate selection processes. We, too, recognize filtering factors in mate recruiting (see Table 19.1). The criteria for mate recruiting in his study were grouped under five factors; sociocultural, economic, physical traits, psychological attributes, and emotional factors. The effect of filtering is dependent upon the number of these factors used and their influence on circumscribing the field of eligible mates.

The purpose of filtering is to make mate seeking efficient and effective toward finding a suitable marital partner. There seems to be a conscious effort to seek congruence through the filtering process. For example, sociocultural factors narrowed down the field of eligible mates in India, and psychological factors did the same in the United States. Physical traits and emotional factors circumscribed the number of eligibles in both Western cultures while economic factors bounded the eligibles in all three cultures. Female mate seekers from West Germany seem to be applying the least filtering by explicitly prescribing the least number of characteristics desired of eligible marital partners. The males of India seem to filter the most by giving a lot of information about themselves and about desired characteristics of their future mates. Economic and physical traits were prevalent at this stage of recruiting in all three cultures. Sociocultural factors were least operative, and emotional factors were most operative in the United States, which is considered an individualistic society. Using these factors in the recruitment of mates in various cultures suggests that matrimonial advertisers consciously seek congruence in their mates.

Although the filtering process operates in every culture, the filtering factors and their importance are culture specific. For example, the sociocultural factor is of major importance in India, while the emotional factor is of major importance in the United States and West Germany. Economic factors weigh much more in India than in Western nations. The opposite seems to hold for the physical attribute factor.

The findings and the proposed conceptual framework were bounded by the scope of this study. This research was enveloped by the cultures of three nations and a sample of matrimonial advertisements in newspapers and magazines. Future research in the field of recruiting marriage partners through a variety of applicable channels in many cultures and subcultures is needed to test and refine the proposed theoretical frameworks. Longitudinal studies of the entire process of mate selection (from recruiting to the final marriage decision) in different cultures could not only provide a broader theoretical framework for marriage, but also for studying the cultures themselves as well. On the pragmatic side, these kinds of studies may lead to successful approaches for intercultural marriages.

REFERENCES

AGRAWAL, K.G. (1964) "Marital choices in India." *Indian Journal of Psychology,* 39: 107-112.

ANAND, K. (1965) "An analysis of matrimonial advertisements." *Sociological Bulletin,* 14: 59-71.

AUKEN, K. (1964) "Time of marriage, mate selection and task accomplishment in newly formed Copenhagen families." *Acta Sociologica,* 8.

BIELEFELDER ANZEIGEN (April, 1977).

BIRCHINAL, L.G. (1960) "Research on young marriages: Implication for family life education." *The Family Life Co-ordinator,* 8.

BLOOD, R. A., Jr. (1967) *Love Match and Arranged Marriage.* New York: Free Press.

BRIGITTE (Jan. 27, 1977: Feb 10,1977; Feb. 24, 1977).

CAVAN, R.S. (1953) *The American Family.* New York: Crowell.

CHAKRABARTI, T. (1974) "Attitudes reflected in matrimonial advertisements."
   The Australian and New Zealand Journal of Sociology, 10.
CHEKKI, D.A. (1968) "Mate selection, age at marriage, and propinquity among the
   Lingayats of India." *Journal of Marriage and the Family,* 30.
CHRISTENSEN, H.T. (1964) *Handbook of Marriage and the Family.* Chicago:
   Rand McNally.
DAS, B. (1964) "An analysis of the matrimonial column advertisements of news-
   papers." *Indian Journal of Psychology,* 39.
DELORA, J. (1963) "Social systems of dating on a college campus." *Marriage and
   Family Living,* 25.
DIE WELT (April, 1977).
GIST, N. (1953-1954) "Mate selection and mass communication in India." *Public
   Opinion Quarterly* (Winter): 481-495.
GLICK, P. and LANDAU, E. (1950) "Age as a factor in marriage." *American
   Sociological Review,* 15.
GOLDSTEIN, R.L. (1972) *Indian Women in Transition.* Metuchen, N.J.: The
   Scarecrow Press.
HAAVIO-MANNILA, E. (1964) "Local homogamy in Finland," *Acta Sociologica,*
   8.
HEIM UND WELT (April, 1977).
HOROSCOPE (May, 1977): 78-80.
JACOBSON, P. and MATHENY A. (1962) "Mate selection in open marriage
   systems." *International Journal of Comparative Sociology,* 3.
KATZ, A.M. and HILL R. (1958) "Residential propinquity and marital selection: A
   review of theory, method, and fact." *Marriage and Family Living,* 20.
KERCKHOFF, A.C. and DAVIS, K. (1961) "Value consensus and need complemen-
   tarity in mate selection." Paper presented at the annual meeting of the American
   Sociological Association, St. Louis.
MICHEL, A. (1964) "Mate selection in various ethnic groups in France." *Acta
   Sociologica,* 8.
MIDNIGHT (April 19, 1977):38-39.
MINDENER TAGEBLATT (April, 1977).
NEUE WESTFAELISCHE (April, 1977).
RAMSOY, N.R. (1966) "Assortative mating and the structure of cities." *American
   Sociological Review,* 31.
RYES-HOCKINGS, A. (1966) "The newspaper as a surrogate marriage broker in
   India."*Sociological Bulletin,* 15.
SULLIVAN, J.A. (1972) *Selection of Dates and Mates.* Ohio: Ohio State University.
THE TIMES OF INDIA (October, 19,1977; November 9,1977; November16,
   1975).
WALLER, W. and HILL, R. (1951) *The Family: A Dynamic Interpretation.* New
   York: Henry Holt.
WIEBE, P.D. and RAMU, G.N. (1971) "Marriage in India: A content analysis of
   matrimonial advertisements." *Man in India,* 51: 111-120.

20

CULTURAL SELF-COMPREHENSION IN ETHNICALLY PLURAL SOCIETIES: THE CASE OF SUB-SAHARAN AFRICA

AKINADE O. SANDA

University of Ibadan, Nigeria

It is most difficult to be comprehensive and certainly impossible to be exhaustive in any discussion of African culture which is limited to a few pages. This is mainly due to both the richness of the culture concerned as well as the extensive literature which currently exists on the subject. Any intellectual concern with African culture must therefore necessarily limit itself to a few cultural phenomena which are manageable or which can adequately be subsumed under the immediate area of discourse. Consequently, this paper will be concerned with only a few aspects of African culture as they relate to the problem of cultural self-comprehension in the multiethnic societies of sub-Saharan Africa.

Our concern with cultural self-comprehension in black Africa should be perceived to be concern with the nature of self definition of Africans by Africans in relation to cultural forms, values, and attitudes which are peculiarly African. Before we consider such definitions of African culture by Africans in our research areas, however, it may be helpful to consider initially some of the existing definitions of African culture by both Africans and non-Africans. Such a concern will be followed by a consideration of some of the self-definitions of African culture which are reflected in oral literature (proverbs) that transcend ethnic divisions. Subsequently, we shall summarize the core arguments of the paper in a concluding section.

AUTHOR'S NOTE: *This is a revised version of a paper presented at the International Symposium on the Self-Comprehension of Nations, Innsbruck, Austria, July, 1974.*

CULTURAL DIVERSITY IN BLACK AFRICA

The designation of specific patterns of culture as African is sure to elicit considerable criticism from scholars who ascribe greater significance to ethnic pluralism and to assumed diversity of cultures in black Africa. For instance, Meyer Fortes, (1972: IX) has raised the relevant issue in a cogent way. He asks,

> by what criteria can we include under this rubric, both the culture of the Kung Buah men of the Kalahari—those gentle, peaceful, propertyless, hunting and collecting folk . . . and the traditional patterns of life and thought of the sophisticated, materially wealthy, politically and socially complex, militarily organized Kingdoms of West Africa—Ashanti, Benin, Yoruba and Hausa."

This skepticism expressed by Fortes did not prevent him from writing an introduction to Ayisi's (1972) book on African Culture. But similar recognitions of the degree of cultural diversity in black Africa are contained in the works of Murdock (1959), Turnbull (1962: 19), Bohannan and Curtin (1971: 17), Hunter (1963: 323), Levine (1966), Olorunsola (1972), Brown and Ford (1964), Middleton (1970), and Cohen and Middleton (1970). In addition, series of monographs and journal articles on individual and labeled African Societies (e.g., Ethnographic Survey of Africa edited by D. Forde), also convey the impression of both linguistic[1] ethnic and cultural diversity in Africa. Each of the ethnic groups identified is therefore assumed to be heir to distinctive cultural traditions. As far as scholars in the above category are concerned, therefore, it may be more appropriate to talk of African cultures rather than talk about African culture which, to them, appear more of a myth than a social reality.

However, another group of scholars would accord partial recognition to some cultural patterns which are believed to retain some distinctively African (rather than ethnic) characteristics. This category of Africanists suggest in addition that the cultural interaction of Africa with the West, especially during the colonial period, has resulted in tremendous modification or transformation of traditional African culture, including the economy, religion, education, technology, and communication of Africans. Turnbull (1962: 35), for instance, contends that the contemporary African stands in between the African tradition and the Western tradition; that he belongs to neither of the two traditions, and consequently experiences some feeling of loneliness—"a sense of a lack of something in their lives."

Also, in the same context, both Wole Soyinka's *The Lion and the Jewel* (1963) and Chinua Achebe's *No Longer At Ease* (1960) depict the conflict of cultures—especially the value conflicts—which the authors perceived as attendant on the process of cultural interaction between Africa and the West. Alain Richard (1970: 1) has vividly described this in connection with African writers:

> The writer thus finds himself in a very ambiguous situation, particularly in Africa. On the one hand, he affirms the dignity of his own culture and that of his language. On the other hand, he uses a Western language, and often his cultural references are Western.

Similar emergent dualism in value systems, preferences, social institutions and styles of life have been ably described by Hunter (1963: 317-318). In music, in art, in literature, in dance, in normative orientations, this second group of authors question the extent to which the various aspects of African culture are totally African.[2] They either recognize both African and Western culture patterns as coexisting in the contemporary context, or suggest that a hybrid culture is emerging in Africa.

In addition to the propositions of the preceeding two categories of social scientists who either overremphasize the salience of ethnocultural pluralism or cultural marginality in Africa, a third group of scholars have recognized the reality of African culture as distinguishable from either the cultures of the African ethnic groups or from Western, Eastern, and other cultures. Leslie (1973: 5), for example, while assuming the existence of African culture and an African world view, suggests that there is "the need to attain self definition and knowledge of African culture while Africa undergoes change and external influence. . . " However, she failed to spell out both the African culture and African World view discussed in connection with her main subject of concern.

Sofola (1973) while relying considerably upon the Yoruba experience, suggests that certain ideas and philosophies of life transcend ethnic divisions in Africa. He emphasizes in particular the functional nature of African art, the role of the African family in uniting lineages or groups (and not merely individuals, as in some other cultures), the distinctive modes of dress, concern with good character and good neighborliness ("African personalism"), concern with absolute justice, and the fact that both the opposition and the government are not structured as antagonists in African Councils.[3] All these were considered by Sofola to be distinctively African. As already indicated, however, Sofola's evidence was mainly based on Yoruba expressions of African culture. Nevertheless, his exploration of the field constitutes one of the few that have been devoted to African culture as a distinct social reality.

Ayisi's (1972) consideration of African culture though significant, also had the shortcoming of deriving most of his evidence from Ghananian materials (especially from Akans and the Ashantia). Ayisi's conception of African culture involves the consideration of marriage as a group phenomenon, extended family as being characteristic of African societies, kinship ties as being salient, festivals and ceremonies as being prominent in the commemoration of important social events, religion, law, and other issues of belief and practice as being initimately interwoven with other aspects of the African way of life.

A similar acceptance of the reality of African culture is contained in the works of Hunter[4] (1963: 325), Ademuwagun St. Claire Drake (1963, 1971), Diop (1962), Shelton (1970), Jahn (1961, 1964), and Maquet (1969, 1972). Ademuwagun, for example, has contrasted different aspects of African culture as manifested by African students in the United States, to aspects of American culture as reflected in American Students behavioral patterns. One of the cultural attributes which he identified as typically African is polygyny (1971: 28). His position on this aspect of African culture agrees with those of Turnbull (1962: 28), Ayisi (1972), Bohannan and

Curtin (1971: 101-108), Southall (1969: 52), Mair (1969: 1), and Maquet (1972: 73). Among other things, Ademuwagun also suggests that there is considerable deference to age and seniority in Africa. Consequently, first-name relationships are usually between those who are age mates, and that all these facets of culture are different from what prevail in the United States. This author, too, did not present crossethnic evidences of the pervasiveness of these aspects of African culture.

In Jahn's (1961: 237) view, however, African culture differs in significant respects from the European and other cultures. "African culture is . . . a culture of the 'How', of the Kuntu, while present day European culture has become a culture that emphasises the thing, Kintu, above everything."[5] As evidence of the transethnic nature of African culture, Jahn (1961: 99) notes the degree of agreement between different researchers working on African philosophical systems:

> Five entirely different authors—Belgian Monk, a French ethnographer; a North American actress, an African sage . . . and an African scholar . . . these five from different motives, have presented the philosophical systems of five different people—Baluba, Ruandese, Dogon, Bambara, and Haitians—who live far from one another. And for all the differences in detail, these systems agree basically with one another

Jahn (1961: 211) also recognises the impact of other cultures on African culture and he predicts the assimilation of such functional but alien cultures into African culture.[6] Jahn's emphasis was upon the philosophical foundations of African culture which he considered to be basic to the understanding of all aspects of the culture.

Another author who has recognized the reality of African culture is Maquet. Maquet (1960: 7) notes that a description of African culture from the point of view of individual "global" societies—about 800 or more of them—is inadequate even if it was possible since "cultural identities would be concealed by societal diversity." Marguet also notes that even where monographs on the cultures of certain individual African societies exist, their comparison reveal tremendous similarities of cultural forms across the separated societies.[7]

Maquet further suggests that African culture therefore has a distinctive quality that is different from those attributes of the component ethnic or societal groups. For instance (according to this author), a specialist in African Sculpture can identify up to 200 types from a museum selection, "Yet in a museum of 'primitive' art it is easy to perceive a certain relationship between African works, a common quality that distinguishes them from works of different origin" (Maquet, 1972: 5).[8] Maquet (1972: 6) argues that similar inferences could be drawn from the same kind of underlying similarities in other areas of African culture like marriages, family, belief systems and world views. This unique cultural form in black Africa is what the author terms Africanity, which is reflected in various dimensions of culture (1972: 8; 54). For instance, Maquet considers marriage as a group affair, ancestors as respected parts of the community, polygyny as being all-pervasive, and monarchical forms of government as characteristically African. All these and other aspects of African culture which constitute Africanity distinguish black African culture from those of either its component ethnic groups or those of non-African societies.

Maquet and other authors in our third category all recognize the reality of African culture and these authors' position is distinguishable from those of the initial two categories of authors. We are now in a position to state our problem much more clearly. From our preliminary considerations, we intend to suggest that ethnic pluralism certainly militates against the creation of a unifying culture and identity in multiethnic societies. However if, as some authors have suggested, there are cultural values and attitudes which transcend ethnic boundaries in Africa, then it could be suggested further that ethnically plural societies have potentials for either a unified culture or a group of segmented and ethnically based cultures, depending upon whichever aspects are emphasized by the societal elites (or power groups) and the society's educational processes. This consideration therefore raises two questions: since the transmission of culture in multiethnic societies demands a definition of which aspects of what facets of whose culture are to be transmitted, which culture is to be transmitted by our educational institutions in Africa? Second, the adoption of a certain type of cultural policy by the state takes for granted an adequate recognition of what the culture is as well as a decision as to which aspects of the culture are to become objects of policy. Where there is little or no awareness or knowledge of the culture of a people, the government is certain to project a false cultural image abroad and an unrealistic cultural policy at home. Hence one can raise the question of what is the cultural policy of the African States in both the domestic and foreign fronts? Is the cultural policy of the state geared toward the promotion of cultural pluralism at home and a similar projection abroad?

Any aspect of the questions raised suggests a dire need for an adequate awareness (or comprehension) of the cultural attributes which transcend ethnic divisions in the plural societies of black Africa in the attempt to reach an answer. In this section, we follow the pioneering work already done in other spheres of culture by Diop, Jahn, and Maquet, and offer an aspect of African oral literature—proverbs—which are expressions of some cultural values that transcend ethnic and linguistic divisions in Africa. This endeavor, we believe, will assist not only in revealing some underlying unities in African culture, but also in aiding Africans to comprehend them.

Patience as a virtue:

Yoruba:	Suru ni baba iwa
trans.:	Patience is the 'father' of character
Hausa:	Hankuri magani du niya
trans.:	Patience (is) the universal remedy,
	or
	Komi ya bachi hankuri ne babu
	Lack of patience upsets everything
Wolof:	Mongne a guenne
trans.:	Patience is good
Kanuri:	Gedi kanadiben tsannawa
trans.:	At the bottom of patience there is heaven (i.e., the greatest reward)
Fulani:	Munyal Wonnata
trans.:	Patience will not bring destruction
Nupe:	Hankuri yi cigbe yizele o
trans.:	Patience is the medicine for living (in the world).

Honesty as a virtue:

Yoruba: Puro ki o niyi, ete ni ikehin re
trans.:   Telling a lie in order to receive honor subsequently ends
              with disrepute (for the liar)
Hausa: Fadi gaskiya ko do zo a che da kai Allah wadai ba komi
trans.:   Speak the truth, though (even if) they say God curse you, no
              matter (i.e., tell the truth and shame the devil).
Hausa: Gaskiya ka fi dokin kasfe kasfi
trans.:   Truth is stronger than an iron house.
Kanuri: Son nga fai key gnou di jou; sou nga thia farey wajatey
              deuguegua
trans.:   If you find yourself in a situation where there are two sides
              to a quarrel, you may take either side, but at least speak the
              truth.
Ashanti: Nokware mu nni abra
trans.:   In truth there is no deceit,
                                        or
Ashanti: Otorofo de nfe apem tu kwam a onokwafo de dakoro tiw no
              to no
trans.:   Whereas the liar takes a thousand years to travel on a
              journey (i.e., to accomplish a task), the truthful person
              follows and overtakes him in a day.
Fulani: Feutere te an amma jo'inta
trans.:   Telling a lie may help you to marry a wife, but not to keep
              her.

On gratitude and ingratitude:

Gratitude:
Yoruba: Bi a ba se ni l'ore ope ni a da
trans.:   When someone does a good turn for us, we usually express
              our gratitude, or
Yoruba: Bi omode ba dupe ore ana a ri omiran gba
trans.:   When a child shows his gratitude for a benefit which he
              received yesterday, he will receive another (benefit).
Ashanti: Obi kye wo ade a na woda n'ase
trans.:   When somebody presents you with a gift, you (ought to)
              thank him.
Zulu: Ukubon' ukuzibekela
trans.:   To express one's gratitude (for a benefit received) is to
              provide for one's future.
Ingratitude:
Yoruba: Enia kukuru ki i yin olorun; o di igba ti o ba ri arara.
trans.:   A short man does not praise the lord until he sees a dwarf.
Fulani: Dokko yettata Allah sei yii bumdo
trans.:   A one-eyed man does not thank God until he sees a blind
              man.

Hausa: Daidai majinyachi ba shi gode Allah sai ya da wanda ya mutu

trans.:   Frankly, the sick man does not thank God until he sees a person who has just died.

Cooperation and reciprocity in human relations:

Yoruba: Otun we osi we otun ni owo mejeji fi nmo

trans.:   The right hand washes the left hand, and the left hand washes the right hand (in this way); the two hands become clean.

Ibo: Akanni kwo ada ekpe, aka ekpe akwo aka nni

trans.:   The right hand washes the left hand, and the left hand washes the right hand.

Fulani: Nano lota nyamo bo lota nano

trans.:   Left hand washes the right, and the right hand washes the left.

Zulu: Isandla sigez' ensinye

trans.:   Hands wash each other.

On ignorance:

Yoruba: Bi omode ko ba fi oju kan oko elomiran yio so wipe ko so oko bab eniti oju ti bab on lo.

trans.:   If a child has not seen (or visited) the farm of another person's father, he will say (conclude) that no other person's father owns a farm that is larger than that of his own father.

Ashanti: Wonko bi a fum da wose mi enku ni kuafo

trans.:   If you had never been to another Man's plantation, then you would say that you're the only planter.

Fulani: Kardo anda ko belado wondi

trans.:   A satisfied man does not understand the plight of a hungry man.

Nupe: Dzakangi dzum m'bo a u ga a de za na ma je bo kun nna nwi na a.

trans.:   A child who never left home says nobody cooks as well as his mother.

On lack of information:

Yoruba: Eni ti a nbo ko mo wipe iyan nja

trans.:   He who is being fed does not know that there is famine.

Hausa: Machiyinka ba ahi ganin remakka

trans.:   He who eats (feeds on) you will not see your leanness.

Wolof: Poudhie ou maigue de na jaja ah taw, tey sailo yagoul

trans.:   The house roof struggles to keep off the rain, but he who is protected ignores the situation (or takes it for granted.)

Experience as the best teacher:
Learning from the experiences of self and others.
Experiences of self.

Yoruba:	Ohun to s'eni l'ekan ki ise eni ni ekeji
trans.:	One does not fall into the same mistake twice.
Ashanti:	Moko efee kolo si i enyo
trans.:	Nobody is twice a fool.
Zulu:	Ukubona kany' unkubona kabili
trans.:	To see once is to see twice.
Nupe:	Ema go po za le u ga le tutumpere ye u yaba
trans.:	If a person was once scotched, when next he sees ashes he will be careful.

Experiences of others:

Yoruba:	Eni t'o jin si koto ka ara y'oku l'ogbon
trans.:	The person who falls into the pit teaches others a lesson.
Ashanti:	Obi anko na obi amma a; anka yebeyebe den ahu se okwan mu nye
trans.:	If no one had gone and no one had returned, what should we have done to find out whether or not the road is safe.
Hausa:	In ka ga gemun dan-uwanka ya kama wuta zuba na naka ruwa
trans.:	If you see the beard of your brother in flames, pour water on your own.

Leadership (chiefs and councilors):

Yoruba:	Oba ko buru emewa re ni ko sunwon
trans.:	The chief is not wicked; only his advisers are inadequate.
Hausa:	Ba a mugun sarki sai mugun bafada
trans.:	There is no bad chief, only a bad councilor (exists).
Ashanti:	Ohen—mone nni babi, na osafohene-bone na owo babi
trans.:	There is no such thing as a bad king even though a bad subordinate may be found.

or

Ashanti:	Ohene nya ahotrafro pa a na ne bere so dowo
trans.:	When a king has good councilors, his reign is peaceful.

Respect for elders:

Yoruba:	Bi omode ba te'riba fun agba, ojo re a pe
trans.:	If a child respects the elders, he will live long.
Ashanti:	Abofra eni anso panyin a ofre ampopa se haha
trans.:	It is when the child does not respect the elders that he calls the palmfrond useless.

or

Ashanti:	Abofra nte ne na ne n'agya osema eye mmussu

trans.:   When a child does not listen to the words of his father, he eats food which has no salt (faces untoward consequences).

Efik-Ibibio: Kpuno owo eke osonode fi fi koru osono owo oson ifiok

trans.:   Give respect to the elders because the older man has more wisdom.

Wolof: Waje y mague doyoul vaidi

trans.:   You should not interrupt the speech of an elder.

Hausa: In badan mutane kunka gani ku garmama shi

trans.:   If you see a man's father, give him respect.

Kikuyu: Hari muthuri hatiitangaguro maai

trans   One must not pour water in the presence of elderly people (i.e., one must not speak angrily before elders).

Wisdom or discretion expected from elders:

Yoruba: Agba ki iwa lo'ja, ki ori omo titun fo

trans.:   An elder cannot be in a market where the head of a newly born baby gets broken.

Ashanti: Opanyin ntra ofie na asadua nfow

trans.:   An elderly person does not sit in the house and allow the loom to get wet.

Nupe.   Dzakangi ga egun 'na tsutsu, nusa 'a da bo u gauy

trans.:   If children are kindling the fire of death, if an old man is there, he should scatter it.

Wolof: Jalele sainou ane na sainou guissetil dara, tey nague dieky thy soufe guissa yope.

trans.:   The child looks everywhere and very often sees nothing; but the elderly man while sitting down sees everything.

Self-respect expected of elders:

Yoruba: Agbalagba ki ifi ara re se langbalangba

trans.:   An elder does not make fun of (or ridicule) himself.

Kikuyu: Kiama gitirugaga ruui

trans.:   The elders of the council do not jump over a brook (hastily).

Ashanti: Opanyin didi adibone a oyi nasanka

trans.:   When an elder eats (all his food) with greed, he carries his own plates (i.e., he clears his own table).

On representations:

Yoruba: Enikan ki i je awa de

trans.:   A single individual does not bear "we come" (i.e. should not pretend to be equivalent to a group)

Ashanti: Dua bioko nye kwae

trans.:   One tree does not make a forest

Nupe: Cigban nini jin kuso a

trans.:   One tree does not make a forest.

Hausa: Itache daya ba ya kurmi
trans.:   One tree does not make a forest

On the force of gravity (used to indicate the inevitable):

Yoruba: Lala t'o r'oke ile ni o nbo
trans.:   Anything that goes high into the sky will (subsequently)
                    come down to the earth.
trans.:   Everthing up in the air falls to the ground at last.
Ashanti: Biribi we soro a, et wa se abeba
trans.:   Whatever object is above must come down (in the end).

On hope and perseverance:

Yoruba: Bi emi ba wa ireti nbe
trans.:   When there is life, there is hope.
Hausa: Inda rai da rabo in babu rai rabo ya kare
trans.:   Where there is life there is hope; if there is no life, hope
                    ends.
Zulu: Ithemba kalibulali
trans.:   Hope does not destroy (kill).

On the "bommerang":

Yoruba: Agba ti o ba gbin ebu ika,ori omo re ni yio hu si
trans.:   When an elder plants the seeds of wickedness (or cruelty), it
                    germinates on the heads of his children.
Hausa: Kowa ya yi keta kansa
trans.:   Evil recoils on the evil doer.
                                           or
                    Yadda aka dama a sha hakansan
                    As you mix, so you drink (i.e., you reap whatever you sow).
Fulani: Komoi defi nyiri nganyandi sei bakke wala ha jiba mum
trans.:   Whoever cooks the food of malice will have some of it
                    sticking to his pocket.
Zulu: Uzidlise ngobuthi bakhe
                                           or
                    Iquili lidliwa ngamany' amaguili
trans.:   He (who attempts to poison others) poisons himself with his
                    own poison.

In the preceding section, we have tried to demonstrate the degree of agreement between the different linguistic and ethnic groups in Africa on some of the philosophical and normative ideas which are characteristic of African culture. Although the data cannot be said to be conclusive, they are indicative of the general pattern which underlies the seeming heterogeneity of ethnocultural forms in sub-Sahara Africa.

CONCLUSION

Of the numerous factors which militate against the awareness and manifestation of a unifying culture (and as a result an undivided identity) in sub-Saharan Africa, two appear to be most salient. One is concerned with the dynamics of cultural interaction between the West and Africa; the other is concerned with the dynamics of ethnicity. Both phenomena have seriously impeded the full development of a unified cultural awareness among Africans.

This chapter has tried to consider the ethnic aspects of the problem, leaving aside the problem of cultural marginality that results from Africa's cultural interaction with other cultures. We have argued that the nature of cultural self comprehension in sub-Saharan Africa will depend on the policies of our power elites and educators. This is because there are both divisive elements as well as unifying elements in African culture. Depending on which aspects of African culture are emphasized, cultural self-comprehension will be more or less problematic and more or less functional in ethnically plural societies of sub-Saharan Africa. Our preceding considerations further indicate that we can talk intelligently about African culture, in spite of the ethnic pluralism in the continent.

NOTES

1. Alain Ricard (1970: 7) recognizes 200 languages in Africa; Basil Davidson (following Greenburg) suggests that all African languages could be traced to four language families. However, the former author warned against equating language differences with cultural differences and language similarities with cultural similarities: as put by Ricard, "It is wrong to identify language and culture in a rigidly reciprocal way" (1970: 1).

2. Writing on the experience that resulted from his attempt to write a work with "a truly Nigerian flavour," Samuel Akpabot (1972: 177) moaned his predicament: "I was myself in two minds as to the real value of my work but I could not get away from the fact that there was too much European influence in my effort."

3. Sofola (1973: 11-31) also recognized the effects of the contact of Africa with the West on African culture—especially on the economy, religion, education, and mass media.

4. Hunter (1963: 338) in addition identified some forces which militate against the persistence of African culture. These are "the idea of free and responsible individual personality, the idea of deomocratic authority, the idea of economic competitiveness. Marked with them are the institutions which have in the past expressed them in the

West: the nuclear family, universal education, the ballot box, the individual ownership of landed property, and the industrial corporation."

5. Jahn (1961: 16-17) asserts that neo-African culture is built on "two components"—the European and the African. On the African component, he asserts that philosophical categories explain African culture. These he found in "Muntu," "Kintu," "Hantu," and "Kuntu," which he suggests provide the main categories of African philosophy.

6. He was, in fact, writing on African poetry and prose, on the writers and their acceptance or reflection of African tradition in their works. Another author—Shelton—makes a slightly different suggestion. He recognizes support for traditional African values in the works of the African authors that he studied. See "Behaviour and Cultural value in the West African Stories: Literary Sources for the Study of Culture Contact," in Middleton (1970).

7. Maquet's (1969: 7-8) real examples here were the kingdoms of the lacustrine area where the descent systems, marital relations, mythical and cult relations, social stratification, and political systems have been found to be similar across the societal boundaries.

8. See also Hill (1963).

RERERENCES

ACHEBE, C. (1960) *No Longer at Ease*. London: Heineman.

ADEMUWAGUN, Z.A. (1971) "Miscommunication in cross-cultural context: The dilemma of African students in the U.S.A." *Ibadan*, 29 (July): 27-32.

AKPABOT, S. (1972) "The conflict between foreign and traditional culture in Nigeria." *Presence Africaine*, 81 (First Quarter): 177-182.

AVERY, G.M (1970-1971) "African oral traditions." *African Research Bulletin*, 1, 1 (October): 17-36.

AYISI, E. (1972) *An Introduction to the Study of African Culture*. London: Heineman.

BOHANNAN, P. (1964) *Africa and Africans*. New York: Natural History Press.
    and CURTIN, P (1971) *Africa and Africans*. New York: Natural History Press.

BUSIA. K.A. (1951) *The Position of the Chief in the Modern Political System of Ashanti*. London: Oxford Univ. Press.

CASTLE. B. (1966) *Growing Up in East Africa*. London: Oxford Univ. Press.

COHEN. R. and MIDDLETON, J. (1970) *From Tribe to Nation in Africa*. Scranton, Penn.: Chandler.

DAVIDSON, B. (1969) *The African Genius*. Boston: Little, Brown.

DIOP, C.A. (1962) *The Cultural Unity of Negro Africa*. Paris: Presence Africaines.

DRAKE, A.S.C. (1965) "Traditional authority and social action in former British West Africa," in P.L. vander Berghe (ed.), *Africa: Social Problems of Change and Conflict*. San Francisco: Chandler.

EGUDU, N. (1972) "Proverb and riddle in Igbo traditional verse." *IKENGA*, 1, 1 (January): 101-108.

EMENANJO, E.N. (1972): "Some notes on the use of repetition and contrasts in Igbo proverbs." *IKENGA*, 1, 1 (January): 109-114.

FORDE, D. (1954) *African Worlds*. London: Oxford Univ. Press.

FORTES, M. (1972) "Introduction," in E.O. Ayisi (ed.), *An Introduction to the Study of African Culture*. London: Heinemann.

HILL, J.N. (1963) "African Sculpture: An Aesthetic Evaluation," in *African Seen by American Negro Scholars*. New York: Presence Africaines.

HUNTER, G. (1963) *The New Societies of Tropical Africa: A Selective Study.* London: Oxford Univ. Press.

JACOBSON, D. (1970) "Culture and stratification among urban Africans." *Journal of Asia and African Students,* 5: 176-183.

JAHN, J. (1964) "Value concepts in Sub-Saharan Africa," in F.S.C. Northrop and H.H. Livingston (eds.), *Cross-Cultural Understanding: Epistemology in Anthropology.* New York: Harper & Row.

———— (1961) *Muntu: An Outline of Neo-African Culture.* London: Faber & Faber.

LESLIE, O. (1973) "African aesthetics and literature. *UFAHAMU,* 4, 1 (Spring): 4-7.

LEVINE, R. (1966) *Dreams and Deeds.* Chicago: Univ. of Chicago Press.

LLOYD, P.C. (1967) "The elite," in P.C. Lloyd et al. (ed.), *The City of Ibadan.* London: Cambridge Univ. Press.

MAIR, L. (1969) *African Marriage and Social Change.* London: Frank Cass.

MAQUET, J. (1972) *Africanity.* New York: Oxford Univ. Press.

———— (1969) "The cultural units of Africa: A classificatory problem," in M. Douglass and P.M. Kaberry (eds.), *Man in Africa.* London: Tavistock Publications.

———— (1971) *Power and Society in Africa.* New York: McGraw-Hill.

MIDDLETON, J. (1970) *Black Africa: Its Peoples and Their Culture Today.* New York: Macmillan.

MURDOCK, G.P. (1965) "Uniformities in culture," Pp. 51-54 in Obrien et al. (eds.), *Readings in General Sociology.* Boston: Houghton Mifflin.

OLORUNSOLA, V. (1972) *The Politics of Cultural Sub-Nationalism in Africa.* Garden City, N.Y.: Doubleday.

RADCLIFF, B. and FORDE, D. (1964) *African Systems of Kinship and Marriage.* London: International African Institute, O.U.P.

RICARD, A. (1970) "Literature and cultural pluralism." Talk on African and Afro-American studies at the University of California, Los Angeles (translated by A.R. Oyowe).

SANDA, A.O. (1973-1974) *The Dynamics of Ethnicity Among the Yorubas.* Unpublished Ph.D. thesis, University of California, Los Angeles.

———— (1972): "Education and social change: some problems in class formation. *Ufahamu* 3, 1, (Spring): 73-86.

SHELTON, A.J. (1970) "Behaviour and cultural value in W. African stories: Literacy sources for the study of culture contact," in John Middleton (ed.), *Black Africa.* New York: Macmillan.

SMYTHE, H. and SMYTHE, M. (1960) *The New Nigerian Elite.* Stanford, Cal.: Stanford Univ. Press.

SOFOLA, J. (1973) *African Culture and the African Personality.* Ibadan, Nigeria: African Resources Publishers.

SOUTHALL, A. (1969) *Social Change in Modern Africa.* London: Oxford Univ. Press.

SOYINKA, W. (1963) *The Lion and the Jewel.* London: Oxford Univ. Press.

TRIANDIS, C. (1972) *The Analysis of Subjective Culture.* New York: Wiley.

TURNBULL, T.M. (1962) *The Lonely African.* New York: Simon & Schuster.

21

NATIVE AMERICAN COMMUNICATION PATTERNS: THE CASE OF THE LAKOTA SPEAKERS

BEA MEDICINE

University of Wisconsin

The Lakota speakers are commonly referred to in the anthropological literature as the Teton Dakota or the Western Sioux. At present, they inhabit the reservations of Pine Ridge, Rosebud, Cheyenne River, and Standing Rock in South Dakota and the northern portion of Standing Rock in North Dakota. It is in the latter part of Standing Rock reservation that the dialects referred to by the indigenous peoples as the *Isanteye* and *Wicheyela* are still maintained. This fact presents an interesting implication for dialect durability and linguistic boundary distinctiveness. Generally, however, the vernacularly specified "L dialect" is universally understood by those native peoples who speak Lakota. Lakota is the language of the people who primarily fall into the category of the people who are called "full-bloods," and these persons are often termed "traditionalists." In this segment of the populations, which varies according to the reservation, Lakota is the language of family and kin, socialization and interpersonal interaction, ritual expression and identity of those people who recognize themselves as "Lakota."

Most Siouan-speakers of these nothern dialects often ask each other, "Do you speak 'L' or 'D'?" The latter dialect reference is to the ethnographically designated Dakota speakers who live in the area east of the Missouri River in the states of North and South Dakota and Minnesota, and the Canadian provinces of Manitoba and Saskatchewan. Seemingly relegated to noninclusion is the "N" dialect of the Assiniboine Sioux in Montana and the Stoney Indians in Alberta, Canada. Many linguists and anthropologists often forget the remnants of the Hunkpapa and Sihasapa (Blackfoot Sioux) who live in southwestern Saskatchewan. There are a number of Lakota speakers in the area of Fort Quepple, Saskatchewan. It is difficult to assess the precise number of persons speaking either Lakota or Dakota in that area. To my knowledge, no one dealing with Siouan dialects of the Northern Plains takes into consideration the language use of the Metis peoples of Canada.

Additionally, the range of speaker—including nonnative traders, missionaries, anthropologists, linguists, hobbyists, and singers of native songs—may be seen as another aspect of the use of a native language by persons in a contemporary native American community. Moreover, the utilization of Lakota as a foreign language in Ph.D. programs for native students and the teaching of Sioux in Native American (Indian) Studies Programs raises interesting issues in the use of native languages.

It is obvious, therefore, that each native linguistic stock surviving in North America has its own distinctive characteristics reflected in the native speakers. The degree of adaptation to the dominant societies and the functional utilization of language in each speech community poses great research potential to the interface of Anthropology and Linguistics. Creative research techniques in sociolinguistics are sorely needed.

Decades of language suppression have taken their toll on the Lakota. In the first wave of wrenching children from parents when the Lakota were placed on the reservations, the eradication of savagery and the mark of civilization was explicitly seen by the oppressors to be correlated with the Lakota student's ability to speak English. One need only look at such poignant expressions written by Lakota speakers going through a secondary socialization process (Standing Bear, 1928: 122-150; and other writers) to appreciate, but not internalize, the trauma associated with this psychological passage and linguistic limbo. In rereading these accounts, the cutting of the Lakota male's hair (which symbolized manhood, warriorhood, and protectorhood of the Lakota people) plus the denigration of language, culture, and kin must have been an almost intolerable situation.

In the 1930s and 1940s, the data indicate that it was a mark of "acculturation" to claim to be a non-Lakota speaker. There are instances of many Lakota speakers who went away to boarding schools or to a first semester at a university, who, upon return to their natal communities, indicated that they were unable to speak or understand their native language. As a counter-balance, many Lakota speakers have indicated that native langage use was an adaptive strategy in dealing with boarding-school personnel and intertribal interaction.

However, pressure to conform to the dominant society was great—whether it was a Bureau of Indian Affairs boarding school, a parochial boarding school, or a public school. Facility in the English language was still a criteria of an educated native. Religious denominations and schools were institutions which were instrumental in continuing the civilization process. In all fairness, many Christian religions conducted services in Lakota. As an index of the times, it was in this period that many Lakota individuals changed their culturally significant names to Anglicized versions.

It was shortly after the enactment of the Indian Reorganization Act of 1937, which posited an appreciation of native languages and cultures, that bilingual readers appeared in many schools operated by the Bureau of Indian Affairs for the Lakota. In a true spirit of sharing, many of these books found their way into the homes of public school children. It would be helpful to assess the effects of those readers in light of the present emphasis on bilingualism in native American communities.

To those "full-bloods," however, utilization of Lakota was ongoing. Many of these people lived in isolated communities on the aforementioned reservations. In many cases, Lakota was the first language of these persons. The "mixed bloods" (*hanke-wichasa*—literally, "half-men") had often worked as *eyeska* (translators—a name also applied to this mixed blood Lakota) in the agency towns. This fostered a core of "half-breeds" who are still working in the agency towns. This is not to say, however, that there is a neat correlation to this

Handbook Of Intercultural Communication

dichotomy. Incidentally, the Lakota word for "full-blood" is
wa-ozula (blood full) or *Lakota kexe* (Lakota—true or ultimate).

Thus, the universe of the Lakota speakers is diverse and
variable from community to community on the contemporary
reservations. There are many Lakota who are monolingual in
English. Conversely, there are some individuals who speak
only Lakota.

The perceptual parameters of blood quantum figure significantly in the linguistic interaction in present day reservation
life. Identity is also tied to natal reservation, i.e., "Pine Ridge
Sioux" is often given as a Lakota's affiliation. This means that
the person is enrolled on Pine Ridge reservation. There are,
however, many Lakota speakers who know their band affilia-
tions and can relate their genealogies. These are tied to the
placing of the seven bands of the Lakota on the reservation.
These persons tend to be individuals who are bilingual with a
first-language proficiency in Lakota.

Fortunately, for the Lakota speakers, there have been
several sources written by native Lakota scholars which
present a unique perspective on language, language acquisition, and speech patterning. The current renaissance of native
ritual and expressive culture combined with the thrust of
bilingual education has resulted in the production of many
dictionaries for all bands of the Lakota.[1]

An early "informant-collaborator" with Franz Boas was
Ella Deloria, whose linguistic works have been a bench mark in
Siouan linguistics (Boas and Deloria, 1941). Much of Deloria's
linguistic data was obtained from Standing Rock, where her
father, *Tipi Sapa* (Rev. Phillip Deloria), was a Dakota
Episcopal missionary among the Lakota speakers.

In discussing cultural transmission in the *tiospaye*, E.
Deloria (1944: 43) writes:

> Nor was it any wonder that small children learned their social duties,
> since the training constantly given them was calculated to condition
> them and direct them in that way. All grownups by tacit consent seemed
> to "gang up" for this purpose. Even before a child was aware of his
> kinship obligations, they made sentences and put the correct word and
> formal speeches into his mouth for him to repeat to this or that relative. It
> was their informal but constant system of education in human relations
> and social responsibility.

Essentially, this is the enduring pattern of speech and behavioral learning exhibited by many of the more "traditional" Lakota. The interesting evidence of "baby-talk" for the Comanche (Casagrande, 1964: 245-250) is lacking for such groups as the Lakota and another Siouan-speaking group, the Hidatsa. There is no "baby-talk" allowed in the majority of the Lakota speaking families. There is continued use of the diminuitive ending *la* to refer to youngsters and when addressing them—as *hokshila*—little boy. Increasingly, such words as *baby-la* (little baby) crop up in vernacular useage. Many Lakota have commented upon the use of kin terms which incorporate English kin terms—such as *sister-mi-ta-wa-ki* (my sister). Such terminology completely obliterates the traditional terms for older sister (*chu-we*) and younger sister (*mi-tanka-la*). In most instances, proper kin terms are used.

Generally, the frequent utilization of Lakota is operative in most of the home labeled as "full-blood." Although much of the native belief system (the Sun Dance and its related rituals) was suppressed in the 1880s, with the concomittant superimposition of Christian values, such mandates for social action based upon the four cardinals are eroded, but still remain viable in the implicit rules for expected behavior.

The remainder of this chapter will focus upon one class of Lakota speech category, the factors constituting the context of occurrence, the range of functions served by this category, and the contemporary cultural background. Selection is upon the action term *eyak' sapa*—"to speak wisdom to one." When asked to explain this term, most Lakota speakers replied "to give advice," or "to explain something to someone," or "to enlighten," or "to make someone behave."

Colloquial Lakota is necessarily on a different dimension than Lakota of ritual expression. Colloquial Lakota also suffers from what some writers have termed "reservation English." This reflects generations of poorly taught English with no esteem for the richness of expression in the native tongue. Moreover, the translation of native phrases into English equivalencies was seldom, if ever, treated as a learning experience in bilingual and bicultural adeptness and adaptation. The area of segmentalization of language and behavior needs amplification in adaptive strategies of native Americans as individuals and as tribal communities.

The phrase as it is articulated on the personal level will be presented and this is often the expectation of a Lakota community. A Lakota speaker—of either gender—may seek help in asking another Lakota to *eyaksapmey* (*e*-female speaking; *o*-male speaking). This is an appeal for aid and is usually directed to an older person, or in some instances, someone in his peer group, whom the individual making the appeal, respects. This person may be in the *tiospaye* (extended kin group) or it may be a person outside the kinship circle. This appeal for aid is often utilized by English-speaking Lakota who very often are monolingual in English. This dyadic relationship is often activated by the request, "I want you to speak (talk) to me." This request, either in Lakota or English, may be interpreted to mean that the person making the request is in need of guidance, advice, reassurance, or wishes help in a decision-making or a stressful situation. The person who is asked to "advise" or to "speak" often only fulfills the role of listener. In many cases, the individual seeking aid or advice simply reaches an autonomous decision without any direction by the advisor. Often, the initiator of advisory action may weep, in which case, the advisor is expected to join in the weeping. In the majority of cases, however, the cause of seeking advisory aid merits a dialogue between the two persons in this instance of interchange. The cause of the stress, unhappiness, or need for counsel is presented by the individual seeking help. The advisor listens carefully. S/he may respond by first delineating the individual's social role—in family and community, the probable reasons for uneasiness or the psychic state, and often alternatives to alleviate the situation. This self-actualization utilizing this class of interaction is truly a reflection of the tremendous value placed on the autonomy of individuals. It is also a manifestation of the native Lakota phrase—*Ho! hecha kin ka sha.* "Thus, s/he desires the situation to be so. It is so." This is the ultimate statement regarding individual autonomy.

The second category of events in which this linguistic term is invoked can be correlated with contemporary rites of passage.

The most common ones are the naming ceremonies for children and adults. Adults include many nontraditionalists who are responding to this event increasingly since the 1960s. Adult adoptees into the tribe are also obtaining Lakota names. In the latter two cases, however, the verbal interchange of the *eyaksapa* is seldom enacted. For children, however, the ceremony is an eventful one. A person in the *tiospaye* (usually one of the grandparents) tells the history of the family and the place of that name. If it is a male grandparent, he makes a public announcement. If a female grandparent acts as the oral historian, she relays this information to the *eyapaha* (herald or announcer). He relays this information to the group of people, first in Lakota, and then in English. The grandparent then lectures the child about the Lakota lifeway and the expectations involved. Then an honoring song is sung in which the words reinforcing the Lakota lifeway and all members of the *tiospaye* dance in honor of the newly named.

In wedding ceremonies, the same linguistic term is used to ask an elderly couple of high esteem to publicly advise the young couple as to the proper behavior for a long, successful marriage. This is often done with humour and may be in the English or Lakota language, depending upon the linguistic ability of the bride and groom. Again, this behavior is observed only in "traditional-type" marriages of the legal variety. It was not witnessed in the so-called (again in the Lakota-English vernacular) "shack-ups" or consensual marriages, or the newly designated "Indian marriages" of urban Indians, or the militant group.

Eyaksapa assumes a different affect when utilized at funerals —more specifically, the all-night wakes which precede burial. The performance of this verbal presentation is strictly voluntary. The person (of either sex) who is so inclined will speak to the mourning family sometime during the night. This form of *eyaksapa* assumes a more personalized rendition based upon the qualities of the deceased and the role this person played in the life of the deliverer. It assumes a tranquilizing aspect, and is meant to solace and strengthen the bereaved persons.

A more formalized usage of *eyaksapa* occurs at the currently designated "memorial feasts" (*washapayampi*—literally, "to cook over"). Deloria (1944) refers to these as "ghost-keeping" ceremonies. At present, before this ceremony begins, a native religious practitioner seats the soon-to-be-released mourners. Their year-long apartness from the Lakota community will soon be terminated. There is a prescribed seating arrangement. After the ritual offering of water and native tobacco to the mourners (*washigla*—"the affronted"), he offers prayers which are stylized and uttered in Lakota. Often he will offer a tribute to the deceased person and welcome the *washigla* back to the Lakota lifeway. After these statements, he brushes the mourners with a feather fan. They are formally reincorporated into the community and the ritual cycle. In rare instances, this ceremony may be performed at the "feeding the mourners" ceremony after the funeral of a Lakota. This decision is at the discretion of the religious leaders with the agreement of the community. The bereaved family has no option. This releases them from their year-long mourning period. They are free to participate in the Lakota traditional events. The extent of their involvement is an individual choice.

Another aspect concerning this speech category occurs when a member of a family asks someone to *wahokiya* (advise some person) a member of the kin group. This native term elicited these translations: "to lecture," "to give advice," "to scold," and "to bawl out." This request usually occurs when a member of a *tiospaye* transgresses or someone in the extended family fears that s/he might transgress. In this instance, the aura of the verbalization is meant to change behavior or to prevent deviant behavior. The person to whom the appeal is made is often a respected elder member of the community or one who has undergone recent ritual involvement. The latter example indicates that the supernatural contact adds much to the verbal impact. This is often an ongoing role for the participant who has been involved in rituals. This aspect of stress alleviation on the part of the person making the request and aspects of anticipatory social control via verbal intervention are important parts of *tiospaye* life in the present day.

By concentrating upon one aspect of a class of Lakota utterance, the parameters of contemporary language use among the Lakota speakers have been delineated. It seems apparent that one could select any similar concept, as for example, *wa eya*—"gossip" or *wa one han*—"to honor" and arrive at several contextual frames to better understand the words and actions of contemporary Lakota speakers.

The paramount research need for Lakota speakers is an assessment of the rate of bilingualism and a careful socio-linguistic analysis of comparative speech patterning in the communities of the western reservations. This investigation should go beyond the setting out of speech patterns of one community. A stringent analysis of the degree of viability and functions of speech in native American communities of the present time is sorely needed. This is becoming even more critical in view of the emphasis upon bilingual and bicultural programs which are currently being funded by the federal government.

NOTES

1. There have been recent attempts by the Lakota people to publish dictionaries. A *Dakota-English Dictionary* (1969) and LAKOTA WOONSPE WOWAPI (L. Hairy Shirt et al., 1974) are examples. In 1975-1976, the American Indian Higher Education Consortium (Denver), which provides technical assistance to native American community colleges, of which *Sinte Gleska* (Spotted Tail), is one, held several meetings which centered upon problems of orthography encountered by native teachers on all levels of instruction. Participants included persons from the communities of the western Lakota reservations, teachers and aides in elementary bilingual programs, and instructors in colleges, including the community colleges.

REFERENCES

BOAS, F. and DELORIA, E. (1941) "Dakota Grammar." Memoirs of the National Academy of Sciences, 23.

CASAGRANDE, J.B. (1964) "Comanche baby language," Pp. 245-250 in D. Hymes (ed.), *Language in Culture and Society.* New York: Harper & Row.

CAZDEN, C.B. and JOHN, V.P. (1971) "Learning in American Indian children." Pp. 525-572 in M.L. Wax and L.S. Diamond, and F.O. Gearing (eds.), *Anthropological Perspectives on Education.* New York: Basic Books.

Dakota-English Dictionary (1969) Pierre, S. Dak.: Working Civil Association.

DELORIA, E. (1944) *Speaking of Indians.* New York: Friendship Press.

HAIRY SHIRT, L., ONE STAR, L., SR., DONVILLE, V., STANDS, C., SUSNOWSKI, S., and BRENNAN, T. (1974) *Lakota Woonspe Wowapi.* Rosebud, S. Dak.: S.J. Sinte Gleska College Center.

STANDING BEAR, L. (1928) *My People, The Sioux.* Boston: Houghton, Mifflin.

22.

BLACK-WHITE COMMUNICATION: AN ASSESSMENT OF RESEARCH

DORTHY L. PENNINGTON

University of Kansas

The purpose of this chapter is to examine communication between black and white Americans in terms of some of the basic assumptions guiding investigation into the area and their application, and in terms of some of the methodological concerns; and finally to posit suggestions for future consideration. Because research in the area of black-white communication is relatively recent, examples will often be cited not only as support, but also to provide information which illuminates terms and concepts, as opposed to making sweeping statements which assume broad reader familiarity with the literature.

Upon examining the literature on communication between blacks and whites, one is struck by its dearth. In acknowledging the many definitions of communication provided by scholars, one can see that throughout the literature, black-white communication, in a broader sense of race relations, has been treated by scholars in other disciplines as sociology, psychology, psychiatry, and anthropology. Thus, the area, as treated by communication scholars, is in a state of infancy and, of necessity, suffers something of an identity crisis in terms of theory and research generation, as well as integration.

Also lacking are consensual answers to the questions, "Why black-white communication? What are its objectives? Is its accomplishment an end in itself, or a means to an end?" That such epistemological answers are needed became evident when a participant at a recent seminar on racism posed the question, "Will interracial communication really solve the difficulties in relations between whites and blacks?" This obviously focuses attention to the definition of interracial communication, an issue to be addressed later in this chapter. Also accompanying any stated objectives of black-white communication is the skepticism of some blacks that increased understanding of them by whites will only lead to greater manipulation by those in power.

Thus, any serious attempts at black-white communication must be played against the traditional patterns of communication between the two groups in which motives have been suspect and in which blacks have had to strategically develop subversive and in-group communication symbols and signals which could only be understood by other blacks. Designed in part to exclude whites, as well as being a reaction to the norms established by whites, this use of communication by blacks was an answer to their perceived insincerity of whites. The result is the transference of inauthentic information, based not so much upon what is available, but rather upon what is expedient in a climate of suspicion.

In a general sense, scholars and participants in black-white communication recognize that there are difficulties between the two groups, and various attempts have been and are being made to provide greater understanding of interracial communication. Many of the attempts to improve the communication between whites and blacks seem to rest on certain basic assumptions.

The attempts to facilitate the communication between blacks and whites generally assume, though by no means exclusively, that the communication difficulties are attributable to two factors: (1) cultural differences and (2) racism. Let us then look at these assumptions.

CULTURAL DIFFERENCES

Exploring the many definitions of culture is not the concern here, so culture shall generally be viewed as learned and shared patterns of perceiving and behaving which are transmitted by a common symbolic code. As examples of some of the cultural differences between blacks and whites seen as significant, we shall use those of language and perception, nonverbal, temporal, and family structure and relationships.

Language and Perception Differences

The language of blacks is shown to differ from that of whites in ethnography, grammar, and style. Much research has been conducted in recent years on what is now referred to as Black English, as it is estimated to be used by about 80 percent of blacks in America (Dillard, 1972: 229). From its origin, Black English is seen as being a mixture of African languages and American English, developing through a systematic, orderly process of pidginization-creolization-decreolization. (Dillard, 1972). Pidginization, in this instance, refers to the language of the slaves which no one spoke originally but which resulted from the mixing of speakers of a large number of languages where no one language dominated and where various forms of such mixtures were spoken within a speech community (Dillard, 1972: 74, 303). Creolization resulted when the pidgin became the only language of a speech community (Dillard, 1972: 303) and decreolization refers to the influence of the English used by whites on the creole of the slaves (Dillard, 1972: 83). Thus, Black English is sometimes informally referred to as *patois*.

Though Black English first served an adaptive function, it has now achieved cultural significance, often serving as a symbolic rejection of standard English. Since the speaking of standard English by blacks can be interpreted to mean that they agree with or identify with the norms of whites, blacks often deliberately reject standard English out of a type of psychological consciousness and also out of peer group pressure (Dillard, 1972: 238). While much of the use of Black English may result from such a consciousness, an important unconscious use of it is also recognized: "In this sense one important unconscious use of *patois* rests on the Negro's perception, and, in fact, his white confrere's perception, as well, that the true status of the races in the United States at this time is that Negros are regarded as slaves who are no longer officially enslaved" (Grier and Cobbs, 1968: 105). Many of the actual differences between Black English and standard English, therefore, have become symbolic differences.

Some of the significant structural differences include the absence of the copula in Black English and the distinctive use of the verb "to be," as in "he busy'' or "he be busy" (Baratz,

1973: 134). Phonologically, although Black English is seen in many ways as being the same as standard English, the distribution of the various phonemes is different in terms of vowels and consonant sounds. For example, in Black English, in some regions, /i/ and /e/ sounds are not clearly distinguished before nasal consonants (Baratz, 1973: 140-141). In terms of consonants, some of the many differences which are noted to distinguish Black English are nasals being lost in the final position, so that "ng" becomes "n" in such words as "sing"; in fricatives, "th" sounds often become "d," as in "den" for "then" and "udder" for "other"; and final consonant clusters are often simplified, such as in "must" and "muss," "ben" and "bend" (Baratz, 1973: 144).

Grammatically, the Black English is observed to often omit the linking verb in such instances as "he goin'", instead of "he is going"; the possessive marker is often omitted, such as in "John cousin," rather than "John's cousin"; and the subjects and verbs sometimes disagree, such as in "she have a bicycle," instead of "she has a bicycle"; and double negatives are noted in such uses as "It ain't no cat can't get in" for "No man can get in" (Baratz, 1973: 144).

Although to some, these differences might seem insignificant, they can contribute to communication difficulty. For instance, concerning intonation and pronounciation, Asante writing under the name Arthur Smith (1973: 75-76) calls attentions to the misunderstandings that occur each day and cites an example of a black girl who nearly missed an important meeting because she did not recognize her name being called over a public address system due to intonation and pronunciation. And linguists hasten to point out that although Black English differs from standard English, it is not inferior and does not suggest cognitive deficiency.

Some of the significant stylistic differences noted are those of precision being emphasized in verbal production by whites, while often "Fancy Talk," a tradition of utilizing improvisation, is emphasized on the part of blacks. And the call-response tradition of interaction is seen as being a distinct feature of blacks. Though not exhaustive, these examples provide insight into how Black English is shown to differ from standard

English. Since language greatly determines how one perceives the world, differences in language are believed to lead to differences in perception.

Nonverbal Differences

Specific nonverbal differences between blacks and whites are noted in kinesic features such as eye movement, walking, gestures, and interaction postures, as well as in temporal use. Concerning eye movement, for example, the practice of "rolling the eyes" (Blubaugh and Pennington, 1976: 71-72); Johnson, 1972: 183-184) and of avoidance of eye contact are common to black Americans and are subjected to different uses than those of whites. "Rolling" of the eyes by blacks is a nonverbal means of communicating impudence and disapproval of the person in the authority role, according to Johnson (1972: 183), and is carried out by moving the eyes from one side of the eye socket to the other and by lowering the eye lids. Unlike the "cutting of the eyes" used in the dominant culture in which eye movement is always toward another person, in "rolling the eyes," eye movement is always away from the other person. Or, another difference in communication noted through use of the eyes is that whites, being a part of the dominant culture, emphasize having direct eye contact with the person with whom one is communicating, while avoidance of direct eye contact is common among blacks, particularly vis-à-vis someone of a higher status.

Briefly turning the back on others while interacting with them is often observed among blacks, a sign of trust, which is different from the face-to-face emphasis of the dominant culture (Johnson, 1972: 183).

As far as the attitude toward and use of time are concerned, blacks have a somewhat cavalier approach, contrasted to the more conscientious attitude of the dominant culture (Smith, 1973: 31). Since a group's concept of time is determined, in part, by their world-view, by the amount of control which they perceive themselves exercising over their lives, and by the significance of events, blacks have not historically felt that their destinies or time were in their own hands and thus, the less than commercial attitude toward time (Pennington, 1974: 155-161).

The differences in nonverbal communication between blacks and whites are important not only because some of the nonverbal behaviors are foreign to the other group, but also because those which have a resemblance may convey an altogether different message.

Family Structure and Relationships

When viewing the family structure and relationships of blacks and whites, general descriptions often characterize black families as being extended and many times matriarchical, while white families are characterized as being more nuclear. While these characterizations are often traditional generalizations which should be subjected to systematic investigation (since systematic social research shows that there are few significant differences between black and white families strictly attributable to race), clinicians who treat blacks have recognized concerns which seem unique to blacks. Citing one of the primary purposes of the family as the protection of its young, Grier and Cobbs (1968: 68) argue that

> the black family cannot protect its members. Nowhere in the United States can the black family extend its umbrella of protection over its members in the ways that a white family can. In every part of the nation its members are subjected to physical and verbal abuse, humiliation, unlawful search and seizure, and harrassment by authorities. Its members are jailed, beaten, robbed, killed, and raped, and exposed to a kind of jeopardy to a degree unheard of in white families.

This is an important distinction in that it calls attention to the ways in which, for the black family, outside forces can interfere with the very concept of unity and protection around which families are built. The foregoing cultural differences between blacks and whites are cited as examples of one of the trends in black-white communication research which assumes that because cultural differences are a source of communication difficulty, isolating important factors within the cultures can facilitate closer examination and understanding.

Assuming that there are cultural differences, scholars demonstrate that racism occurs when whites, who are in the majority and in the more powerful positions, view themselves and their culture as being superior to that of blacks, thus using race as a criterion for awarding goods, privileges, and services. Racism, then, is seen as another major cause of white-black communication difficulties.

> I will say that in addition to this that there is a physical difference between the white and black races which I believe will ever forbid the two races living together on terms of social and political equality. And in as much as they cannot so live, while they do remain together, there must be the position of superior and inferior, and I as much as any other man am in favor of having the superior position assigned to the white race.
> —Abraham Lincoln [Jones, 1895: 283]

While the thorny problem of relating culture to race is clearly recognized, racial identification in America is facilitated greatly by the symbol of skin color, which becomes the basis for placing persons into "superior" and "inferior" positions. Because the awarding of goods, privileges, and services on the basis of skin color is seen as being fortified by the presence of certain phenomena, researchers delineate the negative aspects of prejudice, stereotypes, and assumptions as factors in interracial communication. The link between these phenomena and racism is clearly pointed out.

Prejudice, Stereotypes, and Assumptions

While it is recognized that individual personalities can be shaped in childhood toward being prejudiced or unprejudiced, tolerant or intolerant (Allport, 1954: Frenkel-Brunswick, 1948), the apparent influence of the racial basis of prejudice is clearly demonstrated. For instance, one of the earlier reports on prejudice shows that high school students from all parts of the United States indicate by an overwhelming majority that they believe blacks to be members of an inferior race (Allport, 1954: 75). After reviewing the results of many studies on prejudice, such as those by Hartly (1946), and Bettelheim and Janowitz (1950), as well as based upon his own works, Allport estimates that four-fifths of the American population harbors racial prejudice (1954: 77). Bettelheim and Janowitz (1950) indicate that racial prejudice is expressed in various stereotypes held by other groups. Of significance here is the fact that whites believe blacks to be dirty and superstitious (Allport, 1954: 76).

Contemporary scholars in communication find that prejudice, stereotypes, and assumptions still exist on the part of whites and blacks toward each other, though perhaps not to the same degree. While some of the prejudices, stereotypes, and assumptions may be considered as positive, some which have a negative impact on black-white communication are obvious. For example, white Americans believe blacks to be argumentative, aggressive, defiant, and hostile (Ogawa, 1971), while blacks believe whites to be evasive, boastful, aggressive, and arrogant (Rich, 1974: 58). More specifically, with unquestionable links to racism are the assumptions made by whites that "white society is superior to black society," "blacks can be stereotyped," "blacks are trying to use whites," and that "blacks must be controlled"; and the assumptions made by blacks that "all whites are racist," "honkies have all the power," "all whites are alike," "whites are trying to use blacks," and "whites are united in their attitudes toward blacks" (Lee and Schmidt, 1969: 4).

While there is some question concerning the present pervasiveness of racial prejudice, stereotypes, and assumptions, such as those cited above, scholars continue to provide descriptions of how they operate and how their existence can often be determined through verbal and written indices.

Symbols

The symbols linked to racism are often easily determined in terms of both the linguistic and nonverbal forms. Realizing that the symbols within a society determine the ways of perceiving and responding to phenomena, it is possible to show how many of the symbols of the American society are designed to portray the superiority of and accommodate the needs of whites, while at the same time derogating and failing to accommodate the needs of blacks. This use and control of symbols by whites is referred to as "symbolic imperialism" (Smith, 1973: 85-86). Some of the American symbols designed by whites for whites are the Constitution, Santa Claus, and standards of beauty (Smith, 1973: 87-95).

Linguistic connotations found within the color of each race, such as black as evil and dirty or white as good and clean, the knight on the white horse who performs the heroic deed, or the black sheep of the family all point to differences in evaluation. Written laws designed to exclude blacks from certain facilities, unwritten public policies, and the nonverbal messages communicated by de facto segregation in such things as housing, schools, and other agencies are also seen as fortifying racism. Attitudes and assumptions expressed in symbols can continue to perpetuate racism by governing and manipulating our perceptions and behaviors. Symbols are thus portrayed as linking persons to each other and to reality, and thus, the role of their negative use in separating blacks and whites from each other is kept well in view by most researchers in white-black communication.

Power

Though more elusive to get a handle on, power is recognized as a key variable in black-white communication. Power is linked to racism in the sense that just as the language defines the perceptions and roles of the races, power provides those elevated to the "superior" position with the ability to carry out the perceptions and role definitions. Though elusive to capture, power is generally conceptualized as the ability to exercise control over one's own perceptions, behavior, and destiny, as well as over those of others, even against their will (Blubaugh and Pennington, 1976: 32). Further insight into the concept of power is provided by scholars pointing out its psychological as well as physical, coercive dimensions. That the equal distribution of power across racial lines will be difficult is acknowledged because of the deeply embedded traditional role relationships, as well as because of the threat which inheres to whites when they are urged to relinquish some of their power.

While blacks are seen as having power over whites, this power is described as, by and large, reactionary, that is a response to the uses and abuses of power by whites (Blubaugh and Pennington, 1976: 38). Thus, the power of blacks is believed to be confined to such exhibitions as protesting, demonstrating, or subversive defiances.

Race, or skin color, then, becomes the basis for determining one's potential for being a power wielder or recipient in black-white communication, and being placed in the "superior" position gives whites the ability to legislate, execute, and judiciously enforce the laws by which blacks are governed, according to the general findings in the literature.

A TOTAL PERSPECTIVE

By pointing to cultural differences and how they are compounded with racism to cause significant communication difficulties between blacks and whites, it is possible to conceptualize issues in interracial communication. All of the foregoing may be considered as strengths in terms of bringing to focus behavioral impediments to black-white communication. Conceptually, however, systematic investigation and hypotheses are needed which go beyond the behavioral manifestations to their underlying bases. First, the concept of culture needs to extend beyond that of such components as discussed above the the central core of a culture: that of its world-view or what is referred to by several scholars as the "deep structure" of a culture, which is often unconscious, even to the persons within the culture (Daniel and Smitherman, 1976: 28). Thus while probing the "deep structure" of a culture, a paradoxical effect is that of also bringing to surface some of the underlying assumptions of it. (Some may go so far as to argue that if persons are unhappy with the underlying assumptions governing their behavior, this, in itself, will create the anxiety necessary for change in a positive direction, in this case, the elimination of racism [assuming that those persons have a sense of conscience], but the validity of such an argument should be subjected to systematic investigation.) At any rate, returning to the need to probe the "deep structure" of a culture and showing how it relates to racism, the important question would become not only whether or not there are cultural differences beween blacks and whites, but significantly, whether or not there are world-view differences between the two groups. This has several merits: (1) it points to the unquestionable, though often ignored fact that cultural behaviors are based in a world-view; the underlying assumptions unifying a culture; (2) it calls attention to the need to determine what the world-views are of both blacks and whites, since many participants in black-white communication do not know what their own world-view is, not to mention knowing that of the other group; and (3) it allows the world-views of whites and blacks to be systematically compared in terms of such central issues as those of our relationship to nature, to divinity, to other humans, to inanimate objects, and to activity. One often hears the statement that racism is a basic American value, thus treating racism as something of a given transmitted from generation to generation. Racism, however, is only symptomatic of and one step removed from the real source of values. A more basic concern needs to be that of answering the question of what world-view allows racism to develop in the first place? Then, the question should be do blacks and whites objectively share that world-view? For example, expressing a question asked in black-white communication, if blacks, instead of whites, were in the position of control, would they (blacks) practice racism and discrimination against other groups? A strategic reply is another question: " Would their world-view allow them to comfortably practice racism?" In other words, something inherent in a group's world-view conduces it to or precludes it from the ability to comfortably practice the subordination of one group to another. Systematic determination of the world-views of blacks and whites, then, would aid in answering such questions and in providing a greater understanding into the dynamics of culture and racism in black-white communication. Once the world-view or underlying assumptions of blacks and whites are determined, they should be articulated and stated in a systematic way so as to provide analytical constructs, rather than being merely empirical generalizations.

On a related chord, one can note that among communicationists the treatment of racism often focuses upon the dynamics involved without always focusing equally as importantly on the origin of racism in America. The problem inherent in taking racism where it is presently and treating it as something of a given, without historically tracing its origin is that of provoking white guilt. Assuming racism in America to be something of a given (when, in fact, its origin was quite arbitrary) automatically creates two categories: those of racists and victims, without giving the "racists" a foundation for determining how they may be caught up in a process which they had no part in creating. Thus, the response of many whites in refusing to accept the blame for the racism of their ancestors should come as no surprise. This indicates the need to arrest the process and to encourage detachment from it long enough to study its origin, for such a study would reveal that many of the negative attitudes of whites toward blacks did not originate in sacred, absolute pronouncements, but rather, had arbitrary origins in the historical need to expediently provide free labor. Since blacks were convenient sources of labor, the attitudes toward them as being inferior resulted primarily from the need to justify enslaving them in order that they would continue to provide free labor by thinking of themselves as inferior and deserving of no better station in life. In terms of dealing with racism from the point of view of understanding it, then, insight can be obtained by probing beyond its behavioral dynamics to re-constructing its origin in America, thus showing that the whole mythological superior-inferior hierarchy of whites and blacks had a purely arbitrary origin and can perhaps be just as arbitrarily changed in the positive direction of establishing equality.

METHODOLOGICAL CONCERNS

Methodologically, the concern in black-white communication is, in part, the standard controversy which has caused a schism within the communication discipline, as well as across disciplines: how to identify the problem, whether through experimental quantitative methods or through more qualitative, humanistic ones.

The experimental method is seen as being more scientific, with its strengths being those of rigor, quantification, and the ability to isolate and measure variables. The humanistic approach, on the other hand, is viewed as being more qualitative, inventive, generative, and creative, thus allowing researchers to achieve a better, more introspective examination of humans in their wholism (Bevilacqua, 1972).

In the applied sense in black-white communication, the experimentalists are seen as being mechanistic in their outlook, and the humanists are seen as being experiential in this approach. And, in part, the methodologies have been allowed to determine the realities of the researchers, particularly among the mechanists. Philosophically, the mechanist says that in order for something to become real, it must be situated in time and space, and it must lend itself to isolation, measurement, and quantification (Pepper, 1942). By contrast, the experientialist says that if one has experienced something, then the existence of that phenomenon for that person becomes real, although not quantified, necessarily. Of course there are experimentalists and humanists who do not conform to clear lines of demarcation.

That the two methodological orientations can lead to the perception of different realities in black-white communication can best be illustrated by using a true incident as an example. At a recent seminar on racism attended by whites and blacks, the mechanistic and experimental orientations were clearly evident. Blacks often cited personal examples of what they and other blacks had experienced and perceived as racism in the organization complex—thus, the experiential approach. Many whites, on the other hand, especially those trained in psychometrics, psychology, and business, failed to find creditable the black's reality because such experiences had not been experimentally quantified and measured in controlled, replicable conditions. There were, clearly, two perceptions, with the tendency to deny the validity of the others' perceptions existing more heavily on the part of the mechanists.

One cannot help believing that the persons present at the seminar represented a microcosm of the black-white communication difficulties in the larger society where the different methodological orientations shape different realities. Obscured in the same interaction is the less obvious problem of how persons' positions as senders or receivers across racial lines may influence their perceptions of racism. That is, are receivers or "victims" of racism more sensitive to perceived acts of racism than are the senders of such acts/policies? Are there factors inherent in the sending of racism which contribute to the senders' being less sensitive, or cognizant to the reality perceived by the receiver? Therefore, recognizing how methodological orientations can be allowed to determine one's sense of reality is needed for researchers and participants in white-black communication. The problem seems prevalent in the applied sense and is compounded when the methodological orientations become mutually exclusive.

Regardless of the methodological approach used, a common problem for researchers and participants in black-white communication is that of specifying and operationalizing the concepts in question. The major concern of operationalism is that of being able to trace the researchers and participants' conceptualizations back to what is immediately observable, and if it were possible to do so, much of the ambiguity of concepts would be avoided. The fact is that such is not always the case, and in spite of carefully delineated operations, unclarity of what is meant by some terms still results. For example, the term "interracial communication," itself, has not been clearly defined, either in nature, intent, or effect. While all definitions of "interracial communication" are behaviorally oriented in the sense that they involve a sender and receiver who affect one another through symbolic means, some view it as a form of interpersonal communication between cultural or racial groups (Blubaugh and Pennington, 1976: 13; Smith, 1973: 14), while others view it as having societal dimensions. While for some "interracial" is seen as being almost interchangeable with interethnic (Rich and Ogawa, 1972: 27), others see the two terms as being different. Also, it is not clear when interracial communication has actually occurred. Does it occur whenever there is increased understanding between races or does it occur whenever races interact with each other, regardless of the intent or effect? Although interracial communication is seen as involving senders and receivers of different races affecting each other through symbolic means, Scheidel (1976: 381), though speaking of intercultural communication, warns against a tendency which is also applicable to interracial communication (inasmuch as interracial and intercultural communication communication between blacks and whites in America are often seen as being nearly synonymous).

> The greatest enemy of intercultural communication, as of all communication, is the illusion of its occurrence. When you originate a message, you understand perfectly what you said and you know exactly what you meant. Consequently, you might suppose that the same levels of knowledge and understanding are true for the listening agent. While this position may have merit in some settings, it is one to guard against when messages occur across cultures.

Interracial trust, anxiety, and attitude demonstration are other examples of concepts difficult to operationalize in interracial communication. As an instance, we can take attitude demonstration. Although the term attitude has been well-defined, difficulty arises when attempts are made to measure attitudes and to correlate them with behavior. For example, LaPiere concludes, based upon investigation, that attitudes of whites expressed toward a certain racial group in written-response situations are not always the same attitudes seemingly demonstrated by whites in the behavioral situations (LaPiere, 1934). Put more succinctly, in black-white communication, it is difficult to determine how participants best communicate their true attitudes or whether certain behaviors can be attributed to the existence of certain attitudes. The problem is compounded by the fact that some attitudes have more of an action structure than others (Cartwright, 1949). And because some attitudes have more of an action structure than others, a challenge for researchers in white-black communication is that of operationalizing the behavioral aspects not only in terms of physical and verbal indices, but also in terms of nonverbal indices.

Another problem for researchers in white-black communication is that of the multidimensionality of variables, particularly in experimental research. Both independent and dependent variables are not unidimensional, but are multi-faceted and complex and may interact with one another in many ways. Thus, inferences about cause-effect relationships cannot always be safely made, since one does not always know what dimension of a variable is causing the observed effect. Progress has been made, however, in recognizing the multi-dimensionality of some of the variables studied in interracial communication. Again, using the study of attitudes, although much of the large-scale research on the racial and ethnic attitudes has been done by social scientists, we can differen-tiate some of the major components of attitudes, such as the cognitive, affective, and the conative, as Harding et al. (1969), explain:

> The cognitive components are the perceptions, beliefs and expectations that an individual holds with regard to various ethnic groups. The beliefs and expectations of an individual with regard to members of a particular ethnic group . . . may vary along a number of dimensions. Probably the most important of these are . . . (1) simple (or undifferentiated) versus complex (or differentiated), (2) central (or salient) in consciousness versus peripheral (or embedded), (3) believed tentatively versus believed with assurance, (4) inadequately grounded versus grounded with appropriate evidence, (5) accurate versus inaccurate, and (6) tenacious versus readily modified.
>
> The affective components of an ethnic attitude include both a general friendliness or unfriendliness toward the object of the attitude and the various specific feelings that give the attitude its affective coloring. On the positive side they include such feelings as admiration, sympathy, and "closeness" or identification; on the negative side they include feelings like contempt, fear, envy, and "distance" or alienation.
>
> The conative components of an ethnic attitude include beliefs about "what should be done" with regard to the group in question, and action orientations of the individual toward specific members of the group. The former type of component is sometimes called "policy orientation" and is typically investigated by means of "third person" questions in attitude surveys (for example, "Should Negros be allowed to . . .?"). The latter type of component includes both general action orientations toward "typical" members of an ethnic group (for example, "How would you feel about working under a Negro supervisor?") and specific action orientations toward particular members of the group in question (for example, "Do you know any Negro well enough that you might invite him to your home?").

Because of the various dimensions of popularity researched variables such as that of attitudes, as just shown, researchers in black-white communication can profit by giving heed to "multidimensionality" signposts, thus avoiding the pitfalls of treating such variables in amorphous, confounding ways. Any method which permits more insight into problems of interracial communication is useful.

SUGGESTIONS FOR FUTURE CONSIDERATION

Inasmuch as communication scholars often define interracial communication on the interpersonal arena and often rely upon interpersonal relation theory, this tendency needs to be closely examined. Since race and culture have group dynamics and social dimensions, and inasmuch as some writers make distinctions between the interpersonal and the other levels of communication, perhaps the focus should also be upon the group and social dimensions of black-white communication, which are seen as being different than the interpersonal level. For example, Ruesch and Bateson (1968) identify and distinguish four levels on which communication takes place: (1) the intrapersonal, where the focus is limited by the self, and the various functions of communication are found within the self; (2) the interpersonal, where the perceptual field is occupied by two people; (3) the group level, where the perceptual field is occupied by many persons; and (4) the cultural level, where the perceptual field is occupied by many groups. They indicate that "concomitantly, in each of these fields, the importance of the single individual diminishes, and at the higher levels one person becomes only a small element in the system of communication" (1968: 274). Of further significance to black-white communication, in terms of the dynamics, is the fact that at the group level, the identity of persons is unspecified by name, and persons are known by role, just as at the cultural level, many groups are unspecified by name, but are known by role, which expresses moral, aesthetic or religious views (Ruesch and Bateson, 1968: 277). A relevant question to be answered is whether black-white communication is a form of intercultural communication, rather than or in addition to its being a form of

interpersonal communication, since participants do not always
see each other in terms of individual persons, necessarily, but
in terms of symbolic, representative roles (Vontress, 1967)?

The concern here is to address the black-white communication which occurs on levels other than the interpersonal. If race
and culture have social dimensions, it would seem that the
theory on black-white communication should also address
itself to these dimensions, determining, out of interest, if the
theory can remain the same across all levels.

In terms of methodology which can be used to arrive at a
wholistic perspective on the cultural and racial dynamics of
white-black communication, it would be useful to determine,
from a conceptual point of view, the simultaneous relationship
among the variables seen as being important. For example, is
there a relationship, say, between language, assumptions,
temporality, and family relationships when they are viewed in
terms of their simultaneous, dynamic interaction with each
other? What multivariate approaches can be utilized to focus
upon the simultaneous interaction? Can the multivariate relationship be integrated into a coherent theory?

CONCLUSION

The area of black-white communication is relatively new in
the communication discipline, and those who have pioneered
have made significant contributions in pointing out important
issues. Work is yet to be done in developing taxonomical
hypotheses, theories, and concepts which focus not only upon
descriptions of the behavioral dynamics involved, but also
upon the underlying assumptions and bases. If understanding
the sources of the communication difficulties between blacks
and whites can lead to the ability to propose ways of eliminating
them, then understanding the roots of those difficulties is of
primary importance.

REFERENCES

ALLPORT, G. (1954) *The Nature of Prejudice.* Garden City, N.Y.: Doubleday.

BARATZ, J.C. (1973) "Language abilities of black Americans," in K.S. Miller and R.M. Dreger (eds.), *Comparative Studies of Blacks and Whites in the United States*. New York: Seminar Press.

BETTELHEIM, B. and JANOWITZ, M. (1950) *Dynamics of Prejudice*. New York: Harper.

BEVILACQUA, V.M. (1972) "Vico, rhetorical humanism, and the study of our times." *Quarterly Journal of Speech*, 58: 70-83.

BLUBAUGH, J.A. and PENNINGTON, D.L. (1976) *Crossing Difference . . . Interracial Communication*. Columbus, Ohio: Merrill.

CARTWRIGHT, D. (1949) "Some principles of mass persuasion." *Human Relations*, 2: 253-267.

DANIEL, J.L. and SMITHERMAN, G. (1976) "How I got over: Communication dynamics in the black community." *Quarterly Journal of Speech*, 62: 28.

DILLARD, J.L. (1972) *Black English*. New York: Vintage Books.

FRENKEL-BRUNSWIK, E. (1948) "A study of prejudice in children." *Human Relations*, 1: 295-306.

GRIER, W.H. and COBBS, P.M. (1968) *Black Rage*. New York: Bantam.

HARDING, J., PROSSHASKY, H., KUTNER, B. and CHEIN, I. (1969) "Prejudice and ethnic relations," in G. Lindzey and E. Aronson (eds.), *Handbook of Social Psychology*. Reading, Mass.: Addison-Wesley.

HARTLEY, E.L. (1946) *Problems in Prejudice*. New York: Kings Crown Press.

JACKSON, J. (1973) "Family organization and ideology," in K. Miller and R. Dreger (eds.), *Comparative Studies of Blacks and Whites in the United States*. New York: Seminar Press.

JOHNSON, K.R. (1972) "Black kinesics: Some nonverbal communication patterns in the black culture," in L. Samovar and R. Porter (eds.), *Intercultural Communication: A Reader*. Belmont, Cal.: Wadsworth.

LEE, B.M. and SCHMIDT, W.H. (1969) "Toward more authentic relations between blacks and whites." *Human Relations Training News*, 13: 4.

LINCOLN, A. (1895) "Fourth joint debate at Charleston (Illinois) September 18, 1858." P. 283 in A.T. Jones (ed.), *Political Speeches and Debates of Abraham Lincoln and Stephen A. Douglass, 1854-1861*. Battle Creek, Mich.: International Tract Society.

OGAWA, D. (1971) "Small group stereotypes of black Americans." *Journal of Black Studies*, 1: 273-281.

PENNINGTON, D.L. (1974) "Temporality among black Americans: Implications for intercultural communication." Unpublished Doctoral Dissertation, University of Kansas.

PEPPER, S.C. (1942) *World Hypotheses: A Study in Evidence*. Berkeley: Univ. of California Press.

RICH, A.L. (1974) *Interracial Communication*. New York: Harper &Row.

_____ and OGAWA, D.M. (1972) "Intercultural and interracial communication: An analytical approach," in L. Samovar and R. Porter (eds.), *Intercultural Communication: A Reader*. Belmont, Cal.: Wadsworth.

RUESCH, J. and BATESON, G. (1968) *Communication: The Social Matrix of Psychiatry*. New York: W.W. Norton.

SCHEIDEL, T.M. (1976) *Speech Communication and Human Interaction*. Glenview, Ill.: Scott, Foresman.

SMITH, A.L. (1973) *Transracial Communication*. Englewood Cliffs, N.J.: Prentice-Hall.

VONTRESS, C.E. (1967) "Counseling negro adolescents." *School Counselor*, 15: 86-91.

PRACTICAL APPLICATIONS: TRAINING METHODS

The compression of time and space and increasing human contact across national boundaries is characteristic of life in the twentieth century. Rising ethnic consciousness and awareness of ourselves as people with an individual history and culture calls for new approaches in our daily interactions. The body of theory and knowledge gathered from our research investigations must not lie dormant in textbooks or research articles. One of the seminal characteristics of intercultural communication is its ability to chart new horizons and understanding of human interaction in contemporary societies. Through applied strategies intercultural communication can significantly contribute to developing alternative approaches to social issues arising in multicultural, interdependent societies.

An important task for intercultural communicationists is to bring together the theoreticians and practitioners as they approach the issues of human interaction in culturally diverse settings. We are interested in how our theories and specific research will be translated into the operation of our daily institutions, interpersonal relations, involvement with international politics, diplomacy, and counseling. We have only begun in the development and application of intercultural principles to these settings.

In this section, Pedersen begins by presenting a training design for counselors who work with clients from different ethnic, racial, or socioeconomic groups. His training program is based on a triad model consisting of the counselor, the client, and an anti-counselor who is of the same culture as the client. Through the use of simulation and video, the counselor trainee is able to view the client's problems from their cultural perspective as well as his or her own. According to Pedersen, this affords better understanding of the cultural aspects of counseling problems and resistances to counseling. The model gives us an innovative approach to training methodology.

DiStefano's article surveys different types of international management training in the public and private sectors and presents the case study method as a viable approach for such training. He believes the public sector provides more thorough and competent training than the private sector whose emphasis lies mainly on the management issues. The case study approach facilitates acquiring skills in decision-making, problem-solving, judgment, and development of useful attitudes. DiStefano calls for a greater interchange between public and private sector senior people to increase the value of training programs.

Finally, Schnapper's essay identifies the needs, challenges, resistances, and goals of multinational corporation training. He describes a 10-step training model with a logical and disciplined approach to the special nature of multinationals. The model includes four basic criteria: managerial aspects, international business, language, and intercultural communication, deemed essential by Schnapper to any training program. The complexity of the multinational system requires the trainer to have a variety of approaches that can be modified for the particular situation. These articles should provide the reader with several approaches for putting intercultural communication principles into practice.

23.

COUNSELING CLIENTS FROM OTHER CULTURES: TWO TRAINING DESIGNS

PAUL PEDERSEN

University of Minnesota

There is an increasing need for a model to train counselors for work in multicultural populations. There is a growing awareness of institutional racism in the traditional selection, training and certification of mental health professionals, resulting in counselors who are inadequately trained to work with clients coming from racial, ethnic or socioeconomic groups whose values, attitudes, and life-style differ from those of the counselor (Pedersen, et al., 1976).

This article describes two training models that will help counselors understand coached clients in several different cultural contexts. Both designs apply one particular training model matching the counselor trainee from one culture with a coached client and anti-counselor from the same other culture in a simulated counseling interview. The objective of this simulation is to build a coalition between the counselor and client from another culture in spite of interference by an anti-counselor from the client's culture (Brislin and Pedersen, 1976).

This model, developed by Pedersen (1973), is designed to explicate cultural aspects of a counseling problem and resistance to counseling through an open struggle for power between the counselor and anti-counselor. The unique element in this design is the role of the "anti-counselor." The anti-counselor is encouraged to prevent the counselor from coalescing with the client toward a "solution" of the problem by increasing the client's dependence on the problem. The trainee in a counselor's role is encouraged to accept help from both the counselor and the anti-counselor according to which of these two persons seems to offer a more satisfactory alliance. The client is finally forced to choose between the counselor from another culture or the anti-counselor from his or her own culture. A counselor-client coalition against the problem or anti-counselor becomes the vehicle of effective counseling, whereas ineffective counseling results in a client/anti-counselor coalition that isolates the counselor.

The triad training model has been used for the last three years in several hundred workshops throughout the United States. Persons who have used the model report that they are better able to articulate the problem after a series of cross-cultural interviews with the client/anti-counselor teams. The client's problem as *I* see it from my own cultural viewpoint, is almost certain to be different from the way that problem is viewed from within the client's culture. Participants also reported increased skill in anticipating the resistance to counseling persons from other cultures. Otherwise, counselors may complete a crosscultural interview knowing they failed but never knowing *why* they failed. Immediate feedback from the anti-counselor confronts a counselor with the mistake even before the counselor has finished a poorly chosen intervention. Other recent research indicates statistically significant growth on the three Carkhuff scales of Empathy, Respect, and Congruence as well as the Gordon seven-level measure of understanding affect. There are indications that participants in the counselor role become less defensive after training and are less threatened by working with clients from other cultures. Finally, there is evidence that participants' real and ideal view of themselves as counselors becomes more congruent after training with the model (Pedersen, Holwill, and Shapiro, 1976).

A demonstration one-hour videotape has been developed, including four interviews with the counselor, client, and anti-counselor, and commentary on the triad model design. This videotape and an accompanying manual is available through the International Student Advisor's Office at the University of Minnesota. The manual and demonstration videotape provides a necessary introduction to this training model that should accompany either of the two suggested training designs described in this article.

The first training design described is appropriate for a small group of about 10 or 12 counselors working together for a one-day intensive training experience. The second training design is appropriate for a larger group of about 30 or 40 counselors working together for a two-day workshop experience. In either design there are advantages and disadvantages which will be described. The key element in both designs is the selection and training of coached client/ anti-counselor teams. These teams of resource persons should be as close to one another as possible, such as one team from the same ethnic group, nationality, socioeconomic group, age level, life-style, or sex role. In previous workshops teams of prisoners have been used to train social workers, and teams of handicapped persons have been used to train rehabilitation counselors. These teams of resource persons should be acknowledged as the trainers in the workshop. The coached client/anti-counselor teams should be carefully selected, paid as professionals, and should be trained in their coached roles as client and/or anti-counselors. The training involves showing them the demonstration videotape and rehearsing their roles according to directions on the accompanying manual prior to either training design. The manual will provide additional information about the triad model with illustrative examples. Each of the training designs described should be led by a facilitator who is already familiar with the triad model. The purpose of this article is to suggest a framework for bringing counselors together with coached teams from other cultures in a simulated counseling interview.

INTENSIVE ONE-DAY LAB FOR SMALL GROUPS OF COUNSELORS

Requirements

(a) Three trained client/anti-counselor teams from three different cultures.

(b) One large meeting room to view videotapes and a small
    nearby video lab to videotape triads.
(c) Ten rolls of videotape, two video recording decks, one
    camera and at least one monitor.

Design

Following an introduction and presentation of the video
demonstration of the triad model, the facilitator answers
questions while one of the counselors leaves the room with a
client/anti-counselor team to make the first videotape. The
counselor and team return to the group after having produced a
10-minute videotape of a simulated counseling interview and a
5- to 10-minute videotape of the three participants debriefing
one another. The 20-minute videotape is shown to the larger
group for comments and discussion. While the tape is being
viewed another counselor leaves the room with the second
client/anti-counselor team to produce a second tape. By the
time the group has discussed the first tape the second counselor
has returned with a second tape. While the second tape is being
viewed, a third counselor will leave with the third client/anti-
counselor team to make a third tape. Each counselor participant will take a turn in making a tape with one of the client/anti-
counselor teams in sequence. There are three client/anti-
counselor teams so that every three simulations, each team will
have a brief rest. After all the counselor participants have had a
chance to make, view, and receive feedback on their videotape,
there is a general plenary session to summarize insights from
the variety of videotapes and to answer questions.

Advantages

Assembling counselor colleagues interested in crosscultural
training for a day together discussing the special circumstances
of cultural differences in the counseling process is in itself a
useful experience, resulting in on-going contacts and professional relationships that are extremely useful later. By allowing
each participant to produce a tape and receive feedback from
colleagues, the experience becomes intensive and specific to
the individual counselor. By including three different teams

from three different cultures, the trainees are allowed some flexibility in matching themselves with a particular culture. At the same time, the group is able to compare and contrast how counseling clients from one culture is different from counseling clients from another culture. The videotapes produced during such a workshop can themselves provide a valuable resource, depending on the willingness of participants and the client/ anti-counselor teams to allow the videotapes to be used.

Disadvantages

It is sometimes difficult to secure the facilities to run such a workshop. It requires considerable videotaping equipment, one larger meeting room and a nearby videotaping studio room. The client/anti-counselor teams must be paid as professional resource persons. This is particularly true if the workshop organizer is being paid, but in any case it establishes the role of the resource persons as central to the instruction funtion of the workshop. In this particular design, each participant will miss the group feedback on one tape, while they are producing their own videotape. The advantages of making and discussing the videotape while it is still fresh outweigh the disadvantage of the participants missing one session, however. It is essential to select and train the client/anti-counselor teams with extreme care. Some teams are able to role-play the "problem" more easily than others, but in all cases the training includes viewing models of how the anti-counselor should function on videotape and then rehearsing their roles until they are comfortable with the roles. They should have several preselected problems that they would be able to present to the counselor trainee. The anti-counselor and clients should have selected one another and be able to anticipate what the other team member will do or feel in as many situations as possible. The anti-counselor should be verbally articulate, although some anti-counselors have used nonverbal approaches very effectively.

INTENSIVE TWO-DAY LAB FOR LARGE
GROUPS OF COUNSELOR TRAINEES

Requirements

(a) One trained client/anti-counselor team for the same culture for every eight counselor trainees.

(2) One large meeting room, large enough for everyone to meet together, and adjoining smaller rooms that would allow groups of 10 persons to meet with a minimum of distraction from one another.

(c) One videotape play-back deck and monitor.

Design

The first session would begin with an introduction of the client/anti-counselor teams to the participants, a statement of the agenda for the workshop, a clear statement of the workshop goals, and time for questions. Then the video demonstration of the triad model would be shown to the total group with time for questions and some discussion. After the discussions there can be a demonstration by the facilitator and a team of the crosscultural triad model in front of the entire group, or the entire group may be instructed to divide themselves into triads so that they may briefly experience the model with the facilitator and coached resource teams circulating among the triads to answer questions. Once the group participants have a clear notion of the model, they will be divided into groups of eight according to prearranged assignments to insure that each group will be as heterogeneous as possible in terms of culture, age, sex role, life-style, training, socioeconomic status, and other available characteristics. The coached client/anti-counselor teams will be assigned to each of the different groups for a period of 45 minutes. During this time the coached team will elect a volunteer from their group to function as counselor. The team will have prepared three or four problems beforehand that they can develop in a crosscultural simulated counseling interview. They will role-play the interview for five or 10 minutes and then go out of role for a five- or 10-minute debriefing of one another without the triad. After the three participants have had a chance to give feedback, they will call on the other seven group members for additional observations and discussion. The coached team will then elect a second volunteer from the participants and repeat the cycle of a simulated interview, debriefing, and discussion. The team should have time to complete at least two interviews before the 45-minute period is complete. At the end of 45 minutes the team will rotate to another group in ordered sequence for a second 45-minute period. The rest of the first day will be spent in three small groups with the client/anti-counselor teams with lunch and coffee breaks at convenient points. The last 30 minutes of the day will be spent bringing the total group together to share their experiences, ask questions, or share insights.

The second day will begin with a general session of the total group with opportunity to ask questions and suggest insights that might be useful to other participants. The participants will then divide into their same groups of eight participants and continue meeting with the coached client/anti-counselor teams until each of the teams has met with each of the small groups. By this time each of the eight participants in each small group should have had a chance to role play the counselor in a triad.

After the small groups have been completed, the total group will come together for a discussion and the participants will be asked to form their own triads either with one another or including members of the coached client/anti-counselor teams, but with freedom to assume any of the three roles of counselor, clinet, or anti-counselor. If the participants wish to experiment with a triad design in which the third person acts as a *pro-*counselor to *help* the counselor do a better job, they will be encouraged to do so. Participants not wishing to role play will be encouraged to organize their own triads in client or anti-counselor roles with problems they have identified out of their own background. This less structured session will be concluded with the lunch break.

After the lunch break, the client/anti-counselor teams will be assembled as a panel in front of the total group. Each team member will be given a chance to speak briefly on what they observed during the training process. After ech team member has had a chance to speak, there will be an opportunity for participants to ask questions and discuss the training process within the larger group. By this time participants should have numerous questions on the specific ways that culture differences between the coached teams affected the counseling relationship. At the end of the discussion evaluation, forms will be distributed among the participants asking them to complete the evaluation before leaving the workshop.

Advantages

Alternating the small-group and large-group experience allows both intensive interaction where participants can learn from one another's style in some detail and still have the benefit of insights by other participants outside their immediate small group. By presenting more than one client/anti-counselor team to each small group, participants can see how different cultures approach the same problems or counselor-style in different ways. By going for two days, participants have a chance to assimilate the training data and to think about questions they might want to ask during the last session. Each participant will have a chance to be the counselor in a simulated interview at least once and possibly more often. Participants will also have a chance to experience the roles of client and anti-counselor after the small group sessions are completed. Participants will also have a chance to experience a triad where the third person takes on the role of a pro-counselor from the client's culture which might be useful in actual therapy. Participants will be encouraged to present counseling problems they have actually experienced in their own counseling experiences for feedback and suggestions on appropriate intervention.

Disadvantages

Participants will not have a chance to make their own videotapes and see themselves working with clients from other cultures. The logistics of assembling small groups, assigning participants, and rotating the client/ anti-counselor teams can become complicated. The small groups can become so involved in discussion of issues that they avoid the role-playing tasks and need to be reminded to save their discussion of issues until the last session. The facilitator can circulate among the groups to help them get into role-play as much as possible during the small group sessions. Sometimes participants are not able to attend the workshop the full two days, so the small groups may fluctuate in size. The interaction is extremely intensive and liberal allowance should be made for coffee breaks between sessions while keeping as much pressure on the participants as possible. The facilitator should be able to guide discussion during the last session to provide closure to the workshop experience and summarize insights that have occurred during the sessions. The triad model should serve to stimulate interaction between the coached teams and the participants by directing the participants toward these resource persons as the primary teaching resource for the workshop.

Evaluation

The triad-training mode has been used as an in-service training mode with a number of different populations training foreign student advisors to work with foreign students, training counselors to work with clients from other ethnic minority groups, training counselors to work with alcoholics and other drug-dependent clients, training counselors to be more sensitive to sexist attitudes, and training prisoners at a federal prison to train social workers to become more sensitive to prison as a culture. The range of possible applications extends to any situation where the values of the counselors are likely to be different from those of their clients. The counselors are allowed to make mistakes in the "safe" context of a simulated interview with clients from the target culture. The counselors receive immediate and direct negative feedback from clients on each mistake as they are in the process of counseling so that they can learn not only to recognize possible mistakes beforehand but also recover from mistakes they have made without destroying the interview. Perhaps the two most valuable specific skills a counselor can learn through the triad model are (1) how to become less defensive when under direct attack or when receiving strong negative feedback from a client, and (2) how to recover from a mistake once it has been made.

While the workshops have tended to be limited to one or two days, there is some evidence that the experience was judged to be useful by participants. Two of the workshops were held in Hawaii where a two-page questionnaire was distributed to the participants, soliciting their reaction to the training process. These data describe the responses of 39 mostly Asian-American counselors in the Department of Social Welfare on Maui, working with counter-culture clients, and 40 counselors for a variety of backgrounds working with clients from a variety of cultures in Hilo. Both workshops were two days in duration and included four trained client/anti-counselor teams from the local culture. Data from these two in-service training workshops will illustrate typical responses from trainees describing their training experience.

The participants from Maui were given a semantic differential and asked to describe the training mode on twelve dimensions according to a seven-point scale. These data are reported on Table 23.1.

Table 23.1: Semantic Differential Responses by Counselor Trainees in Maui Describing the Triad Model

		N X	1	2	3	4	5	6	7	
1	Pleasant	39/2.7	10	9	8	7	2	3	0	Unpleasant
2	Friendly	39/3..0	8	11	9	6	4	0	1	Unfriendly
3	Accepting	39/3.0	8	9	8	6	5	3	0	Rejecting
4	Enthusiastic	39/2.6	10	10	8	6	4	1	0	Unenthusiastic
5	Lots of fun	39/3.7	4	8	5	11	5	2	4	Serious
6	Relaxed	39/3.3	5	10	7	7	5	3	2	Tense
7	Cooperative	39/2.6	11	13	2	7	4	2	0	Uncooperative
8	Supporting	39/3.0	4	12	9	6	2	3	2	Hostile
9	Interesting	39/2.4	11	12	8	6	1	1	0	Boring
10	Harmonious	39/3.7	2	9	8	8	6	3	3	quarrelsome
11	Self-assured	39/2.8	5	14	7	8	1	3	0	Hesitant
12	Efficient	39/3.0	4	9	14	6	5	0	1	Inefficient
13	Open	39/2.8	10	10	6	6	3	2	2	Guarded

The responses were widely distributed with a tendency to favor positive rather than negative or punishing characteristics. While the participants describe the experience more in positive than negative terms, there was also some recognition of the tension and pressures in the training design.

When the Maui trainees were asked whether the training model helped them anticipate resistance in clients from other cultures, 28 responded "yes," four responded "no," and the other seven trainees did not respond. When the trainees were asked whether the training model helped them to articulate the problem from the client's cultural viewpoint, 25 responded "yes," six responded "no," two responded "somewhat," and the other six trainees did not respond. When the trainees were asked whether they would like additional training in this model, 22 responded "yes," eight responded "no," one responded "maybe," and the other eight trainees did not respond. The trainees were consistent in evaluating the training experience as useful even though many of them had earlier described the experience in more punishing terms on the semantic differential.

The Maui trainees were asked to describe the three roles of client, counselor, and anti-counselor on the basis of their experience. In terms of the "most powerful," two selected the client, nine counselor, and 24 the anti-counselor; in terms of the "most interesting," 10 selected the client, 12 the counselor, and 10 the anti-counselor; in terms of "most educating," 17 selected the client, nine the counselor, and six the anti-counselor; in terms of "most threatening," 13 selected the client, three the counselor, and 16 the anti-counselor. While the anti-counselor was perceived as most powerful and the client as most educating, both the client and the anti-counselor roles were perceived as threatening, and all three roles were described as interesting.

When the trainees from Maui were asked about the most serious weaknesses of the training model, they volunteered criticism that was coded into several categories. According to 14 trainees, there was a problem in role-playing correctly or successfully. According to five of the trainees, other groups beside the social welfare staff should have been included in the training. Other responses suggested that the model was not well explained beforehand, that the discussion wandered from the central focus of the training session, and that there was not enough time for the training.

When the trainees were asked about the most promising advantages of the training model, they volunteered benefits that were coded into several categories. According to 22 of the trainees, the model made all persons more aware of each other and the problems of counseling. According to seven of the participants, the model made the counselor more responsive to reacting to the client. Other responses were that the model illustrated cultural differences and a unique approach to counselor training.

When the trainees were asked what new insights they had gained as a result of using the model, 12 emphasized the importance of understanding cultural differences, eight emphasized the importance of in-service training for counselors, five emphasized an increased awareness of problems, and three emphasized the value of a third person in simulated counseling interviews. These observations are generally consistent with the stated goals of the workshop.

The participants from Hilo were also given the same semantic differential and asked to describe the training model on 12 dimensions according to a seven-point scale. These data are reported on Table 23.2.

Table 23.2: Semantic Differential Responses by Counselor Trainees in Hilo Describing the Triad Model

		N X	1	2	3	4	5	6	7	
1	Pleasant	38/2.7	10	9	7	5	6	0	1	Unpleasant
2	Friendly	39/2.3	14	11	7	5	0	1	1	Unfriendly
3	Accepting	38/2.6	6	14	9	7	2	0	0	Rejecting
4	Enthusiastic	37/2.7	9	9	8	6	5	0	0	Unenthusiastic
5	Lots of fun	38/3.2	6	8	8	9	3	2	2	Serious
6	Relaxed	38/2.9	10	6	8	5	7	2	0	Tense
7	Cooperative	37/2.2	14	10	5	6	2	0	0	Uncooperative
8	Supporting	38/2.6	10	9	9	7	2	1	0	Hostile
9	Interesting	39/2.0	17	11	5	5	1	0	0	Boring
10	Harmonious	38/2.7	8	8	9	9	2	2	0	Quarrelsome
11	Self-assured	37/3.0	2	13	9	8	5	0	0	Hesitant
12	Efficient	38/2.9	6	10	10	5	5	2	0	Inefficient
13	Open	40/2.5	14	9	7	4	3	2	1	Guarded

The responses by Hilo trainees were also widely distributed but somewhat less negative in their description of the experience as punishing. We do not yet know whether an effective workshop should be described in more or less punishing terms and these data only serve to illustrate the range of neutral categories by which trainees describe their experience.

When Hilo trainees were asked whether the training model helped them articulate the problem from a client's cultural viewpoint, 32 responded "yes," one responded "no," one responded "maybe," four responded "somewhat" and "don't know," and one did not respond. When asked if the training helped them anticipate resistance in clients from other cultures 34 responded "yes," and two responded "no." When the trainees were asked whether they would like additional training in this model, 28 responded "yes," one responded "no," one responded "don't know," and 10 did not respond. Again, the trainees were consistent in evaluating the training experience as useful to them in specific ways.

The Hilo trainees were asked to describe the three roles of client, counselor, and anti-counselor on the basis of their experience. In terms of the "most powerful," four selected the client, eight the counselor, and 24 the anti-counselor; in terms of "most interesting," six selected the client, nine the counselor, and 17 the anti-counselor; in terms of most educating, three selected the client, 16 the counselor, and 12 the anti-counselor; in terms of the most threatening, five selected the client, 14 the counselor, and 17 the anti-counselor. While the anti-counselor was again selected as most powerful and most interesting, the counselor role and anti-counselor role were both selected as most educating and threatening.

When the trainees from Hilo were asked about the most serious weaknesses of the triad model, they volunteered criticism that was coded into several categories. According to 12 trainees, there was a problem in role playing correctly or successfully. According to six trainees, the model was not well explained beforehand. Other criticism included that there was not enough time, that the discussion wandered from the workshop objectives, that there was not enough discussion,

418 Handbook Of Intercultural Communication

that the problems lacked solution and that the training might intensify stereotypes of some ethnic groups.

When the trainees were asked about the most promising advantages of the training model, they volunteered benefits that were coded into several categories. According to 12 of the trainees, the model made all persons more aware of each other and the problems of counseling. According to 10 of the trainees, the model made the counselor more responsive in reacting to the client. Other responses were that the model illustrated cultural differences and suggested alternative approaches to counseling.

When the trainees were asked what new insights they had gained as a result of using the model, 17 emphasized the importance of understanding cultural differences in counselor/ client confrontations, seven emphasized an increased awareness of problems, five emphasized the potential for in-service training, and three emphasized the value of a third person in simulated counseling interviews. Again, these observations are generally consistent with the stated goals of the workshop.

CONCLUSION

The two training designs described in this article suggest two ways in which counselors might learn about counseling clients from other cultures. The emphasis is on rehearsing both good and bad interventions so that counselors can become more confident in working with clients different from themselves. Either design will result in new insights by counselor trainees that need to be explored and made explicit through discussion with the larger group. Counselor participants should also develop skills in learning *about* counseling clients from other cultures *from* members of those cultures, which should make them more attentive to cultural aspects of their own client population.

Both training designs suggested emphasize a crosscultural triad with the anti-counselor in the third role. Crosscultural dyads or triads with a pro-counselor would suggest alternative variations in simulated interviews. After using these variations, it seems that the triad with an anti-counselor should never be used in real counseling because of possible dangers to a client. A pro-counselor might prove extremely useful in actual counseling interviews. We know that cultural values make a significant difference in the counseling relationship. Either of these two designs should help the counselor trainee identify in specific terms how the counselor's own values as well as the values of a client might effect the counseling process.

REFERENCES

BRISLIN, R.W. and PEDERSEN, P. (1976) *Cross-Cultural Orientation Programs.* New York: Gardner.

PEDERSEN, P. (1973) "A cross-cultural coalition training model for educating mental health professionals to function in multicultural populations." Paper presented at the Ninth International Congress of Ethnological and Anthropological Sciences, Chicago, September.

_____ HOLWILL, F. and SHAPIRO, J. (1976) "A cross-cultural training procedure for classes in counselor education." Unpublished manuscript, University of Hawaii.

PEDERSEN, P., LONNER, W. and DRAGUNS, J. (1976) *Counseling Across Cultures.* Honolulu: Univ. Press of Hawaii, Culture Learning Institute.

24

CASE METHODS IN INTERNATIONAL MANAGEMENT TRAINING

JOSEPH J. DiSTEFANO

The University of Western Ontario

Competent management is probably the world's scarcest resource. This deficiency is felt both in communist and capitalist societies and takes its toll in nonprofit institutions— from government to hospitals, from universities to churches— as much as it affects business and industry.

The problem becomes even more critical when we consider managing on a global scale. And when we tally the growth of international activities on the part of business, government and other nonprofit organizations, the scarcity of management talent capable of dealing with worldwide problems becomes acute.[1] Whether we concern ourselves with food, energy, industrial or consumer goods and services or even with human rights, the essential ingredients to meet our objectives in any of these areas of endeavour are the ability and skills to organize efficiently and effectively human, physical and financial resources. More simply put, it is management. But either plainly or elaborately stated, it is a rare commodity.

Fortunately, management is a developable skill. As the challenges to human survival and advancement grow more complex and as concomitant growth occurs in the numbers, size, and scope of human organizations attempting to meet these challenges, there evolves a vastly expanded need for training. In the post-war world which has experienced these remarkable changes there has been a serious lag in the training of managers who are able to define, analyze, and take effective action with regard to international problems.

AUTHOR'S NOTE: *The author gratefully acknowledges the helpful suggestions of his colleagues Blair Little and Peter Newson.*

Therefore the purpose of this chapter is to survey the types of training currently available and to examine in some depth the use of case studies in training managers for international assignments. In the first section on training, differences in the public and private sectors and their implications for training are examined. Various types of training and examples of the programs available for each are described. The special opportunities and needs of the private sector will be noted.

The second section of the chapter focuses on the role of case studies in such programs. The case method is described, and various types of cases and their sources and diverse uses are discussed. Implications of the current state of training for practitioners and educators will conclude the chapter.

TRAINING FOR INTERNATIONAL ASSIGNMENTS[2]

Differences in the Public and Private Sectors.: There are significant differences between public and private sector organizations that have important implications for training.

Consider, for example, the situation of a large beer company operating mostly in the United States and Canada.[3] After several months of negotiating with an African government for partial ownership and for expansion of the government-run brewery, a settlement had been reached rather abruptly and the company found itself scurrying to find a general manager to head the operation and to represent their interests. Without a manpower planning system and with no information available pertinent to the overseas qualifications of their people, they made their decision on the basis of technical qualifications.[4] The man selected was a very successful production superintendent from one of their Midwestern breweries. He had been born in a neighboring state and had received his engineering education there. His whole working career had been at the local brewery. Neither he nor his wife knew any foreign languages, and their travel experience was limited to the surrounding regions in the United States.

Soon after the executives persuaded him to accept the assignment "for at least two years," they approached a professor in a nearby university for help in preparing the man for his new location. "By the way," they noted after a lengthy list of topics they wanted covered, "he has to leave in two weeks." Needless to say, the training he received was as inadequate as the company's preparation.

Unfortunately, even in more experienced multinationals such occurences are not atypical. Unlike the high and predictable volumes of military personnel regularly assigned overseas, private corporations usually have a very small number of expatriates in their foreign subsidiaries. The numbers going to any single country are even smaller—in sharp contrast, for example, to the Peace Corps or Canadian University Services Overseas (CUSO) or to U.N., A.I.D., or Canadian International Development Agency (CIDA) projects.

Sharp differences are also likely between the orientations and motivations of the people involved in the two types of organization. The commitment of a rising young hopeful in the State Department toward learning foreign languages or adapting to other cultures might be expected to vary markedly from a manager who sees his assignment to launch European operations for his U.S. firm as only a stepping stone to his rapid advance in the headquarter hierarchy back home. The career diplomat, the missionary, the teacher-volunteer, and so on, all have personal and professional interests that are directly related to the very substance of international training programs. Most are already sensitive to intercultural issues and are eager to acquire more knowledge and skill. On the other hand, the manager in the private sector is more likely to have previous experience and training only indirectly related to the social system and cultural variables which preoccupy his public sector counterparts.

Similarly, the domestic superiors of these two types of people are likely to view the training needs of their personnel quite differently and therefore to provide different types of resources and expertise for the preparation for overseas assignments. Their selection procedures and criteria are also likely to be dissimilar with public sector screening procedures being more formal and with more comprehensive criteria being employed.

Consequences for Training: The differences noted above influence training programs in the public and private sectors in several ways (see Table 24.1). Public sector training is more likely to consist of two- or three-week, formally structured, and

Table 24.1: Training for International Assignments in the Public and Private Sectors: Differences and Their Consequences

| Unit of Analysis | Dimension | Sector* | |
		Public	Private
Individual	Relation of pre-employment education/training to international assignments.	Moderate to High	Low to Moderate
	Extent of Career Commitment to International Activity	Moderate to High End in Itself	Low to Moderate Means to End
	Perception of International Tasks	Broad: Includes Socio-cultural Variables	Narrow: Emphasis on Business and Technical Factors
	Who Initiates International Assignment	Self or Superior	Superior
Organizational	Criteria for Selection	Broad	Narrow
	Process of Selection	Formal	Informal
	Training Program Structure	Formal	Informal
	Duration of Training Program	In Weeks	In Days
	Numbers of People per Country of Destination	Small to Moderate	Very Small
	Predictability of Training Needs	Moderate to High	Low to Moderate
	Frequency of Programs	Moderate to High	Low
	Regularity of Programs	Moderate to High	Low
	Content of Training	Broad	Narrow
	Training Resources Employed	Permanent, Internal Staff full-time plus external resources	Internal Personnel Part-time plus external resources

*Differences indicated in "Public" and "Private" Sector columns are meant to be indicative of general trends and are relative to each other. Obviously, individual cases will vary from this table.

professionally prepared and presented programs. These tend to include country-specific information as well as general, crosscultural orientation. In addition to technical data of relevance to each particular group receiving the training, there is usually broad coverage of historical, legal, socioeconomic and cultural factors. Language training is frequently held prior to the international program. These programs conducted by public organizations are usually repeated frequently on a regularly scheduled basis. A cadre of permanent staff whose main responsibility is to design and run the programs thereby build considerable experience. Their knowledge and skills are supplemented by outside experts who deal with specialized topics or particular countries or regions.

In contrast, preparation for overseas assignments in the private sector is much more likely to be an ad hoc, informal, unstructured series of meetings, briefings, and individual exploration and search. It will include discussions with others in the company who have been to the country, briefings by personnel staff and "line" officers responsible for the country at the headquarters, and reviews of whatever files the company may have accumulated. (Increasingly, staff departments are being created to advise international executives on social and political developments in the world. But rarely do such units include cross-cultural factors in their range of information.) Occasionally a short-term assignment at headquarters or in the international division, if there is one, is featured to "round-out" areas where there are perceived weaknesses (DiStefano 1975a). In those cases where there is sufficient planning, companies usually provide support for language training out-side the firm.

The primary focus of all these activities, however, is usually technical in nature and business-oriented. While some time may be spent on learning local customs and history, it usually is done by the interested manager on his own time outside of work. Of necessarily greater concern to the company will be its business objectives and the economic and organizational plans and resources to accomplish these. While an understanding of sociocultural variables is very important to effective manage-ment abroad, awareness of the impact of these factors has not penetrated the business community sufficiently enough to be included as high priority items in training.

Relative to the needs of individual managers, only a few companies send their international personnel to external, formal programs like those described for the public sector. Only in rare instances do private firms provide their own internal programs of training for international duties. The more usual practice is to rely on preemployment education and training, informal coaching by those already experienced internationally, and general purpose management development programs. Specific examples of these and other training approaches are described below.[5]

Types of Training Available: As noted above, the most comprehensive preparation for an assignment abroad combines general crosscultural training with country-specific orientation and information. This type of program is regularly provided in the U.S. military, for overseas volunteers (e.g., CUSO and Peace Corps) and for those on limited-term contracts for foundations and government agencies.

The "Adaptation Programs" conducted by CIDA are good examples, perhaps the best, of what can be accomplished even under relatively tight budget and time constraints. The two-week programs are designed for those under CIDA contracts with foreign governments, although participants from private companies headed for overseas assignments are sometimes included on a fixed fee-for-costs basis. A distinctive feature is the inclusion of whole families in the program. Separate portions of the program are oriented to elementary school children and to teenagers, to spouses of volunteers, and to problems encountered by the whole family unit.

The content of the program emphasizes general crosscultural training, but there are significant amounts that are country-specific. Different offerings over the year feature different regions of the world depending on the needs at a given time. The country-specific parts of the program cover a wide range of topics from food and games to health considerations. Staff for these aspects of the program include natives from the countries involved and are available to the participants during the whole program. Canadians who have worked in the countries, usually on similar tasks or assignments, also confer with the new volunteers. As well, embassy representatives are usually included and make presentations to the volunteers about their countries. In addition to these sources of information, library materials, films, and video-tapes are also available at the training site.

The more general, crosscultural portions of the program include case studies of real situations faced by others working overseas, simulations and other involvement exercises, and more traditional lectures, books, films, and so on. These are provided by a mix of CIDA permanent staff and external consultants. The latter are usually engaged over several programs.

Although post-assignment participant evaluations indicate that these programs are highly valued, opportunities for training of comparable breadth and depth are rare in the private sector. Two organizations which attempt to fill these needs are the American Graduate School of International Management (Key Manager Program) and the BCIU Institute in Washington, D.C.[6] But the market for such programs in the private sector is still very difficult to serve because of its diffuse and decentralized nature (in addition to the complicating features summarized in Table 24.1.) The private sector simply is not very aware of the need.

The main sources of international training for those in the private sector are "in-house" programs run by the companies themselves and those offered by universities or nonprofit institutes. Almost all of these are general in orientation (no country-specific data) and are designed either to deal with technical problems of international concern (such as underwriting for global insurance companies) or to provide general management development for corporate personnel drawn from several countries.

Examples of both the technical and the general programs can be found in most large multinationals. A typical firm whose activities have been reasonably well documented is Commercial Union Assurance Company (CU) headquartered in London, England (DiStefano, 1975b). Their first training of

international scope started in 1972 with a two-week, integrated, case method general management program which
included components of marketing, control and financial
analysis, and organizational behavior. The latter subject area
was, as is typical of such efforts, the portion which dealt with
intercultural issues. This program was conducted three successive years in Canada, Australia, and Denmark, and each
session was attended by 70 middle managers from all over the
world. In 1975 and 1976 four-week programs were held for
more senior managers of the firm including those responsible
for the major territorities of United States, United Kingdom,
Europe, and the Far East. These, too, were integrated case-
method programs. The content included higher level problems
in the previously mentioned areas to which were added
sessions on decision analysis and business-government relations. A unique feature was the inclusion of especially prepared cases on some of the most current and important
international problems faced by the company. All the programs were designed and conducted by a team of business
professors in consultation with CU corporate staff and executive directors.

Although the primary purpose of all these programs was the
development of managerial skills, an important secondary
purpose explicitly stated and highlighted by the chief executive
who initiated and supported the programs was to sensitize and
to train their managers (who had previously been relatively
provincial in outlook and experience) about the international
and intercultural realities of the company's operations around
the world. The expectation that future international appoint-
ments to senior positions would draw heavily from those who
had attended these programs was already being fulfilled by the
fourth year and continues to be realized. There was a significant increase from before to after the training programs in the
percentage of managers who were eager, or at least willing, to
accept an international transfer.

Midway through this five-year effort the director of their
international personnel department and his senior researcher
took a separate course on casewriting,[7] and subsequently
wrote CU cases for use on technically oriented short programs

which have since been conducted around the world using in-house instructors.

Concurrently, the company featured an "International Management Development" program of work assignments for a small, but select group of managers. These consisted of short assignments of six months to a year in a country different from the manager's current location. The program had dual objectives of completing a specific task for the country which could not be fulfilled domestically, and of exposing the manager to international operations, usually for the first time in his career.

The combination of these activities served to dramatically and quickly transform this huge organization. It turned from a mature company which, in spite of its operating in over 100 countries, had had a narrow, nationalistic view of itself to a more effective multinational which could better serve, as well as profit from, its customers around the globe.

This example has been developed in some detail because it illustrates activities undertaken by many multinationals in training their personnel for international responsibilities. They were painstaking in designing a program to meet their management development needs and simultaneously educate their managers concerning the international problems and opportunities facing the corporation. Although CU was late in entering the ranks of truly multinational operators compared to many manufacturing companies, it was ahead of most other insurance giants and of many international banks.

A similar range and mix of international training activities is duplicated in virtually every industry. Among the prominent multinationals who conduct programs like these are such diverse firms as Nestle, Citibank, Gulf, Coca Cola, IBM and Bata Shoe. Case-method, two-to three-week general management programs is the one area where private organizations are way ahead of the public sector in international training activities.

Universities and related institutions also provide international management training through their continuing education activities and, to a lesser extent, in their degree programs. In the area of continuing education where efforts are more likely to be directed toward practical, current issues, the important distinction to be drawn is between (a) those activities which are primarily oriented to general management development and are only "international" by virtue of the range of countries from which the participants and faculty are drawn; and (b) those programs which are designed and developed with the international objective primarily in mind. The former vastly outnumber the latter. And even in the cases where participants and faculty come from a mix of countries, the number of really integrated programs which address the needs of the practitioners who attend, rather than the concerns of the academics who staff them, are very rare.[8]

In North America the universities with the best known degree programs in management, with special strength in training for international activities, are (in aphabetical order) Columbia, Harvard, Indiana, Stanford, Western Ontario, and Wharton. Lesser known institutions which have research and teaching programs of note in international management are the American Graduate School (Glendale, Arizona), Kent State, and the University of Georgia.

Of all the institutions in the United States and Canada, the only two which regularly operate management training programs (of the type described above) throughout the world are Harvard and Western. Both of these institutions have also helped establish management development centers with an international reach . . . Harvard in Europe and most recently in Iran, and Western in Europe, the West Indies, and most recently in Brazil.

There are several centers and programs which provide international management training in Europe. Together, they offer both degree and continuing education programs in a wide range of languages. The best-known programs are in England (IMP[9]), France (INSEAD[10]), Norway (NEMI[11]) and Switzerland (CEI[12]) and IMEDE[13]). Harvard also has its own program in Switzerland, and there is a program in Barcelona. All of these feature an international faculty and student body. Except for INSEAD and the Spanish program, the courses are conducted in English.

However, it should again be noted that almost all the programs and insitutions referred to above have their primary commitment to general management training with their interest in international management as a specialty. The major exceptions are the previously mentioned Key Manager Program at the American Graduate School with its distinctive language component, and the University of Western Ontario, which inaugurated in 1978 an annual three-week program designed to address directly the special problems faced by international managers.[14]

Needs of the Private Sector: Two conclusions about private sector training can easily be deduced on the basis of this review. (1) When one considers the availability of general management training for those responsible for international business, the overall judgment of the current state of the art is reasonably positive. (2) But if the criterion variable is the adequacy of these programs either with regard to country-specific orientations or with respect to crosscultural sensitization and training, then the judgment is more harsh. At best, there are serious shortcomings; at worst, the deficiencies are dangerous. The gap between what is, and what is needed, widens automatically as nationalism burgeons in the Third World, as political systems antagonistic to Western values gain strength, and as the challenges and opportunities of new human needs arise around the globe.

Yet, neither educators in North American business schools nor managers in its enterprises are sufficiently aware of the culture-bound nature of much of what is taught and practiced. Thus it should hardly be surprising, especially given the heavy pressures of day-to-day demands, that training programs fall woefully short in preparing or helping managers to deal sensitively and effectively with people in other countries. Too often the businessman who experiences difficulties while working abroad explains away the problems by a pejorative litany of natives' shortcomings. Furthermore, both he and his business professors falsely assume (or at least behave as if they did) that U.S. business practices are the only means to accomplish tasks efficiently. They mistake their own unexamined cultural values for business imperatives and thereby frequently miss opportunities to learn new approaches to effective problem-solving, to say nothing about the by-passed enriching of their own lives.

But the situation is far from hopeless. We only have to introduce these topics into already existing programs and curricula. The problem is one of altering or adding to on-going activities, not of convincing the business community or governments to support massive new programs.

Fortunately, there is available a well-tested and widely used methodology for adding crosscultural training to on-going programs, viz, case studies. It is no accident that nearly all the management programs mentioned above employ the case method to a significant extent. This pedagogical approach which requires the active involvement and participation of the students is highly appropriate to the needs and temperaments of action-oriented managers. Furthermore, case studies are a natural vehicle for capturing the richness, subtlety, and breadth of substantive material necessary for effective intercultural training. Hence it is to this teaching methodology, so highly amenable to the subject requirements and so highly accepted by those who have experienced it, that we now turn our attention.

CASE STUDIES IN INTERNATIONAL TRAINING

Clarification of Terms: While there is widespread use of case studies in both public and private sector international training, what is labelled "case-method" varies widely with regard to the cases themselves and how they are used (Dooley and Skinner, 1977). With respect to the case itself, the range of meanings consists of, at one extreme, a brief description of a page or two of a critical incident with little or no supporting data or contextual information, to a middle position of

> a record of a business issue which actually has been faced by business executives, together with surrounding facts, opinions, and prejudices upon which executive decisions have to depend. These real and particularized cases are presented to students for considered analysis, open discussion, and final decision as to the type of action which should be taken. [Gragg, 1954][15]

to the opposite extreme of a lengthy, historical review of an organization or a situation without clear focus or perspective and usually attempted from an objective point of view of a researcher.

How cases are actually used varies equally widely. At one end of the spectrum is the nondirective approach where the instructor is relatively passive and acts primarily to record the comments of the discussants on a blackboard or flip chart and to facilitate the exchange among the participants. Most case instructors tend to describe themselves this way, although their actual behavior is rarely as nondirective as they imagine. On the other end of the scale, the professor merely uses the case study as a springboard for his own analysis which frequently turns out to be a full-fledged, traditional lecture with the students taking notes and asking occasional questions. More instructors who call themselves case teachers display this tendency, albeit rarely to this extreme, than care to acknowledge it.[16] Most professors, of course, tend to behave somewhere in between. The variations in the middle ground are primarily (1) in the amount of time spent in placing the case in the context of the course or program, or in summarizing the discussion at the end of class, and (2) in the extent to which the content and flow of the discussion are directed.

Even this brief discussion of variations in definition and use of case studies should amply demonstrate the errors made by those who pronounce glib generalizations about "the" case method and characterize (or caricature) individuals or institutions as "case method."

When to Use (Which) Case Methods: The main consideration in deciding whether or not to use case studies in international or intercultural training is the educational objectives one has. If your chief objectives are to acquire knowledge, develop concepts, or understand techniques, then you are probably better off using a different pedagogy. However, if you aim to help others (1) acquire skills in using techniques, in analyzing problems, or in making decisions and plans, or (2) develop useful attitudes or mature judgment and wisdom, then case studies are likely to be an effective vehicle (Dooley and Skinner, 1977).[17]

However, educational objectives are not the only factors which should influence the choice of case studies and how they are used. Other considerations include

(1) the fit of cases with other methods being used
(2) the personality of the professor
(3) the expectations and experience of the participants
(4) the time available
(5) the number of people involved, and even
(6) the physical facilities

The relation of cases to other teaching methods being employed is important because of the active role demanded of students in case discussions. If all other faculty are given lectures, the lone case teacher will have a difficult time motivating students to break from their passive, dependent mode. Even if one other professor uses cases or other methods requiring students to participate actively, then case studies are likely to be more effective.

Of equal importance are the needs of the professor. If one has high needs for power or low tolerance for ambiguity, then cases are less appropriate. This is true because student interpretations of case events and their conclusions about the best action to take are often markedly different from the professor's views and from each other. Only rarely does the discussion end with a clear consensus. Even if the professor is secure psychologically, the discrepancy between the way the discussion unfolds and what was anticipated can be unnerving. On the other hand, it is never boring. No matter how often one teaches the same case, the discussion always reveals unexpected views. The challenge of responding and of shaping the flow is stimulating and refreshing.

Student expectations are a factor, too. If they perceive the professor as the expert (as they often do), then the students can be very frustrated if he does not provide "the answer."[18] The resulting anger can be most threatening, especially for less experienced teachers in untenured positions. Furthermore, since many of their past educational experiences have reinforced a passive role for students, they, too, can feel threatened by a method which requires them to prepare their work carefully and regularly and to expose their ideas and logic to rigorous challenges from their peers and professors. The shaking of self-concepts which results is most often visible in younger participants, but it is even manifested among experienced managers. However, as they gain confidence and become adept at the give and take of case method learning, they strongly resist professors who try to impose their views on the group.

One must recognize, too, that effective use of cases takes a fair amount of time both in preparation and discussion. In addition to individual preparation, it is highly advantageous for small groups to meet prior to class to share their ideas. This provides each with additional perspective which, in turn, contributes to a better class session. The classes also require more time than the usual 50-minute lecture period. Minimum time for most types of cases is an hour and a quarter with additional time required as the number or complexity of issues in the case increases.

For good discussions, a minimum of 15 to 20 participants are needed. The classroom layout should facilitate and encourage exchange among the students. Under the best conditions (semi-circular, tiered seating, amphitheatral arrangements supplemented with large name cards and swivel chairs) up to 100 people can be included in a class run by a skillful teacher. However the ideal size for most case discussions would be set between 40 and 60 participants by most experienced case professors.

There are several other advantages and disadvantages also to consider. Among the chief advantages are the development of analytic skill and of decision-making and planning abilities. The fact that these skills are developed with less dependence on the professor than is usual with other approaches, better prepares the participants for the realities of assignments abroad where they are isolated from much of what is familiar and supportive. Further, if the use of small discussion groups is encouraged, the students also gain experience in cooperating, leading, sharing, arguing, and generally understanding and managing group dynamics. This, too, is invaluable training for most tasks they are likely to face. Finally, if the mix of cases is chosen carefully, a by-product of the method is an unconscious absorption of a significant amount of contextual information. Participants learn about how people behave in different organizations, situations and cultures. They learn the jargon of different industries and specialities. They discover later that all kinds of data, which they treated as peripheral information when they prepared the cases, are unexpectedly recalled when needed or relevant.

There are serious disadvantages as well. The most obvious are its low efficiency for acquisition of facts, the special skills and facilities required for effective teaching, and the high level of commitment required among a large majority of the participants. Another significant disadvantage is that the case study reveals no information about the distribution of the phenomena it contains (Chandler, 1976: 37). We don't know how often the issues occur or how significant they are in general. Nor do we get much sense of the effect of different conditions.[19] The instructor can counter these deficiencies by choosing a variety and mix of cases with these limitations in mind. This particular disadvantage is also offset by the fact that the dynamics of a social situation can be illustrated much more effectively in a case than through the traditional lecture. A combination of cases with role playing, videotaping, or simulations further enhances the learning of social dynamics.

Cases for Intercultural Training: If one compares the usual objectives for intercultural training with the Dooley and Skinner list noted above as appropriate for case studies, the high applicability of the method becomes clear. However, even after the decision is made to use cases in a training program, a number of choices about the kinds of cases to choose and about the style and context of their use still have to be made.

The situation the participants are likely to experience after the training helps resolve some of the questions. For example, most people being trained for international assignments will be interacting with members of a different culture and will be making decisions that affect these people in less predictable ways because of the cultural differences. It therefore seems sensible to select cases which require participants to analyze and make decisions about similar situations and face the reactions of their colleagues.

Similarly, since few will have crosscultural experts to advise them when they reach their new locations, it seems appropriate for the instructor to choose a style of case-teaching that is relatively nondirective.

An equally fundamental choice has to do with the content of the cases. Of course, the educational objectives (general crosscultural sensitization versus country-specific briefing) and the type of participants (Peace Corps volunteers versus international bankers) determine a large part of the appropriate content.[20] One of the most difficult problems regarding content, however, is the choice between cases describing behavior within a single foreign culture or a member of that culture— such as difficulties faced by a Nigerian bureaucrat in running one of his departments—and those which illustrate the problems of people from two or more cultures interacting—such as CUSO volunteer teaching in an African school run by English nuns (DiStefano, 1972b). Although the latter type of case would seem to be the obvious choice for intercultural training, there is a serious shortage of such material. Most cases available are of the former variety (Davis, 1971). The explanation for this fact, which seems strangely discrepant with training needs, lies in the long tradition of comparative studies in the disciplines from which these materials first emerged. Whether in psychology or education, political science or business administration, a standard academic device has been to study a given phenomenon across a series of different cultures and then to prepare an article, book, or course by comparing the results seriatim.

But unfortunately such an approach has only limited usefulness for international training. While it may help trainees understand the behavior of those in other cultures, it doesn't do much to assist them in seeing the cultural determinants of their own behavior. More importantly, it doesn't show the frequently unexpected and dysfunctional consequences of their behavior.

Succinctly put, the single culture case doesn't illustrate the problems the trainees are likely to experience—hence the importance of case studies which show people from different cultures interacting with one another.

Another important factor in choosing the cases to use is the identification that course participants can make with the principal actor in the case. Although it is neither necessary nor even desirable to have all the cases identically matched with participant backgrounds and occupations, it is important to have cases with which the participants can generally identify. Thus if the participants are all teachers destined for African schools, it would be better to use a case describing a Peace Corps nurse working in a foreign clinic or a North American advising a government agency than one with a Japanese pharmaceutical executive trying to decide on a Brazilian advertising campaign for his product.

The use of supporting materials and related teaching methods in addition to the cases is also important. The inclusion of theoretical readings and the applications of the ideas to particular settings (e.g., Rhinesmith, 1970) is advisable in order to provide conceptual frameworks within which to incorporate and organize the learning from cases and the information from lectures, films, and the like. Role-plays, involvement exercises such as BAFA-BAFA,[21] and actual field work interactions with subcultures within the trainee's culture are all important adjuncts to the practice and experience of the case classes. Such experiences also permit the introduction of the notion of culture shock (Oberg, n.d.; Sargent, n.d.) on something other than an abstract, arms's length basis. Additionally, trainees are forced to come to grips with the difficulty of changing one's own behavior.

An Example: In order to illustrate the kind of material available and the context in which cases might profitably be used, an example of a typical case might be helpful. One case frequently used in training programs, especially for people going to Third World countries is "International Bank of Malaysia Ltd." (DiStefano, 1974). The principal actor from whose point of view the case is written is a white, expatriate general manager who is experiencing two major problems. The less serious one is an interpersonal conflict between department heads which is causing disruptions in the work and morale of the office. The fact that one of the men is of Chinese origin while the other is Bumiputra (literally, "sons of the soil," meaning an indigenous Malaysian) mirrors the larger problem the manager faces in trying to meet government-imposed quotas on Bumiputra employment at every level in his hierarchy.

The case contains the history of the three men, the tasks, interactions, and interdependencies required in their work, pertinent data about the organization, and a brief summary of the political, religious, and racial factors underlying the legislation. The case also includes several exhibits of demographic data and describes the general manager's views of the two men as well as some of the possible approaches he was considering at the time the case was written.

The student is charged with analyzing the 16 pages of text and quantitative data and deciding on a course of action to deal with the two interrelated problems. In doing so, he must consider the juxtapositions of three cultures and the consequences of his actions from the point of view of all three.

The case is suitable for courses in both degree and continuing education programs. It has been successfully used with undergraduates and top executives, with government bureaucrats and with entrepreneurs. It is especially effective where quota systems are in force or are being considered.

In most instances this case has been preceded by ample amounts of theoretical material and by cases with simpler issues. Usually it is followed by cases of similar complexity (Evans, n.d.) where participants are requested to role play their solutions in class. [22] Experiential learning through simulation exercises and required field work have also typically followed the use of this case.

Sources of Case Studies: While literally hundreds of cases are being written around the world, access to appropriately indexed and categorized information about this growing output is relatively simple. There are two main sources of information and published cases (in the English language). The larger, which also gathers cases written in other countries, is the Intercollegiate Case Clearinghouse (ICH) at the Harvard Business School in Boston. The other source is the Case and Text Division, School of Business Administration, the University of Western Ontario in London, Canada. Both will publish and ship cases anywhere in the world and will also fill orders for inspection copies. Each of these sources also publishes an annotated bibliography of the cases available. These are referenced by topic and author and provide brief summaries of the contents of each case. ICH also publishes several separate volumes of bibliographies where the cases from given regions of the world are listed. In Europe an excellent source of international cases written in English is IMEDE at Lausanne. Although they do not publish a bibliography, lists of their cases are available.

Each of these sources provides a steady output of cases containing up-to-date problems of interest to those teaching international or intercultural subjects. The Harvard and Western cases cover every kind of setting and organization in both the public and private sectors.

Cases are also available in books on international management (see, for example, the previously cited Davis, 1971; Knudson, 1967; Wadia, 1970; Sethi, 1972). However, nearly all of these collections suffer from defects of inconsistent quality (some of the cases have obviously been "armchaired" rather than written from true experiences) and most are of the single culture, comparative type described earlier.

Another good source of cases is your own experience. If you choose to write your own cases, however, some notes of caution are in order. First, be prepared to write several before you are satisfied. You can lower your error rate and frustration level by reading (Leenders and Erskine, 1973) before you start. Second, avoid using student reports unless you are prepared to engage in substantial writing and additional research. Third, never "armchair" a case or fabricate one from several different situations. They are easily transparent and destroy the credibility of subsequent cases. Finally, be prepared to spend money and time and to learn a great deal. The new case-writer and the novice case-teacher can profit from reading the Andrews (1953) volume, too.

SUMMARY AND CONCLUSIONS

This review of current practices in international management training through case studies suggests that although there are a number of areas for improvement, the overall record is resonably sound.

Training Programs: It is clear that there are substantial differences in how (and what) the public and private sectors are providing for international training and that the strengths of one are the weaknesses of the other. In the public sector preparation for the intercultural dimensions of overseas assignments seems particularly thorough and competent in its execution. In the private sector the forte is in the emphasis on management training for the international executive.

One suggestion for the exchange of these strengths is a greater interchange of senior people between the two sectors. One way such mutually beneficial transfers of skills and perspectives can occur is through a formal exchange such as those occurring between industry and the Canadian Department of Industry, Trade, and Commerce. In a recent case, a senior member of a multinational holding company joined the government Department, while one of their most experienced commercial officers who had had postings throughout Europe and the United States went to the headquarters of the corporation. The exchange was for a period of two years, time enough for the men to adapt to the different jobs and environments[23] and for their families to become part of the community to which they moved. The government man became an "in-house" consultant and took on a number of special projects, a large percentage of which dealt with international issues. He also provided sound advice on improving the selection process and training of the managers being chosen for overseas assignments . . . exactly the input being suggested here.

The company felt that the experience was so successful that they offered the civil servant a very senior position, which he chose to decline in favor of returning to the government. He is now serving as senior commercial officer in a country of significance to Canada's economy. He has brought back to the government important understanding of how business really operates and has left the company more informed about dealing with the government and more sensitive and competent in its international operations. While the company felt that the man was an unusual talent, they also were convinced that the program itself was most valuable. The proof of their conviction is evidenced in their current proposal to DITC for another exchange.

The corporate manager also found his experience of use. The government assigned him a difficult project of promoting an important Canadian product internationally. Although he made significant contributions with respect to this task, he was used to a more free-wheeling environment and felt increasingly frustrated by the bureaucratic processes of the government. However, he completed the two years convinced that it was a most worthwhile experience. He, too, returned to his organization with a better understanding of how his counterparts in the public sector worked.

The exchange program merits consideration by international managers in other organizations and countries. It has the potential to crossfertilize institutions and add significantly to their capacity to serve society better.

Cases: In reflecting on the discussion of case studies in this chapter, one is likely to conclude that cases appropriate for use in international training are broadly available, but underutilized. Part of the explanation has to do with the negative image of business among academics in general and social scientists in particular. This bias colors their view of methods associated with business administration. Another factor is the reciprocated suspicion of businessmen for academics, especially those they perceive as left-leaning. Taken together, these two factors have tended to isolate the two groups and have slowed communication about the availability of suitable case studies for use in public as well as private sector training.

Then, too, there has been a paucity of good cross-cultural (as distinct from single culture) cases in international settings. Until the mid-sixties very little except comparative case-writing was being done. Even now the output, much of it from Western, is modest.

Conclusion: If the needs for international training are to be met to the full extent of our capacities as educators and practitioners, we still have ample room for improvement. Those who have misinformed views about cases and case methods would do well to suspend their assumptions and test their applicability to international training. In particular the use of such methods for management development and international education in the public sector and in disciplines outside of business administration warrants serious consideration and encouragement.

Similarly, those in the private sector need to examine critically the serious omission of crosscultural components in their training of managers for overseas assignments. They would do well to borrow from the useful experience of their public sector counterparts in this regard. The exchange of efforts and learning between these institutions cannot help but improve the effectiveness of our international activities. In the end both the societies served and the individuals who serve will be richer and more humane.

NOTES

1. One indication of the magnitude of this phenomenon is the prediction (Kahn, 1969) that by the year 2000 approximately two-thirds of the noncommunist output of goods and services will be produced by 300 to 500 multinational firms. This compares with $300 billion, 15% of the output, by multinationals in 1970, an estimate of $1 trillion in 1980, and over $2 trillion by 1990 (one half the free-world output).

2. This section takes the perspective of managers in North America. Please note that language training has been omitted from the discussion. For a book-length treatment of the whole subject of cross cultural training, see Brislin and Pedersen (1976).

3. The situation cited here was reported to the author and verified by him. In another example, the personnel department of a large Canadian bank was asked how many managers were working in the foreign countries where the bank operated. Not only were they uncertain about these data, but they were unable to provide even an accurate list of the countries involved. For a general discussion of these difficulties, none of which is atypical, see DiStefano (1972a).

4. For a superb research study which reports that this criterion is normally used as a key factor in selections for overseas assignments, see Miller (1973).

5. No attempt was made to be exhaustive. The selection of examples was taken from the author's knowledge and experience as representative of those generally available.

6. Business Council for International Understanding, American University, 5010 Wisconsin Avenue, N.W., Washington, D.C. 20016, U.S.A.

7. A one-week program is offered annually by Professior M. Leenders at the School of Business Administration, The University of Western Ontario. He has conducted similar programs in the United States, Europe, West Indies, and Brazil.

8. In this context "integrated" means that faculty and teaching materials come together in a cohesive package. Operationally, this requires faculty who know and respect each other and who develop the program design through considerable discussion and exchange. It requires intimate knowledge of both content and style and an active relating of the academic content and processes across disciplines. It frequently results in team-teaching efforts. It is essential that all faculty decisions are firmly anchored in the problems of the clients. Since none of these qualities is found in surplus among highly competent academics, it is no wonder that such programs are rare.

9. IMP—International Marketing Program, 2 Seaforth Place Buckingham Gate, London SW1E 6JP, England.

10. INSEAD—Institut European d'Administration des Affairs, Boulevard de Constance, 77300 Fontainebleu, France.

11. NEMI—North European Management Institute, Oslo 3, Kongeveien 26, Holmenkollen, Oslo, Norway.

12. CEI—Center for Education in International Management, 4 Chemin de Conches, 1211 Conches-Geneva, Geneva, Switzerland.

13. IMEDE, Management Development Institute, P.O. Box 1059, Ch-1001, Lausanne, Switzerland.

14. For information about this program direct inquiries to Dr. Harold Crookell, Director, Centre for International Business Studies, School of Business Administration, The University of Western Ontario, London, Ontario.

15. For a discussion of the case method from the point of view of the philosophy of education, see Dewing (1931).

16. Case instructors who feel sure about their style and who are unafraid of disconfirming data should submit to Chairman Mao-like self-criticism with the assistance of a videotape of their actual classroom behavior.

17. See Table 2 (Dooley and Skinner, 1977) for an excellent display of case method considerations. For each of eight educational objectives they describe the (1) kind of case which might be used, (2) degree of applicability of case studies, (3) appropriate roles of teachers and students, (4) skills, knowledge and preparation required by the teacher, (5) problems frequently encountered, (6) requirements for success, and (7) standards for judging success.

18. For the classic reply from a professor to his students who were pressuring him to give his "answer" to the case, see "Memo on a Session with Section E" (Bailey, 1962).

19. Of course the same is true for the lecture method unless the professor chooses to find out and provide such information. Furthermore, the very choice of lecture topics is often made on bases other than how representative of the real world the phenomenon is!

20. However, it is not always (or even usually) desirable to provide all the cases in the same working context of the participants. For example, in the programs for CU mentioned in the first part of the Chapter, only a very small percentage of the cases were

set in the insurance industry. The reasoning is that it is too easy to rely on old habits and knowledge when the situations are familiar. New settings frequently provoke new insights about old behavior.

21. BAFA-BAFA is an excellently designed simulation available from SIMILE II, 1150 Silverado, La Jolla, California 92037 U.S.A.

22. For an excellent case for the use of role-playing, see "Showa-Packard (A) and (B)" (Yoshino, 1973). The two cases describe the same events and problems from the contrary point of view of the Japanese and U.S. executives who are about to meet to settle several outstanding issues in the joint venture of their two respective companies.

23. The terms each used to describe his entry to the new organization were nearly identical to those employed by people moving to new cultures. In fact, the two settings of government and business have been described as different cultures in a recent report (Cawsey, et al., 1976).

REFERENCES

ANDREWS, K.P. [ed.] (1953) *The Case Method of Teaching Human Relations.* Cambridge, Mass.: Harvard Univ. Press.

BAILEY, J. (1962) "Memo on a session with Section E," EA-A 408, Boston, Mass.: Intercollegiate Case Clearing House, Harvard University.

BRISLIN, R.W. and PEDERSEN, P. (1976) *Cross-cultural Orientation Programs.* New York: Gardner Press.

CAWSEY, T.F., HODGSON, R.C., LORD, R.J.A. and PEACH, D.A. (1976) *Managing the Political/Regulatory Environment.* London, Canada: University of Western Ontario, Research and Publications Division, School of Business Administration.

CHANDLER, D. (1976) *Capital Punishment in Canada.* Toronto: McClelland and Stewart.

DAVIS, S.M. (1971) *Comparative Management.* Englewood Cliffs, N.J.: Prentice-Hall.

DEWING, A.S. (1931) "An introduction to the use of cases," in C.E. Fraser (ed.), *The Case Method of Instruction.* New York: McGraw Hill.

DISTEFANO, J.J. (1975a) "Worldwide goes to Iran," restricted case study. School of Business Administration, University of Western Ontario, London, Canada.

_____(1975b) "Manpower planning and management development at C.U. (A) and (B)." London, Canada: Case and Text Division, School of Business Administration, University of Western Ontario.

_____(1974) "International bank of Malaysia." London, Canada: Case and Text Division, School of Business Administration, University of Western Ontario.

_____(1972a) "Managing in other cultures: some do's and some don'ts." *Business Quarterly* 37, 3: 22-29.

_____(1972b) "A pregnancy at St. Theresa's." London, Canada: Case and Text Division, School of Business Administration, University of Western Ontario.

DOOLEY, A.R. and SKINNER, W. (1977) "Casing casemethod methods." *Academy of Management Review* (April): 277-289.

EVANS, G. (n.d.) "The road to hell. . . " 9-403-097, ICH DC 3H13. Boston, Mass.: Intercollegiate Case Clearing House, Harvard University.

GRAGG, C.I. (1954) "Because wisdom can't be told," in McNair, M.P. and Hersum, A.C. (eds.) *The Case Method at the Harvard Business School.* New York: McGraw-Hill.

KAHN, H. (1969) *Year 2000.* New York: Macmillan.

KNUDSON, H.R. (1967) *Organizational Behavior: Cases for Developing Nations.* Reading, Mass.: Addison-Wesley.

LEENDERS, M.R. and ERSKINE, J.A. (1973) "Case research: the case-writing process." London, Canada: University of Western Ontario, Research and Publications Division, School of Business Administration.

MILLER, E.L. (1973) "The international selection decision: A study of some dimensions of managerial behavior in the selection decision process." *Academy Management Journal* 16, 2: 239-252.

OBERG, K. (n.d.) "Culture shock and the problem of adjustment to new cultural environments," unpublished mimeo.

RHINESMITH, S. (1970) *Cultural-Organizational Analysis.* Cambridge, Mass.: McBer.

SARGENT, C. B. (n.d.) "Psychological aspects of environmental adjustment," unpublished mimeo.

SETHI, S. P. (1972) *Advanced Cases in Multinational Business Operations.* Pacific Palisades, Cal.: Goodyear.

WADIA, M. S. (1972) Cases in International Business. Scranton, Penn.: Intext.

YOSHINO, M. Y. (1973) "Showa-Packard, Ltd. (A) and (B)" 9-373-348 (349), Boston, Mass.: Intercollegiate Case Clearing House, Harvard University.

25.

MULTINATIONAL TRAINING FOR
MULTINATIONAL CORPORATIONS

MELVIN SCHNAPPER

*Mel Schnapper Association, Inc. and
G.D. Searle and Company*

One of the more recent exciting and challenging applications of intercultural communication is multinational training. This chapter will show the student of intercultural communication how the theory and concepts, as applied to managerial development, permeates the pragmatic task of designing, implementing, and evaluating effective multinational training. This paper will identify the needs for, challenges and goals of, and resistances to such multinational training. Then it will describe the criteria for effective training and a 10-step multinational training model along with multinational/intercultural considerations, problems, and paradoxes. Much of this has been drawn from the author's own experience in multinational corporations and international development agencies.

Multinational training is intended for the multinational manager who must be knowledgeable and skillful in a number of areas. Therefore, multinational training must include an appropriate blend of training areas which are typically mutually exclusive:

1. *Managerial training* typically focuses upon the managerial functions of leading, controlling, planning, and directing regardless of the language, cultural differences and the business.

AUTHOR'S NOTE: *This chapter is a revised and expanded version of a monograph published by the American Society for Training and Development entitled "Multinational Training for Multinational Corporations / International Organizations." Copies of the monograph are available from ASTD in Madison, Wisconsin.*

2. *Intercultural training* typically focuses upon cultural differences such as values, perceptions, assumptions, style regardless of the language, managerial role, and the business.
3. *International business training* typically focuses upon business practices/functions across national boundaries such as production, marketing, financing regardless of the managerial role, or language, with perhaps some attention to cultural differences.
4. *Language training* typically focuses upon developing language fluency in the social and technical areas regardless of the managerial role, or the business, though some attention may be given to culture.

All of these areas, as parts of a total comprehensive development program, are necessary for adequately preparing the multinational manager. The comprehensive foci of multinational training is summarized below (Figure 25.1), where "Yes" indicates that the area is focused upon and "No" indicates typical exclusion.

FOCUS / TRAINING	MANAGERIAL ROLE	CULTURAL DIFFERENCES	BUSINESS	LANGUAGE
1. Managerial	Yes	No	No	No
2. Intercultural	No	Yes	No	No
3. International Business	No	No	Yes	No
4. Language	No	No	No	Yes
5. Multinational	Yes	Yes	Yes	Yes

Figure 25.1: Multinational Training Foci

NEED FOR MULTINATIONAL TRAINING

Examples of Waste

*   A Venezuelan vice-president of marketing for an American-owned multinational is fired by the president because he refuses a promotion, which would mean abandoning his parents in Caracas and moving to Boston. In Venezuela, where children are expected to take care of their parents, "abandoning them" would be shameful. The American president of the company is angered and confused by the Latin American's "lack of appreciation and loyalty,"

- A German engineer, thinking he has successfully negotiated a joint venture with a Japanese firm returns home to await the Japanese signatures on the contract, and discovers several weeks later, that the Japanese have not agreed to over half of the contractual conditions. While in Tokyo, the Japanese smiled and nodded approvingly all during his presentations. They also wined and dined him very graciously, and never hinted at being resistant to his proposal. He had no idea that during the brief time of their acquaintance, they were not yet ready to disclose their serious reservations.

- A sale of millions of tons of wheat to the Soviet government results in severe price increases for bread in the United States. The U.S. businessmen, in their eagerness to close a profitable deal, assumed that once the major agreement was finished, they and their Soviet counterparts would work out the fine details quickly and with little difficulty. Later on, the Americans found themselves yielding on many minor aspects of the total agreement because the Russian negotiators went over the contract with painstaking thoroughness, and were ready to cancel the whole contract, based on an impasse over any one of these fine points.

- A British supervisor of a bridge-building project in Nigeria was shocked when his team of Nigerian workers refused to continue the project after he had encouraged them to pick their own team leader. He knew that his Nigerian work team was a mixture of several tribes, but he did not expect that tribal rivalry would be so significant that competition for a leader role would bring work to a halt.

Crucial business mistakes like these occur daily in some part of the world, be it Caracas, Tokyo, Moscow, or Lagos. These misunderstandings result in needless wastes of time, effort, and money that one or both sides of an international transaction must bear. The examples cited above are but a few of the thousands of anecdotal stories of otherwise successful multinational corporate executives/managers/employees who daily commit disastrous or near-disastrous mistakes in dealing with business counterparts from different cultures.

Very often entire businesses get wrecked on the shoals of the intercultural misunderstandings which occur in the multinational business world. Careers are often ended abruptly because managers interpret cultural differences as personal and attitudinal manifestations of "disloyalty," "lack of proper leadership," or "poor judgment." Contracts are often concluded based on faulty assumptions and on misinterpretations of the legal, personal, and cultural aspects of the negotiation process.

All of these factors contribute to multinational managers becoming frustrated, angry, and even racist, because they have little appreciation of how crosscultural differences effect managerial style. Frequently these feelings result in an early return for the manager and his/her family, causing a waste of managerial talent and money to the company.

Growth of Multinationals

Another reason for the growing need of multinational training is the accelerated pace of growth of the multinational. It is becoming increasingly critical that multinational managers get the kind of training and development that will enable them to manage the complex and ever-expanding entities. The last several decades have shown an impressive growth of the multinational corporation.

> Multinational conglomerates are absorbing domestic companies and corporations with such rapidity that even business leaders in our country have expressed alarm lest the anonymity and transnationalism afforded by multinationals allow potential political adversaries to gain economic influence which might be translated into social and political influence. Multinational corporations have recently been the target of political attacks and investigators. Each year billions of dollars, pounds, deutsche mark, yen are being invested abroad. The international or multinational exists and continues to grow. [Vansina, 1975]

The following statistics are but a few of the many which demonstrate how much of an impact this contemporary business form is having upon national and international economic life.

> Of the 120 largest industrial corporations of Belgium, 48 are controlled partly or wholly from abroad. And it is forecast that in a few years one of every five Belgain manufacturing workers will work for a foreign . . . company.

> German corporations now have more capital invested in South Carolina (U.S.A.) than anywhere else in the world except Germany.

> Some 90% of Europe's production of microcircuits is controlled by American companies.

> Switzerland's largest corporation, Nestle Alimentana S.A., does 98% of its business outside Switzerland. [Fest and Robbins, 1976]

For all of the growth of the multinational, its size and complexity are often bewildering to those who must manage it. Even conceptual frameworks about the nature, scope, and function of the multinational do not have wide acceptance. It is in this context that the multinational trainer must face the unique and often pioneering efforts of developing effective and credible training for the multinational manager who must try as best s/he can not to drown in a sea of ambiguity.

UNIQUE CHALLENGES FOR THE MULTINATIONAL TRAINER

Along with the usual challenges of the training process, the multinational trainer faces some unique variables. Some of these have resisted resolution and solutions, yet they must be faced. These relate to (a) defining the multinational, (b) complexities of the multinational, and (c) cultural stereotyping.

Defining the Multinational

Unfortunately, there is no widely shared conceptual notion of a multinational enterprise.

> Furthermore, it is very difficult to group the total system. The mere size, the geographic distances between operating companies and headquarters make it difficult to gain intellectual and psychological understanding of the functioning of the total system. The environment of the international organization is a complex pattern of nation states and state nations, which affect differentially the various parts of the organization ... (Many) try to manage the international firm as if it were a large national enterprise, applying old solutions to new or different problems. [Vansina, 1975]

Thus, within the context of conceptual ambiguity about the nature of the multinational, the trainer's task is to evolve a clear and precise notion of appropriate training. What a task indeed!

For purposes of identifying an appropriate training model, *multinational* is defined as a business entity whose main operational functions (such as production, marketing, selling, and purchasing), embrace at least two nation-states whose

managers and employees differ in cultural orientation. It is also
assumed that these differences will translate into differences of
business and managerial style, such as work norms, interpersonal and intergroup relations, communication, and decision-
making. Because subsidiary organizations may have a nearly
peer relationship to the headquarters, managers of various
national and cultural backgrounds have a significant input into
decisions, with great impact upon organization. The multinational is distinguished from the (1) *national* enterprise
within one country, though not excluding the possibility of
great internal cultural diversity; (2) the *international* enterprise where the home office exercises extreme authority over
its branch offices, licensees, sales office, or wholly owned
foreign subsidiaries; and (3) the *transnational* enterprise
where "the distinction between the home office and subsidiaries is obliterated so that the organization entities transcend
national boundaries . . . In a transnational organization managers are developed in such a way that they could serve in any
or all of the locations" (Nath, 1977).

Complexity of the Multinational

Since the trainer's main function is to help managers and
employees gain better knowledge, skills, and understanding of
their multinational corporate environment, s/he is faced with
the challenging task of selecting training priorities from an
infinity of choices. The graphic illustration (see Figure 25.2) of
how four systems (technical, cultural, economic, political)
influence managerial practices in any one country is impressive. Consider how these variables may be multiplied as
manyfold as there are significantly different "intermeshing
systems" which impact upon corporate norms, policies, and
procedures. This presents a staggering array of variables for
the trainer to integrate.

There have been many different attempts to understand and
operate the multinational. Among these are thousands of
studies of the values, beliefs, and espoused behavior patterns
of managers in almost every country in the world. There are
thousands of studies identifying the training needs of various
nationals going overseas to work in a foreign country. In

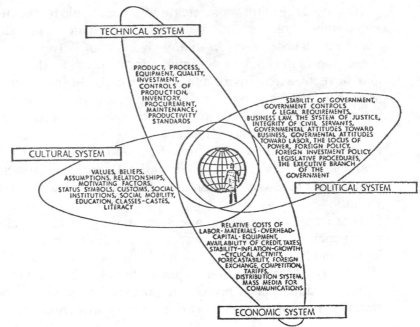

Figure 25.2: Four Intermeshing Systems Which Influence Managerial Philosophy and Practice

addition there are hundreds of lists on how to cope with general and specific cultural differences for managers and business-persons. And there are many, many theories about how to improve the multinationals' effectiveness. However, for all of the work in these areas, *there is very little about a pragmatic multinational training approach!* Hopefully, the model presented here will make a useful contribution toward this end.

Cultural Stereotyping

The folk wisdom of most multinational training is to prepare managers to cope with the "German" or "French" personality, and there are many studies which show that managers in different countries will exhibit common responses to questions concerning their values, motivations, and style.

However, the more sophisticated trainer should be skeptical about these studies and their often simplistic conclusions about managerial practices in any given country. Even though these studies may have a common approach and methodology and have research instruments which have been translated appropriately from one language to another, the research instruments may not have used exactly equivalent terms. This inescapable crosscultural research dilemma of being certain about "functional equivalents" (Fest and Robbins, 1976) is even more crucial for the multinational corporation where conclusions based upon such research must have operational validity.

These crosscultural management studies which conclude with generalizations, may have some validity, but only as lightly and briefly heeded guidelines. In addition to managing effectively where normative behavior may be different, multinational training must prepare managers for the unique personality and unique sets of variables they will encounter.

> Holistic descriptions of cultures are of little value to the trainer for they do not take account of the diversity within a culture. In fact, there may be more cultural variation within a culture than between cultures. Any description of a culture which does not accommodate variations is of little value and may be more harmful than helpful. [Fest and Robbins, 1976]

In the business context, two persons from very different countries and cultures may communicate with each other better about a professionally related problem or task than they can with their respective bosses within the same culture. This is because the same professional group has been exposed to much of the same education, training, and even social acquaintances. All of these factors contribute to their becoming a "perceputal group—a number of individuals who perceive some aspect of the external world more or less similarly" (Singer, 1965). This understanding of cultural stereotyping and shared perceptions of professionals in the same or related fields will help the trainer design appropriately balanced multinational training, and give him/her a general model for anticipating trainee responses to the training content/process and to each other.

Within a national company, tremendous gaps may exist between headquarters and subsidiaries and even between functional units within the same operational branch. The knowledge of "perceptual groups" will help the trainer be aware of the even greater gap within his/her client population that is inevitable when professional backgrounds, national backgrounds, and cultural backgrounds are different!

GOALS OF MULTINATIONAL TRAINING

From the previous discussion about the enormous task of understanding the multinational organization, it should be obvious that there are too many variables to allow any one training approach to be valid across different nations, cultures, organizations, and departments. The trainer must hold lightly to models, techniques, and philosophies of training and select the appropriate blend of each to fit the needs of the organization, trainees, and training staff. Nevertheless there are certain basic goals which must be achieved. What and how will be discussed in the remainder of the chapter.

What Multinational Training Must Accomplish

Perhaps a brief aphorism will establish a framework for the multinational training model:

Telling is helping to know.
Teaching is helping to know and to grow.
Training is helping to know, to grow and do and inevitably becoming a different person.

Thus, training must have an element of doing and "inevitably becoming a different person." These "becoming" processes are not occurring very much in programs that are largely didactic in nature. The nature of effective training demands that the person not only:

(a) *know*—about the crosscultural management differences, intercultural communication skills both verbal and nonverbal, and business— markets, laws, economics, and so on.

(b) *grow*—have awareness of self and others in the environment, knowing how managerial behavior affects others; and

(c) *do*—effectively fulfilling the job mission, making friends, and satisfying personal needs; but the manager must also

(d) "utilize different behavior"—through the process of intercultural adaptation, the manager learns to internalize and/or accept new values, assumptions, perceptions, and to risk different and more appropriate behaviors. All of these processes will in some way help the trainee cope more effectively than the person who first entered the program.

These necessary personal change processes are often ignored by programs intended to help prepare the multinational manager for the intercultural encounter. Such programs often present a great deal of necessary and useful information about the laws, business practices, employee expectations, government regulations, taxes, and profit issues as well as important data for almost any business function. These seminars may also include detailed discussions about history, customs, and cultural data about working and living successfully in the multinational/multicultural environment. Most companies will give the employee an adequate orientation related to the terms and conditions of the assignment including compensations, travel and shipping arrangements, special allowances and employment conditions, overseas and upon return home.

All of this information is necessary but not sufficient. In almost all cases, this information is presented in a traditionally academic manner. This approach will not enhance the manager's personal/cultural self awareness, will not give him/her specific interpersonal/intercultural skills, and will not help to initiate and/or facilitate the personally profound insights, awareness, and dynamics that will change a domestic manager into a truly competent participant in the multinational management world. This kind of preparation has marginal utility and does not meet the previously identified criteria of effective training.

Experiential Training

There is growing evidence (Schnapper, 1972) to support the contention that in the hands of skilled, interculturally sensitive, and empathic trainers, the experiential or laboratory method of training will accomplish these personal change processes which were identified as so critical for effective multinational management.

> A new form of interpersonal training is emerging. Its technology is borrowed from organizational development efforts, and many of its tools are taken from the laboratory techniques of the behavioral scientist. It is possible to expose the future expatriate to training sessions on relating authentically to people in different cultures, the value of candor and interpersonal feedback in crosscultural communications, and how to understand what your foreign counterpart is really saying. [Noer, 1975]

However, the trainer must be very cautious about which techniques to use and how to make them appropriate for a specific or multicultural group of managers. The next section, which explains the 10-step multinational training model, will suggest how to make this happen.

A 10-STEP MULTINATIONAL TRAINING MODEL

As has been discussed, there are a variety of training approaches that span the continuum from purely academic to purely experiential. Preferably the training is an appropriate balance of the two. Whatever the approach, this 10-step multinational training model will help insure an effective program. Unique considerations for the multinational context will be posed for each step.

Step 1. Client Request: Generally, a client (individual, group, department, or total organization) will request training as a solution to a problem, even when the problem does not have a training solution. Often problems of poor performance, low morale, breakage, waste, and conflict have a systems-wide source and may originate with poor procedures and policies. The trainer should not respond to the client's request with immediate delivery of a training program, for no matter how well the training is performed, it may be irrelevant. The trainer should explore the needs behind the request, define mutual expectations, mutual and mutually exclusive areas of responsibility, seek for "hidden agenda," and identify critical managers who need to approve and support a training intervention.

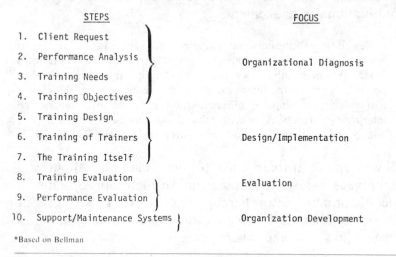

*Based on Bellman

Figure 25.3: A Ten Step Multinational Training Model*

MULTINATIONAL CONSIDERATIONS

- Poor performance in a multinational situation may have causes that are very different from those expected. Employees may not perform beyond a certain level because to do so would make others "lose face" or embarrass "elders" or other high status individuals.

- Training may be seen as "meddling" in very private or intimate areas or will be seen as futile since the status quo is seen as unalterable.

- The trainer/consultant may be seen as working for the requestor in order to insure the requestor's control over employees.

- On the other hand, employees may overwhelmingly accept new training norms which will be disruptive of the organization.

- In many transitional societies like Nigeria, where middle level managers may be more educated and innovative than senior managers, immediate adaptation may lead to greater organizational conflict and the training may be blamed.

Step 2. Performance Analysis: Most training requests are a result of perceived discrepancy between what is and what should or could be better performance. Performance analysis, sometimes referred to as "front end analysis" or "task analysis," is a process of observing the work itself. Performance analysis focuses upon identifiable behaviors and not upon

hidden thought processes such as attitude or motivation. All conclusions should be tested with the employees, supervisors, peers, and any customer of the performance. Perhaps "poor" performance was really a question of misunderstanding between these persons.

MULTINATIONAL CONSIDERATIONS

- Very often, performance deficiencies in a multinational result from traditional practices and values and not from inadequate training or unwillingness to cooperate. For example, a new product's poor performance in the consumer market (though extremely successful in another country) could be due to its image and/or need for consumers to change habits. Assuming that the salesmen need to improve their selling skills would be invalid and unproductive.

- Observing performance may be impossible and/or very discomforting to employees who do not have familiarity nor tolerance for a "fishbowl" experience.

- Open discussions about "poor" performance may be very inappropriate, as in Japan where not embarrassing fellow employees nor being embarrassed by them is very important.

Step 3. Training Needs Analysis: Johnson (1967) has identified over 33 ways to determine training needs. Some of these are: (1) analysis of activity, (2) analysis of problems, (3) analysis of behavior, (4) analysis of organization, (5) appraisal of performance, (6) brainstorming, (7) buzzing, and (8) card sort. Each of these techniques offers advantages and disadvantages with regard to efficiency, cost, subtleties, depth, breadth, open-endedness of analysis and other variables. These analyses will give the trainer an opportunity to match training needs with his/her client's objectives, unit's performance with unit's functions. These processes of analysis will also determine which performance problems actually lend themselves to a training solution and which lend themselves to more of an organization or systems development approach. Feedback of this analysis to the client is done to get commitment and ownership.

MULTINATIONAL CONSIDERATIONS

- Often persons unfamiliar with approaches which utilize questionnaires will try to respond with the "correct" answer instead of describing a work situation. If questionnaires or any paper and pencil instruments are to be used, they must be explained in depth, even by going though a trial run.

- Interviews also must be designed to elicit critical data without offending existing norms and values about not betraying one's boss or the company. This is especially true where companies provide lifetime employment and encourage high levels of boss-subordinate loyalty patterns.

- Group analysis, where employees publicly identify their own and company shortcomings, may be a nearly impossible approach as in Viet Nam where company, familial, social, and political considerations are so intertwined.

Step 4. Training Objectives: Training objectives are the specifiable, measurable, and attainable statements about the training outcomes. They can be stated in terms of what people will know, be able to do, and even feel/think about something. The more specific and observable they are, the better training can be evaluated. Vague objectives diminish the focus of both trainees and trainers about the ultimate outcomes of training. Objectives must also be realistic in terms of systems support. If not, trainees with new skills, knowledge, and awareness will feel frustrated and discouraged as they try to use what they have learned. Objectives must be limited to the few of many which may have been identified. These critical objectives must be accomplished within the limits of time, energy, resources, and budget.

MULTINATIONAL CONSIDERATIONS

- Since objectives are typically value-laden, they must be negotiated and agreed upon with key managers who are to support the training and its outcomes.

- A paradox of including key managers in the objectives-setting process is that the trainer's expertise may be seen as lacking, since so much help was needed. In many cultures the consultant is expected to act like "l'expert," as in France.

- When managerial training has objectives related to "successful confrontation or feedback skills," these skills and their inherent values may be anathema to certain cultural norms.

- Objectives must be stated in language that is understood by the client group, even though they are stated in ways generally unaccepted by the training professional.

Step 5. Training Design: Though it was stated previously that training must inevitably facilitate change in the trainee and that the experiential approach is most effective, the variables in any particular situation may indicate that the most appropriate approach is to focus on knowledge and concepts with a nonthreatening and low risk-taking discussion approach. The design must always be appropriate for the trainer's skill level, style, and comfort, while challenging to the trainee population. The number of techniques that are available to the knowledgeable trainer are many; and by modifying, synthesizing, and sequencing these techniques, an almost infinite variety of training experiences can be provided (Schnapper, 1973). To get the greatest mileage out of the training, the design ought to include supportive material which the trainee can use after training. Ideally, the design would include a project to demonstrate application of training objectives with a follow-up session for trainees to share their project experience and learn new skills and/or sharpen old ones. Also, the design might include cooperative and supportive action from the trainee's supervisor to build system support.

MULTINATIONAL CONSIDERATIONS

- All aspects of the design need to be scrutinized to insure that intercultural misinterpretations do not occur. Experiential group dynamics may be seen as a "brainwashing" attempt; film produced in one country may communicate a very different message in another; media colors, shapes, symbols, images may provoke a very different response from that intended; using pictures of people may be offensive in a Moslem culture.

  The whole notion of attending a training session, especially if more than one level of management is present, may be so different as to influence all responses, no matter what the design(!).

- Frequently, the logistics of trainee travel and lodging will determine the length of training programs and even individual sessions, especially when a multinational has small offices in several neighboring countries and training requires staff attendance from each office.

Step 6. Training of Trainers: Though often neglected as an integral part of the training process, training of line managers or participants to train may be the only way to insure the survival of the initial training efforts. The program they have been through can do a lot to increase the credibility and desirability of the training function. This is not only a good strategy for gaining organizational credibility, but allows a trainer to multiply potential training efforts. When training of trainers is accomplished by utilizing the model described here, and when the potential trainers are also graduates of the trainee group, the training itself is more likely to be acceptable, appropriate, and effective.

MULTINATIONAL CONSIDERATIONS

- As a developmental opportunity for the trainer, this level of training legitimizes more detailed and intimate feedback while having a "laboratory" to experiment with host national[1] reactions to his/her own training style.

- Multinationals typically do not have a lot of internal training resources, especially for managerial training. If training is to be seen as valid and useful, persons other than those in the training and development department ought to be involved. This will help insure that all training aspects have the greatest input from a wide variety of staff and line management. Using line managers may ultimately support the survival of the training function.

- Since training with host national trainers presents a lot of dilemmas and paradoxes, this area will be discussed separately in the next section.

Step 7. The Training Itself: All of the best preparation in the world will go by the wayside if the actual implementation of training is poor. It is important to check and double check all facilities, equipment, provisions for refreshments, and norms around starting and ending times of each session. Seating may also be a critical variable, especially if done in a way which departs from the typical classroom style which still dominates in so many training facilities. The staff must attend to the learning climate to insure that expectations are identified and clarified and all learning objectives are understood. This will help the trainees take responsibility for their own learning and clarify mutual and mutually exclusive areas of staff and trainee responsibility. Since the design may have lacked some critical inputs from the trainees themselves, the staff must always entertain the possibility of changing the design midstream, and be sensitive to trainee reactions to each part of the training as it continues.

MULTINATIONAL CONSIDERATIONS

- The training itself is the area where many of the unknowns surface as trainees interact with and react to the staff and each other. When the trainee group is multicultural, certain training techniques such as simulation, role-play, encounter, and feedback which are comfortable for some groups/individuals may be discomforting to others. The multinational trainer will have to make special inquiries periodically to maximize everyone's comfort and attention. Host national co-trainers, are a good source for this kind of data.

- The trainer must also attend to his/her language even when speaking the trainees' language which s/he learned in a different country. Just as "America and England are two countries separated by the same language" so do varieties of Spanish and French differ from country to country.

- Also, the trainer must attend to nonverbal behavior which differs widely from culture to culture (Schnapper, 1975).

Step 8. Training Evaluation: Evaluation of training is typically the weakest link in the whole training process, though critical for assessing the value of trainee time and organization expense. Training must make a difference to the trainee or it is a waste. Evaluation, which usually occurs either during or immediately after the training program, will measure either knowledge, skills, and/or attitude. Typically, evaluation is in terms of reactions to staff and particular sessions. A more valuable approach would be to evaluate the actual skills and knowledge learned by the trainees. When learning objectives are a clear part of the initial design phase of the training, these objectives can readily become the evaluation criteria for successful training. Different techniques can be designed, such as role-playing, observation of trainees during a subsequent task, or more conventional paper and pencil techniques to evaluate the actual learning. Clear objectives also enable the trainees to evaluate their own success or achievement. When evaluation is done within the training program itself, feedback can enable the staff to further emphasize something not learned well or to change their approach to some subsequent objective.

MULTINATIONAL CONSIDERATIONS

- Evaluation in a multinational setting is subject to all of the same mistakes as Step 3—Needs Analysis, and the techniques must be selected appropriately. Very often, trainees will see the evaluation process as reflecting solely upon their learning abilities as opposed to reflecting upon the skills of the trainers. The author's experience with Samoans and Swazis bears this out.

- Participants may also be "polite" during the evaluation phase and give the responses which they believe are expected. The evaluation approach must be designed to filter these responses out and/or trainees must be convinced that the *staff* are the focus of the evaluation process.

- In a multinational context all of the variables which are hitherto unknowable may suddenly surface, e.g., the training was good, the objectives were achieved, but because of factors related to the selection process, the learning is irrelevant to the trainee.

Step 9. Performance Evaluation: Though training evaluation is seldom done, performance evaluation is hardly done at all. It is very challenging to try to see what actual changes come about in a person's performance as a result of a training experience. Sometimes these changes are so subtle that change is almost impossible to observe and must be reported by the participant. Ideally, part of the training design includes supervisory or peer ownership for giving the participants and/or staff feedback about changes on a post-training basis. Minimally, the staff should build long-term interviewing into its plan so it can follow up on participant performance at a later date.

One way of evaluating post-training performance is to assign on-the-job projects for trainees to complete after the training is over. In this way, the trainer knows that at least the project itself represents new performance. Hopefully, the participant can relate improved performance on the project to the training experience. Another difficulty with performance evaluation is that certain concepts and skills related to management may not emerge until some critical number of situational variables awaken the latent learning which has occurred.

MULTINATIONAL CONSIDERATIONS

- This kind of evaluation is very difficult to accomplish in a multinational, especially when so many corporations have an inadequate system for evaluating any kind of regular performance. So often the idea of supervisors evaluating, discussing, and planning for improvement of training is very rare; and to expect this to occur because the training staff needs the data to evaluate its training is often unrealistic.

- In a multinational European setting it was only after a second training program that participants engaged in a candid evaluation of the organization.

- Additionally, cultural norms, apart from organizational norms, may prove very punishing to the participant who returns to work and tries to implement the new learnings.

Step 10. Support/Maintenance Systems: If training is to be truly effective, it must be supported by reward systems which are part of the trainee's environment. The skills from a session on "Evaluating Subordinate Performance" are much more likely to be carried back to the job if the organization has a formal performance evaluation procedure that forces the supervisor and subordinate to examine the subordinate's performance. A training session on "Planning the Work" is often dependent on a variety of system-wide planning procedures that will impact on how well newly learned planning procedures can be practiced and mastered. One way to get some system support for training behaviors, when such supportive systems are generally absent, is to build in the support and cooperation of the participant' s supervisor. Designing new support and maintenance systems is a challenging and often frustrating activity and requires a whole other set of skills usually referred to as organization development or O.D. A good trainer should have enough O.D. skills, such as survey feedback and analysis skills, to make structural changes to help the organization support the training objectives.

MULTINATIONAL CONSIDERATIONS

- Since many multinationals do not have the kinds of support systems which would help the training outcomes be more utilized, this area may be truly vexing. Initiating system-wide support and support systems is the focus of the O.D. specialist who may try to initiate system change through structural changes or process changes and probably a combination of both. The field of O.D. is a fairly new one which utilizes a lot of behavioral sciences concepts and approaches to help organizations plan change.

• Since the multinational's environment is so fraught with unpredictable change, utilizing O.D. strategies requires a great deal of flexibility and patience. Also, O.D. strategies are very value-laden and may be very inappropriate for the multinational environment unless drastically modified.

• In a South Pacific country, organization changes had occurred so frequently for so long that there was little faith in the basic idea of planned change.

Paradoxes of Multinational Training

The 10-step multinational training model just presented also presents a unique set of dilemmas and paradoxes when applied to multinational training. Many multinational trainers ignore the paradoxes of preparing persons for working and living together in a multicultural setting, especially when such preparatory activities includes different nationalities. The paradoxes which exist within the goals and the processes of training are:

• When managers who make requests for training are not culturally representative of the vast employee population, such training may be insensitive to and unwelcomed by the trainees, thus setting up dynamics for failure.

• If cultural relativism (the idea that all cultures are equally valid patterns of survival within their environment) is a "truth" held by multinational trainers, then preparing managers to help their culturally different subsidiaries change (typically in the direction of buying into the value and belief system of North American behavioral sciences) is a violation of this "truth."

• The "belief" that multinational training is valid and accomplishable, is a basically North American belief, which like other North American beliefs, is being sold to other countries.

• When host nationals are used as part of the training staff, they typically have little decision-making power about training design and implementation. The message to trainees is subtle but profound—these nationals do not share "valid" perceptions of what is important in their culture. This is often what Ivan Illich would call the "hidden curriculum" of education/training. Is this what the training staff wants to communicate?

The host national role has not been fully exploited. They have more potential for serving as culture role models that managers can observe, interact with, become sensitive to, and learn to cope with. Even though allowing and encouraging host national involvement in decision-making may result in the compromise of basic experiential training beliefs/ values, confusion, and entail lengthy negotiations, the resultant training model could have impressive and truly multinational outcomes.

Some trainers have even advocated that host nationals share an intense T-Group (or sensitivity training) experience with the trainees.

> Human relations training for overseas work can probably be enriched by incorporating foreign nationals into the training groups. T-Groups of mixed nationalities, for example, may represent a microcosm of a crosscultural encounter that can provide an in-depth cultural learning experience for the participants. Under skillful guidance, such a strategy may integrate the substantive content of cultural learning with the situational requirements for behavioral change. [Foster and Danielian, 1966]

This approach, using a modified T-Group, has often been used successfully for integrating many Peace Corps training staff, though in some cases, it has proved traumatic for host nationals, especially if they have not been familiar with experiential techniques. (Though the Peace Corps is a unique phenomenon with an unusually strong emphasis on intercultural competency, multinationals could benefit immensely from Peace Corps' multinational staff integration experience.) On the other hand, if host nationals are involved completely with all aspects of training, they will be forced to engage in processes that may be prohibited in their culture, such as expressing conflict openly in a group, giving personal feedback to a fellow staff member about how his/her behavior affects others, engaging in egalitarian interaction with different levels of the staff hierarchy. In other words, to the extent that host nationals become truly responsive to the North American agenda for the training program, they become less congruent with and/or authentic to their cultural origins. In considering this approach, the training staff will have to face the dilemma of perhaps losing the value of host national staff modeling their culture as well as offending their cultural sensitivities.

If, on the other hand, the host national staff have ultimate decision-making power about the training program, the design might well resemble a highly structured, academic lecture/discussion approach void of innovative experiential group-process training techniques. Is the gain of host national cultural biases worth the loss of what most experientially oriented trainers consider to be effective training? These questions with regards to training goals and processes are always implicitly or explicitly posed for every multinational training program. Unfortunately, many trainers do not recognize these issues or are uncomfortable in dealing with them, even though they do not have the choice *not* to deal with them. There is no way to escape the "double bind" posed by the paradoxes raised here, but one can benefit from recognizing them and discussing them with the host national members of the training staff.

RESISTANCES TO MULTINATIONAL TRAINING

Given the earlier examples of intercultural problems which continue to occur in the ever-expanding corporate world of the multinational and the training model previously described, how can we explain the continued low priority given to developing comprehensive training which promises to considerably reduce the waste caused by inappropriate behavior exhibited by multinational managers?

There are obviously some resistances to introducing this kind of training, and the trainer must be aware of these in order to convince management of the need for multinational training. Though these resistances are not new ones, they continue to be vexing ones both for those in line management with operational concerns, and for those in the human resource development field.

The lack of an effective orientation and training program not only causes home and host country management headaches but has serious productivity implications. Why spend a great deal of money to select and transport an expatriate to his new assignment only to have him spend an inordinate amount of time just learning to cope with his new environment? [Noer, 1975]

There are two major areas which account for the resistances and low priority given to multinational training: (1) the structure of the multinational, and (2) the assumptions held by key decision makers, most of whom are not crossculturally sophisticated, even though many of them are world traveled.

Structure of the Multinational

The structural reasons why multinationals do not have multinational training include:

(1) Multinationals typically have a headquarters office staffed by a predominance of one nationality. This group often dictates world-wide policies, procedures and practices. In other words, the critical decision-making arena is not multinational. The structure and staffing (and consequently information flow) of the corporate offices may keep decision-makers ignorant of the cultural differences which exist between headquarters and foreign offices.
(2) Multinational corporations are committed to the profit motive which often ignores or minimizes nonprofit-making activity. It is difficult to prove the contribution of multinational training to the profitability of the company.
(3) Most multinationals attend to the *business* of the business first and managerial development second in terms of short-range succession planning and reassignments. Quite frequently the expedience of a business decision requires that someone be transferred to another country immediately, with no time for predeparture orientation.
(4) Multinationals have few internal development and training personnel who have a truly multinational perspective on the business and its training needs.
(5) Even when the internal training staff has a truly multinational perspective, coordinating training on a world-wide basis is conceptually difficult, logically demanding, and often organizationally/politically impossible.

Assumptions of Key Decision Makers

The assumptions area of resistances relates to management's lack of understanding and appreciation of cultural differences. Figure 25.4 describes some of the more commonly articulated reasons for resisting multinational training with the

STATEMENT	ASSUMPTION	CONTRASTIVE ASSUMPTION
(A) "Our people have already proven they can work with people no matter what their race or culture."	Evidence has already been demonstrated that the person has proven his intercultural skills by working with a variety of fellow nationals. People are not so radically different, at least on the job.	Professional and/or interpersonal success in one's own country does not guarantee similar success in a different culture. The cultural differences between people are so profound that significant new skills and behaviors are necessary for effective intercultural interaction.
(B) "Nothing can be done for the person until he is overseas and is in the actual situation."	Only the reality of the job situation will produce learning. People will not accept the "reality" of the training situation.	People can learn these new skills and behaviors before they get into the actual setting. Training which emphasizes new behavior in a supportive environment will help the trainee carry these behaviors into a new work situation.
(C) "We're sending mature adults whose basic personality is already set."	Mature adults cannot learn or unlearn behaviors even when such changes are to their advantage.	Though the prepatory activity cannot and should not attempt basic personality restructuring, even mature and "set" persons can change and modify their behavior when they see it as serving their purpose. So-called set personality traits such as sensitivity to others, creativity, tolerance for ambiguity and ability to cope with stress can all be strengthened by a training process.
(D) "Our personnel will get along with the host nationals by living and working with them."	People learn to like each other and work together by being together.	Working and living with people who are different does not mean that people will learn to love each other or cooperate. There are numerous examples that indicate the contrary.
(E) "There is no proof that any kind of preparation makes a difference."	This is largely true. Most studies have either evaluated change immediately after training itself, or lacked controls or other "hard research" essentials.	There is data that effective training can improve the functioning of managers.
(F) "People are about the same everywhere."	People differ only superficially in regard to foods they eat, the language they speak, and the clothes they wear.	Beyond the obvious difference of clothes, physical appearance and overt behavior are differences of how the world is experienced, of assumptions, and of cognitive structures.

Figure 25.4: Contrast Assumptions Which Support and Confront Resistances To Multinational Training

underlying assumptions, and also the contrastive assumption, which is more supportive of training. This figure is not assumed to be exhaustive.

Feldman (1976) observed:

> Many key management and HRD specialists either failed to recognize a need for crosscultural training; or if they did, did not provide training in a way that took advantage of the available research, knowledge and experience for conducting effective HRD programs designed to improve crosscultural adjustment and interaction.

Hopefully, the trend is toward greater intercultural sensitivity.

A survey of 33 major U.S. international companies recently released by the Conference Board, a nonprofit research organization, indicated that they were putting greater emphasis on executives' ability to adjust to the customs and environment of foreign companies. This does not mean that these companies would support greater training efforts. They could rely on more sophisticated selection procedures. Unfortunately, when a foreign subsidiary or office is demanding a manager to fill a vacant slot, and that slot requires rare business, technical, and/or managerial skills, multinational managerial sensitivity is seldom the key variable in the decision to fill that slot. Thus a large part of the burden is still on the training function to help managers manage more effectively, but to do so trainers need to understand what multinational training should accomplish, as has been previously discussed.

CONCLUSIONS

The world of the multinational corporation is too vast, complex, and changeable for one training model to have universal application. Multinational training must, however, focus on four major areas: managerial, intercultural, business, and language. No one of them alone is sufficient to cope with (1) the managerial role of planning, controlling, directing; (2) the intercultural variables effecting communications related to problem-solving, conflict resolution, and decision-making; (3) such business issues as profits, investments, national and international tax, labor contracting laws, marketing, and production; and (4) language fluency—especially knowing unique business, managerial, and cultural terms for effective communication. Too often multinational managers receive lopsided preparation that leaves out at least one of the four areas and most often only includes the business preparation.

On one hand, the evidence of costly mistakes and career failures in the multinational grows while research flourishes which points out the vast cultural differences between managerial counterparts from different nations. These differences are often the cause of unnecessary waste. On the other hand, in spite of the data showing how critical the cultural variables are, multinationals give multinational training low priority. This low priority is a result of general multinational structure and attitudes. The multinationally oriented manager and trainer have a great challenge to influence both so that sound multinational training is valued as essential for increasing individual and organization success. Unfortunately, "proving" the relationship between multinational training and effectiveness is difficult. There are usually too many uncontrollable variables to draw sound behavioral science conclusions.

There are several things the multinational trainer can do to enhance the credibility of the function. Some of these were mentioned in the training model. These are: (1) include line managers as trainers; (2) make sure that management (at least the next level above the trainees' level) supports the training; (3) design, implement, and evaluate training using an organization development strategy; (4) look for and initiate systems-wide leverage to support training goals; (5) follow all steps of the training model to insure effective training that trainees will support; (6) include work-related projects so trainees will apply newly acquired knowledge and skills to their job; (7) have trainers show cost-savings results of applying learnings from the training; (8) have follow-up training sessions to reinforce knowledge and skills; (9) become knowledgeable about the business so line managers will recognize him/her as understanding their operational problems; (10) become an articulate spokesperson for multinational training using the language of the business environment and avoiding jargon.

This paper contends that experiential training is the most effective way to confront managers with the intercultural coping and personal change process so critical for the multinational working and living situation. However, training must ultimately have an appropriate fit with organizational norms or it will not be supportive or supported. A great deal of critical information about the employees' contract, business issues and conditions, foreign laws and regulations, multinational regulations and procedures can appropriately be presented by the traditional approach, utilizing lectures, discussions, readings, and case studies. There are many foreign language learning approaches which are very effective.

The 10-step multinational training model represents a logically sequenced and disciplined way to develop sound and credible training which attends to the unique nature and environment of the multinational. The examples of multinational considerations for each step are not nearly exhaustive and are meant to suggest possible *caveats*. The actual numbers of considerations may be considerable.

Currently, most multinational trainers with a training or behavioral science background tend to use an experiential approach. Many values and techniques of this approach may not be supported by the host national culture. The multinational trainer will have to decide how to use host nationals as co-trainers and as trainers who may eventually assume full authority for training. The multinational trainer will have to resolve how to train them appropriately without being interculturally insensitive.

However, the most critical variable for successful multinational training is the trainer who must be crossculturally knowledgeable, wary of using cultural stereotypes, interculturally sensitive, highly skilled in the training profession, familiar with the commercial, legal, and operational aspects of the business world, able to use a systems or organizational development approach, and must possess a wide repertoire of approaches and techniques which can be modified for the always unique, ever-changing, multinational training situation.

NOTE

1. The term host nationals refers to the majority of the nationality of the local company or division personnel, e.g., a company headquartered in Ottowa with a subsidiary in England would refer to the British employees in the U.K. office as host nationals.

REFERENCES

BELLMAN, G. (1977) "A ten-step training process." Skokie, Ill.: G. D. Searle.

FELDMAN, M. J. (1976) "Training for cross-cultural international interaction in the federal government." *Training and Development Journal* (November).

FEST, T. B. and ROBBINS, J. G. (1976) *Cross-Cultural Communications and the Trainer.* Monograph prepared for the International Development Session ASTD National Convention, New Orleans, Louisiana.

FOSTER, R. J. and DANIELIAN, J. (1966) *An Analysis of Human Relations Training and Its Implications for Overseas Performance.* Washington, D.C.: Human Resources Research Office.

HOWARD, C. G. (1975) "Major personnel problems of U.S. multinationals abroad." *The Personnel Administrator* (May).

JOHNSON, R.B. (1967) "Determining training needs," in R.L. Craig and L. R. Bittel (eds.), *Training and Development Handbook.* New York: McGraw-Hill.

NATH, R. (1977) "Training international business and management personnel— An overview." Paper presented at Third Annual Conference of the Society for Intercultural Education Training and Research (SIETAR). Chicago, Illinois, March.

NEGANDHI, A. R. and ROBEY, D. (1977) "Understanding organizational behavior in multinational and multicultural setting." *Human Resources Management,* 16, 1 (Spring). University of Michigan, Graduate School of Business Administration.

NOER, D. M. (1975) *Multinational People Management: A Guide for Organizations and Employees.* Washington, D.C.: Bureau of National Affairs.

RHINESMITH, S. (1967) "The development of intercultural sensitivity through human relations training." University of Pittsburgh, Graduate School of Public and Intercultural Affairs. (mimeograph)

SCHNAPPER, M. (1975) "Nonverbal communication and the intercultural encounter," in J. E. Jones and J. W. Pfeifer (eds.), *1975 Annual Handbook for Group Facilitators.* La Jolla, Cal.: University Associates.

—— (1973) "Culture simulation as a training tool." *International Development Review,* 15, 1.

—— (1972) "Experiential intercultural training for international operations." Unpublished Ph.D. dissertation, University of Pittsburgh.

SINGER, M. R. (n.d.) "Culture: A perceptual approach," in D. S. Hoopes (ed.), *Readings in Intercultural Communication,* vol. 1, Pittsburgh, Penn.: Regional Council for International Education.

SKINNER, C. W. (1964) "Management of international production." *Harvard Business Review* (September/October).

STABLER, C. M. (1973) "Talk of the Globe," *Wall Street Journal* (April 18).

VANSINA, L. S. (1975) "Improving international relations and effectiveness within multinational organizations," in J. D. Adams (ed.), *New Technologies in Organization Development,* vol. 2. La Jolla, Cal.: University Associates.

ABOUT THE AUTHORS

STEVEN M. ALDERTON is a teaching associate of Communication at Indiana University. His research interests include small group, interpersonal, and interracial communication, primarily attribution processes.

MOLEFI KETE ASANTE is Professor and Chairperson, Department of Communication, State University of New York at Buffalo. He is also the first Chairperson, Society for Intercultural Education, Training and Research.

NJOKU E. AWA is Associate Professor of Communication at Cornell University. His primary research interests include communication and development, language and cross-cultural behavior, and transactional communication. He is the Treasurer of the Society for Intercultural Education, Training and Research and a consultant for several organizations.

ALENE BARNES is a Ph.D. candidate in Communications at the State University of New York, Buffalo. Her work continues in *What's in Small Talk?: Revolutionary Communication in Black Children's Games*, a volume on children folklore.

CECIL A. BLAKE is Assistant Professor and Director, Communication Research Center, Department of Communication, State University of New York at Buffalo.

JERRY L. BURK is Associate Professor at Boise State University. His interests are in theoretical work in intercultural communication.

JOSEPH J. DiSTEFANO is Professor of Organizational Behavior at the School of Business Administration, University of Western Ontario. His special interest in the problems of cross-cultural management have taken him on management development and consulting assignments in twelve countries over five continents. Professor DiStefano is Director of the Senior University Administrators' Course, the only national program for university academic administrators and business officers in Canada.

LAWRENCE W. HAAPANEN is Assistant Professor, Department of Communication, Utah State University. His research includes political communication and the role of values in communication.

PEGGY HALL (SMITH) was associated with the Language and Intercultural Research Center at Brigham Young University during 1976 and 1977. She is currently working on her Ph.D. in linguistics at the University of California, Los Angeles.

WILLIAM S. HOWELL is Professor of Speech-Communication at the University of Minnesota. Dr. Howell's interests are in interpersonal communication, persuasion, motivation, and domestic and international intercultural communication. His major interest in intercultural communication is task-oriented interaction involving managers of multinational corporations and managers from other countries.

K. KYOON HUR is Assistant Professor of Radio-Television-Film at the University of Texas at Austin. His research interests include international and intercultural communication and social impact of mass media with emphasis on minority groups.

STANLEY E. JONES is Associate Professor, Department of Communication, University of Colorado. Dr. Jones' work has concentrated on theoretical problems in the literature of intercultural communication.

DAN LANDIS is Professor and Chairperson, Department of Psychology, Indiana-Purdue University at Indianapolis. Dr. Landis is Editor and Founder of the *International Journal of Intercultural Communication.* His present interests include intercultural communication and research, social theory, and research design and analysis.

JANET G. LUKENS is associated with the University of Wisconsin, Milwaukee.

BEA MEDICINE is Professor of Anthropology, University of Wisconsin. Dr. Medicine is a leading scholar on native Americans and has published widely in the field.

EILEEN NEWMARK has a B.A. and M.A. from the State University of New York at Buffalo and is completing her Ph.D.

dissertation at the same institution. She has taught international communication at the United Nations.

DENNIS M. OGAWA is Professor of American Studies at the University of Hawaii and a consultant for the East-West Center Communication Institute.

PAUL PEDERSEN is Counseling Psychologist for the International Student Office at the University of Minnesota.

DORTHY L. PENNINGTON is Assistant Professor in Speech Communication and Human Relations and African Studies, University of Kansas. Her ongoing research interests include the variable of temporality in intercultural communication and the historical approach to enhancing intercultural communication.

SHEILA J. RAMSEY is an Assistant Professor of Communication at the International Christian University in Tokyo, Japan. Dr. Ramsey's research interests include nonverbal aspects of intercultural communication, the development of intercultural communicative competence, and exploration of communicative styles in different cultures. She is the author of several articles on nonverbal communication.

GEORGE O. ROBERTS is Professor of Comparative Culture and Social Science at the University of California, Irvine. Dr. Roberts has concentrated his research and teaching activities on ethnic relations, human resources development, and evolving societies in Africa and the Middle East.

AKINADE O. SANDA is Lecturer in Sociology and a Senior Research Fellow at the Nigerian Institute of Social and Economic Research, University of Ibadan. Dr. Sanda is Editor, *Nigerian Behavioral Sciences Journal.* His current research interests include development studies, and the needs, problems, and interests of Nigerian youth, and ethnicity in relation to national integration.

TULSI B. SARAL is Professor of Communication Science at Governors State University where he teaches courses in intercultural communication, interpersonal and personal growth, therapeutic communication, cultural aspects of mental health, and communication and human sexuality. Dr. Saral is the recipient of the International Development Fellowship from the Institute of International Education in the year 1967-1968.

MELVIN SCHNAPPER is President of Mel Schnapper Associates, Inc., a Chicago based consulting firm which specializes in delivering organization/development and training programs to multinational corporations and international organizations.

ROBERT SHUTER is Associate Professor and Chairperson, Department of Interpersonal Communication, Marquette University. Dr. Shuter has published widely on interpersonal and intercultural communications. Specializing in intercultural interaction, he has conducted research in Latin America and Western and Eastern Europe, and has examined selected American ethnic groups.

K. S. SITARAM is Professor of Communication at Utah State University. He was the founding Chairman of ICA Intercultural Communication Division (1970-1972). He has presented papers on intercultural and mass communication at professional associations.

JAMES S. TAYLOR is Professor of Spanish and is associated with the Language and Intercultural Research Center at Brigham Young University. He has written widely on the teaching of foreign language and intercultural communication.

V. LYNN TYLER is Director, Language and Intercultural Research Center, Brigham Young University. Dr. Tyler has been working with intercultural communication concerns for thirty years. He currently serves on the Governing Council of The Society for Intercultural Education, Training, and Research.

OLIVER C. S. TZENG is Associate Professor of Psychology at Indiana-Purdue University at Indianapolis. In addition to research in quantitative psychology, he has been actively engaging in various intra-and intercultural comparative studies on semantic differential data, as well as implicit cultural theories of personality, dynamics of subcultural changes, social indicators, attitudes, and intercultural communications.

ERIKA VORA is Assistant Professor of Speech Communication, St. Cloud State University. She has organized special topic seminars and presented several papers on intercultural and interpersonal communication at various national and international conferences.

JAY A. VORA is Associate Professor of Management, St. Cloud State University. He has published several articles in *Management Science, Managerial Planning,* and other journals.